Photojournalism
An Introduction

Fred S. Parrish

WADSWORTH

THOMSON LEARNING ™

Australia • Canada • Mexico • Singapore • Spain
United Kingdom • United States

Production Service: York Production Services
Text and Cover Designer: Hespenheide Design
Photo Acquisition: Elsa Peterson Ltd.
Copy Editor: Julie Kennedy
Illustrator: Illustrated Arts (UK)
Custom Photographers: Thomas Graves, Frederic Petters,
 and Simone Associates
Front Cover Photograph: David Leeson/*The Dallas Morning News*
Back Cover Photograph: Thierry Orban/Corbis Sygma
Compositor: York Graphic Services
Cover Printer: Phoenix Color Corporation
Printer: Quebecor World, Taunton

About the front cover photograph: Tannie Shannon (left) cradles grandbaby Andrea while his wife, Frances, leads the family sheepdog, Amadeus, from their flooded home in search of higher ground after the floodgates to Texas' Lake Conroe were opened in October 1994 following three days of torrential rain. The Shannons made it safely across this swollen waterway, but their home was destroyed by more than seven feet of water.

Printed in the United States of America
1 2 3 4 5 6 7 05 04 03 02 01

For permission to use material from this text, contact us by
 Web: http://www.thomsonrights.com
 Fax: 1-800-730-2215
 Phone: 1-800-730-2214

Library of Congress Cataloging-in-Publication Data
Parrish, Fred S.
 Photojournalism: an introduction / Fred S. Parrish
 p. cm.
 Includes bibliographical references and index.
 ISBN 0-314-04564-3
 1. Photojournalism. 2. Photojournalism—Vocational guidance.
TR820 .P294 2001
070.4′9′023—dc21
2001023535

Wadsworth/Thomson Learning
10 Davis Drive
Belmont, CA 94002-3098
USA

For more information about our products, contact us:
Thomson Learning Academic Resource Center
1-800-423-0563
http://www.wadsworth.com

International Headquarters
Thomson Learning
International Division
290 Harbor Drive, 2nd Floor
Stamford, CT 06902-7477
USA

UK/Europe/Middle East/South Africa
Thomson Learning
Berkshire House
168-173 High Holborn
London WC1V 7AA
United Kingdom

Asia
Thomson Learning
60 Albert Street, #15-01
Albert Complex
Singapore 189969

Canada
Nelson Thomson Learning
1120 Birchmount Road
Toronto, Ontario M1K 5G4
Canada

For
Mae,
Jean and John,
And most of all
Theresa (Tad)

Contents

Photojournalism: An Introduction is a richly illustrated book that encourages aspiring photojournalists to communicate to readers the most appropriate truth fairly represented, through an eye-catching personal style, with technical proficiency, within legal and ethical restrictions, and with an appreciation of what came before in photography and photojournalism.

Photojournalism: An Introduction reaches out to bring you the commentary and thoughts of some of the most talented visually oriented journalistic professionals of contemporary and past times.

A wealth of photographs is reproduced to illustrate points, serve as examples of what others have done, and stimulate you to visually communicate effectively. Taken as a whole, these images are a portfolio of some of the best photojournalism anywhere.

Photojournalism: An Introduction begins with a meaty overview of photojournalism. Chapter 1, "An Overview," introduces you to six areas in which photojournalism is used—newspapers; wire services; picture agencies; magazines; books; and the Internet. You will learn about the editorial photo operation of a medium circulation general interest daily newspaper from *The Arizona Daily Star*'s assistant photo editor, David Poller, about being an Associated Press photographer from Amy Sancetta, and about picture agencies and the Internet by other contributors. Immediately after the chapter is a Q&A with Bryan Grigsby, regional photo editor of *The Philadelphia Inquirer*. The topic: "Do You Really Want to Be a Newspaper Photojournalist?"

The next two chapters, "Cameras, Lenses, and Related Hardware" and "Film and the Digitalization of Photo-

journalism" cover "nuts and bolts" of journalistic photography—cameras, lenses, F-stops, shutter speeds, film, and digital processing, for example. You need to know about these so you can more accurately convert what you personally viewed at a scene into photographs viewed by readers. In a "Focal Point" at the end of Chapter 3, you will accompany three-time Pulitzer Prize winning *Dallas Morning News* photographer William Snyder as he digitally covers the Atlanta Olympics and processes images in *The News'* electronic darkroom. The piece's title is "Digitalization—A Real-Life View."

In Chapter 4, "Composition Broadly Construed," you will briefly explore the nature of composition, central perspective, photographic seeing, and creativity before turning to 27 specific composition techniques broken into three broad categories.

"Light and Color" is covered in Chapter 5—fundamentals first, then specific light-related picture-taking considerations with which photojournalists need to be familiar. A Q&A ends the chapter. It is with Charlie Riedel, photo editor at *The Hays* (Kan.) *Daily News* and is titled "Life at a Small Circulation Newspaper."

Journalistic photographers regularly gather caption information, the subject of Chapter 6, "Gathering Caption Information." In a Q&A, "The Road to Success," at the end of the chapter, Thomas R. Kennedy, director of photography at Washingtonpost.Newsweek Interactive shares his views about preparing for a career as a photojournalist, about looking to the future, about doing freelance work for his organization, and about the importance of personal interaction skills.

The next two chapters deal with subjects and forms. Chapter 7, "Major Subjects," is constructed around nine subjects beginning with spot news and ending with illustration. Three practicing photographers, Randy Hayes with the *Post Register,* Idaho Falls, Idaho, Scott Wheeler with *The Ledger,* Lakeland, Fla., and Fred Conrad with *The New York Times,* bring a down-in-the-trenches realism into the chapter as they write about covering spot news (Hayes), gathering features (Wheeler), and making portrait/personality images (Conrad). Chapter 8, "Major Forms" starts with the single picture, moves on to picture groups and picture sequences, and ends the "forms" with photo essays and picture stories. Special attention is paid to photo essays and picture stories, including suggestions by the author on how to be a one-person reportorial act—how to gather text and photographs together. Also in this chapter is the book's other "Focal Point," a detailed, illustrated how-to piece, "The Picture Story and Design," by an award-winning *Dallas Morning News* photo editor, Leslie White.

Two particularly thought-provoking chapters come next: "Law," and "Ethics and Taste." Chapter 9, "Law" zeros in on five areas you likely will encounter as you practice photojournalism: Access; Privacy; Libel; Three Procedural Areas; and Copyright. Your author's commentary is augmented by case summaries by a practicing attorney of several real-life legal cases. Chapter 10, "Ethics and Taste" includes thought-provoking photographs, basic ethical theory, practical ethical considerations, and an argument for limited invocation of taste to self-censor images. A Q&A titled "One Woman's Road in Photography" ends the chapter. It is with Erica Berger, who is based in New York City.

The last two chapters of *Photojournalism: An Introduction* are about history. Chapter 11 explores selected aspects of photography and photojournalism before the 20th-century and Chapter 12 does the same with the 20th-century. Both are well-illustrated. You should leave your course with a good sense of what came before and, hopefully, a strong desire to flesh out this exciting part of photography and photojournalism by exploring it on your own.

Photojournalism: An Introduction ends with two appendices: "Tips for Operational Success," and "Selected Readings."

Most academic endeavors build on what has come before. But, hopefully, new efforts look at existing knowledge in a little different and in a little better way and perhaps also add something new. In this sense and spirit, this book is constructed on the work of many people who came before. I am most grateful to them.

A particular debt of gratitude is owed to the photographers whose work appears in this book. These talented people breathe visual reality into a visually-oriented book. Please note their names near their photographs. Also owed thanks are the owners of the pictures in this book—newspapers, wire services, picture agencies, museums, photographers and others—who made them available.

In addition, *Photojournalism: An Introduction* was constructed with the help of many people who contributed in one way or the other to this project; my thanks to all. Particular thanks go to: William Albert Allard, freelance; Al Anderson, *USA Today;* Erica Berger, freelance; Bernie Boston, *Los Angeles Times;* Joan Carroll, AP/Wide World Photos; Ben Chapnick, Black Star; Fred Conrad, *The New York Times;* John Davidson, *The Dallas Morning News;* Tina DeBakey; Steve Dozier, *Florida Today,* Melbourne, Fla.; Lowell Elsea, Pitman Photo Supply, Miami, Fla.; Patricia Fairchild; Denis Finley, *The Virginian-Pilot,* Norfolk, Va.; Dr. Bob Gassaway, Department of Communication and Journalism, University of New Mexico; Thomas Graves, freelance; Bryan Grigsby, *The Philadelphia Inquirer;* Craig Hartley, freelance; Randy Hayes, *The Post Register,* Idaho Falls, Idaho; Gary Hershorn, Reuters; David Hobby, *The Baltimore Sun;* Brian Horton, The Associated Press; Tim Janicke,

The Kansas City Star; Thomas Kennedy, Washingtonpost.Newsweek Interactive; Kim Kulish, Saba Press Photos; Bob Lawrence; David Leeson, *The Dallas Morning News;* Catherine Mohesky, School of Journalism, University of Missouri-Columbia; Mike Morgan, Rodey, Dickason, Sloan, Akin & Robb, P. A., Albuquerque, N.M.; Mike Pease, *St. Petersburg Times;* Monique Heijmans Pease; Sylvia Plachy, *The Village Voice;* David Poller, *The San Diego Union-Tribune;* Loretta Provencio; John Reidy; Charlie Riedel, The Associated Press; Naomi Rosenblum, author, *The World History of Photography;* Jack Rowland, *St. Petersburg Times;* Amy Sancetta, The Associated Press; April Saul, *The Philadelphia Inquirer;* Flip Schulke, Flip Schulke Archives, Inc., West Palm Beach, Fla., Bob Self, *The Florida Times-Union,* Jacksonville, Fla.; William Snyder, *The Dallas Morning News;* Craig Walker, *The Denver Post;* Scott Wheeler, *The Ledger,* Lakeland, Fla.; Leslie White, *The Dallas Morning News;* Bradley Wilson, National Press Photographers Association; Alan Youngblood, *Ocala* (Fla.) *Star-Banner.*

Without diminishing in any way the help given by everyone noted above, several people deserve special mention:

*Hal Buell, former assistant general manager for news photos at The Associated Press and a distinguished figure in photojournalism, graciously helped with great patience.

*Howard Chapnick, former president of Black Star, columnist and author. Another generous and gracious photojournalism giant who unselfishly and patiently helped.

*James (Jim) Gordon, editor, *News Photographer* and former photojournalism professor. His always timely help was given in the best spirit of collegialism.

*Dave Hertzel and Barbara Rosen, ever helpful, ever patient University of New Mexico librarians. No one could ask for better assistance.

*Don Sider, consummate journalist and long-time friend, who read an early manuscript and offered valuable suggestions.

*Rex Throckmorton, managing director and a senior attorney at the law firm of Rodey, Dickason, Sloan, Akin & Robb, P. A., Albuquerque, N.M., who provided wise legal counsel on business matters related to this project.

Thanks go to three Wadsworth staffers. Deirdre Cavanaugh and Peter Marshall were in charge of the project at different times; each in their own way offered wise guidance that was much appreciated. Cathy Linberg, Wadsworth's production chief on the project, gave insightful comment and friendly support that likewise was much appreciated.

Carol Eckhart, this book's ever-cheerful project manager at York Production Services, York, Pa., took a genuine personal interest in the book and met the challenge of shepherding a novice author through the book-production process while efficiently moving the project to completion. I am grateful for her firm but fair approach.

The last and most important acknowledgment goes to my wife, Theresa (Tad) Parrish. Without her empathetic support, continued encouragement, and down-in-the-trenches help, this book would be just another dream.

An Overview

**Q&A: Do You Really
Want to Be a
Newspaper
Photojournalist?**

Bryan K. Grigsby—
regional photo editor,
*The Philadelphia
Inquirer*

Spot news events—events that typically happen unannounced with little or no time for coverage to be planned—occur every day all over the country. Among other things, cars collide, people jump off bridges, businesses are robbed, swimmers drown, trains wreck, and structures burn. Photojournalists must picture the obvious—the flames and smoke and firefighters battling them, for example. But in addition, photojournalists always should be alert for human involvement and human emotion—for portraying the human condition of these unfortunate, often tragic happenings. Here Jonathan Sneed, an anguished Washington, D.C. firefighter is held back—and comforted—after his attempt to rescue a firefighter friend from a burning building was unsuccessful.

© 1997 THE WASHINGTON POST. PHOTO BY DAYNA SMITH.
REPRINTED WITH PERMISSION.

Overview

Photography, from the Greek *pbos*, meaning "light," and *graphein*, meaning "writing," has had a tremendous effect on the world since its introduction more than 160 years ago.

Photography stops time and allows people to see what they did not witness in person (Figure 1.1). Philosopher George Santayana made the point in a 1912 speech to the Harvard Camera Club: "Photography is . . . helpful to every intelligent man because it enables him to see much that from his station in space and time, is naturally invisible."[1] Back in 1857, one commentator made clear how common photography had become, even so close to having been introduced to the world in 1839. Here is how she put it: "Photography has become a household word and a household want; is used alike by art and science, by love, business, and justice . . . ."[2]

Photography also enlivens the past by jogging our memories of personal experiences. Photography is an integral part of contemporary life, helping people to better understand each other and themselves. Photography plays a part in medical, business, social, and economic development, bettering and enriching our lives.

At its best photojournalism, the journalistic part of photography, is visual reporting of the most appropriate truth. The most appropriate truth, fairly represented, is the coin of the realm of contemporary photojournalism. The journalistic still photograph is a representation of reality. It is, in the words of Hal Buell, the savvy and thoughtful former assistant general manager of news photos for The Associated Press, "a moment in time . . . memorable, lasting, a fraction of a second isolated from the many other seconds. It is there forever to consider, ponder, re-examine."[3]

Journalistic Uses for Photography

Journalism's use of photography dates to the 19th century, when impressions were handmade in wood—the woodcut —from a photograph that could not it-self be mass-reproduced on a printing press. In the 1890s increasing use of the halftone process, which allows direct mass reproduction of impressions of photographs, sent photography on its long journey toward becoming a major factor in contemporary journalism.

Of course, photographs are meaningless unless people see them. Portraitists claim the family dresser and the wallet; public relations practitioners have the annual report and the meeting room display; the FBI has the post office wall. Photojournalists have six major outlets for their work. Newspapers, magazines, books, and the Internet deliver photos directly to readers; wire services and picture agencies are wholesalers.

Newspapers

The United States has approximately 1,500 general interest daily newspapers and well over 5,000 other newspapers.

Small-circulation newspapers—dailies or weeklies—may employ only a part-time photographer or a combination reporter-photographer. Large-circulation daily papers in metropolitan areas may employ 15 or more full-time photographers, several photo editors, photo support staff such as technicians and secretaries, and one or more photo managers.

Newspapers offer the most entry-level jobs for photojournalists right out of college. Typically, graduates start at small- or medium-circulation papers. After a few years they may move to large-circulation papers, earning more money and reaching more readers with their photography.

To help maintain—and enhance—photography's position in journalism, those who value photojournalism must educate themselves well in the liberal arts and all aspects of journalism. They should be at least as knowledgeable of the world and the journalism business as their word colleagues. Photographer-as-unthinking-button-pusher at many—it is hoped all—newspapers is as outdated as the manual washing machine and as undesirable as Typhoid Mary.

FIGURE 1.1

One of the great photographic achievements—the pictures were made by U.S. government-employed photographers—was the documentation in the 1930s and '40s of America on hard times, particularly rural America and its farmers. This is one now-famous image, "San Francisco Bread Line," from this now-famous coverage. For more photographs from this project and additional information about it, see Chapter 12.

DOROTHEA LANGE. FARM SECURITY ADMINISTRATION / © DOROTHEA LANGE COLLECTION, THE OAKLAND MUSEUM OF CALIFORNIA, THE CITY OF OAKLAND, GIFT OF PAUL S. TAYLOR.

David Poller, Assistant Photo Editor

At *The Arizona Daily Star* photographs are an integral and highly valued part of the newspaper (Figure 1.2) We believe we serve our readers best by making photos both compelling in content and artistic in appearance and that also complement stories rather than simply parroting them. Photographers are encouraged to produce photographs that add to our readers' understanding of our community and the issues we all face. We realize that a photograph with visual impact can grab the readers' attention and draw them into the page so we try to make sure both the journalistic content (the storytelling elements of who, what, where, when, why and how) and the graphic ingredients (composition, lighting, visual appeal, etc.) are of the highest quality. We try to shy away from literal images, favoring instead a more thought-provoking approach. We give our readers credit for being visually literate, surrounded as they are by well-produced and attention-getting images in magazines, movies, television and on their computer monitors. We are constantly challenging ourselves to bring our readers a fresh view of the commonplace. This philosophy drives the decisions we make on a daily basis, from how we assign photos to the photographers' approach to shooting them, all the way to deciding which photos run where in the paper.

The Arizona Daily Star is a 100,000-circulation A.M. daily (185,000 Sunday) owned by Pulitzer Publishing Co. Founded in 1877, the *Daily Star* is located in Tucson, a sprawling desert com-

FIGURE 1.2

The front page of the Thursday, April 8, 1999 *Daily Star*. It is not unusual for the front page to look similar to this, or with a single large image dominating the page.

Aaron Latham/*The Arizona Daily Star*

munity of nearly a million only an hour north of the border with Mexico and roughly the same distance from Phoenix. The *Daily Star* serves all of southeast Arizona and circulates in parts of northern Mexico as well, with most of our readers in Tucson. The *Daily Star* publishes seven days a week. Some of the issues we cover regularly are development, water use and immigration. Tucson is home to a thriving arts community, the University of Arizona's (UA) 35,000 students and a U.S. Air Force base. In the heat of the summer the city slows down. There are fewer college students in town and our "snowbird" seasonal visitors have returned to more comfortable northern climes.

The *Daily Star* is a photo-friendly newspaper. The Photography Department is led by Photo Editor Linda Seeger Salazar. She and I work with a talented staff of eight full-time photographers, a full-time prepress technician plus several part-time freelance photographers (Figure 1.3). Springtime is busy here with Spring training baseball, PGA golf tournaments and the UA's basketball teams often involved in the NCAA playoffs and championships. During this time we hire two full-time college interns for the Photography Department. Linda reports directly to Managing Editor Bobbie Jo Buel, who reports to the Editor, Jane Amari. Among our duties, Linda and I assign work to the photographers, edit their film, regularly evaluate their performance, communicate with editors and reporters from other departments, set the photographers' work schedules, attend daily budget meetings (in

which we and other editors decide what photos, stories and graphics will appear in the next day's paper) and run the department on a day-to-day basis. Linda prepares a working budget for the department, including such items as salaries, film and chemical purchases, new equipment purchases and equipment maintenance. She also attends regular meetings with other editors to plan for our editorial needs over the long term.

A photo assignment at the *Daily Star* can have its genesis in any one of a number of places. Reporters know it is part of their job to come up with ideas to illustrate the stories they produce, and often a reporter who is working on a story will simply fill out a photo assignment request form and bring it to either Linda or me. If it looks like the reporter has pinpointed the best way to illustrate the story, we'll give the assignment to a photographer as it stands. Sometimes, however, Linda

or I will see there may be a better way to illustrate the story than the approach the reporter is taking and we'll ask if our idea fits the story. If it does, we'll pursue that avenue instead. Open communication is an important part of our close working relationship with the *Daily Star*'s reporters.

City Editor Ann-Eve Pedersen and the assistant city editors work closely with us to make sure stories are illustrated, and we often hear from them about a story a reporter is working on before the reporter gets in touch with us to request a photo. Linda and I come up with photo and story ideas from things we hear about. The photographers themselves develop ideas for stories, projects and small feature packages. When a photographer develops a story idea he or she wants to work on, a reporter will be assigned to write a story that accompanies and complements the photos. Most of the *Daily Star* photographers have deep ties to the community that go back many years so they keep an ear to the ground for story ideas. We encourage the photographers to develop their own ideas for projects they want to pursue. Working on these self-assigned ideas is part of their jobs and can be very rewarding to them on a personal level (Figure 1.4).

Photographers usually have two or three assignments per day on average. We try to make sure they have appropriate time to shoot the assignment plus enough time for travel to and from their assignments. We also make sure they have time to process, edit and scan their film, computer process their selected images and take an hour-long lunch or dinner break. The newspaper business being what it is, it doesn't always work out this way but that's what

we strive for.

The photographers usually shoot their assignments on color negative film and sometimes on color slide film. At the *Daily Star* they use an automatic processor to develop their film. Then they cut their processed film into strips and place the strips in clear pages for editing and filing. Then they make a preliminary edit, going through the film to pick their favorite images.

Sometimes photographers shoot their assignments on a digital camera, a technology that uses electronics in place of film to make an image. Using a digital camera means there's no film to be stored, just electronic files, which can be opened in a computer. The photographer using such a camera makes his or her preliminary edit on a Macintosh workstation and selects several photos to choose from.

Linda and I try to make it a priority to have a thorough editing session with each photographer on every assignment (Figure 1.5). The photographers tell her or me about the story they photographed and collaboratively we pick the photos to be scanned and put into our computer system for printing in the newspaper and archiving. Using a grease pencil, we mark directly on the clear plastic pages which photos are to be printed, including a suggested crop if we think the photo needs to be cropped smaller than full frame.

The photographer then uses a film scanner at a Macintosh workstation to read the negative or slide and make a computer file of the resulting digital picture using Adobe® Photoshop® software. At the *Daily Star* we don't have a chemical darkroom to make paper-based pictures. Instead all the photographs we publish are

Photographer Sarah Prall was visiting an acupuncturist friend at her office. While there, Sarah saw a spaghetti sauce jar filled with live honeybees and, curious, asked why they were there. Her friend told her that a young woman was coming to her to have acupuncture performed—using bee stings instead of the traditional needles—as therapy for her illness. Sarah knew it could be a good story for our newspaper and she pursued it. She pitched the idea to Photo Editor Linda Seeger Salazar, who okayed the idea. Sarah secured the cooperation of her friend, the acupuncturist, and the patient, Krista Martin, and her family; she did research on bee therapy.

Sarah spent months photographing, exposing dozens of rolls of film. Krista's therapy took time to show results, and Sarah worked many angles to the story. This in-depth look could not be achieved by visiting the subject just once or twice. It is important that subjects understand ahead of time that serious photo coverage demands considerable photographer access.

She was allowed to schedule her time with Krista herself and to work at her own pace. The resulting photographs were edited by Linda, Sarah, and me. The photo story was published in the December 6, 1998 issue of the *Daily Star*. It began on the front page (1A) and continued inside the paper on two facing pages—a double truck. A *Daily Star* reporter, Jill Jorden Spitz, was assigned to write the text to go with the photographs. *Daily Star* designer Gawain Douglas did the layout.

Sarah's photography earned her a second place in the picture story category of the 1998 Arizona Press Club's annual contest. More importantly, the story brought to our paper's readers a visual and word package that presented a much more in-depth look at this subject than would be possible with a single photograph and its accompanying caption.

SARAH PRALL/*THE ARIZONA DAILY STAR*

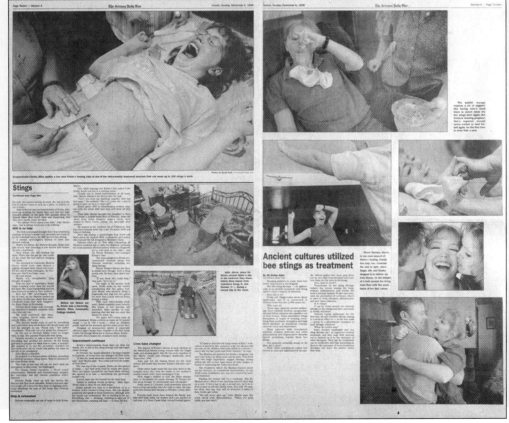

FIGURE 1.5

Along with photographer Benjie Sanders, I edit his film at a light table. Linda or I go through a photographer's film with the photographer after it is developed, and discuss the photos. We edit film with the photographers because each of us brings valuable insights to the process. The photographers are journalists on the scene and know important story details that often make a difference in choosing pictures. Linda and I know what other photos and stories will be used in the next day's paper and how they must work together with the photos being edited.
AARON LATHAM/*THE ARIZONA DAILY STAR*

computer files that are sent electronically to the newspaper's engraving department, where the plates are made for our presses.

When scanning the photograph, the photographer only does minimal tonal and color correction adjustments, if needed, to make sure the picture will reproduce well. More extensive photo manipulation occurs only if the finished work is to be used as a photo illustration, which will be clearly labeled as such. We're committed to being honest and fair in our photography, just as we are in the rest of the newspaper. Other than clearly labeled illustrations, *Daily Star* photographers stay

away from setting up situations for a photograph, or altering an image digitally so as to make it appear different than reality.

After the photograph has been scanned, the photographer adds complete caption information including the "5 Ws" (who, what, where, when and why) to the photograph. This information will later be used by the copy editors to write a caption that goes with the photograph on the page. Files are saved in color and archived to the *Daily Star*'s electronic picture library as well as saved into a computer folder appropriate for the assignment. For example, if a photographer shot a

picture of a play rehearsal for *icaliente!* (the *Daily Star*'s weekend arts and entertainment section) and then stopped at the police department to copy a booking mug for a daily news story, he or she would save those photos in two different places; one folder for our weekly arts and entertainment section and another folder for daily news photos. Later, the person doing electronic prepress (final preparation of the photographs for printing in the newspaper) will know where to find the photos.

Depending on the story, we may either use a single image or a package of two photos or more. We like to make sure the photos get the display they deserve. If more than one photo is going to be used, we pick a dominant image as well as a second, third, etc., and clearly mark them as such so the page designer knows how to run them.

Daily Star page designers, the people who lay out the photographs and stories on the pages, are asked to not second-guess our editing decisions when it comes to picture usage. In addition, designers for the feature sections of the paper know that they need to consult with Linda or me if they want to design a page with type on a photo in any way. This respect for the integrity of the image is a direct result of our overall philosophy of photos being valued for their content.

The photographer then makes a low-resolution color print, including caption information, and delivers this to the appropriate section editor or the picture desk if it's for the Metro section (for most local stories) or the A section (for big local stories as well as national and international stories). These low-resolution prints don't look as good as the photographs will once they're published, but they're good enough for us to have an idea of what the photo will look like, and they're inexpensive and quick to make.

Linda or I bring these color prints to the daily budget meeting to show Managing Editor Buel what we have to offer for the next day's paper, and what we plan to use as our dominant, or "lede" photos on the front pages of each section (Figure 1.6). We'll also bring the best photos from The Associated Press and other wire services to the budget meeting, especially if they go with a story that looks like it'll be played on the front page. After the meeting

we give the low-resolution paper prints to the designers of the various sections so they can design their pages. They measure the photos and return the paper prints to our prepress technician, who then calls up the image files, sizes them according to the designer's needs, does final tonal and color adjustment and converts them to CMYK or grayscale

files before sending them to the back shop where the color separations and black-and-white halftones are made. CMYK refers to the four colors of ink (cyan, magenta, yellow and black) used to reproduce colors when printing, and all photographs must be converted to a file comprising these four ink colors before they can be printed. Grayscale is a black-and-

FIGURE 1.6

Photo editor Linda Seeger Salazar shows two photos that are available to be published in the next day's paper during an afternoon budget meeting. In addition to staff-produced photos, the *Daily Star's* editors have available to them photographs from The Associated Press and other wire services. Budget meetings are each morning and afternoon. The morning budget meeting is to discuss what the editors of the different departments have planned, and the afternoon budget meeting is to discuss the final lineup of stories, photos, and graphics for the next day's paper. It is important to say that nothing coming from a meeting is etched in stone. News happens regardless of our deadlines and changes are made when necessary. We remain flexible right up to the last minute trying to make the paper as newsy and fresh and interesting as possible. Typically, Managing Editor Bobbie Jo Buel makes the final decision on what will be published in the paper and how it will be displayed.

AARON LATHAM/*THE ARIZONA DAILY STAR*

white image, actually made of many shades of gray in addition to black and white. We use color film for all of our assignments since good quality black-and-white photos can be made from color film.

Daily Star photographers use 35mm Nikon cameras. Each is given an outfit with two bodies, dedicated flashes, a variety of lenses from wide angle to tele-photo and a portable lighting kit for making studio-quality lighting possible on location. Also available to all the photographers is an extensive set of additional lenses, from ultrawide to super telephoto, a Nikonos underwater camera outfit and other items. Some photographers prefer to use their own equipment as well—for example, Jeffry Scott often uses a small, quiet Contax rangefinder camera for his assignments.

The *Daily Star* has set up strobes in the University of Arizona's McKale Center gym to bring our readers higher quality photos from the sporting events there. Also we have a large studio at the newspaper for shooting portraits and illustrations.

There are nine Power Macintosh workstations in the *Daily Star* photo department. They are part of the comprehensive and flexible newsroom network, linking our Macs with the *Daily Star* photo archive, the page designers' Macs, and the newspaper's production facilities. In addition, every photo department Mac has a fast con-nection to the Internet, which makes each workstation ideal for researching picture story ideas, planning out-of-town trips and communicating with others via e-mail.

Photographers use Nikon NC2000e digital cameras in addi-tion to their regular film cameras. They use these cameras for as-signments where tight deadlines take priority over quality, such as when a photographer is traveling out of town to shoot news or sports on deadline. Since digital cameras don't use film that must be processed, using these cameras saves time for the photographers. The NC2000e technology is get-ting somewhat long in the tooth and we're currently looking into the newer-generation of digital cameras. But as of this writing it's not worthwhile for us to switch over to digital cameras entirely—quality still seems to be better us-ing film.

For occasions when a *Daily Star* photographer is out of town on assignment, we use three Mac-intosh Powerbook computers so the digital images can be trans-mitted directly to the *Daily Star*'s prepress operation using phone lines and the Powerbook's modems.

Speaking of computers, it's im-portant to mention the *Daily Star*'s online presence and how it impacts our operations. StarNet (http://www.azstarnet.com) pres-ents the daily content of the newspaper in a format well suited to the online experience. Paid sub-scribers to this service have access to the online version of the entire contents of the daily newspaper, plus other features that are of-fered online only. Those who are not paid subscribers can access some of the *Daily Star*'s content, but not all of it. StarNet has its own editorial employees working separately from the newspaper, and *Daily Star* photographers are sometimes assigned to the proj-ects they are pursuing. StarNet can be a great forum for *Daily Star* photographers' work, as pho-tographers have the ability to run more photos online than they do in print, since space isn't an issue. Most of the work that runs online will be picked up by the print ver-sion of the paper around the same time it is published online. *Daily Star* photographers' portfo-lios are available for viewing through StarNet as well.

At *The Arizona Daily Star*, pho-tos are a valued means of telling stories about people who make news and those who are affected by newsmaking events. *Daily Star* photographers also create inform-ative, visually pleasing slice-of-life photographs that aren't tied to any news events. Newspaper pho-tographs illustrate, educate, de-light and enrage. They bring life, color and emotion to a newspaper page that otherwise would be gray and stale without them.

Author's note: David Poller now is a picture editor with *The San Diego Union-Tribune*.

Wire Services

Three major wire services widely dis-tribute photographs by satellite to clients in the United States. In alpha-betical order they are Agence France-Presse (AFP), Reuters News Pictures Service, and The Associated Press (AP). Other organizations, such as Gannett News Service, Knight-Ridder/Tribune Photo Service, and The New York Times News Service also distribute photo-graphs by satellite. Some organizations distribute photographs by nonelec-tronic means—by the U.S. Postal serv-ice, for example.

Agence France-Presse is owned by French media businesses and is head-quartered in Paris. Reuters News Pictures Service is a unit of the publicly held London-headquartered company Reuters Holdings PLC. The Associated Press is a New York City-based cooperative owned by its American newspaper members. Wire services are wholesalers of information, serving newspapers, magazines, and other organizations that choose to receive their pictures, either as member organizations or as independent purchasers of images.

A wire service's daily generation of photographs is prolific. For example, any one of the more than 1,100 domestic journalistic organizations taking the AP's 24-hour PhotoStream picture service—PhotoStream is the AP's name for its high-speed digital picture service—receives about 300 pictures of international and national interest in any 24 consecutive hours of transmission, 98 percent in color (Figure 1.7). In addition, these organizations, mostly newspapers, have their own PhotoStream "address," which allows them to receive pictures of interest only to their region, state, and locality. Recipients may, at their discretion, use color photographs in black and white.

It takes 5 minutes for AP New York to electronically receive a color photograph from an originating point and fewer than 2 minutes for a black and white. When New York retransmits the pictures to its members, PhotoStream color photos move in 15 seconds, whereas black and whites take only 8 seconds. These incredibly fast transmission times allow wire services to electronically transmit mainstream photographs as well as more offbeat ones that only more avant-garde publications are likely to use.

AP New York gathers images from around the world. After appropriate captioning and editing, they go by satellite to receiving organizations' AP Leaf Picture Desks, the AP's name for its computerized receiving equipment. A computer called a *file server* receives and stores the images. This machine holds 1,600 transmissions (a color image is three transmissions, a black and white is one). Many receiving organizations use more than one file server.

Local editors retrieve images from computer storage in a variety of ways: by topic, originating city, geographical interest, name of photographer, dateline, or reference to a specific story, for example. Computer screens display the images. Editors can crop and do other image-processing chores, such as lightening and darkening areas and correcting color, on the computer. Editors then transmit the images electronically to computer pagination programs or print them on specialty printers.

AP operates a commercial satellite service, PhotoExpress. Other journalistic organizations, such as Gannett News Service and Knight-Ridder/Tribune Photo Service, pay the AP to transmit their images by PhotoExpress. The AP also sends photographs to more than 100 countries around the world. The bulk of photographic coverage by a major general interest wire service deals with news events, but wire service photographers also provide feature images.

Many wire service photographers have worked at newspapers, where they probably provided photos to one or more wire services from time to time. Wire services often obtain photographs from newspapers they serve. The newspapers' photographers usually receive fees for pictures they took that are provided to wire services.

Some services offer individual pictures that are stored on a computer that can be accessed by publications. This eliminates the need for publications to pay a flat yearly subscription to a photo service. For example, a newspaper interested in a certain event connects with a service's computer bulletin board. The bulletin board lists the photographs available from that event. Newspaper editors call up low-resolution digital pictures of those images that are of particular interest to them.

Once editors have made their selections, the service transmits high-quality images to the newspaper's computers. The publication is charged for an image, the connection time, and telephone toll costs.

FIGURE 1.7

Major wire services heavily cover major events. This is one of the many photographs of the 1996 Summer Olympics in Atlanta taken and disseminated by The Associated Press. Emotion overtly displayed can be a powerful storyteller as is the case with the U.S.'s Kurt Angle weeping after winning a close wrestling match—and a gold medal. While the actual action is important in sports as well as in other events, never forget the emotional aspect that may surface, often after the action.

MICHAEL LIPCHITZ/AP/WIDE WORLD PHOTOS

Amy Sancetta, The Associated Press

I am one of The Associated Press's two enterprise photographers, a position I've held since 1994. I generate, shoot, and write feature packages that go out over the AP wire to our member newspapers across the U.S. and the world. Prior to 1994, I spent 10 years as a staff photographer in the Philadelphia bureau on a staff of four photographers and one photo editor.

The AP has some 120 photographers assigned to bureaus across the U.S. We have many other photographers in cities around the world. The Associated Press is the world's oldest continuously operating news-gathering organization. Newspapers, magazines, radio and television stations join The Associated Press and in return receive words, pictures, and audio and video of news, sports and feature stories from around the world.

In the U.S., photographers are assigned to specific bureaus and are responsible for coverage of all events which occur in the region around their bureau. For instance, the photographers in Philadelphia cover eastern Pennsylvania. The photographer in Des Moines covers all of Iowa and Nebraska. Photographers are assigned to bureaus around the country based on population, the number of newspapers in the state to be served, and on the amount of news and sports that comes out of the region. New York City, the financial and fashion capital of the U.S., the headquarters of the United Nations, and home to a myriad of professional sports teams requires more staff for coverage than a smaller city.

The AP brings together photographers for the coverage of big events like an Olympics, a political convention or a major flood. We have the ability to pull people together—photographers, editors, writers, and technicians—at a moment's notice when the news calls.

The AP has two enterprise photographers. I am based in Cleveland, Ohio, and Eric Draper is based in Albuquerque, New Mexico. We work a little differently than other photographers in the company who are primarily responsible for coverage of the region in which they work. I work from home, rather than in a bureau. I photograph and write feature picture packages on stories anywhere in the country. I shoot pictures for our national and regional writers. I'm also involved in the coverage of major sporting events like the Super Bowl, the World Series, and the Olympic Games.

I've always enjoyed sports—in fact, that's what spawned my interest in photography back in high school—so I'm very happy to be able to be a regular contributor to our coverage of major sporting events (Figures 1.8 and 1.9).

The type of stories I work on varies to a great degree. I enjoy light-hearted stories, like the package I just completed on the inventor of the yard art pink flamingo, or the story I did several years ago about a camp in Vermont for people and their dogs.

I also do my share of serious work. I spent the better part of five months last year working closely with reporters on a series of stories about child labor in the United States (Figure 1.10).

For these stories, a reporter and I would go to specific areas where migrant workers were employed. We garnered the assistance of the local migrant advocacy organization to help us identify particular fields and workers. And then we just went out and talked to people. Most were very open about their situations. In the fields, I never shot pictures without first asking permission, and found that I was never turned down. I felt this was important so as not to invade the privacy of my subjects. The work we were doing might in the long run jeopardize the employment opportunities of these workers. I felt they should have the final word on whether or not to be involved in the story.

Technology has progressed to the point that I use all digital equipment in my work—a digital camera and a laptop computer free me from the long hours spent in the old chemical darkroom. When on an assignment, I can pop my camera disk, a PCMCIA hard disk drive, which is a mini hard drive that can hold 71 images, into my laptop, and edit the day's work. This quick, on-the-spot editing lets me know what pictures I have and what others I might need to complete a story while I'm still on the scene. I can see on the spot if a subject blinked during a portrait, or if I did not have enough depth-of-field in a particular picture to produce the results I wanted.

On some assignments, I transmit pictures immediately to my supervisor, enterprise photo editor Claudia Counts, in our New York

FIGURE 1.8

St. Louis Cardinals first baseman Mark McGwire watches the flight of his record-breaking 62nd home run in St. Louis on Sept. 8, 1998. This homer broke New York Yankees' right fielder Roger Maris' single-season record of 61 home runs, set in 1961. The fact that McGwire hit most of his home runs to left field made my position, which was on a stool in the aisleway of the front row of seats half way between the third base bag and the left field corner, a good one for his swing, follow through and reaction. I shot this picture with a long telephoto lens, which allowed me to record the scene from such a long distance. I used a digital camera.
AMY SANCETTA/AP/WIDE WORLD PHOTOS

office. I do this using my laptop, a modem card, and a telephone line.

Most of my work is done on an advance basis—I shoot a story and interview the subjects, go home to write the story and edit the pictures, and then send the words and pictures to our New York office for final editing and scheduling on the wire.

I recently completed a photo package on how young girls are getting caught up in basketball fever with the growing popularity of the Women's National Basketball Association (WNBA). I had been noticing an increased number of ads in the newspaper for girls' basketball camps. I had been to some WNBA games and saw the enthusiasm of the young fans. So I set out on my story.

I went to a popular girls' basketball camp, shot pictures of the campers working out in their WNBA T-shirts and in jerseys bearing the names of their favorite female stars. A star college player came to the camp to talk to the girls and give them a

FIGURE 1.9

In a ceremony following the game, Mark McGwire kisses the ball that he hit over the left field wall for his record-breaking 62nd home run. I worked my way down the third base line and lined up just inside the third base bag to make this digital image, also with a long telephoto lens. It was a spontaneous response by McGwire after receiving the ball, which was retrieved by a member of the Busch Stadium grounds crew.

AMY SANCETTA/AP/WIDE WORLD PHOTOS

shooting lesson. I interviewed some of the girls about what it's like having female role models, and asked what they wanted to be when they grew up. Most mentioned a professional basketball player.

To round out the story and pictures, I went to a WNBA game, photographed young female fans decked out in team apparel cheering or seeking autographs, and talked to a few of the pro players about what it's like being a role model to these youngsters.

As I proceeded through the story, I made a series of sketches on paper of the pictures I had already made. This gave me an idea of what storytelling pictures I was

missing and also showed me how a newspaper might actually use the work.

Once I felt I had the pictures and interviews to tell the story, I set about to edit my photos and write a story.

When I edited the pictures, I first looked for content and then made sure my selected images were shot with a range of lenses and that I had both vertical and horizontal pictures. It is very difficult for a newspaper designer to put together a page of pictures if they are all horizontals shot with the same lens.

Once the pictures were edited and I had written the story, I transmitted them to my supervisor in New York. She re-edited my pictures, selecting eight and removing two that were redundant with other images that she liked better.

The words were sent to a sports editor for a similar edit before the whole package was scheduled on the wire for use by our members.

Since most of my work consists of a story and five to nine pictures, it is "advanced" on the wire. This means that a notice of the package is sent to the member papers several days before the recommended usage date. The package and advance note will run on a Tuesday if the package is to be used the following weekend. This advance warning and arrival of the work gives a newspaper time to make space on their pages.

Any AP photographer covering a spot assignment—one that needs to be moved instantly for use in the next day's paper—must work at a quicker pace.

With the current technology—digital cameras, laptops, and cell phones—a shooter can photograph a plane crash and transmit it from his car without any outside

power or phone lines. The car's battery provides the power needed to run the laptop computer and the cell phone provides the wireless transmission capability.

In experienced hands, a photo can travel from a photographer's camera, to her laptop, and over phone lines to our hub bureaus in New York and Washington, and back out through the satellite and phone lines to newspapers across the globe in a matter of minutes.

When a newspaper is on deadline and its presses are aching to roll, a minute here or there can mean the difference between our picture appearing on the front page or inside or not at all.

In Cleveland local AP staffer Mark Duncan is able to use a phone line, which is run into his dugout photo position at Jacob's Field, home of the Cleveland Indians. He can shoot early action of an Indians game, transmit a picture over the wire from the dugout, and go back to shooting the game without ever leaving his position.

The quality and speed of the new technology make this an exciting time to be a photojournalist. Yet it is still the eye of the photographer that is of the greatest importance—the ability to see a good picture, to relate to the subject, and to understand what image best tells the story.

For young photographers entering the business, my suggestion is to shoot, shoot, shoot. There are a number of colleges with wonderful photojournalism programs, but whether you go to school in photography or not (I was a history major at Ohio State University), your own enthusiasm and hard work will be your best friend.

I was given a great gift while I was in college to be able to work with and learn from the two AP photo staffers who worked in the

FIGURE 1.10

Migrant worker Laura Mares, 10, holds up her self-portrait outside the one room farmer-provided building where she lived in August 1997 with her parents and two siblings in the cucumber fields of northwestern Ohio. Though she traveled from Florida with her family to work in the fields all summer and into the fall, Laura hopes one day to become an artist. I wanted to show how she saw herself, and saw hope for herself, despite the rigors of migrant life, so using the self-portrait in place of her own face seemed like a natural. I used a digital camera.
Amy Sancetta/AP/Wide World Photos

Columbus, Ohio bureau at that time—Brian Horton and Harry Cabluck. Both were marvelous teachers and very patient. I was enthusiastic and wanted to learn. Together, we were all a very good combination.

You should get a portfolio together, one that you can update often as your work improves. It should contain some features, some sports, some news, if possible, and a picture story of some kind. As well as your professors and peers, show working photographers your work, and take from their comments those things that will help you to become a better shooter. Most good photojournalism is a healthy combination of talent, knowledge, empathy, planning, and luck. You have the opportunity through your own hard work to put yourself in the best position to make the best pictures possible.

Picture Agencies

Picture agencies are divided into two categories: stock and assignment. Stock picture agencies are the libraries of the agency world—obtaining photographs, usually on consignment, and splitting sales with photographers.

Stock agencies range from large national and international organizations that sell pictures covering a broad range of subjects to national agencies that specialize in particular subjects or particular applications (such as public relations, advertising, sports, animals, and medical and scientific subjects) to regional and state agencies specializing in pictures of their geographical areas. Assignment picture agencies usually have photographers on staff as well as stringers. These agencies search out work for their photographers. They handle all the paperwork, including collecting payment from the client. Assignment agencies generate additional revenue when they sell to other publications the so-called secondary rights to their photographers' work. Assignment agencies also act as stock agencies, selling pictures previously taken by their staffers and stringers, both on assignment and speculation.

Two venerable American-based assignment picture agencies are Black Star and Magnum, the former headquartered in New York City and the latter in Paris and New York City. Black Star is a privately held company contracting with its photographers. Magnum is a cooperative, owned and managed by its photographers.

In the past few decades French-based or -connected picture agencies specializing in news coverage have secured a firm foothold in the American and European markets. Gamma (known as Gamma-Liaison in the United States) was the first of these agencies in the United States. Other major agencies include the French-based Sipa Press and the U.S.-based Corbis Sygma.

Contact Press Images is another major New York City-based agency with French ties. It was formed by Robert Pledge, who was with Gamma until he left to form Contact Press Images with the American photographer David Burnett. Whereas Gamma, Sipa Press, and Corbis Sygma emphasize news coverage, Contact Press Images emphasizes in-depth coverage of continuing subjects of personal interest to its relatively few photographers. Saba and Matrix are two important new players in the picture agency arena. Four premier U.S. stock agencies oriented toward commercial (as contrasted with editorial) accounts are Comstock, Inc., The Image Bank, The Stock Market, and the Free Lance Photographers Guild. Many other picture agencies, a number of which are headquartered in New York City, also vie for business.

Most agencies operate in the same way. Typically, upon receiving an inquiry about photographs of a particular subject a picture agency will send—by whatever means the client wishes—a selection of pictures held in house. The buyer will look at the selection, picking one or more and purchasing the right to use them.

Assignment picture agencies also provide photographers. An organization that needs custom photography—for example, photos for the company's annual report—might prefer to contact an assignment agency rather than hire a nonagency photographer. The agency sends a photographer who takes the pictures and sends them to the agency, where they are edited and then sent to the client.

This simplifies the process. The well-regarded and long-time former head of Black Star, Howard Chapnick, explains:

> Assignment agencies provide geographical diversification of photographers, bringing the photographer closer to the job, thus lowering expenses to the client. Assignment agencies do an important job in representation and promotion of the photographers and must be out on the firing line showing portfolios, marrying client and photographer, and finding the right photographer

for specialized kinds of photography, among other things.

Picture agencies are keeping up with the world of computers and the Internet. For example, Black Star touts its assignment capabilities on the Internet and allows potential customers to tour its library of 40,000 images.

Magazines

The demise of the large-circulation photo-oriented magazines of general interest—the weekly *Life*, *Look*, and *Colliers*—was a sad event for photographers. When these magazines folded, photojournalists lost important outlets for their work to be seen by hundreds of thousands—even millions—of readers. (See Chapter 12 for more about *Life* and *Look*.)

National Geographic, a specialized magazine, and a limited number of newspaper Sunday magazines continue to be important outlets for in-depth visual stories (Figure 1.11). Almost all *National Geographic* photography is done by a few staffers or by contract photographers. The *New York Times Magazine* tends to use well-known freelance photographers, whereas other newspapers' Sunday magazines tend to use their paper's staff photographers.

News-oriented photography for magazines is alive but largely limited to the weekly newsmagazines—*Newsweek*, *Time*, and *U.S. News & World Report*. Much of these magazines' photography is the work of staffers or is done by assignment picture agencies that have the money to send photographers anywhere in the world.

Specialized publications are another major outlet for magazine photography, but these tend to run more limited photographic undertakings rather than lengthy visual stories. *Arizona Highways, American Horticulturist, Conde Nast Traveler, National Wildlife, Sports Illustrated, Surfing, Town & Country, Vogue,* and *Wildlife Conservation* are examples.

FIGURE 1.11

Cover of the March 29, 1998 issue of *The New York Times Magazine*. Photograph of United Nations Secretary General Kofi Annan by Nigel Parry/CPI/for The New York Times.

COVER OF THE MARCH 29, 1998 ISSUE OF *THE NEW YORK TIMES MAGAZINE* COPYRIGHT © 1998 BY THE NEW YORK TIMES CO. REPRINTED BY PERMISSION.

Kim Kulish, Saba Press Photos

I am a journalistic photographer based out of Los Angeles, California.

Working for a picture agency, Saba Press Photos, is the latest stop in my photojournalism career.

I started this journey back in 1978 when I was in high school; I took pictures for the *Hollywood* (Fla.) *Sun-Tattler*'s high school section. During breaks from classes at the University of Florida, I interned at *Florida TODAY* in Cocoa, Fla.; the *Jackson* (Miss.) *Clarion-Ledger*; *The Arizona Daily Star* in Tucson, Ariz.; the *Gainesville* (Fla.) *Sun*; and *The Orange County Register*, in Santa Ana, Calif.

Then, in 1985, I was ready for the world of full-time photojournalism.

After what seemed a long search, I took a job at the *Post-Herald*, a medium circulation daily in Birmingham, Ala. I worked at the *Post-Herald* for almost 2 1/2 years.

I left the *Post-Herald* to work at the *Daily News*, a larger circulation daily in the Los Angeles area. I spent nearly nine years at the *Daily News* shooting primarily news, personality portraits, sports and feature picture stories.

I reached a point where I felt burned out in my daily newspaper job and lost some of the drive I had back in my early days in the business. I toyed with the idea of becoming an independent photojournalist—a freelancer—but was concerned about how successful I would be. I knew that the freelance business was quite competitive, especially in Los Angeles.

I overcame most of my fears and made the decision to begin freelancing after attending a photography seminar presented by prominent photojournalist Eugene Richards.

During the program, I sat down with Richards and we talked about my future in photography. "Are you ready to leave your comfortable 9 to 5 job and starve for your photography?" was his question. "You will know when to make the next step in your career."

Following that week-long workshop, I spent a lot of time thinking about my photography, personal goals and finances, and I decided it was the right time for me to take a big risk, to leave a steady job and "take the next step."

For the next two years as a freelance photographer, I shot whatever I could for almost anyone I could, making contacts along the way. My work was getting noticed by picture agents including Marcel Saba, owner of Saba Press Photos.

In 1997 I was asked to join the ranks of the talented photojournalists represented by Saba. I quickly jumped at the opportunity. Saba, founded in 1989 by Marcel Saba, a prominent figure in photojournalism and one of the most talented people I have met in the business, is based in New York City. It represents a small group of photographers throughout the world. Although the main emphasis is on editorial work particularly for magazines, Saba represents its photographers to corporate and advertising agencies for projects such as annual reports and executive portraits. Marcel Saba believes in personal and one-to-one contact with the photographers and clients and is respected for the professionalism of his agency. Although Saba is not as large as some other agencies, it remains just as competitive by having savvy people who know what is important and using photographers who cover assignments well.

Saba has a staff of 15, which includes picture editors, researchers, librarians and accountants.

The editors at Saba handle the editing and captioning of photographs after they arrive from photographers and make sure they get to the client. Each editor works with a group of magazines to keep continuity with their editors. But since Saba has such a small staff, the agency's editors work together to get the job done, especially on big breaking news stories.

As a photographer for Saba, I get assignments from various publications; these come through the agency. Plus, I generate my own news and feature story ideas. If Saba editors like an idea, they in turn contact the magazines for an assignment, or if I had gone ahead and shot the idea on speculation, they try for a sale. In addition, I do work for several large newspapers that need photo assignments shot in southern California (Figure 1.12). Their picture editors contact me directly and we go over the details of the shoot. Typically, faxed assignment sheets are sent after our conversations. I always keep my copyright. Once the photos have been published, the newspapers return the pictures to me and if there are any resale possibilities, I send them on to Saba for their New York photo

FIGURE 1.12

Actor Tom Hanks poses for a portrait in a Pasadena, Calif. hotel suite to promote his Oscar-winning movie "Saving Private Ryan." Since the movie's publicist ruled that no photos were allowed during the reporter's interview with Hanks, my assistant Rebecca and I quickly set up two flash units (strobes) in the corner of the hotel suite prior to his arrival. We were told to wait outside in the "holding area" until Hanks was ready. We had only five minutes to make the photo. I shot quickly as Rebecca held a fill card—a white card that reflects light into the subject's shadow area and brings out detail—and adjusted the strobes. It is hard to capture the "real" person with so little time, but I think this image has a nice feel to it. It was the last frame on the roll. The photo was shot on assignment for the *San Francisco Chronicle* and was later marketed by Saba around the world.

Kim Kulish/Saba for the San Francisco Chronicle

library files. In addition to sales in the United States, Saba makes copies and sends the photographs to picture agents around the world working for Saba to sell.

When an assignment comes from the agency, Saba calls or pages me with details and follows-up with a fax noting the client, subject information, contact phone numbers, deadline and shipping information.

On fast-breaking news stories most of the details are communicated via cell phone while I am heading to the scene. If deadlines are real tight or if there are problems in getting film back to New York City, I use my portable computer and film scanner to transmit to Saba's computer system. But as a rule, having an original slide in hand is always preferable to both magazine editors and Saba because of the higher quality of the image, especially if the picture will be reproduced large.

Saba photographers primarily shoot color transparency (slide) film because of its excellent reproduction quality. Color negative film is used when deadlines are tight and we are transmitting from the field or when lighting conditions are poor. Today's high-speed color negative films offer increased exposure latitude and about a 15-minute processing time. In comparison, slide film takes at least an hour. Since time savings is critical, negative film typically is used on tight deadlines. Even though the market is limited, selected stories are shot in black and white if it seems appropriate for the subject matter or if requested by the publication.

I get my photo story ideas from various sources. They range from daily newspapers and television reports to the alternative press and the Internet.

Using the ever-increasing variety of Internet resources has made researching information for assignments easier than going to the library. I have used the Internet numerous times to help me locate people, organizations, and even maps with driving instructions to locate unfamiliar locations. Plus, some publications request photos be scanned and sent via e-mail to meet their tight deadlines.

Besides Saba-assigned photos, I shoot stock pictures including such topics as people working, playing and protesting. I also shoot social issues such as wealth, poverty, teenage smoking and pollution. My stock photographs are sent to Saba to be edited, captioned and filed in the agency's photo library and scanned into its growing digital database. The photos are sent to publications when Saba receives a request for images like the ones I shot.

As a Saba photographer, I am paid monthly for assignment and stock photo sales collected from the previous month. I receive a 70/30 percent split, plus expenses for all Saba-assigned work and a 50/50 split for stock photo sales.

There is no base salary or medical or retirement benefits paid by Saba. If I want to make a living, I need to aggressively go after work, not just sit at home waiting for the phone to ring.

When I shoot stock or self-assigned work, I pay for my film

and Saba pays for processing. Other expenses, such as airfare and hotel room costs, are usually split 50/50 with the agency.

I work closely with Saba to constantly update my portfolio with fresh images. I promote my work through annual visits to editors, by direct mailings to them of recent work, and by a personal website on the Internet. I consider these efforts important to being a successful agency photographer. Some magazine editors prefer only to look at portfolios, but others won't hire you for an assignment unless they have met you—even if it is only five minutes over a cup of coffee. Sometimes they just like to put a face to the portfolio and name. This meeting can help to break the ice with a new client and secure that first assignment.

As a Saba photographer, I do not work a set number of hours a week. I am always on call for a breaking story and have to move quickly to remain competitive. Let me give you three examples.

A phone call from Saba came at dinnertime as CNN and wire stories relayed on-going details of a mass suicide. I was told I was on assignment for *Newsweek* magazine and to get to the scene ASAP.

The Heaven's Gate cult mass suicide occurred geographically close to me—San Diego County, Calif.—but driving through three counties' rush hour traffic made for a long nervous trip as the story continued to unfold over my AM radio.

I arrived as police and coroner officials were still making their way through the maze of television trucks, reporters, and photographers. I stayed up all night on the site not knowing when the coroner would remove the bodies from the scene. For the next 72 hours I recorded every significant

aspect of the story from the suicide scene to the coroner's office. *Newsweek* ran a cover and several pages inside on the tragedy. I don't think I will ever forget the smell from the truckloads of bodies being unloaded at the coroner's office.

Another story I worked on, quite opposite of the mass suicide, was the birth of septuplets in Iowa.

When the story broke that the Iowa septuplets were born healthy, Saba knew it was an important story and I was on a plane within hours. I left without an assignment, but by the time I arrived, Marcel Saba had gotten me an assignment from *Time* magazine.

I hit the ground running, locating and photographing the family, doctors, neighbors, local residents and the happy parents. I also coordinated photo coverage with *Time's* Chicago bureau chief and a *Time* contract photographer who arrived a day later. Our combined team efforts produced a cover story on the historic births.

Another tragic story I covered was the Columbine High School shootings.

On a Tuesday I was photographing a press conference in downtown Los Angeles. I was paged by an editor at Saba. She told me that there was a major school shooting that was happening in Colorado and asked if I could go. I said yes and quickly drove home to gather my clothes and my travel computer and scanner kit. I caught the next non-stop flight to Denver and was making photos on the scene within five hours of that first call.

One local Saba photographer had been at the school all day and captured great images of the day's events. Another was coming from New York and was still on a

FIGURE 1.13

Classmates of Isaiah Shoels, a student athlete killed in the Columbine High School shooting, slowly carry his casket from the church following his funeral service. I made a few images inside the church. I then left through a side door to take a position behind a row of Isaiah's friends and quietly waited for the procession to make its way past me. The sky was overcast and threatening to rain. *U.S. News & World Report* ran this image in the following week's issue.

KIM KULISH/SABA FOR *U.S. NEWS & WORLD REPORT*

plane. We were all put on assignment for *Newsweek* magazine.

As I drove from the airport to Littleton, Colo., I listened to radio news reports that the shooting scene was calm following the day's earlier events and that people were gathering at a local church to pray. I made my way past the school to the church and photographed students and parents embracing during the vigil. Plus, I went to a nearby elementary school where parents were reunited with their children.

In the several days following the shooting, the three of us worked with reporters from *Newsweek* to track down various

leads on what was now a cover story for the magazine. Plus, we interviewed and photographed several of the victims' family members (with their permission) and attended memorials that grew around the school daily.

On Wednesday and Thursday we shipped film to New York for the *Newsweek* editors to review. On Friday and Saturday morning we transmitted the images in order to make *Newsweek*'s deadline. The magazine was putting together a special fold-out section and needed the images as soon as possible.

I was off the *Newsweek* assignment Sunday, but decided to stay

in town for a couple of days to see if I could get another assignment. It was still a very fluid story and my agent, Marcel Saba, thought I would be back on for another publication very quickly.

He was right. I ended up getting a week's assignment from *U.S. News & World Report.* I was given free rein by the magazine to photograph what I thought was important for a follow-up story.

The *U.S. News'* picture editor was great to work with. She trusted my judgement and I don't think I let her down. One day late in the afternoon as rain clouds gathered, I spent over five hours on the side of a hill overlooking Columbine waiting for the right moment as lines of people filed past crosses erected for those killed. The image I made ran across two pages in the magazine.

I also attended the funeral of Isaiah Shoels, a football player killed in the shooting. I really hate to cover funerals. But it was part of the story. Plus, when I met the parents the week before they asked me to attend and photograph the funeral to "show everyone our son did graduate from high school." He was laid to rest in his cap and gown.

I quickly processed my film and sent low-resolution scans back to *U.S. News* so a layout could be done. I then shipped the film by a local courier arranged by the magazine so *U.S. News* could make its own high quality scans.

The magazine ran a half-page photo of his classmates carrying his casket out of the church as rain clouds filled the sky (Figure 1.13).

Newsweek and *U.S. News & World Report* editors—and Saba —were happy with my work. I was mentally drained from the tragic events of the past two weeks.

FIGURE 1.14

The "Pope Mobile" carrying Pope John Paul II arrives at the Plaza de la Revolución in Havana, Cuba for the final mass of his historic visit in 1998. Thousands filled the plaza overshadowed by a building sculpture of deceased Cuban hero Che Guevara. Following the early morning security sweep, I waited several hours with other journalists to be in the right position to take this photograph of the Pope, the large crowd, and the Guevara image. I was on assignment for Saba.

KIM KULISH/SABA

Being an agency photographer can have its own set of frustrations. I was used to getting feedback from my fellow staff photographers when I worked for newspapers. At times early in my freelance career it was difficult to get used to little or no feedback from magazine editors following an assignment. I was told by one of my editors at Saba, "magazine editors are usually too busy with deadlines and photo shoots that did not work out. They usually only call when something is wrong, so relax." Plus, as a newspaper photographer I was used to practically every assignment I shot getting published. As an agency photographer, I had to get used to not being published as much. News holes are smaller in magazines and layouts and stories change constantly. My work can be scheduled to run in a publication one moment and be out the next.

I have learned most magazine editors I work with don't want to hear how high the mountain was or how deep the water—they just want the photos on their desk so they can do their thing. If I have concerns about my shoot I call the picture editor at Saba handling the film before it is sent over to the magazine to discuss the edit, verify caption information or check on critical exposures.

I thought I worked hard as a staff newspaper photographer. But as an agency photographer I now work each assignment—whether assigned or self-generated—as hard as I possibly can. I approach each job with a new vigor, always exploring new angles and techniques and researching each subject when time permits. I believe that this pressure has pushed me to produce some of my best work.

When I decided to be a photojournalist, I wanted to be the eyes of my community. As an agency photographer, my mission has remained the same, except my community does not end at the city limits (Figure 1.14).

When I was a newspaper photographer, I was not at all concerned with journalism as business. But now as an agency photographer I am very aware of the business side of photography. If you do not pay attention to business issues (i.e., invoices, expenses and taxes), you fail or end up in jail. Working for Saba allows me the chance to concentrate more on my photography while the agency handles the marketing and sales of my pictures. I still need to send billing information to Saba for prompt processing by the accounting department.

One long-time Los Angeles agency freelancer told me that "you must think of each assignment as a baseball game and must go out and try to hit a home run each time . . . because you are only as good as your last shoot."

Saba is a good fit. The staff is a talented team working with me for both our benefit. Plus, I like that I can call Marcel Saba on the phone anytime to discuss an idea or concern.

Being a freelancer can be one of the most difficult paths a photojournalist can take—it can also be one of the most rewarding. In the end, I like that I am the one person ultimately in control of my career.

Author's note: CORBIS acquired Saba in 2000.

THE PICTURE AGENT

Howard Chapnick—Former President, Black Star

In my book *Truth Needs No Ally: Inside Photojournalism* I have described a picture agent as "mentor, psychiatrist, financier, researcher, idea person, negotiator, stimulator and the quintessential middle-man." This description applies particularly to picture agents at assignment agencies. Stock picture agents need other attributes, primarily the recognition of good and saleable images, their proper cataloguing for easy retrieval, the generation of a good clientele, and handling picture requests with efficiency and dispatch.

The picture agent in an assignment agency like Black Star has first to recognize potential talent, then use all of his or her creativity, business acumen, and editorial talents to advance and enhance the photographer's career. Ideally, the picture agent helps the photographer to generate saleable editorial ideas, facilitates the photographer's access to existing markets, aids in the development of a portfolio, arranges assignment fees, assists in logistical organization of travel and other details related to assignments, edits the pictures in the photographer's absence, oversees residual sales of the photographs in foreign markets, and maintains the files for secondary sales of the pictures as stock pictures after first publication in the assigning publication. A good picture agent is the photographer's alter ego, doing whatever is needed to contribute to the photographer's creative and financial success.

Books

An important outlet for in-depth photographic projects is books. Authoring a picture book is not easy. Usually, the subject must be compelling and the photography superb.

But doing a picture book is possible, and it is one of the few ways for newspaper and wire service photographers to perpetuate their work. An important reason that so many newspaper and wire service photographs are lost to posterity is that they typically are published on newsprint, ensuring that their exposure is short-lived.

A number of outstanding picture books have been published in the past few decades. Arguably, the most prominent and influential in the contemporary photojournalism world is the 1975 book *Minamata* by W. Eugene Smith and Aileen Smith. It is the story of the people of a Japanese fishing village who were poisoned by their mercury-contaminated bay (two *Minamata* photographs are in Chapter 8).

An earlier influential picture book was *The Americans*, a Swiss-born photographer's look at the United States in the mid-1950's. Robert Frank, using a small, relatively unobtrusive camera— a Leica—photographed throughout the Unites States in 1955–1956 thanks to his receipt of a John Simon Guggenheim Memorial Fellowship. When he finished his picture-taking, Frank could find no U.S. publisher who would take on his book. His photographs were too controversial—stylistically they were considered compositional heresy and the technical quality flowing from his 35mm film was poor compared with the reigning larger size 4×5 inch and $2^1/_4 \times 2^1/_4$ films so popular at the time. Perhaps even worse, Frank's choice of subjects left the impression in the publishers' minds that his pictorial effort showed the United States in a skewed, unfavorable, and unfair light—his work was called anti-American among other things.

Frank's book was published in France in 1958 with the title, *Les Americains*. Then in 1959 his subjective—ever so subjective—look at America was published in the United States Its title was *The Americans*. Frank's book—hard-hitting, subjective, and with a then-unconventional approach toward composition—has survived the test of time and in doing so has influenced many photojournalists, one of which is Bryan Grigsby of *The Philadelphia Inquirer*, whose Q&A "Do You Really Want to Be a Newspaper Photojournalist?" ends this chapter. According to photographic historian Beaumont Newhall, "Frank had no interest in beauty, but rather in stark realism, however unpleasant or common."[4]

As with all the other picture books noted here—and the many other good ones available to you—you really should read Frank's book yourself, draw your own conclusion about the worth of the photography and accompanying text, and about the overall worth of his endeavor. In doing so, you may glean some ideas about the photographic road you want to travel or do not want to travel.

Other contemporary journalism-oriented picture books of note— among many others—are, by date of publication, *The Family of Man* (1955), Edward Steichen; *Yankee Nomad* (1966), David Douglas Duncan; *Telex: Iran* (1983), Gilles Peress; *Vanishing Breed: Photographs of the Cowboy and the West* (1984), William Albert Allard; *King Remembered* (1986), Flip Schulke and Penelope Ortner McPhee; *Other Americas* (1986), Sebastião Salgado; *Deeds of War* (1989), James Nachtwey; *In Our Time: The World as Seen by Magnum Photographers* (1989), Magnum; *Unguided Tour* (1990), Sylvia Plachy; *Living With the Enemy* (1991), Donna Ferrato; *The Russian Heart: Days of Crisis and Hope* (1992), David C. Turnley; *Americans We* (1995), Eugene Richards; *Sleeping With Ghosts* (1996), Don McCullin; *LIFE Photographers: What They Saw* (1998), John Loengard; and *Migrations: Humanity in Transition* (2000), Sebastião Salgado.

FIGURE 1.15

This is a screen capture of MSNBC.com front page, April 10, 1999, updated 12:55 Eastern time. Representatives from three departments—a producer, a multimedia producer, and a designer—work together to create MSNBC.com front pages. SCREEN CAPTURE COURTESY OF MSNBC.COM, MAIN PHOTO BY ATTILA KISBENEDEK/AGENCE FRANCE PRESSE (AFP).

The Internet

The newest outlet for photojournalists is the Internet, specifically that part of the Internet deemed the World Wide Web. The World Wide Web delivers photographs with only captions or with a package consisting of a combination of two or more of these: captions, stories, graphics, sound, and user interactivity, meshing together to convey an arguably more rounded communication than photographs and captions alone permit.

One important Internet outlet for photojournalists is any organization that disseminates newspaper-like publications. This new kid on the journalistic photography block is just an infant. But young as it is, its delivery of photography to "readers" is now a reality. Three prominent players—there are many others including major wire services and many newspapers—in this new publishing endeavor are Discovery Communications, Inc., through its Discovery Channel Online, MSNBC (a joint venture of Microsoft Corp. and the National Broadcasting Co.) through its MSNBC.com, and The Washington Post Co. through its Washingtonpost.Newsweek Interactive.

The president of Discovery Channel Online's creative division described its genesis in a *Washington Post* article:

> It all grew out of an observation that the Internet is this amazing new channel we need to take advantage of. We knew we could tell stories in a different way and attract new audiences when we all realized how powerful a transmission medium it could become.[5]

Discovery Channel Online, MSNBC.com, and Washingtonpost. Newsweek Interactive employ picture-oriented people. One of these, MSNBC director of multimedia, Brian Storm, sees this new outlet for journalistic photography as:

> just a beautiful place to publish pictures. There is a luminosity behind pictures that newspapers don't have. Not only would I say, "Yes, this is another place to publish pictures, but I would say, Yes, this is a GREAT place to publish pictures."

According to Storm, breaking news photos on MSNBC.com typically "live

Thomas R. Kennedy

I am director of photography for Washingtonpost.Newsweek Interactive, the online publishing group of The Washington Post Company. I oversee the creation of visual content for our websites, directing both photography and multimedia areas.

The vision of interweaving audio, video, still photography, and text into powerful new narrative combinations is often more grand than the daily reality of trying to organize and send it easily to an audience. Nonetheless, the challenge and opportunity to realize such visions are what make this an exciting experience. My own interest was piqued by a workshop experience in the early 1990s, and I have moved inexorably toward this medium since that first encounter. There is something enormously liberating and invigorating about career migration into a completely new area where the communications possibilities are still largely unformed. Before this, I was on the print side of journalism for my entire career.

By combining and using the best of the elements available to us—video, audio, still photography, animated information graphics, and typography—we can rearrange the narrative structure used to tell stories and thus better communicate information to our viewers. The interactivity capability of our medium opens up possibilities for dialogue between photojournalist, subject, and a larger audience in ways far different from what is possible with most print experiences. Then there is the immediacy. This entire package of information can be communicated globally almost instantaneously, and unlike print, it is almost limitless in its capacity to present content. Time and production tools, rather than physical space, are the current, primary limiting factors (Figure 1.16).

I am very happy to have a chance to contribute personally to the evolution of photojournalism in this medium. I consider that an enormous privilege and opportunity. In many respects, I think society, throughout the world, is at the beginning of experiencing a force that will be as reshaping in its time as the automobile or film have been. The globalized economy will almost certainly be speeded in its evolution by the Internet. I also think it is likely that the Internet will play a role in revitalizing photojournalism as a communications medium and strengthen its value in expressing fundamental truths about the human condition. Many people have learned to read photojournalism as an expression of reality. I think it is important to preserve that function of photojournalism and to encourage the furtherance of its dissemination while also extending career opportunities and options for individual practitioners.

Thus far, this digital world has been as complete and interesting a challenge as I have found in my career. I only hope other professional colleagues will make the same journey and find the same experience. Together we can do great things in this new medium.

from 1 to 24 hours and special reports, 7 to 10 days." This turnover means that MSNBC (and other similar organizations in Internet photojournalism) has a constant hunger for images (Figure 1.15).

Storm is wildly enthusiastic about what he is doing. He particularly likes the multimedia aspects:

> There is no manual in this medium. We're defining it right now. We are asking, "How can we best tell the story? How can we add more context?" Sometimes this is accomplished by adding a sound clip of the photographer discussing background issues or the subjects telling their story. Maybe it's an event-associated sound like a train rolling by. Maybe we use information from the sound clip as text instead of as a sound clip.

> The key is to use the best possible media element to tell the story. Still images are only one option. If video says it best, fine. Maybe a sound clip drives the point home. Multimedia is most successful when these elements are integrated, each providing insight to the story.

Information accompanying photographs clearly is a key to material being used by MSNBC.com. Storm drives this

An August 1998 Washingtonpost. Newsweek Interactive page featuring people trying to find relatives and friends in the Nairobi, Kenya city morgue who were victims of the bombing of the American Embassy. This photograph, taken by Associated Press photographer Jean-Marc Bouju was one of a group of photos that won for The AP the 1998 Pulitzer Prize for Spot News Photography. The small photos above the large one give page viewers an idea of other related photographs available to be viewed with the click of a mouse.

SCREEN CAPTURE COURTESY OF WASHINGTON POST INTERACTIVE, MAIN PHOTO COPYRIGHT JEAN-MARC BOUJU/AP/WIDE WORLD PHOTOS

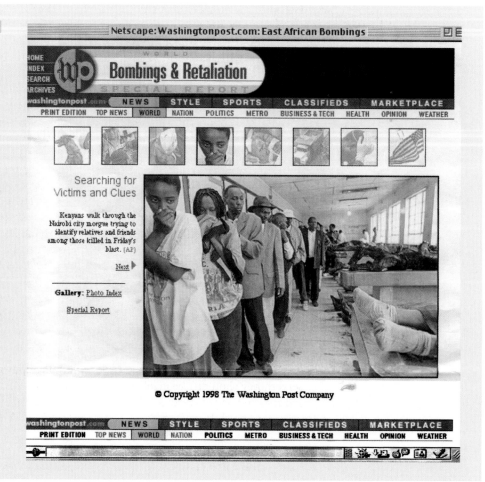

point home when he maintains that "great pictures are obviously important, but it's often the supporting material such as strong captions or compelling audio interviews that determine whether or not we publish a package."

There seems no doubt that to really succeed in the Internet photojournalism arena you must not only be a good still photographer, but you also must know how to gather information and turn it into well-written captions or longer text, you must have a good quality tape recorder and know how to use it, and you must know other skills such as how to use a video camera.

Only time will tell whether this fledgling computer-driven publishing endeavor is going to be a success. Certainly, it has disadvantages—it's hard to get comfy with a computer monitor like you can with a newspaper, magazine, or book, and downloading pictures can be slow. But improvements surely will come, and with the legions of computer users around the world and well-financed, big-name companies betting their money on Internet publishing, every forward-looking photojournalist is well advised to prepare to successfully work in this new journalistic environment.

Reflections on Photojournalism

Before moving on to Chapter 2 and some technical concerns you need to know to do your assignments in this course, let's consider the words of six current and former photojournalists—words that are food for thought. As with everything presented for your consideration in this book, read these quotations with a critical, inquiring mind.

Likewise, consider with a critical and inquiring mind everything in this book. Then, along with all the other information you undoubtedly will have obtained, decide upon the best road for you to take, the best approach that will lead you to a distinctive—and hopefully successful—photojournalistic career.

- You're usually in someone else's backyard, and I think you always have to remember that and treat your subjects with respect, the same respect that you hope they would afford you. **William Albert Allard**[a]
- No matter what it is I am photographing, I try to understand both intellectually and emotionally the person or situation and through this understanding to visually interpret what I see and feel, not just do photography from a so-called objective point of view. **Sylvia Plachy**[b]
- The media should be an objective observer; they shouldn't be involved or participate in any way [in what they are covering]. **Gary Hershorn**[c]
- Some photographers justify a picture as being honest if they didn't arrange or change the scene in any way. They feel a picture is honest if it happened in front of their camera. I point out to them that if it happened in front of them it doesn't necessarily represent the truth of the situation. **Flip Schulke**[d]
- A journalistic photographer should give the readers a window on the world. I've always thought the idea was to show the readers something that they wouldn't ordinarily see—to give them insights into the way other people live and to make them think. **April Saul**[e]
- To be in the journalism business a person has to be a curious individual and an individual who is very comfortable in all situations, someone who is able to meet and deal with people. You really do need to have a love for people. **Bernie Boston**[f]

Final Thoughts

Photography gave the world a lifelike memory. It is especially well suited for journalism, but serves other areas exceptionally well also. Legions of photojournalists have used the medium with great energy; many also have used it with great thoughtfulness and ethical integrity. The heirs of earlier photojournalists continue

[a]William Albert Allard has long been associated with *National Geographic* magazine, both as a staff and contract photographer. He also has been a freelance photographer. He believes that people who want to be great journalistic photographers must discipline themselves, must be willing to become their own toughest critics. He works only in color and is the author or *Vanishing Breed: Photographs of the Cowboy and the West, The Photographic Essay, A Time We Knew: Images of the Basque Homeland*, and his most recent book, a memoir: *Time At The Lake/A Minnesota Album.*

[b]Sylvia Plachy is a staff photographer for the New York City weekly newspaper *The Village Voice*. She studied art at the Pratt Institute in Brooklyn, and is a John Simon Guggenheim Fellowship recipient. She likes to use three types of cameras—35mm, $2^{1}/_{4} \times 2^{1}/_{4}$, and a panoramic—because she feels "some subjects look better in one or the other format." Various publications have used her photographs, including *Life, Ms., Newsweek, The New York Times Magazine, Wired*, and *The Washington Post Magazine*. She is the author of two books, *Unguided Tour* and *Signs and Relics*, and is coauthor with James Ridgeway of *Red Light.*

[c]Gary Hershorn, a Canadian, is a photographer for the London-based worldwide wire service Reuters and formerly worked for another wire service, United Press Canada. He is fond of the 400mm lens, both to produce a "clean" background and to give the reader a front row seat. He is based in Washington, D.C. and has covered many national and international events.

[d]Flip Schulke is vice president of Flip Schulke Archives, Inc. a picture agency marketing his photographs. Prior to his current position, he covered the U.S. civil rights movement on assignment for *Life* and *Ebony* magazines and became a personal friend of the Reverend Dr. Martin Luther King Jr. He was associated as a photographer with Black Star Picture Agency for more than 30 years. He is the author of four books, including *Martin Luther King Jr.: A Documentary—Montgomery to Memphis* and *He Had a Dream: Martin Luther King Jr.*

in their footsteps, taking advantage of the significant improvements in technology to better communicate to readers and with heightened ethical awareness.

Although photojournalism is usually a team endeavor, the individual remains important—the single person who photographs, edits, makes assignments, or manages so these can be accomplished in the smoothest fashion possible. Good photojournalism always comes back to individuals who push themselves to the limit, who love their work and want to succeed.

Being a photojournalist is not easy—the labor often is stressful and dangerous, and the hours are sometimes long. The pay often is moderate or worse, and the upward mobility limited. But perhaps for some the feeling of contributing, of being a part of living history, overcomes the disadvantages.

Whatever you plan to do with the photojournalism you learn in this course—photographer; photo editor; reporter who takes pictures or makes thoughtful photo assignments; editor or manager overseeing a photo department; public relations; advertising; agricultural extension; engineering; art; anthropology; or sociology; among others, or simply recording your family over the years in photojournalistic style—always keep in mind that there is more than one way to reveal the truth of your subject, and that your subject presents you with more than one truth at any given time. The burden you bear is to ferret out the most appropriate truth and visually present it in a fair way. This is the challenge—and the reward—that awaits you. Throwing yourself heart and soul into this course should go a long way to preparing you to meet the challenge and reap the reward.

NOTES

1. John Lachs, ed., *Animal Faith and Spiritual Life: Previously Unpublished and Uncollected Writings by George Santayana With Critical Essays on His Thoughts* (New York: Appleton-Century-Crofts, 1967), p. 401.
2. Lady Elizabeth Eastlake, "Photography," *Quarterly Review* (London) 101 (April 1857): 442–68, quoted in Beaumont Newhall, ed., *Photography: Essay and Images* (New York: Museum of Modern Art, 1980), p. 81.
3. Hal Buell, "Moments," in Dan Perkes, *Moments in Time: Fifty Years of Associated Press NewsPhotos* (New York: Gallery Books, 1984), p. 4.
4. Beaumont Newhall, *The History of Photography,* rev. ed. (New York: Museum of Modern Art, 1982), p. 288.
5. Kara Swisher, "Discovery Channel Charts New Territory in Cyberspace," *Washington Post,* 1 January, 1996, Washington Business sec., p. 9.

and the Civil Rights Movement. He is coauthor with Penelope Ortner McPhee of *King Remembered,* and is author with Matt Schudel of *Muhammad Ali: The Birth of a Legend, Miami, 1961–1964.* In 1994 Schulke won the prestigious Kodak Crystal Eagle Award for Impact in Photojournalism for his work titled "Martin Luther King, Jr., and the Southern Civil Rights Movement."

eApril Saul is a photographer for the large-circulation daily newspaper, *The Philadelphia Inquirer.* She specializes in black-and-white photography of non-news subjects, particularly for the newspaper's award-winning Sunday magazine, *The Inquirer.* She also does daily assignments and has used them as the starting point for her much longer projects. She is the recipient of numerous awards, including the Robert F. Kennedy Journalism Award and the first NPPA/Nikon Sabbatical Grant. She was five times the Pennsylvania Press Photographers Association's Photographer of the Year and, along with two of her co-workers, won the Pulitzer Prize for Explanatory Journalism in 1997.

fBernie Boston, before his retirement, was the Washington, D.C.-based photographer for the *Los Angeles Times,* covering the nation's capital, the east coast, and midwest. He was chief photographer of the *Washington Star* until it ceased publication and earlier in his career was a staff photographer for the *Dayton Daily News.* He won numerous prizes over the years including the National Press Photographers Association's prestigious Joseph A. Sprague Memorial Award. He is a two-time Pulitzer Prize finalist. Boston served four terms as president of the White House News Photographers Association. His work is published in various books.

Do You Really Want to Be a Newspaper Photojournalist?

Bryan K. Grigsby—regional photo editor,
The Philadelphia Inquirer

Author's note: Grigsby was a photographer at *The Inquirer* and a photographer, chief photographer, and director of photography at other newspapers.

Q: *Tell me some things aspiring photojournalists should know that they might not find elsewhere.*
A: My advice to them is to do something else. If they are going into newspaper photography with the intention of capturing the world and making life better for their fellow man, forget it. That is not what happens. I've discovered that most newspapers are run by former reporters for current reporters.

If they do go into photojournalism, they need to know about the political makeup of the newsroom. They need to know about gatekeepers who also are responsible for the daily compromises that are necessary for just getting the work done. They need to know there are lots of people "in charge" in the newsroom and they often have agendas of their own.

Q: *Tell me about those agendas.*
A: Power. You've got people running different departments within the framework of the newsroom who are into being "in charge" of those departments, protecting their spheres of influence. I remember one newspaper I worked for years ago where I came to the conclusion that it was not a single newspaper but rather a collection of smaller papers run by individual editors. These people

weren't dishonest. They still believed in the basic tenets of journalism, only it was "their" department and they were going to run it their way. This division of power in the newsroom can present special problems to a photo department, which has to deal with it on a daily basis. Each different department can reflect the different biases each editor has towards photography. Because the photo department is often operating as a service department, the photo editor often has little, if any, say-so about the eventual use of photographs in those different sections. At many newspapers, this lack of editorial power means the photo editor can't kill bad photo assignments or have any input into how a story can be better illustrated.

Q: *What would a novice photojournalist need to know to weave his or her way through this labyrinth?*
A: You can't successfully navigate it as a photographer without a power base at the very top of the newsroom editorial chain of command. The photo department needs to be as equal and as autonomous as the other departments. Section editors don't like to have photo people argue picture content or question the relative importance of particular photo as-

signments. As a photo department manager, you must have this top-level editorial backing. If it is lost for some reason, then you may find yourself at the mercy of fellow editors bent on getting even. It can get quite personal. You can find yourself completely at the mercy of editors who want illustrative "art" that is pretty or cute. Journalism is not immune to very human drives like professional ambition and jealousy.

Q: *Many people beginning in the business want to be photographers. Tell me about the aspect of photojournalism in which you're involved.*
A: There's more to photojournalism than just taking pictures and covering stories. Sitting behind a desk these past 13 years, I've learned there is a lot involved in just getting that huge mass of information we collect into the paper each day. For example, looking for mistakes in spelling or errors in reporting, not to mention getting names right for captions. This is a very demanding process, and for the people who do it full time there are few rewards or immediate satisfaction. It's certainly not as much fun as being out on the street photographing (Figure A). Being deskbound means dealing with constantly ringing phones that usually are carrying a steady stream of

FIGURE A

Bryan Grigsby at his photo editing area where he works mostly with photographs taken by *The Inquirer*'s **suburban staff.**

ERIC MENCHER

problems. Editors oversee the assigning schedule—the who does what and when of the daily routine. This usually means trying to utilize a finite resource (the day's photo staff) against a seemingly infinite number of demands for their usage. Other editors look at film and decide which frames will be considered for publication. These editors then work with word and design people who have their own problems with limited editorial space and stories that come in longer than anticipated. Ultimately, you find yourself dealing more with production problems than with content.

Q: *You recently left your desk job and became a street photogra-*

pher for a short time. What was that about? Getting back to your photo roots?

A: Clem Murray, the director of photography at *The Inquirer,* decided to give a couple of the photo editors time off from their editing duties to get back out on the street and shoot assignments. It really is a good idea. I think if you have been "deskbound" for too many years you lose touch with the realities of the "gathering" process of journalism. Photo editors can become too production oriented and forget the real-world problems that photographers face while shooting on assignment. Editors work according to office deadlines while photographers have to

deal with a constantly changing "real world," where things don't always happen on time. And, there is the physical reality of just getting the pictures back to the office through the suburban or urban maze of a large metropolitan area. But best of all, getting out and shooting assignments again was a fun break from the regular routine.

Q: *I know you are not in a position now that involves hiring but you have been in the past. If you were hiring now, what attitude, what skills would you want photographers to have?*

A: I would look at their portfolio first. I would want to know how they "see," how they see and record with the camera. I would be interested in how

Photojournalism: An Introduction

they present themselves during the interview; they would have to have a measure of self-confidence. They also would have to have people skills. It's important how you deal with other people both in and out of the office. A good photo department should be a team effort. A new photographer joining a department needs to be part of that team and be able to work with his or her fellow journalists. I might add that while I think a journalism-related degree is important, I don't think it's absolutely necessary. Any journalist should have a wide range of interests. I do think that having a college degree—any bachelor's degree—means a prospective photographer has been exposed to a wide variety of academic subjects, and that is good.

Q: *Let's talk about people skills, and about personality. Tell me more about this.*
A. Over the years I've worked with people in this business, reporters as well as photographers, who are absolute geniuses at what they did, but when it came to dealing with

their fellow human beings—forget it. As a manager, this creates a difficult situation because you are tasked with keeping your department running smoothly as well as professionally. These people may produce work of exceptional quality, but on the flip side, their editors may have to spend a great deal of time making sure they get it done on time or just get it done. I've seen some reporters and photographers who were treated with kid gloves by their editors. Well, this business involves a certain amount of creativity and anyone involved in it has a certain amount of creative ego. Staffers who are treated differently because they tend to be difficult to work with can only cause resentment from the rest of the staff. Consequently, I would avoid using them and avoid hiring them as well.

Q: *What are they? Are they abrasive, abusive, prima donnas?*
A: Prima donna is a good word. Unfortunately, these people can also be antagonistic to the public with which they deal. This only makes getting the story that much more difficult.

Q: *Considering you're someone who has made his living at photojournalism for close to 30 years, do you want to reconsider your rather negative advice at the beginning of the interview?*
A: Don't go into photojournalism with wide-eyed naiveté. Set goals for yourself. Learn the word side of the business and make good friends in the newsroom. Professional respect is something you earn. I love photography in the same way many reporters love writing. It's something you do because you have to. Whatever you do, don't let the system beat that out of you. Once you get into this business, if you're doing it as a photographer, you better plan out your escape route. It's been my observation during nearly 30 years in this business that old photographers don't fade away, they simply disappear. For all practical purposes there isn't any career track into upper management for photographers, and what middle management jobs exist are continuations of the front line of stress and daily chaos ordered by the demands of the newsroom.

Chapter 2

Cameras, Lenses, and Related Hardware

Special federal prosecutor Kenneth Star, who later recommended that President Bill Clinton be impeached, looks out onto a sea of still and video cameras.
Doug Mills/AP/Wide World Photos

Overview

The hardware of photojournalism—the variety of cameras, lenses, and other equipment—allows photojournalists to record what they visualize so that readers can see it. This chapter considers equipment for making photographs and how it is used (Figure 2.1). This equipment includes cameras, lenses, meters, electronic flash, filters, and steadying aids.

Cameras and lenses have greatly improved since the early days of photography back in the 19th century. Exposures in split seconds are the norm in contemporary photojournalism; early photojournalists had to settle for much longer exposures.

Light and electronic flash (strobe) meters remove the guesswork from determining exposure times. Small and portable electronic flash units make picture taking possible in even the darkest circumstances, and when the subject is moving extraordinarily fast. These units allow photojournalists to supplement sunlight and artificial light. The improved technology expands the range of photographers' creativity, hopefully yielding more storytelling images.

Sophisticated filtration corrects problems inherent in picturing real life. It also allows photographers to embellish or alter real life if ethical considerations allow. Filters also serve the important task of protecting lenses.

A camera body with a fixed focal-length lens, a lens that has only one focal length, is the basic image-making unit for photojournalism; however, for photojournalists to use only one body and one fixed focal-length lens is practically unheard of. (More about focal length is in the "Lenses" section that follows shortly.) Typically, photojournalists use two to four camera bodies and four to six fixed focal-length lenses. One or more zoom lenses may be used in addition to these fixed focal length

FIGURE 2.1

On assignments, *Baltimore Sun* photographer Kim Hairston typically carries one camera body (though sometimes two); 24mm, 80–200mm zoom and 60mm macro lenses; a flash and the cord that allows her to shoot with the flash off-camera; pens and notepads. All these items go in a fanny pack with an extra pouch. Two very important items she carries are her cellphone and beeper, for keeping in touch with the office and with subjects in the field. If she needs additional lights or a tripod, she has those in her car and will bring to an assignment when needed.
PHOTOGRAPH BY THOMAS GRAVES

Author's note: Thomas Graves took a number of on-assignment photographs for this book, and he wrote the captions that appear with his photographs. Graves is a former *Baltimore Sun* photo editor who also worked as a staff photographer and photo editor at *The Palm Beach Post*. He is now a freelance photographer in the Washington, D.C. area.

lenses or in place of two or more of them. Zoom lenses have many focal lengths and are popular with many photojournalists.

Exposure meters, also known as *light meters,* trace their heritage to the first exposure-calculating device of the 1880s and the first photoelectric meter of the 1930s. These meters help photojournalists determine the proper amount of light that should strike the film. They usually are built into camera bodies, although external handheld meters continue to aid photojournalists, particularly in special circumstances such as measuring from a long distance the light that is falling on a small area of a person.

Another basic piece of equipment for photojournalists is a device that produces artificial light on demand, the invaluable electronic flash. Nearly all small electronic flash units are semiautomatic or automatic; that is, after being properly programmed, they determine the amount of light needed to properly expose the image.

Particularly when photojournalists use more than one electronic flash at the same time on the same subject, they may determine proper exposure by using an electronic flash meter, sometimes called a *strobe meter.*

Photojournalists use few filters, but those that they do use are important. Lens protection duty ranks first. These almost-clear glass filters are semipermanently attached to lenses. They help prevent accidental scratching and gouging as well as problems associated with cleaning lenses. Filters also compensate for the inherent technical deviations sometimes found in film, particularly color film. In addition, they allow photographers to be creative by, for example, darkening a blue sky to emphasize the whiteness of clouds.

Photojournalists must also be familiar with tripods and other steadying aids. Photojournalists sometimes have to steady their cameras, and platforms can range from people's shoulders to tripods to monopods to tabletops—anything that eliminates camera movement.

Cameras

The 35mm single-lens reflex (SLR) is a widely used camera in photojournalism (Figure 2.2). The SLR camera uses only one lens to both view and record the scene, which is reflected off a movable mirror in the camera before reaching the photographer's eye.

The 35mm single-lens reflex allows photojournalists to view the actual images they are about to record. The image reflects light, which passes through the lens attached to the camera body and strikes a mirror; the camera's sophisticated viewing system reflects and

FIGURE 2.2

35mm Nikon F5 SLR with a 35–70mm zoom lens.

Left, Photograph by Simone Associates. Right, Adapted by Illustrated Arts (U.K.) from *Photography* by B. Warren. © 1993. p. 55. Reprinted with permission of Delmar Publishers, a division of Thomson Learning.

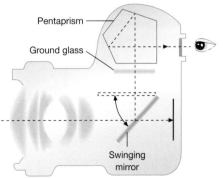

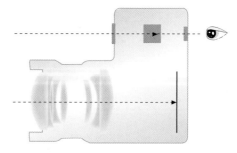

FIGURE 2.3

35mm Leica M6 rangefinder with a 35mm lens.
LEFT, PHOTOGRAPH BY FREDRIC PETTERS. RIGHT, ADAPTED BY ILLUSTRATED ARTS (U.K.) FROM *PHOTOGRAPHY* BY B. WARREN. © 1993. P. 54, REPRINTED WITH PERMISSION OF DELMAR PUBLISHERS, A DIVISION OF THOMSON LEARNING.

reverses the image. What photographers see through the eyepiece at the back of the camera is the image they are about to record. When the photographer presses the release button to take the picture, a mirror that otherwise blocks the image from reaching the film swings out of the way. Light reflected from the image being photographed streams through the camera, ultimately striking the film. The 35mm single-lens reflex camera, as is true of all film cameras of any size and configuration, essentially is a light-proof box containing and positioning film in a way that exposes individual frames. The 35mm camera—or, more accurately, the camera body because to many people *camera* means both the body and a lens—contains a mount for firmly securing a lens to its front. It also contains a shutter that opens and closes for periods of time, thereby controlling how long light strikes the film.

The 35mm rangefinder camera (Figure 2.3) is also used by photojournalists.

FIGURE 2.4

2 1/4 × 2 1/4 Rolleiflex twin-lens reflex camera with its built-in lens.
LEFT, PHOTOGRAPH BY SIMONE ASSOCIATES. RIGHT, ADAPTED BY ILLUSTRATED ARTS (U.K.) FROM *PHOTOGRAPHY* BY B. WARREN. P. 56. © 1993. REPRINTED WITH PERMISSION OF DELMAR PUBLISHERS, A DIVISION OF THOMSON LEARNING.

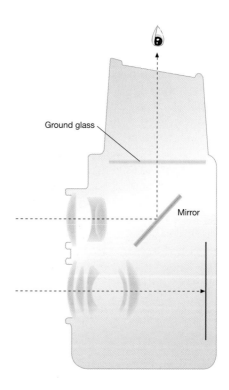

Ground glass

Mirror

FIGURE 2.5

4 × 5 Cambo SCX view camera with a 180mm lens.
LEFT, PHOTOGRAPH BY SIMONE ASSOCIATES. RIGHT, ADAPTED BY ILLUSTRATED ARTS (U.K.) FROM *PHOTOGRAPHY* BY B. WARREN. P. 57. © 1993. REPRINTED WITH PERMISSION OF DELMAR PUBLISHERS, A DIVISION OF THOMSON LEARNING.

Journalistic photographers may set aside their single-lens reflex cameras for rangefinder cameras when the subject matter particularly lends itself to one or more of the rangefinder's key attributes: quiet operation, small profile, and relatively low inherent movement. Journalistic photographers may from time-to-time use larger format cameras than 35mm, such as the 2 1/4 × 2 1/4 twin-lens reflex (Figure 2.4) and the 4 × 5 view camera (Figure 2.5).

Rangefinder cameras cannot, without an accessory attachment, accommodate a type of lens that photojournalists use regularly—the long telephoto. Long telephoto lenses make distant subjects seem close. Typically, they blur anything in front and back of the main subject, especially when the main subject is close to the camera; the more expensive ones also have the capability to gather and pass considerable light to the film. Telephotos (and other lenses) that pass a lot of light to the film are termed *fast*.

A newcomer to photojournalism is the digital camera. This camera, usually somewhat larger than a 35mm SLR camera, does not use film; rather, it is totally electronic, recording and storing images on electronic-based devices. These cameras arguably are the most radical and exciting development in picture-taking since photography began in the first half of the 19th century.

A digital still camera typically used by photojournalists looks and acts much like a 35mm single-lens reflex camera (Figure 2.6). In fact, until late 1999 when Nikon began marketing a built-from-scratch digital camera, the D1, photojournalistic digital cameras typically were conventional 35mm single-lens reflex camera bodies with digital backs. Digital cameras use devices that represent a fundamentally different approach from conventional cameras. They have an electronic light-gathering, processing, and transmission mechanism, and a storage and output mechanism.

Photojournalistic digital still cameras typically use the same lenses as those that attach to conventional 35mm single-lens reflex bodies. But because the light-gathering, processing, and transmission mechanism (digital recording device) is smaller than 35mm film, lenses for 35mm-like digital cameras in effect are longer (their focal length is greater than it would be if used with 35mm film); exactly how much longer depends on the size of the digital recording device used.

This image shows the Nikon D1 digital camera, which appears mostly similar to a standard film-based camera. The difference in appearance is noticeable when viewing the camera back, where there is a small viewing screen and some control buttons not found on film cameras. The memory storage device, an IBM 340 megabyte microdrive is seen beside the camera. It can hold more than 250 images, depending on the compression set by the user. A photographer may carry four or five such "cards" with them. Images can be downloaded into a computer and almost immediately transmitted to a publication, saving nearly an hour of processing and scanning time. This allows users to shoot longer and later at events. They may send their pictures straight from the event over phone lines, thus eliminating the need to leave and drive back to make deadline.

Photograh by Thomas Graves

Lenses

Cameras and lenses typically are packaged, promoted, and sold to amateurs as a package—a single camera body and lens. But photojournalists typically purchase bodies and lenses separately, even though each may be manufactured by the same company.

A normal lens for a camera is one whose focal length—the length from its optical center to the film plane when it is set at the greatest distance at which it can be focused (termed *infinity*)—is roughly equivalent to the diagonal of a frame of imaging material (film or digital recording device) used in the camera. Thus for the 35mm camera a normal lens is 40mm to 50mm because the film's diagonal is 43mm.

Photography commonly classifies lenses according to the amount of a scene that they can record from a given point and the maximum amount of light that they are capable of passing to the film or digital recording device (Figure 2.7). Focal length determines the breadth of the scene that the film or digital recording device will record and the size of the subject on the film or device. Wide-angle (or short) lenses are those whose focal length is less than

that of normal lenses. Telephoto (or long) lenses are those whose focal length is more than that of normal lenses.

Lenses range from the 220-degree, 6mm fish-eye lens, which photographs behind itself, to the super telephoto 2000mm lens to the even longer lenses made by telescope manufacturers.

Excluding specialty lenses—close-up, fish-eye, super telephoto, and perspective-control, for example—photojournalists tend to use only about 10 lenses regularly. These are the 20mm, 24mm, 28mm, 35mm, 85mm, 105mm, 180mm, 200mm, 300mm, and 400mm. Because several of these lenses perform essentially the same function, a photojournalist does not need to own all of them. Also, from a practical point of view it would be inconvenient to lug all these lenses around. It would also be largely a waste of money to purchase all of them.

Different photojournalists prefer different focal lengths. For example, one photojournalist likes a pattern of 24mm, 35mm, 105mm, 180mm, and 300mm, whereas another prefers a 20mm, 35mm, 85mm, 200mm, and 400mm mix, and a third something different from either of these. Whatever the pattern, the lenses may be all

FIGURE 2.7

Baltimore's Inner Harbor and the historic ship U.S.S. Constellation are shown in these four photos, taken with a 20mm (top left), a 35mm (top right), an 85mm (lower left) and a 200mm lens (lower right). With the 20mm lens (top left), the entire ship can be seen, as well as the promenades that line the waterway. In the 35mm view (top right), the Constellation is still visible but some of the mast is excluded from the field of view. The 85mm shot (lower left) goes even tighter, and the water taxi which had been in the lower right of the first two photos becomes more the subject of the photograph with the nearby pedestrians. And in the 200mm photograph (lower right), the departing passengers from the water taxi are prominent in the field of view. PHOTOGRAPHS BY THOMAS GRAVES

fixed focal length, all zoom, or maybe a combination.

As focal length becomes longer, the size of the subject on the film or digital imaging device becomes larger and the view becomes narrower; likewise, as focal length becomes shorter and the view widens, the size of the subject becomes smaller (Figure 2.8). A proportion is involved: subject size doubles when focal length doubles.

Generally, photojournalists choose to use wide-angle lenses over a normal lens for four major reasons:

- To record panoramas
- To get physically closer to subjects
- To emphasize or exaggerate subjects near the lens
- To obtain greater depth of field

Photographers use a telephoto lens to shoot something far from the camera. The image produced is larger, and therefore more recognizable, than is possible with a normal or wide-angle

lens from the same distance. You can also use telephoto lenses to great advantage to emphasize relatively nearby subjects by blurring their foregrounds and backgrounds (Figure 2.9). These lenses also allow photographers to shoot relatively close-up images of people and animals without intruding on their personal space.

Beginning in the late 1980s single lenses that allow a single photographer standing in the same position to shoot a variety of views muscled their way

FIGURE 2.8

Here are two photographs of the same scene, one shot with a 35mm lens (left) and the other with a 300mm lens (right). In the 35mm lens photo, a large area of the scene is shown, and the trees frame the stairway and the person. By contrast, the image taken with the 300mm lens shows a much narrower field of view.

PHOTOGRAPHS BY THOMAS GRAVES

into photojournalism big time (Figure 2.10). These so-called zoom lenses had been around for many years but had found little use in photojournalism because they passed small amounts of light compared to fixed focal-length lenses; this meant that these "slow" lenses precluded their users from photographing in dim light without using often undesirable additional lighting. In addition, the technical quality of the image produced from a zoom lens was sometimes inferior. However, by the 1990s zoom lenses had greatly improved, becoming fast—capable of passing a lot of light—and yielding images of high technical quality.

The zoom lens is now popular with photojournalists and is likely to become more so. But do not confuse true zoom lenses, which maintain their focus at all zoom settings, with variable focus lenses, which must be refocused at each zoom setting.

Before buying any sophisticated lens, a photographer must make a decision about autofocus lenses. The letters *AF*, for autofocus, typically are part of these lenses' descriptions. As their name im-

plies, autofocus lenses focus automatically. One or more tiny electric motors free photojournalists so they can concentrate on more important aspects of picture taking—story substance and composition, for example. Manufacturers sell lenses that do not focus automatically, but photojournalists tend to increasingly use autofocus lenses.

Aspiring photojournalists in their first picture-taking course may not be able to afford even a limited selection of the lenses that photojournalists use. Clearly, sophisticated lenses (and camera bodies) can help novice photojournalists, just as they help those with more experience. But if your funds are limited, you probably can do nicely with an inexpensive normal lens and basic 35mm single-lens reflex camera body or an equivilent digital camera outfit. See Figure 2.11 for an example.

One compromise is to buy a top-of-the-line wide angle lens and if funds allow a top-of-the-line telephoto lens (or a top-of-the-line zoom lens), which you are likely to use for a long time, and a basic camera body that accepts them. As your interest, proficiency, and financial

FIGURE 2.9

Two photographs taken with a 300mm lens, both at the same f-stop. The photograph at left, taken from 60 feet away, gives some feeling for the environment around the subject. The tree in the background, just slightly out of focus, is still recognizable as a tree. In the photo at right, shot from 20 feet, the only objects discernable are the woman and the newspaper because both are in the same plane of focus. The tree in the background is now just a dark fuzzy line. A lens of 300mm or greater is very useful for "cleaning up" selected scenes because depth of field is much more limited than with other lenses, thus throwing objects in the foreground and background out of focus.

PHOTOGRAPHS BY THOMAS GRAVES

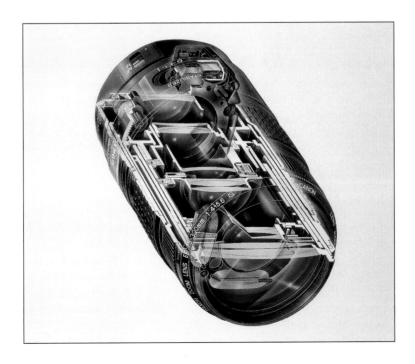

FIGURE 2.10

Cutaway view of a Canon EF 75–300mm f/4–56 IS (Image Stabilizer) USM (Ultra Sonic Motor) zoom lens.

COURTESY OF CANON

FIGURE 2.11

The Pentax 50mm f/2 lens and Pentax K1000 body are an example of an inexpensive outfit.
© PETTERS

capable of passing large amounts of light are complex. Zoom lenses are particularly complex because they have extra lenses that permit focal length to vary. Let's now look briefly at how light and color pass through lenses and how lenses affect light and color. Because zoom lenses are quite complex, this discussion considers only fixed focal-length lenses. Essentially, photographic lenses contain two types of lenses: converging, or positive, lenses and diverging, or negative, lenses (Figure 2.12).

Converging lenses bend light rays entering them parallel to their axes toward their centers—toward their axes. They also bend rays leaving them toward their centers—toward their axes as hypothetically extended in front of the lenses. Diverging lenses bend light rays entering them parallel to their axes away from their centers—away from their axes. They also bend rays leaving them away from their centers—away from their axes as hypothetically extended in front of the lenses.

If lens construction were this uncomplicated, it would be relatively simple to build modern lenses with large apertures—holes that pass lots of light. Unfortunately, this is not the case. Lenses used by photojournalists are quite complicated and become more so as they push aperture extremes.

Two problems—both aberrations faced by designers of the modern lenses coveted by photojournalists—demand subjective compromises, an important reason that lenses vary among manufacturers. These aberrations involve how lenses transmit the color in light and how they focus light.

Chromatic aberrations involve transmission of colors by lenses. Different colors bend differently when passing through a lens, resulting in no focal point at which all rays converge to create a sharp image. To correct this problem as much as possible manufacturers use a lens known as an *achromatic doublet* (Figure 2.13). This lens is different in type and composition from the lens to which it is attached. The achromatic doublet largely corrects whatever prob-

resources increase, you can add more sophisticated bodies and more lenses.

How Lenses Work

No matter how sophisticated or simple photographic lenses are, they are fundamentally alike. Essentially, all lenses collect and bend light and correct—to one degree or the other—inherent problems in the transmission of light through glass.

Because of the way light passes through glass and the way glass transmits light—particularly its colors—modern high-grade photographic lenses

FIGURE 2.12

Drawings illustrating converging (top) and diverging (bottom) lenses bending light.
ADAPTED BY ILLUSTRATED ARTS (U.K.) FROM DAVID FALK, DIETER BRILL, AND DAVID STORK, *SEEING THE LIGHT: OPTICS IN NATURE, PHOTOGRAPHY, COLOR, VISION, AND HOLOGRAPHY* (NEW YORK: WILEY, 1986), PP. 87–88.

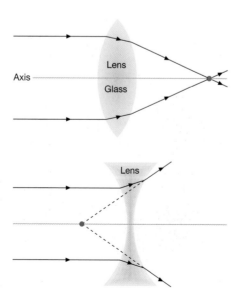

lens in color transmission the designer deems most important to correct.

Spherical aberrations involve light rays that never focus at exactly the same point. Every sophisticated lens suffers from this malady; the trick is designing lenses so that as many rays as possible strike close together. This creates the sharpest image, all things considered.

Lens Protectors

Photojournalists typically protect the front elements of their lenses from scratches and minor gouges by using an ultraviolet (UV) filter. This filter absorbs a minor amount of blue light but is the practical equivalent of clear glass for black-and-white film. Minor filtration of blue light typically is helpful with color films, particularly those that tend to pick up a blue cast from lighting conditions.

After considerable use, a lens-protecting filter—or the front element of the lens if a filter is not used—can become scratched or worse—gouged. UV filters are relatively inexpensive to replace; having a lens's front element ground down and repolished (if this can be done satisfactorily), having a lens's front element replaced (if it can be replaced), or buying a new lens is costly. Although filters do valuable duty as lens protectors, some photojournalists do not use them for that purpose because these photographers think UV filters impair the quality of the image, an arguable position considering publication reproduction limitations.

Lens Shades

Photojournalists almost always use lens shades (Figure 2.14). *Lens shades,* or *lens hoods,* as they are also known, typically are metal or rubber (with a metal threaded ring) and screw into the lens or into the filter that already is screwed into the lens, such as a lens-protecting UV filter. Some lens shades clamp onto the lens; some are built into the lens, particularly telephoto lenses.

A lens shade stops unwanted light rays from entering the lens from extreme angles. Unless blocked, these rays

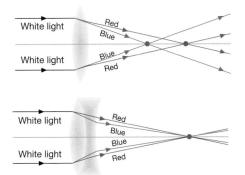

cause lens flare, a lighting condition that film or digital imaging records but that is usually undesirable in journalistic photography.

A lens shade also can act as a lens protector—protecting the lens from a gouging whack, for example. The flip side is that because a lens shade sticks out from the lens, it can lead to damage to the lens and camera if it strikes something that otherwise would have been missed.

Take care to use the lens shade made for each lens you use. Using a mismatched lens shade can cause vignetting, which stops some wanted light rays from striking the film. To one degree or the other this results in the film not recording part of the image being pictured. A mismatched lens shade also can let unwanted rays strike the

FIGURE 2.13

Converging lens and how it transmits red and blue in white light (top); the same converging lens (bottom) but with an achromatic doublet and the doublet's effect on transmission of red and blue light.
ADAPTED BY ILLUSTRATED ARTS (U.K.) FROM DAVID FALK, DIETER BRILL, AND DAVID STORK, *SEEING THE LIGHT: OPTICS IN NATURE, PHOTOGRAPHY, COLOR, VISION, AND HOLOGRAPHY* (NEW YORK: WILEY, 1986), P. 96.

FIGURE 2.14
Lens shade attached to a lens.
PHOTOGRAPH BY FREDRIC PETTERS

film, causing flare. On balance, lens shades are highly desirable in photojournalism.

Light-Controlling Systems

However simple or sophisticated professional lenses and camera bodies are, they have two light-controlling systems: shutter speeds and f-stops. The shutter speed system, typically located in the body of the camera, allows photographers to leave the shutter open for more or less time—to control movement of subject and camera and to assist in determining exposure and depth of field (Figure 2.15).

The f-stop system in the lens works in tandem with the shutter speed system. F-stops allow photographers to control the amount of light passing through lenses by creating smaller or larger openings in the lenses (Figures 2.16 and 2.17). The f-stop system also allows photographers to control the amount of sharpness in front of, and in back of, the point of critical visual focus, the point that is likely to draw the eye; this range of sharpness is termed *depth of field.*

FIGURE 2.15

Shutter speed dial on a Pentax K1000 body.
© PETTERS

Shutter Speed System

Shutter speeds common to most sophisticated camera bodies are 1, 2, 4, 8, 15, 30, 60, 125, 250, 500, and 1000. All are fractions of a second except for 1, which is a full second. For example, 4 is one-fourth of a second. For photographic purposes 1/30 is a relatively long period of time, 1/1000 a relatively short period of time. In addition, these bodies probably have a *bulb,* or *B setting,* that allows the shutter to remain open as long as the shutter release is depressed, and a *time,* or *T setting,* that allows the shutter to stay open until the photographer presses the shutter release again.

State-of-the-art camera bodies used by photojournalists have shutter speeds as short as 1/8000th of a second and as long as 30 seconds. These highly sophisticated camera bodies typically can be used at a wide range of speeds. They can, for example, expose the film for 1/536th of a second. Photojournalists need to be familiar with the shutter speed and f-stop systems, particularly their numbers and what each represents and does, to use these systems to their best advantage to better communicate to readers.

F-Stop System

The f-stop system allows photojournalists to vary the amount of light that passes through the lens. A series of metal leaves works to vary the size of the nearly round opening in the lens. The leaves are known collectively as the *diaphragm,* and the opening made by it is the *aperture.*

A classic f-stop numbering system is 1.4, 2, 2.8, 4, 5.6, 8, 11, 16, and 22. The larger the number, the smaller the opening in the lens. Less expensive lenses are likely to stop at 2.8 and 16. The numbers are derived from fractions. The numerator of the fraction is the focal length of the lens when the lens is focused at infinity. The denominator of the fraction is the diameter of the diaphragm. Thus the formula $fl/d = fn$. For example, when a 100mm lens has a diaphragm of 25mm, the fraction is 100/25, or 4/1, which translates to an f-number of 4, commonly referred to as f/4 (the *f* stands for *fraction*).

The focal length of a lens is determined by measuring the distance from

the lens's optical center to the point, called the *film plane*, where the light rays strike the film at the back of the camera. The optical center may or may not be the center of the lens, but it always is the point at which incoming light rays first bend on their journey to the film plane.

Photographers typically use focal length and the f-number representing the largest f-stop of the lens—for example, an f/1.4 35mm lens—to describe lenses. A lens whose largest aperture is represented by the f-number 1.4 is referred to as a *fast lens* because an f-stop of 1.4 lets a lot of light through the lens relative to most other f-stops. Likewise, a lens whose largest aperture is represented by an f-number of 4 generally would be referred to as a *slow lens*. Fast means that, relative to other similar lenses, the lens has the capability of allowing considerable light to pass through it at any given shutter speed; slow means just the opposite.

In Figure 2.17 with the lens shown, 22 represents the smallest opening through which light passes, and 2 represents the largest opening through which it passes; 8 is a mid-range opening. A good way to remember how the numbers relate to aperture size is this: large number, small hole; small number, large hole.

Systems Working Together

Photojournalists use the shutter speed and f-stop systems in tandem for two purposes: to control the amount of light striking the film or digital recording device and to literally or creatively inter-

pret the scene, for example, by freezing or implying motion, making everything in the picture appear sharp, or making everything except the main subject appear blurred.

The amount of light that strikes the film generally should be that amount that yields an image that shows detail in the light (highlight) and dark (shadow) areas and adequately reproduces the tones between (middle tones), a so-called normal tone image. On the other hand, the photographer may be striving for an image that yields no detail in the shadow areas. Therefore the amount of light that strikes the film for this image must be different from the amount that yields a normal tone image. The point is that photographers must know the image complexion they want to achieve. In

FIGURE 2.16

F-stop scale on the top of a Nikon 35mm lens.

PHOTOGRAPH BY FREDRIC PETTERS

FIGURE 2.17

Three f-stops (left to right)—f/22, f/8, and f/2—on a Nikon 35mm lens.

PHOTOGRAPHS BY FREDRIC PETTERS

f-Stop Scale

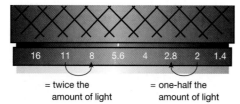

= twice the
amount of light

= one-half the
amount of light

**Shutter Speed
Scale**

= twice the
amount of light

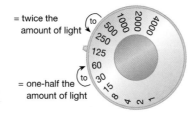

= one-half the
amount of light

FIGURE 2.18

**Unless depth of field
is a real concern in a
given photographic
situation, you most
likely will bracket by
manipulating f-stops
and using the shut-
ter speed you
started with.**

ILLUSTRATIONS BY
ILLUSTRATED ARTS (U.K.)

this sense the exposure of film or digital recording devices is particularly creative.

Bracketing helps ensure that the proper amount of light strikes the film or digital recording device. Light meters sometimes give incorrect readings, perhaps because of photographer misuse or meter malfunction. To increase the likelihood that they are getting the exposure they want, the first picture that photographers take is at the shutter speed–f-stop combination the meter says is correct. Then photographers make a second exposure of the same scene, letting half the light strike the film as in the first exposure. Then photographers take a third picture of the same scene, using twice the light as in the first exposure.

Thus photojournalists bracket the original exposure with other exposures and considerably increase the probability that they will obtain the best exposure possible. Conveniently, changing either the f-stop or the shutter speed to the next setting halves or doubles the amount of light (Figure 2.18). If the light meter is not working or not available and the lighting situation is such that the photographer has no good idea what the exposure should be, the photographer uses more extreme bracketing. After guessing the exposure, the photographer brackets the first expo-

sure with two f-stops or shutter speeds or a combination. Considering the latitude of most photojournalists' film—its ability to produce acceptable images from underexposure to overexposure, particularly when exposed at its normal ISO (International Standards Organization) rating—one of these exposures should be satisfactory. When using color film, photographers may bracket half stops. They may also do more extreme bracketing than what is described here, both with color and black-and-white film.

The second purpose for using shutter speeds and f-stops together is purely creative. For example, should the background be blurry? The foreground? Or both? Should focus, movement, or both help create the intentional blurriness? Photojournalists use depth of field and movement to make creative images that reflect photographers' individual interpretations of the most appropriate truth.

Photographers control depth of field by using focal length of the lens, f-stop of the lens, and distance of the subject from the camera. The shorter the focal length of the lens relative to other lenses, the greater the depth of field, all other things being equal. Telephoto lenses yield little depth of field compared to wide-angle lenses. As a rule, the smaller the aperture in the lens, the greater the depth of field. For example, the smallest aperture in a wide-angle lens, say f/22, yields enormous depth of field compared to the lens's depth of field at a large aperture, say f/2. The farther the camera is from the subject, the greater the depth of field will be at the same f-stop. The photographer has achieved great depth of field when the viewer gets the impression that the foreground, the middle ground, and the background are sharp (Figure 2.19). The photographer has achieved shallow depth of field when the viewer gets the impression that only one plane—or, at most, a few—is sharp and that all other planes are indistinct, as shown in Figure 2.20.

Depending on the message the photojournalist wants the image to convey, depth of field can be good or bad.

FIGURE 2.19

This photo was taken with a Nikon 24mm f2.8 lens using an exposure of 1/250th of a second at f16. The flowers in the foreground, only inches from the lens, are in focus and the church in the background is clear as well.

PHOTOGRAPH BY THOMAS GRAVES

FIGURE 2.20

This photo, made with the same lens as in 2.19, was taken with the lens set at f2.8 to give the minimum depth of field. Adjusting to that f-stop meant also going to a much higher shutter speed, in this case down to 1/8000th of a second! Here, not even all the flowers in the foreground are in focus, and though it is possible to assume that the building in the background is a church, no individual details can be discerned.

PHOTOGRAPH BY THOMAS GRAVES

Shutter speeds and f-numbers (f-stops) are easy to use. The amount of light striking the film is doubled or halved from one number to the next. Imagine an empty bucket and a water faucet. If the faucet drips for a long time, the bucket becomes full. If the faucet is opened wide, the same bucket fills with the same amount of water but in a much shorter time (see Figure 2.21). Essentially, this is how shutter speed and f-stop systems work, except that instead of water photographers use light, and instead of a bucket they use film or digital recording devices.

The manner in which light strikes the film—a large amount over a short time period, a small amount over a long time period, or some combination—can significantly affect what the picture says to readers about the scene. The rule for making easy and creative use of shutter speeds and f-stops is this: the amount of light striking the film doubles or is halved by moving one unit on either scale, excluding the four extremes. (The four extremes on the 4000 to 1 and f/16 to f/1.4 scales are of course 4000 and 1, and 16 and 1.4.)

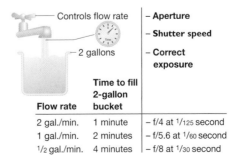

FIGURE 2.21

The bucket ends up with the same amount of water in it whether the spigot is wide open or barely open; the difference is in the time it takes for the bucket to fill.

ADAPTED BY ILLUSTRATED ARTS (U.K.) FROM *PHOTOGRAPHY* BY B. WARREN. P. 31. © 1993. REPRINTED WITH PERMISSION OF DELMAR PUBLISHERS, A DIVISION OF THOMSON LEARNING.

They are excluded from the rule because there is only one way to move; therefore, each is doubled or halved but not both. The amount of light is halved starting with 1 and f/1.4 but not doubled. It is doubled starting with 4000 and f/16 but not halved. Perhaps an example will make understanding this easier.

On an f-stop scale with 16 and 1.4 as the smallest and largest openings, 16 and 1.4 obviously are the two extremes; 16 lets in the least amount of light, 1.4 the most. Say the scale is set toward one extreme at 11—by pure chance after your kid brother played with it (not recommended). When you move the setting to 8, you double the amount of light striking the film. When you move the setting to 5.6 you quadruple the amount of light striking the film. This pattern holds until you run out of f-stops to move to—in this case, 1.4. If your brother set the lens at 4, which is toward the other extreme, when you move the setting to 5.6 you halve the amount of light striking the film. When you move the setting to 8 you quarter the amount of light striking the film. This pattern holds true until you run out of f-stops to move to—in this case, 16. This pattern applies to all the numbers except the two extremes, which in this illustration are 16 and 1.4 (the lenses you use may have different extremes). Because you obviously cannot go beyond 16 and 1.4 with this lens, you can only double the amount of light by moving one f-stop from 16 (to 11), and you can only halve the amount of light, by moving one f-stop from 1.4 (to 2). Using f-stops (in conjunction with shutter speeds) to get the proper amount of light to strike the film and creatively record the scene the way you want may be somewhat confusing. But after working with your camera for a short while, you should be comfortable with these creative controls, which are all but magical.

The name of the exposure game is getting the right amount of light to strike the film while portraying the subject appropriately. One photographer wants the main subject to stand out from the foreground and background; another wants to stop motion without concern for whether the main subject stands out; a third wants both. Thus shutter speeds and f-numbers provide the photographer with great creative potential; familiarity with them is a must.

To stop fast motion, use the shutter speed that lets light strike the film for the shortest period of time. On a 4000 to 1 shutter speed scale, this speed is 4000; 4000 is one four-thousandth of a second (1/4000), a very short photographic time. To get the greatest depth of field, use the f-stop on your lens that lets the least amount of light pass; to get the least depth of field, use the f-stop on your lens that lets the greatest amount of light pass. Two hypothetical but realistic photographic situations can help you understand the creative importance of shutter speeds and f-stops.

Shutter Speed Hypothetical   The assignment is to freeze movement of a high school track star running the 100-yard dash. Thus the first decision is to use the shutter speed that lets light strike the film for the shortest time—the fastest shutter speed stops the most movement. The only other consideration, as far as getting the proper dose of light, is the amount of light striking the film during the 1/4000th of a second exposure. This is where the f-stop system comes in.

The simplest way to determine the proper f-stop number for this situation is to have memorized several of the most common lighting situations in which photojournalists work. To use this approach you must know the intensity and direction of light and a typical shutter speed–f-stop combination for it. For example, a film that photojournalists commonly use yields a normal negative when the shutter speed is 250 and the f-stop is 16 at sea level with strong direct sunlight over the photographer's back and toward the subject. In the mountains at 5,000 feet the exposure is likely to be 250 at f/22. The light is brighter at this elevation because there is less atmospheric interference. Also contributing to its brightness is a shift in the electromagnetic spectrum—radiation waves, visible and invisible—resulting in more light that is ultraviolet, that is, blue.

Because photojournalists know that 250 at f/16 is one shutter speed–f-stop combination that yields proper exposure of the track star—keep in mind the exposure likely would be different if the runner were not facing the sun and the track were not at sea level—they need only adjust both scales to catch the runner in action and get the proper amount of light to strike the film. Of course, they have to focus the lens unless it is an autofocus version, which works with the camera to focus itself. A high-quality autofocus lens should have no problem keeping the runner tack sharp, assuming the photographer keeps the lens aimed at the part of the subject the photographer wants sharp. With a properly used autofocus lens, the depth-of-field concern in this hypothetical is not as important as when using a manually focused lens. To reach 4000, move from 250 to 500 and from f/16 to f/11; 500 at f/11 lets the same amount of light strike the film as 250 at f/16; the difference is that the shutter speed of 500 stops more movement than 250 does, and the resulting image will have less depth of field.

It is likely the runner would still be blurry at 500 because of the movement. So the photojournalist moves yet one unit faster, from 500 to 1000 and likewise one unit more wide open, from f/11 to f/8. This combination stops more movement and yields less depth of field. But two other shutter speeds on this camera allow light to strike the film for a shorter time, 2000 and 4000. So the photographer changes the shutter speed scale to 4000 (two units) and therefore changes the f-stop scale to 4 (two units) to get the right amount of light to strike the film. A speed of 4000 at 4 lets the same amount of light strike the film as 250 at 16 but stops the motion. Because 4000 is the shutter speed that lets light strike the film for the least time, the photographer takes the picture at 1/4000 at f/4. This shutter

speed–f-stop combination stops the runner's movement and lets the proper amount of light strike the film.

But wait. Is 1/4000 at f/4 really the best shutter speed–f-stop combination to use? No. The problem with 1/4000 at f/4 is that the resulting picture will have little depth of field; the likelihood of successfully focusing on someone moving so fast is slim, particularly when using a manually focused lens. To help ensure that the runner is in focus, the photographer needs more depth of field than f/4 permits. Because 1/1000 probably stops enough movement, that is what the photographer uses, gaining two units on the f-stop scale. 1/1000 at f/8 lets the same amount of light strike the film as 1/4000 at f/4 but yields additional depth of field.

Creative use of shutter speeds and f-stops is one reason that photojournalism is more art than science. The opportunity to create something visually exciting while conveying the most appropriate truth fairly represented is there.

F-Stop Hypothetical Joe and Jane Rich, both graduates of Desert University (DU), donated $2 million for a new classroom building. The DU public relations director assigns a photographer to take their picture in front of the new structure to go with a story about the Riches's generosity. (The student newspaper is doing a picture story on how the new building benefits students and faculty.)

The photographer wants the couple to loom large in the foreground so readers clearly see detail in their smiling faces; the building must be tack sharp in the distance. What to do? The primary concern here is great depth of field. F/22 gives the greatest depth of field on the 28mm lens the photographer is using. The photographer sets the f-stop at 22 and poses the Riches so the bright sun shines slightly from the photographer's right toward the couple and the building so that the Riches are not squinting into the sun.

Because the photographer is using film rated at ISO 400, a common practice,

1/250 at f/16 is one shutter speed–f-stop combination that yields proper exposure under these conditions. Because f/22 is a must, the photographer sets the shutter speed at 125. This combination allows the same amount of light to strike the film as 1/250 at f/16 but yields the needed depth of field. To lighten shadow areas on the Riches' faces the photographer also uses an electronic flash. It throws just enough light into the facial shadows to provide moderate detail.

FIGURE 2.22

This image shows the top of a Nikon 43-86mm zoom lens, illustrating the phenomenon of increased depth of field at smaller apertures. At f/16, the image would be in focus from more than 20 meters to about six meters, as seen by following the blue lines on the lens barrel. Similarly, the green line representing f/3.5 shows that using that aperture would only yield a depth of field from approximately 12 to 9 meters. As you use longer and longer focal lengths, your depth of field shrinks, as illustrated by the convergence of the colored lines with the lens at 86mm. (The barrel of this lens pushes away from the camera body to zoom to 86mm as shown here, and is pulled back toward the camera to use the wider focal lengths.)

PHOTOGRAPH BY THOMAS GRAVES

Two traditional methods of focusing ensure maximum depth of field. One way is to look through the camera's viewfinder. Some 35mm single-lens reflex cameras have a device that allows the photographer to manually close the lens's diaphragm to its smallest opening, which permits the photographer to see the actual depth of field. The serious flaw in using this approach, particularly at an extremely small aperture opening such as 22, is that so little light enters the lens. This makes viewing the image difficult, sometimes impossible. Thus it is difficult or impossible to distinguish where acceptable sharpness begins and ends. Some manufacturers are no longer building depth-of-field preview devices in some or all their camera bodies.

The second and better way to achieve appropriate focus for the greatest depth of field is to use the lens's depth-of-field scale (Figure 2.22). This scale—and not all lenses have one—has some of the lens's f-stop numbers

printed on it and has marks for other f-stops. These allow the photographer to focus the lens without looking through the camera. The scale shows the minimum and maximum distances from the camera that are acceptably sharp.

Because the Riches are 6 feet from the camera and the building is 60 feet, the photographer focuses the lens so that at f/22 (the f-stop being used), everything between 6 feet and 60 feet is sharp. To ensure that the couple will be sharp, the photographer builds in a small safety factor. The photographer lines up the number 5 on the lens—which represents 5 feet—so that it is opposite the appropriate f/22 mark, which is a vertical line. The photographer makes sure that the 60-foot mark, which is a guess because it is not marked on the lens, is at or beyond the other f/22 mark. In fact, the sharpness extends well beyond the photographer's estimate of the 60-foot mark. The actual point of focus is somewhat more than 15 feet.

If the Riches and the building were not near enough to each other to be within the lens's depth-of-field capability at its smallest f-stop, in this case f/22, the photographer would have had to move the couple so that they were closer to the building or would have had to move the camera farther away or use a wider angle lens that yielded the depth of field needed.

Meters

Photojournalists regularly use two types of light-measuring meters. Meters that measure continuously produced light are commonly called *light meters*. Meters that measure pulsed light (such as electronic flash light) are called *electronic flash*, or *strobe, meters*.

Light Meters

There are two types of light meters: reflective and incident (Figure 2.23). Reflective meters measure the amount of light that a subject reflects. They are almost universally used by photojournalists because they can be built into camera bodies, which makes them convenient and quick to use.

Incident meters measure the amount of light falling on subjects. Unlike reflective meters, incident meters are not affected by the makeup or complexion of the subject. Because incident meters are not easy to install in cameras, they are separate pieces of equipment. Photojournalists find that incident meters are particularly useful for measuring light from a geographically wide area and when copying paintings and photographs.

Meters can be built into camera bodies or are individual units. Individual meters are self-contained devices that usually are handheld. Built-in meters run the gamut from those that read entire scenes to those that read only a small portion. The most sophisticated and expensive camera bodies contain meters that offer a choice; for example, the light of a small portion of a scene or a balanced light mixture for the entire scene.

Light meters are built so they average to a middle gray all the light that enters them; that is, they assume that

FIGURE 2.23

The way a reflective light meter (left) receives light. The way an incident light meter (right) receives light.

Illustrations by Illustrated Arts (U.K.)

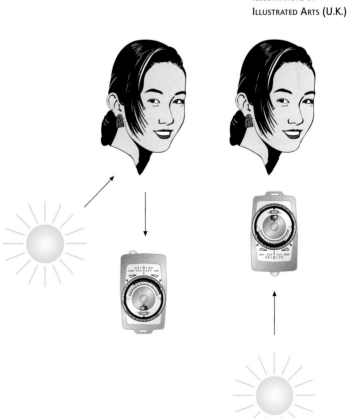

the scene has roughly equal amounts of dark and light tones and recommend f-stops–shutter speed combinations for a compromise middle gray. Photojournalists sometimes are unwilling to settle for this middle gray exposure because they want to be more creative in presenting their vision of the most appropriate truth. In any case they typically make an extra effort to ensure that their light meter readings ultimately produce images that allow readers to see what they visualized.

The trick in the journalistic use of built-in reflective light meters (and all reflective meters) is to measure exactly what you need to measure. For example, if a small shadow area of a person's face is the area for which you need a light reading, you must position the camera so that the meter reads totally or overwhelmingly from that area. If time permits—and often it does not—you should adjust your meter reading to account for the averaging that the meter does automatically. For example, you might want to increase your exposure so that a white area ends up more white than gray.

Correctly using light meters in the quest for proper exposure is a matter of knowing what is most important in scenes and how to convey this.

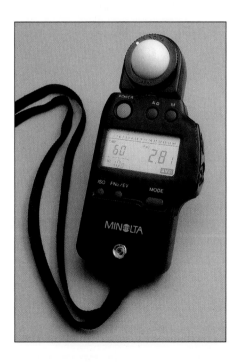

FIGURE 2.24

Minolta Autometer IV F. A combination flash—ambient light meter.
PHOTOGRAPH BY FREDRIC PETTERS

Electronic Flash (Strobe) Meters

Even though, with appropriate adjustment, many lightweight portable electronic flash units determine the proper amount of light striking film or digital recording device, specialized meters for electronic flash light are enormously helpful. Although experienced photographers often can correctly guess the proper exposure for electronic flash, they sometimes need accurate independent measurement of the electronic flash light that is striking their subject and reflecting to their camera. Planned events lend themselves to this measurement, as do portrait/personality subjects and illustrations. Some electronic flash meters double as ambient—existing—light meters; this is a combination popular with photojournalists (Figure 2.24).

Electronic Flash (Strobe)

Contemporary photojournalism is far from the days of the inconvenient and dangerous flash powder that singed eyebrows and worse. Electronic flash units, commonly called *strobes,* store up energy and release it in one great burst. The energy recharges after a short interval—particularly if the unit is equipped with what's called a *thyristor circuit,* which saves any energy that the last flash did not use. The lightweight portable strobes used by photojournalists typically are powered by one or more batteries—some with powerfully high voltage (Figure 2.25). The heavy studio-type units (which also are occasionally used in the field, usually for lighting relatively large areas) are powered by high-voltage batteries or alternating current (A.C.).

Camera stores sell a variety of electronic flash units. Before buying one, check with your course instructor, with students who already use one, and with local photojournalists. Most likely their preferences will lead you to two or three units, any one of which will serve you nicely. Because new and improved models may be available, units that this book could recommend might be outdated by the time you read this. But perhaps some parameters will help. Generally, photojournalists want their lightweight portable electronic flash units to have:

- Powerful and automatic light output
- Wide automatic exposure range
- Variable light output
- Remote sensing capability
- A heavy-duty battery
- Light weight
- A flash head with vertical movement that allows the photographer to bounce flash off ceilings

Students beginning in photojournalism may find an electronic flash with these specifications beyond their financial means. Less expensive units are available and are fine where electronic flash performance demands are limited.

Light from electronic flash traditionally is used in one of two ways: direct or bounced.

Although contemporary photojournalists seldom use a single electronic flash on or near the camera and pointed directly toward the subject as their main light source, this direct technique is useful in some situations. An example is a plane crash at night in a swamp where there is little or no existing light and no ceilings or walls from which photographer-provided light can be bounced. This direct flash technique typically leaves a telltale dark shadow behind the main subject, assuming there is something fairly close behind the subject onto which the shadow falls. Photographers can mitigate this distracting shadow by holding the flash head away from and above the camera (Figure 2.26).

Photojournalists often use a single electronic flash as secondary, or *fill,* light. This technique involves lightening (or opening up) the shadows caused by a main light source, usually the sun or fluorescent lamps. The cardinal rule of fill flash is not to overpower the ambiance created by the main light source. This means that the fill light must not be as intense as the main light; typically, it should be no more than the

FIGURE 2.25
Nikon SB-28 electronic flash attached to a Nikon 35mm F5 SLR camera body.
PHOTOGRAPH BY SIMONE ASSOCIATES

equivalent of one stop less. Doing fill-flash tests in the most common light situations can be immensely helpful later.

Electronic flash units with variable light outputs are particularly helpful in fill photography because they make light intensity easy to control. Incidentally, when subjects are stationary and not pressed for time and the sun is shining brightly, a large piece of cardboard covered with aluminum foil, dull side toward the sun, makes a nice fill setup. Pay careful attention to the amount of light directed toward the subject; it is easy to fill with too much aluminum foil–reflected light.

Another electronic flash technique that photojournalists find useful is using two or more electronic flash units together (Figure 2.27). This is a good way to light large areas as well as individual environmental portraits made indoors.

When photographers need a softer light for relatively close-up work of stationary subjects, such as a portrait, they attach reflectors called *umbrellas* to

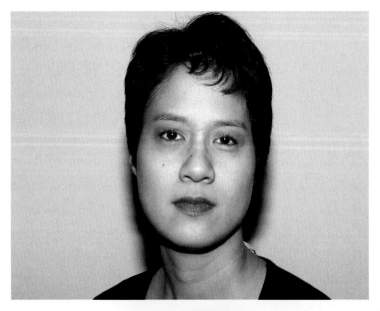

Direct flash from camera position (top) creating distracting harsh shadow; direct flash away from and higher than camera (bottom) with resulting mitigation of shadow.
PHOTOGRAPHS BY THOMAS GRAVES

units, the other units discharge simultaneously. Disadvantages to using several units are the need to lug them and their accompanying stands and umbrellas to scenes and the time required to set them up. Still, photographers must consider using multiple electronic flash techniques in appropriate situations, such as a dinner-dance held in a large, high-ceilinged, dark ballroom where use of existing light and bounced flash is impossible. Take all due care that guests, many of whom may be drinking, do not trip over stands that hold flash units. Generally, the best approach in these circumstances is to use only one additional flash and to have a person hold it rather than place it on a stand. The reporter covering the event may be willing to help.

Bouncing light from multiple electronic flash units can add an illusion of depth by lighting backgrounds that otherwise would be dark in the picture, making images more realistic and believable by imitating the existing light ambiance of the scene. Typically, one bounced electronic flash illuminates only the area around the main subject, leaving background and possibly foreground dark. Using one or more additional flashes simultaneously to illuminate the background, and perhaps the foreground, solves the problem. Again, you must take great care to ensure that passersby do not walk into or trip over your flash stands. Always remember that people could suffer serious injury—and sue you and your publication.

A direct electronic flash technique that yields a relatively soft shadow behind the subject is termed *bare bulb* (Figure 2.29). This technique is the same as that for single direct flash. The difference is that light from the electronic flash bulb is not reflected in a flash head before it strikes the subject; rather, it strikes directly. Because light is emitted for 360 degrees, considerably less of it strikes the subject than when it is reflected. Thus you must adjust your exposure. When using a bare-bulb flash, expect to open the diaphragm about 2.5

light stands (Figure 2.28). The photographer then directs the flash heads toward the umbrellas so that the light bounces off them before striking the subject. Umbrellas of various sizes and reflective surfaces are widely sold and typically yield excellent results.

Skillfully used, multiple direct electronic flash lighting is highly effective. Typically, the photographer discharges the unit nearest the camera through a cord connected to the camera. When the light passes through the photoelectric cells (slaves) attached to the other

FIGURE 2.27

Direct multiple flash setup (top) using three flashes. The subject here was exposed using a cross-lighting setup in which one flash is to the left and slightly in front, and a second is to the right and slightly behind. A third flash illuminates the rose design on the wall behind. Often that third light is useful as a hairlight, placed above and/or behind the subject pointing at the back of the head. This is the setup (bottom) used for the photo above. The flash at left lights most of the subject's front, and the flash at right, set one f-stop brighter, provides a strong sidelight that is almost a backlight. The flash on the floor behind the subject is aimed at the rose and is set to provide wide-angle lighting. It is set to provide the same exposure as the main front light. Keeping the flashes several feet from the subject can help soften harsh shadows that occur with direct flash.

PHOTOGRAPHS BY THOMAS GRAVES

stops more than when you are using a typical reflector flash.

Photographers using bare-bulb units should test to determine the loss of light—or, put another way, the proper exposure—with a bare-bulb flash over a reflector flash. Some photographers may so like the soft ambiance and predictable exposures yielded by a bare bulb that they find the reduced light intensity of little concern except when subjects are at a great distance.

Another approach that softens the relatively harsh light of a direct flash is covering a reflector flash unit's flash head lens with a translucent white plastic cover, as shown in Figure 2.30. These commercially made covers disperse light more broadly and more softly than an uncovered reflector flash.

FIGURE 2.28

Bounced flash using umbrellas (top). Two umbrellas are arranged on the left side of the subject here, one directly left and at waist-level, and the other about 30 degrees off the subject's axis and placed higher up, pointing down slightly. This technique of creating a bank of lights gives a nice soft shadow and good directionality to the light. This is the setup (bottom) for the photo above, showing the placement of the two umbrellas to left of the subject. The flash in the upper left is set so that it will produce about one f-stop more of light than the one set lower. The upper umbrella is also aimed more toward the center of the body than at the head, to provide more even illumination across the scene. Because umbrellas spread out the light so much, photographers will sometimes use them only from one side.

PHOTOGRAPHS BY THOMAS GRAVES

Bouncing—using light from electronic flash units reflected from secondary objects—is an artificial illumination technique popular among photojournalists. Umbrellas bounce light in this way. (Photographers can use other light sources to bounce, but photojournalists almost always use electronic flash.)

Typically, in crowded or hurried circumstances in which using only one flash unit is practical, the photographer directs light from the flash toward the ceiling above the subject as shown in Figure 2.31. Photographers also direct electronic flash light toward a wall in front or to the side of the subject, thus also bouncing it. When the situation is controllable—so that spectators and passersby will not walk into or trip over the stands that hold the flash units—and photographers have enough time, they may use two or more units.

Bouncing flash softens its light and, to one degree or the other, simulates existing light. Photojournalists also use bounced light regularly because they can control it and because it is predictable and often more intense than existing light. Light bounced from ceilings onto people invariably causes their eyes to be dark because the subjects' heads and faces block the light coming from above. Photojournalists have long tried to eliminate, or at least mitigate, this problem by somehow lighting eyes. A popular way to do this today is by attaching a commercial or home-made white or light gray reflector to the back of the flash head. When the photographer aims the head's lens toward the ceiling, the additional plastic or cardboard reflector sends out just enough light to illuminate the eyes (Figure 2.32). Some photojournalists prefer to hold several fingers in back of and above the strobe flash head in lieu of the plastic or cardboard reflector. Evaluation of the reliability of fingers is best left to users. Whatever supplemental reflector a photographer may use, the best way to ensure it works properly—not too little and not too much light striking eyes—is by testing at different distances and different f-stops.

When using electronic flash as the main light source, you usually need not consider ambient light unless it is fairly bright and you're shooting a moving subject with a long shutter speed and large aperture. In this situation you may create what's known as a *ghost image*—usually an unwanted image produced by ambient light and near the electronic flash-produced image. Unless done intentionally, for example, to convey movement, ghost images are undesirable. An example is the ghost image resulting from the intense ambient light at a well-lit basketball court mixed with electronic flash directed at players in action.

Electronic flash units typically require a shutter speed of 1/250 or less with the focal plane shutters of most contemporary 35mm cameras. This relatively long exposure time, combined with a relatively large aperture and a

well-lit gym, produces two images on the film. In this situation the only practical way to avoid imaging from unwanted ambient light, while still using an electronic flash, is to change to a camera with an entirely different kind of shutter. A *leaf shutter* is in the lens rather than in the back of the camera. This shutter allows you to use electronic flash with shorter exposure times. If the

FIGURE 2.29

Bare-bulb strobe flash head.
PHOTOGRAPH BY SIMONE ASSOCIATES

FIGURE 2.30

Translucent cover attached to flash head lens of an electronic flash unit.
PHOTOGRAPH BY SIMONE ASSOCIATES

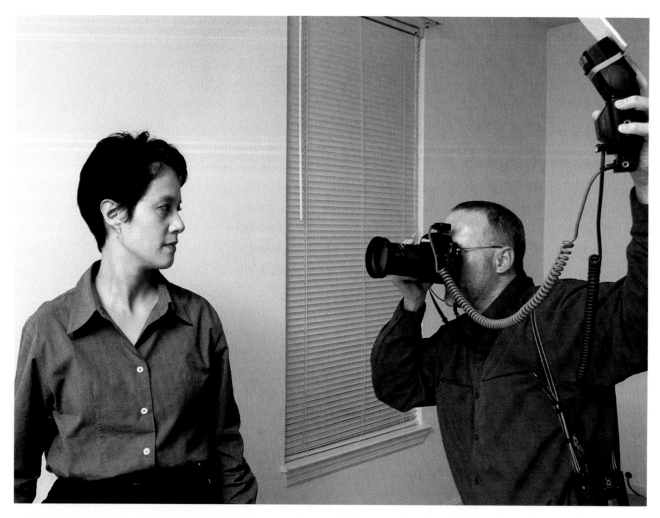

FIGURE 2.31

Bouncing light from the ceiling and on to subject. Here, the flash is directed toward the ceiling, where the bulk of the light produced will then be diffused as it reflects off the large surface area above and down on to the subject. A portion of the light is directed forward by the white "bounce card" attached to the back of the flash and protruding up above it. This will fill in dark areas of the face and produce a more pleasing effect. Holding the flash away from the camera will also enhance the image, because facial features will not be lit from the same angle as the lens is viewing the subject. Thus, the light will create some molding of facial features rather than flattening them out. Make sure you are pointing your flash properly so that the light doesn't fall too far in front of or behind the subject when you are using bounce flash.

PHOTOGRAPH BY THOMAS GRAVES

gym is bright enough, most photographers probably would simply dispense with the flash and use only the existing light.

Coordinating electronic flash light with ambient light can lead to more visually exciting pictures than flash light alone, giving the resulting image a sense of visual depth and richness and relating a storytelling ambiance that is more natural and complete.

Photographers use several methods to coordinate flash exposure with ambient light exposure: by changing shutter speed or f-stop or both; changing the direction of flash light, perhaps by bouncing it; moving flash light closer to or farther from the main subject; diminishing the intensity of flash light striking the subject by adjusting electronic flash controls; placing a commercial diffuser or a thin piece of cloth such as a handkerchief over the unit's lens; or changing to a faster or slower film.

Filters

This chapter considers two aspects of filters: how they work and using them to obtain images that mirror reality or intentionally alter it.

Fundamentals

Filters are transparent material—typically glass, gelatin, or plastic—that are the same color as the color(s) they transmit. Their filtration properties vary, as do their size. Filters stop certain light waves, keeping them from striking film or digital recording devices. Actually, filters tend not to be pure—pure red, for example. Because of this impurity they let some light close to their color, as well as their color, pass through to the film. Therefore a red filter typically lets through some magenta and yellow as well as red. When you use filters, be careful not to change the accuracy of the scene unless you do so deliberately. If you significantly change a scene, the accompanying caption should note that you did so and explain why.

Filters as an Aid in Picture Taking

Filtering light before it strikes film or a digital recording device can help photojournalists more accurately convey their message to readers. Photojournalists usually use filtration to achieve a rendition that comes closer to reality. But sometimes they use filtration to deviate wildly from reality for some particular purpose. Photojournalists typically use a small number of filters when photographing in black and white. Because color photography is more complex, it usually demands a wider range of filtration to obtain accurate negatives and transparencies.

Filters used by photojournalists range in density from light to dark.

FIGURE 2.32

Bounced flash (top) aimed at the ceiling without the use of a supplemental reflector. Here it is seen that the eye sockets and under the nose and chin are in shadow. Often the bounced light will take on the shading of the ceiling or wall off which it reflects, so be careful in rooms painted with bright colors. One common technique is to bounce off a white wall rather than the ceiling. The flash is mounted on the camera in both photographs. Bounced flash (bottom) is seen here again, but a reflector has been placed on the back of the flash to reflect some light into the face, thus reducing the eye socket shadows and those under the nose and chin. Most of the light coming from the flash is still bouncing off the ceiling, but a small amount, perhaps 20%, is being directed forward rather than up by hitting the bounce card on the flash, thus providing some fill light for the facial features.

PHOTOGRAPHS BY THOMAS GRAVES

FIGURE 2.33

Photo (left) taken through a plate glass window without a polarizer; photo (right) taken through the same plate glass window at about the same time with a polarizer.

PHOTOGRAPHS BY SIMONE ASSOCIATES

Typically, they screw directly onto the lens. If the filters are self-standing gelatins, they typically fit into specially made holders that screw onto the lens.

Filters with Black-and-White and Color Film   The most common filter used with both black-and-white and color film is the UV filter. Its main purpose is to protect the front of the lens it covers, not to filter light. With black-and-white film its filtration effect is nil. With color film it filters out a small amount of ultraviolet light. This light typically translates to a blue cast on the film, more so on some color films than others. When using UV filters primarily to protect the lens, be careful to use those that have the least filtering properties—the weakest filters.

Another filter that photojournalists use with both black-and-white and color film is the polarizer. A polarizing filter is most useful to photojournalists for diminishing or eliminating reflection and glare from many nonmetallic smooth or polished surfaces. For example, photographing through plate glass windows often creates a cacophony of reflections; the polarizer largely solves or solves the problem, as Figure 2.33 shows. Photographers also use the polarizing filter to make a blue sky much darker—the filter increases the color saturation, making colors richer—and to decrease or eliminate haze.

A third filter that sometimes comes in handy is the neutral density filter. Photojournalists use it with color as well as black-and-white film because the neutral density filter does not affect the light coloration; it only reduces the amount of light striking the film. Neutral density filters allow photographers to use larger apertures, longer exposure times, or a combination with any par-

Photojournalism: An Introduction

ticular film in any given lighting situation. These filters come in different densities. If a photographer has only one, it may be the 0.9, which allows a three-stop change or its equivalent.

Filters with Black-and-White Film

The three filters photojournalists are most likely to use only with black-and-white film are light yellow, medium red, and medium green. The light yellow filter is helpful on overcast days to increase contrast and on bright sunny days to help ensure that white clouds do not blend with the sky. Photographers use the medium red filter to greatly emphasize white clouds against blue sky or to darken the sky on a sunny day. They use the medium green filter to lighten green foliage, allowing better reproduction of detail.

Filters with Color Film

Photojournalists constantly must decide the color complexion they want to convey and which filter(s), if any, they need to use to achieve it. Fundamental to making an intelligent filtration choice—or the choice not to filter—is knowing that sunlight at different times of the day colors subjects differently and that different kinds of artificial light color subjects differently. The kind of film you're using makes a difference as well.

It is particularly important to consider filtration—you may decide none is needed—if you are shooting transparency color film (slides), even with a single light source. This is especially true when the slide, which actually is the developed film mounted in a cardboard, plastic, or glass holder, is the final product—when someone will look at it directly, either with a magnifying glass or a slide projector.

In photojournalism the rule is—or ought to be—you never use computer image-processing programs as a crutch, justifying sloppy, technically deficient negatives or transparencies. Besides the technical limitations of trying to improve by computer what was not properly done in picture-taking, there looms large the problem of someone other than the photographer computer-processing photographer images. No one except by sheer luck who did not view the scene at the same time and in the same way as the photographer can change what was put into the computer so that the image coming out is a precise image of the photographer's visualization. It is clear that the best way to assure that what comes out of the computer is what photographers want readers to view is to make sure that the image going into it is what they want readers to view. In short, the magic of computer-based processing of images is not a substitute for photographer technical sloppiness. Photographers who take pride in their work will use filters so that their original images on film or digital recording devices reflect the reality they saw in their mind's eye when they tripped the shutter.

Conversion Filters Manufacturers produce two types of color film, each designed for the light for which it is balanced: daylight and tungsten. Daylight-balanced film is designed for the almost white light of a sunny day near noon, when the light usually contains equal amounts of the primary colors—red, green, and blue. Incidentally, photojournalists often take pictures with light from fluorescent lamps. Because there is no "fluorescent-balanced" film, they usually use daylight-balanced film with appropriate filtration. This will be discussed shortly.

Tungsten-balanced film is made for exposure with incandescent light sources that are richly endowed with red and yellow—typically the ubiquitous tungsten bulbs used in household lighting. This film is less sensitive to these colors than daylight-balanced film; it is particularly sensitive to the bluish area of the visible spectrum.

Filters can come close to converting daylight-balanced film to tungsten light and tungsten-balanced film to daylight. However, photojournalists generally are better off using film made for the relevant light source. If need be, you can use an 80A conversion filter to shoot daylight-balanced film with tungsten light. Likewise, you can use an 85B conversion filter to shoot tungsten-balanced film with daylight.

Filters with Light from Single Sources

Light sources, whether used singly or in concert, fall into two categories: natural and artificial light. For the discussion here, natural light is from the sun. Artificial light comes from fluorescent lamps.

FROM THE SUN Color film termed daylight is made for light from the sun near noon on a clear sunny day with a few white clouds. However, photojournalists seldom work in this kind of light. An assignment may be at 9 a.m. or 5 p.m. on a sunny clear day, on a heavily overcast day, or at high noon with no clouds. The subject may be in deep shadow or near a colored object—a piece of clothing or a wall, for example—that reflects its coloration onto the subject.

Light-balancing filters solve these problems—in effect, they convert the light to that for which the film was made. Every photojournalist's camera bag should hold a prudent selection of these filters. They come in two types: amber, which is used to remove bluish light, and blue, which is used to remove reddish light.

Light-balancing filters come in four series. Those most useful to photojournalists are the 81 amber and 82 blue series (the others are the 85 ambers and the 80 blues). Filters in these series range from low filtration to high filtration.

FROM FLUORESCENT LAMPS Photojournalists should filter when fluorescent lamps are the light source. Fluorescent lamps emit light in only some parts of the visible spectrum. They are known as a *discontinuous spectrum source.*

Fluorescent lamps are a particular problem for photojournalists because they often emit light that causes an undesirable green cast with daylight color film, the film typically used (Figure 2.34). This problem is complicated because some fluorescent lamps emit light of different shades of green or of different colors, one of which almost always is a green. This is because they contain more than one phosphor, a light-emitting substance that coats their inside surfaces. These differences in light typically require more than one filter to remove undesirable coloration. Because fluorescent lamps differ in the color of light they emit and because different daylight color films respond differently to the same fluorescent light, choosing the most appropriate filtration can become a little complicated.

For photographic purposes you should disregard manufacturers' color temperature ratings of fluorescent lamps; these ratings are not meant for picture taking. The type of lamp typically is printed on it. Inconvenient as it is, often the only way to know lamp types is to read the information printed on them. The lamps typically are in fixtures, which probably are attached to ceilings. Once you know the type of fluorescent lamp—cool white is one example—you need only follow the chart put out by the film's manufacturer.

Photographers may use color-compensating (CC) filters to filter light from fluorescent lamps. They are numbered 0.025 to 0.50; the weakest filtration is 0.025, the strongest 0.50. CC filters come in six colors, blue, cyan, green, magenta, red, and yellow. Photographers can combine two or three color-compensating filters; the image formed by light passing through them is still high quality. The resulting filtration strength is equal to the sum of each filter used. For example, a 0.50 and a 0.25 equal a 0.75-strength filter. The CC filters that photojournalists typically use are 3-inch-square gelatins housed in commercial holders that fit on the front of the lens. Windy days pose a challenge in using gelatin filters. They are flimsy and blow away easily. They also are susceptible to scratches and gouges, regardless of weather.

Although it is not perfect for all fluorescent lamp situations, a single screw-in filter, known as *FL* (for fluorescent), is an option. When you have neither the time nor inclination to check lamps and carry a selection of CC filters, and when

FIGURE 2.34

The photo (top) was taken using daylight color film and fluorescent lamps as the primary light source and no filter over the camera lens; same scene (bottom) was taken about the same time under the same conditions except the photographer used a CC30M filter over the camera lens. An FL filter could have been used in place of the CC30M filter.
PHOTOGRAPHS BY THOMAS GRAVES

less than optimum but usually quite satisfactory results are acceptable, you can use an FL filter. If you are using daylight film, be sure to use an FL filter made for it; FL filters also are made for tungsten film. Some photographers who want to use only one filter with fluorescent lamps prefer a CC30M filter which comes in a glass screw-in version (Figure 2.34). You may want to try both the FL and the CC30M and decide for yourself which one you prefer.

Because of technical concerns the only way photographers can achieve precise filtration using fluorescent lamps is by testing with specific lamps. The final photographing should be done soon—within a few hours if possible—to avoid light changes. Because of the way fluorescent lamps work, exposures should be relatively long—at least 1/60th of a second, preferably longer.

Filters with Light from Fluorescent Lamps and Electronic Flash   Photojournalists shooting in color often try to preserve the lighting ambiance of a room by combining the relatively low-level lighting intensity of ceiling-mounted fluorescent lamps with the relatively high-level intensity of electronic flash. But using this fluorescent–electronic flash combination with color film usually presents an important technical problem: combining different colored light. One way to take care of this is to convert the usually acceptable light from electronic flash to the usually unacceptable light from fluorescent lamps. The idea is to match the more or less white light of electronic flash with the fluorescent's typically green light. (Not all fluorescent lamps produce a green light, but many used in commercial buildings do.) To do this, place a green filter roughly the shade of a green apple over the lens of the electronic flash, and then filter the light from both sources with a lens filter that filters out the fluorescent's green light.

Filters in Brief Filtration is an important tool for photojournalists. Here is a list of filters you should have available for your use.

For Use with Black-and-White and Color Film

"Weak" UV	Lens protection; slightly diminishes blue light.
Polarizer	Considerably diminishes glare from nonmetallic objects; darkens blue sky; increases color saturation.
0.9 Neutral density	Allows use of slower shutter speeds and/or larger f-stops.

For Use Only with Black-and-White Film

Light yellow	Increases contrast on overcast days; separates clouds from blue sky on bright sunny days.
Medium red	Greatly emphasizes clouds against blue sky on sunny days; darkens sky on cloudless sunny days.
Medium green	Lightens green foliage, yielding more reproducible detail.

For Use Only with Daylight Color Film

81A	Diminishes blue on slightly overcast days.
81B	Diminishes blue on moderately overcast days.
81C	Diminishes blue on considerably overcast days.
82A	Diminishes red and yellow.
CC05Y, CC10Y, or Kodak Wratten 2B	Diminishes blue cast from electronic flash — often permanently installed over flash head lens (specific filter, if any, to be determined by individual photographer's tests).
FL or CC30M	Diminishes or eliminates green cast from fluorescent lamps.
Green	Used over electronic flash lens to create a green cast and in conjunction with an appropriate filter over the camera's lens to filter green from green-producing fluorescent lamps.

Steadying Aids

Mobility is a hallmark of journalistic photographers. Squatting, stretching, leaning, bending and otherwise slowly or quickly moving often makes the difference between an eye-catching story-telling photograph and a ho hum image. But sometimes photojournalists sacrifice some or all their cat-like moving so they can have a relatively solid, or even a rock solid, platform from which to photograph. This sacrifice typically is made when a shutter speed short enough to stop subject motion and photographer and inherent camera movement is not possible or when heavy, bulky telephoto lenses are used for a relatively long time. This is when mobility to one degree or the other is traded for sharpness or practicality, when tripods, monopods, and other steadying aids enter journalistic photography. Let's briefly visit with some of these.

Tripods

The image of photographers carefully and slowly adjusting their cameras, which rest solidly and immovably on tripods, rarely includes photojournalists.

However, occasionally photojournalists are in situations in which they need tripods and time allows their use. Because of this, every photojournalist needs to have a tripod—a well-built tripod. These steadying aids typically spend almost all their time in automobile trunks. But when photojournalists need them, tripods are invaluable.

The reasons tripods rarely are used in photojournalism are because photojournalists seldom have time to use them; films and lenses can record images in extremely low light, making tripods unnecessary; tripods immobilize photographers, lowering their creative potential.

Monopods

Look at the photographers at most any sporting event and you surely will see this single-legged steadying aid helping support their long telephoto lenses (Figure 2.35). The monopod is a good compromise between the rock-steadiness of a well-built tripod and the need for journalistic photographers to move quickly to better photographically position themselves or to get out of the way of danger—a massive fullback running full blast directly toward them, for example. Monopods are extremely popular with photojournalists, helping them (even when using wide-angle lenses) to decrease camera movement when the steadiness of a tripod is not needed or when its use is inconvenient or otherwise undesirable.

Others

Innovative photojournalists use other steadying aids if tripods or monopods are unavailable or are impractical. One such aid is a special tripod less than a foot high that is easy to place on tables, chairs, cabinets, or other surfaces. Be careful not to scratch or gouge surfaces.

FIGURE 2.35

Rick Runion of *The Ledger* covers a Detroit Tigers-Atlanta Braves spring training game in Lakeland, Fla. with the help of a monopod supporting his telephoto lens and digital camera.
SCOTT WHEELER/*THE LEDGER*, LAKELAND, FLA.

Another steadying aid is a C-clamp equipped with a ball-and-socket mechanism that holds the camera and allows it to rotate. Be careful when attaching these clamps; they easily mar and gouge surfaces.

Final Thoughts

Cameras, lenses, meters, strobes, filters, and steadying aids are important tools for photojournalists in their quest for pictures that inform or entertain. Photojournalists must become familiar with the equipment they use but should not become enamored of it for its own sake. It should never become a burden, hindering the goal of communicating the most appropriate truth.

Chapter 3

Film and the Digitalization of Photojournalism

The back of the Nikon D1 digital camera has a small LCD screen that allows the photographer to see what is being shot in "real time," thus eliminating some of the guess work on exposure and composition, and serving as a crude but valuable editing tool in the field.

PHOTOGRAPH BY THOMAS GRAVES

Overview

This chapter deals with film, both black-and-white and color, and with the digitalization of photojournalism.

Color film largely has replaced black-and-white film for photojournalistic use, at least at newspapers. But some subjects demand black-and-white film—not a black-and-white conversion from color—to more fairly, truthfully, and dramatically convey their meaning; because of this, it is unlikely that black-and-white film, which goes back to the beginning of photography, will completely disappear from photojournalism.

Digitalization is used in two ways in photojournalism: picture taking and picture processing. One digital approach involves first using film. After film (and a film camera) is used to photograph the assignment, the film is chemically developed the same way all film of the same type is developed. Then, one or more of the resulting images is inserted—scanned—into a computer and processed using a sophisticated software program. The other digital approach is to use a digital camera with a computer and the processing software, totally bypassing film and all chemical processing.

The chapter ends with a Focal Point section that features William Snyder, three-time Pulitzer prize winner and photographer at *The Dallas Morning News*. (Snyder shared one Pulitzer with another *News* photographer and shared another with a *News* writer and a *News* graphic artist.) Go along with Snyder on his digital coverage of the opening ceremonies of the 1996 Summer Olympics in Atlanta, and visit his paper's electronic darkroom in Dallas.

Back in the 1960s the choice of imaging material was less complicated. Many photojournalists used one kind of black-and-white film. Use of color film was a little more diversified. Today more films are available. However, these films are threatened by a new and entirely different approach to imaging material, one that is electronically based and digitally formulated. Digital picture-taking now is mainstream at all major wire services; many newspapers selectively use digital cameras.

Also back in the 1960s the processing of images after they were recorded on film was done using chemicals in what commonly was called a darkroom—a chemical-optical darkroom to be more formal. Typically, photographs were taken; the photographer, if on deadline, hustled back to his newspaper, put the exposed film in two or three chemicals, washed the chemicals off with running water, immersed the film in a chemical that allowed the water on it to be more evenly removed, applied heat to dry it, or alternatively did the remaining work needed to produce a positive photographic print using the still wet film. A single negative was selected and put into a machine called an enlarger. Adjustment was made to the enlarger so that the desired image in the desired size was projected down onto a sensitized piece of photographic paper called, aptly, enlarging paper. After the negative image was projected on the paper for the appropriate time, the paper was put into two or three chemicals, washed to remove the chemicals, put into a solution that helped it dry evenly and with a high gloss, and run through a machine to dry it—a dryer. With various modifications to fit photographer preference and journalistic needs, this is the way—simplified—a black-and-white positive print that was a photographic representation of the scene the photographer saw and recorded was born.

The digitalization of photojournalism came to practical reality first in the processing of images after they were recorded on film. Now almost all, if not all, general interest daily newspapers and all major wire services use digital processing done in the electronic darkroom in their quest to turn actual reality as viewed by the photographer into representational reality that all can vicariously view. For these journalistic organizations, the more-than-160-year-old chemical print-making process is a thing of the past; photojournalism clearly is in the computer age.

In digital processing, if film is used, the image is put into a computer—it is "scanned" in—and then processed using a software program. Adobe Photoshop is one of these programs; it is extremely popular in the photojournalistic world (more about Adobe Photoshop later in this chapter). If a digital camera is used, the image is put into the computer directly from the camera's memory-storage device—there is no chemical processing. *The Dallas Morning News'* William Snyder goes into detail later in this chapter about digital processing.

Some journalistic organizations, such as The Associated Press and *USA Today,* have for a long time used digital still photography to record real-life news and sports scenes. Use of digital still cameras by wire services and newspapers increased slowly but steadily until 1999 when improved digital cameras accelerated the pace.

Digital picture taking is accomplished by an electronic process. Photojournalists seriously interested in digital imaging—and all photojournalists should be—can follow the progress of the technology by reading publications from the computer world, professional associations, and digital-imaging hardware and software companies. It's also important to keep in close contact with colleagues who stay informed about all the latest developments.

Because photographers don't have to take time to chemically develop film, the use of digital cameras means, among other things, that they can cover assignments closer to deadline or can cover assignments for a longer time, or both. When used in tandem with portable electronic darkrooms and all-but-instantaneous image transmission, digital picture taking can increase the immediacy that for so long has been a pillar of daily print journalism. Use of portable or permanent electronic darkrooms also buys time for photographers who are using film because it is typically faster than making prints in the chemical darkroom. Before turning to the digital arena let's look at film.

Film

Since the early days of photography photojournalists' imaging medium has been light-sensitive emulsions based on silver halides that darken when exposed to light. This medium has vastly improved since photography's birth. Among the more significant innovations was flexible roll film, first introduced in the 1880s, and lifelike, practical and widely used color film, first introduced in 1907. The little rolls of 35mm film, so common to photojournalism, are full of magic.

Black-and-White

Other than the identity of their manufacturer, the primary way to distinguish among the various films is by their sensitivity to light. This sensitivity typically is expressed by a number assigned to each film—400, for example—according to a standard rating system. The system widely used in the United States is that of the International Standards Organization (ISO). A film rated according to this system is described as having an ISO number; for example, a popular black-and-white film used by photojournalists who still use black-and-white is said to be an ISO 400 film.

Some films may use ASA, the rating of the American National Standards Association (earlier the American Standards Association) instead of ISO. ASA was widely used in the United States at one time but has largely been replaced by ISO. The numbers following the acronym—for example, ISO 400 and ASA 400—are from the same scale and therefore are interchangeable in describing light sensitivity of film. A third film sensitivity-rating system uses the acronym DIN for Deutsche Industrie Norm. This is a German-based system whose underlying scale is entirely different from the ISO and ASA scales. Do not substitute a DIN rating for an ISO or ASA rating.

A number of black-and-white films are available for photojournalists, although in practice they use only a few. ISO 400 film provides a good balance between requiring relatively little light

FIGURE 3.1

**Three ISO 400 films:
Ilford's HP5 Plus;
Fuji's Neopan 400;
Kodak's T-Max 400.**
PHOTOGRAPH BY SIMONE
ASSOCIATES

FIGURE 3.2

**Bulk loader, a 100-
foot roll of 35mm
ISO 400 black-and-
white film in its box,
and a cassette
loaded with film.**
PHOTOGRAPH BY SIMONE
ASSOCIATES

to properly expose it and reasonably high technical quality. ISO 400 film is suitable for use in bright sun, in dark areas with electronic flash, and indoors without flash, particularly when room light is relatively bright and ISO speed is effectively increased by a film manipulation process termed *pushing,* in which the film is deliberately underexposed. Figure 3.1 shows three ISO 400 films.

ISO 400 black-and-white films are complemented by films that take much less light to expose them properly than do ISO 400 films. The ISO ratings for two such films are 1600 and 3200. The higher the ISO number the greater the

film's sensitivity to light. The ISO 1600 and 3200 films do not have the relatively high technical quality of ISO 400 films. However, photojournalists are willing to sacrifice some technical quality to preserve the existing light ambiance of scenes. By pushing ISO 1600 film to 3200 or higher, and ISO 3200 film to 6400 or higher, photographers can take pictures in extremely low lighting, thus preserving the lighting ambiance of the scene. Pushing is an exposure-development procedure in which photographers deliberately underexpose the film and use special development to compensate for the underexposure. Typically, photojournalists push film in order to take pictures in dimmer light than they could if they were exposing the film at the normal ISO. Other reasons for pushing these highly light-sensitive films are to use shorter exposure times, smaller apertures, or both. In the past photojournalists were forced to push ISO 400 films, typically to ISO 800 or ISO 1600. With the introduction of the inherently more light-sensitive ISO 1600 and ISO 3200 films, pushing of ISO 400 films became discretionary, based largely on an individual photographer's perception of the best film to push for specific situations and on the convenience of using only one black-and-white film.

Films popular with photojournalists are available from manufacturers in short lengths enclosed in small light-tight containers called *cassettes;* the film is 35mm camera ready. A number of black-and-white and color films popular with photojournalists also are available in 100-foot lengths. The photographer must load this film into cassettes. Light-tight containers called *bulk loaders* hold the long lengths of film and allow photographers to load shorter lengths—the equivalent of 24 and 36 exposures, for example—into cassettes for camera use (Figure 3.2). Buying film in bulk is less expensive than buying it by the camera-ready roll; however, technical problems that may crop up in the loading process—grit scratching film for example—can negate the cost savings. You can buy empty cassettes

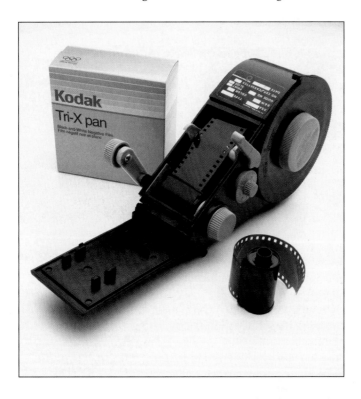

and bulk film at most photo stores that cater to professionals.

Modern black-and-white film traces its origins to the beginning of photography in the 1830s. It changed and improved over the years. Today it is a convenient and reliable product that reproduces real life with amazing fidelity in black and white and shades of gray.

Color

The two types of color film are transparency (also termed *positive, slide,* or *chrome)* and negative (Figure 3.3). Different color processes are used to create images on transparency and negative color film.

Transparency color film long was the predominant choice of newspapers, wire services, magazines, agencies, and commercial organizations that did journalistic-style photography. Then in the 1980s newspapers and wire services began to use more negative color. Negative film is less expensive, faster to process, and has considerably more exposure leeway than transparency color. Now many newspapers use only negative color. Most magazines and agencies continue to use transparency color film because of ease of editing, high technical quality, and financial savings. This is particularly true for the agencies, which incur greater expense with negative color because they have to provide prints to many clients.

Exposing transparency color is much more exacting than exposing negative color. No more than one-half stop overexposed or underexposed is usually acceptable. Arguably, the biggest advantage of negative color film is that it allows much greater exposure latitude than does transparency color film. Negative color film can be underexposed at least one stop and overexposed at least two stops and still produce satisfactory images. This frees photographers from the strict exposure demands of transparency color film and allows them to concentrate more on creativity. But good photojournalists do not misuse the forgiving nature of negative color film. If for no other reason than professional pride, photographers should stretch their talent to produce properly exposed negatives. Color film—transparency and negative—is made by different companies and comes in various ISO ratings.

FIGURE 3.3

Tulips are seen here on transparency film (left) and negative film (right). In the transparency images the colors appear as they did to the photographer's eye when the images were made. The images on the negative film contain colors that are not as they appeared to the photographer when the images were made, but which will produce the same colors as in the transparencies when scanned into a computer or when printed on color photo paper.
PHOTOGRAPH BY THOMAS GRAVES

Digitalization of Photojournalism

From the beginning of photography, latent images were formed by light acting on silver halides; visible images were formed by chemistry acting on the latent images. Things are changing. The era of filmless digital still picture-taking and computer processing in the electronic darkroom is here.

Picture-Taking

Although film still is a widely used imaging medium for photojournalism, it must share its lofty status with a new approach, digital imaging.

Digital picture-taking already is a major competitor to film picture-taking. All major wire services primarily or overwhelmingly use digital cameras. Many newspapers cover selected assignments with digital cameras and a few use them more extensively. Although still more expensive than top-of-the-line photojournalistic film cameras, digital cameras used by photojournalists have significantly dropped in price since first being introduced while having improved greatly in technical quality. While predicting the future can be difficult, it seems highly likely that digital cameras soon will push aside film and the cameras that use it at most, if not all, U.S. daily newspapers, leaving film and its cameras for specialized assignments, if used at all.

Pre-Electronic Darkroom

Not long ago you would not have seen a computer in the photo area you will be working in, and your first photojournalism course might have gone something like this:

On your first day in class the instructor gives you a list of supplies, including black-and-white film, hardware with which to develop it, and costly enlarging paper for making contact sheets and enlargements.

Film developing is a follow-the-instructions affair that takes about an hour to complete, depending on the procedure you use. After you dry your film, you move to the chemical-optical darkroom. This is a dim yellow-lit room in which you work alongside others in your lab. You first make small images the same size as the film; one 36-exposure roll of 35mm film fits on one 8-by-10-inch sheet of enlarging paper (and is called a *contact sheet*).

After properly adjusting a machine called an *enlarger*, you shine its light through a piece of glass or plastic that holds the negatives against the paper. You then put the light-sensitive sheet of paper into three chemical solutions—developer, stop bath, and fixer—for appropriate times and in appropriate ways. You then wash the paper for a certain amount of time, depending on the type you are using. A water-resistant type needs a lot less washing than the more conventional type. You then run the wet paper through a machine called a *dryer,* using the appropriate type for your paper.

You now sit down with a photographic magnifying glass—a *loupe*—to carefully examine each small image, selecting and marking the one or more you want to enlarge, typically from 5 by 7 inches to 8 by 10 inches, depending on your instructor's preference. You also carefully examine the negatives with the loupe to make sure they are appropriately exposed and appropriately sharp.

You go back into the subdued light of the darkroom and enlarge the negative or negatives you chose. This sounds simple and quick to do, but it is not. Enlarging takes lots of practice in manipulating the light passing through the enlarger and striking the paper; you must expose the paper so that the developed image is what you want.

You selectively add light to specific areas—you burn in—and you selectively withhold light from specific areas—you dodge. In enlarging you are using the same chemicals you used to make the contact sheet, and you wash and dry the paper the same way.

After drying your print, you find a typewriter (or a computer in a reporting lab) and write the photo's caption before turning it in for evaluation. Total time as a beginner (depending on the film developing chemicals and process you used, the types of enlarging chemicals and paper, and your proficiency at making enlargements)—from the time you walked into the lab area with your exposed but undeveloped film until you turned your assignment in for evaluation—was two to five hours.

The Electronic Darkroom

Press the fast-forward button and you are in the 21st century. Things have changed and for the better. Photojournalists have a better, easier, faster way of print processing—the electronic darkroom.

The electronic darkroom is not a darkroom at all; rather, at a minimum it is two machines and a computer software program. One machine is a *desktop film scanner*, the other a *computer*. The desktop film scanner is used to put film images into the computer. The software program allows the computer user to process images once they are in the computer. With its sophisticated machinery and pristine working environment the electronic darkroom has gutted chemical darkroom print making—almost all, if not all, journalistic organizations use computers exclusively to process images that once were printed in chemical darkrooms.

Using a computer to process your images is easier than learning the art of making quality enlargements in the chemical darkroom and is far less expensive than buying boxes of silver-based enlarging paper. No more laboring in a dim yellow-lit chemical darkroom, spending all kinds of sometimes frustrating time learning the science—and art—of making enlargements.

With this background, let's briefly consider three key aspects of the new way of doing things—the electronic darkroom. These aspects are the desktop film scanner, the computer, and the image-processing software, Adobe Photoshop.

The Desktop Film Scanner   Unlike images made with a digital camera which can be directly put into a computer, images made with a film camera must be converted into digital form before being put into the computer. In photojournalism, this primarily is the function of the desktop film scanner (Figure 3.4). Once film is developed and ready for use it is edited, and the exposures of particular interest are put into the computer using the desktop film scanner. (Whenever you are working with film, take care to handle it only by its edges to avoid leaving fingerprints on the images.)

A desktop film scanner is a little machine, actually not very impressive. But it does its job. Basically, you insert a mounted 35mm image or put an unmounted image, either singular or in a strip, into a holder. After removing as much dust as possible, you insert the film and holder into the scanner. (Dust is in the air and on everything you work with. Inevitably, it gets on your film image where, unless removed, it shows on your computer image and must be removed then.) Controls on the machine allow you to adjust it for what you think are optimum settings that will insert the best technical image into the computer. The scanner and its software are programmed to dovetail with the computer's software and with the image-processing program you are using.

If possible, you should scan photos into the computer at the size at which the photo will be published. If you don't know what the size will be, always err toward the larger size; that is, scan the images larger than they will appear rather than smaller. Considerable degradation of image quality can occur when an image is published larger than its scan.

In a nutshell, this is the desktop film scanner. Incidentally, different companies make scanners; they vary in quality and in the time they require to scan an image.

The Computer   Once a photograph is in the computer, a proficient operator—photographer, photo editor, editor, technician, whomever—easily changes

FIGURE 3.4

An Electronic Imaging Specialist at *The Baltimore Sun* scans a photograph into the paper's Electronic Darkroom using a desktop film scanner, seen at lower right, and a computer.
PHOTOGRAPH BY THOMAS GRAVES

small or large parts of it. This is the glory and curse of the electronic darkroom. Easy changes of images can lead to both well-informed and poorly informed readers. The photographic computer era raises ethical concerns to a new level. A major concern is how much manipulation—in polite photojournalistic terms, how much processing—is to be done and who should do it.

Some fear that nonphotographers who would never dream of manipulating images in a chemical darkroom will, without hesitation, trample on the integrity of computer images, imposing ill-informed and untrue visual judgments. Similar fears are raised about photographers using computers to correct any substantive and creative errors that they made when taking the picture, or manipulating the image in other ways that degrade the truth in order to ingratiate themselves with editors, win contests, or simply in-

crease their self-satisfaction, however misguided.

But in journalism, with the exception of pictures clearly labeled as illustrations, truth is coin of the realm. If truth—the most appropriate truth fairly represented—is diminished or nonexistent, journalism becomes a curse rather than a faithful light illuminating the way. It becomes worse than no information, worse than ignorance.

Computers and their software are not inherently bad. It is the way they are used that rises to journalistic good or evil. It is journalists—particularly photographers, photo editors, and editors or their technical surrogates—who turn them into a convenient and faithful ally helping to truthfully inform or into tools that hurt, seriously diminishing the journalistic search for the truth.

For image processing, Apple computers are the machines of choice for many photojournalistic organizations. Before Windows®, especially Windows 95,

Apple software made the company's machines the only graphics-friendly computers. Windows 95 considerably narrowed—if it did not close—the gap between Apple's products and the graphics capabilities of other computers.

Adobe® Photoshop®

Adobe Photoshop is not tailor made for most photojournalistic use; rather, it is oriented toward commercial artists who create illustrations for all kinds of users, including advertisers (Figure 3.5). Although photojournalists use the program to create illustrations, thus taking advantage of at least some of this massive program's more exotic features, photojournalism basically piggybacks on the program, using only a small part of it most of the time. Neat as a lot of Photoshop's features are, ethical considerations prohibit using them on most images made by photojournalists. For example, moving one person's head onto another person's body is a serious violation of journalism ethics.

Particularly when its massive capabilities are pared to the limited techniques needed by photojournalists laboring to convey truthful images of real life, Adobe Photoshop offers convenience, speed, and reliability in the processing of images. It allows photojournalists to quickly and easily do everything they used to do in conventional darkrooms. Computer processing of images has freed photojournalists from the time-consuming and darkened environment of the chemical-optical darkroom. It has spirited photo people into the brightness near, or where, reporters and editors work. By doing this it has helped photo people take a giant step in the direction of truly being perceived as equal with their text colleagues.

After Photoshop—or one of the several other photo-processing software programs—is used to make changes, if any, to the image, the image is sent electronically from the computer to the prepress department, where it no longer is the concern of the photo department. Alternatively, it is sent to a printer that makes a high-quality paper-based print. This print is then used to prepare the image for the press.

As anyone who has learned to use a complicated computer program—word processor, design program, whatever—surely will testify, *the* way to learn such a program is to sit at the computer, receive methodical and well-organized instruction, and practice. Once you are proficient in using Adobe Photoshop (and your desktop film scanner), in a rush you can expect to scan and process a 35mm color image in five minutes. For a more leisurely and refined processing, expect to spend no more than 20 minutes, including scanning.

With this background, travel in a Focal Point feature with *Dallas Morning News* photographer William Snyder to the Atlanta Summer Olympics and to his paper's electronic darkroom. See how one of the country's most honored newspaper photographers, a three-time winner of the Pulitzer prize, digitally covered the opening ceremonies. Look over his shoulder as he shares with you how he works in the electronic darkroom at *The Dallas Morning News.*

FIGURE 3.5

Adobe Photoshop is widely used in photojournalism.
PHOTOGRAPH BY SIMONE ASSOCIATES

William Snyder, photographer, *The Dallas Morning News*

The Opening Ceremonies for the 1996 Summer Olympics presented some problems for the three of us sent by *The Dallas Morning News* to photograph the Centennial Games.

The ceremonies began late, around 8 p.m. Dallas time. The two main events of the ceremony—the entrance of the U.S. team and the torch lighting—were scheduled late in the nearly four-hour ceremony. Precious time would be wasted by shooting film, shipping it to the Main Press Center in downtown Atlanta, processing it, scanning it, and sending the images to Dallas.

So we decided to shoot the entire ceremony (Figures 3.6 and 3.7) on digital cameras and transmit the images from a hotel room across the street from the Olympic stadium.

With those problems solved, all we had to do was take the photos, leave our shooting positions, fight the Olympic crowds, run down four flights of stairs, exit the stadium, sprint 50 yards up a side street, cross the main street between the stadium and the hotel, throw our $350 PC cards (which I'll explain in a minute) over the

10-foot-high storm fence that surrounded the hotel, and transmit the photos to Dallas in time for our deadline.

No problem.
Okay, maybe I'd better slow down. No doubt many

FIGURE 3.6

Images of actors dressed in ancient Greek costumes are projected against screens during the Opening Ceremonies of the Atlanta Olympic Games.

FIGURE 3.7

The U.S. Olympic Team, led by wrestler Bruce Baumgartner, marches past President Bill Clinton during the Opening Ceremonies of the Atlanta Olympic Games.

You're probably wondering what in the world does all that stuff mean? How do you scan film? Do you use a radio to transmit a photograph? Or do you move it with a truck? Is a digital camera the same as a regular camera? What the heck is a PC card anyway?

My intention is to give you a basic tour of the world of digital photojournalism as practiced in the award-winning photography department of *The Dallas Morning News*. You'll follow a photo assignment through the *News*'s photo department and on the way be introduced to the basics of scanning film into a computer using Adobe Photoshop. You'll get a glimpse of the equipment used to send photographs through the newsroom, across the country, or around the world. You'll also learn the differences between a film camera and a digital camera. (*Hint:* One uses a PC card.) And finally you'll find out if we made our deadline.

Other systems work as well as the *News*'s system; I encourage you to seek them out and learn about them. This piece is not meant to be the final word on the subject—the world of digital imaging changes rapidly. If you want to stay competitive, it is important to keep up with the technology.

Ethics   Everyone has experienced the awesome power of digital-imaging technology. From movies, television programs, and commercials to arcade games, magazine ads, and flight simulators, digital technology allows artists to unleash their creativity and create images quickly and cleanly with the click of a mouse.

Images that once took months to create are now finished in hours. If a photograph is not exactly what you had in mind, digital technology allows you to change it and make it perfect.

The power to alter an image quickly and cleanly seduces even the most seasoned journalism veterans. *National Geographic* magazine once moved the Great Pyramids for a cover. *Time* magazine manipulated O. J. Simpson's police mug shot in such a way that it made him look darker and more sinister. In both cases a public outcry condemning the publications arose when the manipulations were discovered.

As you can see, it's a slippery slope, this digital technology, so before I get into the bits and bytes, let's pause for a moment and discuss some basic tenets of photojournalistic ethics as practiced at the *News*.

A photojournalist's job at the *News* is to document life, to capture intimate, storytelling moments in a subject's life. The *News*'s readers must believe that what they see is what actually happened. This belief is based on trust, the trust that the photojournalist hasn't altered the image in any substantive way, shape, or form. This trust gives the photojournalist's work power—the power to inform, persuade, and even change society.

As a photojournalist at the *News* I do not create situations to photograph or recreate an event I missed, unless it is for an environmental portrait or an illustration. I do not direct, alter, or "touch" existing situations. I also follow this no-touching rule in the *News*'s

darkroom so that no substantive alterations are made to an image postexposure.

Computers have become today's electronic darkrooms, and—aware that if used improperly this powerful technology can destroy the integrity, the "believability" of a photograph—the *News* continues to err on the side of conservatism. Therefore *News* photographers don't change the color of the sky or erase an unsightly soda can, nor do they remove an offensive sign or gesture in the electronic darkroom. Once started, it becomes easier and easier to rationalize a change here, an addition or subtraction there. Before you know it, you've slipped into unethical territory. When this happens, the trust between the photojournalist and the audience is broken and photojournalism dies a little. Even though using computer technology poses some dangers, it provides many benefits for modern newspapers. It allows photojournalists to spend more time with a subject and increases the quality of reproduction. It cuts costs by lowering the use of photosensitive materials, which indirectly helps the environment by reducing the consumption of silver and the production of toxic waste.

Technology   The *News* still maintains a conventional darkroom for reprint orders and contests, but photographs for the daily newspaper are now produced in the electronic darkroom. Let's see how this new technology works in a daily newspaper by following a photo assignment through the *News*.

Each photographer receives a computer-generated photo assignment sheet with the basics of the assignment—who, what, when, where, why. Since the early 1980s the *News* has run color photos on the cover of each section and sometimes on inside pages. Because of this demand for high-quality color images *News* photographers shoot every assignment on color film so that they have the flexibility to scan and reproduce photos in black-and-white or color. Negative color film is used because it is relatively inexpensive and has more exposure latitude than transparency color film.

After the photographer finishes the assignment, the film is processed in an automatic processing machine in about eight minutes. While waiting for the film to finish processing, the photographer creates a file for the assignment in a computer database. This file contains the who, what, where, when, and how of the assignment plus a file number. This information is then printed on an envelope in which the negatives will be stored.

The photographer slips the processed film into special plastic sleeves to protect it from dust, dirt, and scratches. It is edited by the photographer and then taken to a photo editor. The photo editors are responsible for controlling which images are seen by the section editors and for monitoring the overall photographic content of the newspaper. Using the photographer's suggestions and knowledge as a guide, the photo editor selects the frame, or frames, to be scanned.

At some newspapers lab technicians scan the negatives into the computer system, but at the *News* the photographers scan their own negatives. As you will see, being able to scan their own negatives makes it easier for the photographers to send photographs back to the paper when they travel.

Back at the *News* the photographer goes to a scanning station, a desk with a computer, high-resolution monitor, and a film scanner. The *News* uses Macintosh computers because of the ease of their operating system and several different makes and models of film scanners. I use a Kodak RFS 2035 Plus Film Scanner for this discussion.

Scanning The *News* uses Adobe Photoshop, which makes it possible to do incredible things to photographs. But, as stated earlier, I make only a limited number of adjustments to the photographs.

Before putting the negative in the scanner the photographer wipes it with an antistatic cloth and blows compressed air across it. This gets rid of a majority of dust, thus reducing the number of spots on the photograph that will have to be removed later.

After starting up, or opening, Photoshop I connect to the scanner by pulling down the File menu until I get to Acquire. Once there, I see Kodak RFS 2035 Plus Scanner and select that as my option. The scanner menu appears and is ready for the prescanning process (Figure 3.8).

Although color film can be scanned in color and black-and-white, all images at the *News* are scanned in color so the paper always has the option of reproducing the photograph in color. Because I'm scanning in color, I make sure the B & W box is *not* checked. I also choose Negative in the Film box.

I took the negatives used for these illustrations during the Summer Olympics when Michael John-son received his gold medal for the men's 400-meter run. The Kodak scanner is designed so that a strip of six negatives is placed into the machine horizontally. The Johnson photo is vertical, so I click on the 90 CCW—90 degrees counterclockwise—button to prescan the photo in the proper perspective.

The next step is to click on the Focus button. This ensures maximum sharpness of the scanned image by focusing the scanner on the film plane. Although it is not necessary to focus the scanner for each negative, always do it on the first scan of the day, just to be safe. You don't want to finish the entire scanning process to discover that the beautiful image on the screen isn't sharp. The Focus button also produces the prescanned image. The prescanned image is a small low-resolution image. Large changes are made in the cropping, image size, brightness, and color on the prescanned image.

Make as many corrections on the prescan as possible. When an image is finally scanned, it is made up of a finite amount of digital information. If you make large changes on the final image that should be made on the prescan, you are altering and in some cases removing data from the image. Once the information is removed from the image, it cannot be replaced and the image quality suffers.

The initial prescan is low in contrast and too dark, so I begin by correcting those problems. Using the appropriately marked slider bars to the right of the image, I increase the Contrast and Brightness until the density looks good and the image has some punch—contrast—to it. These changes make the skin tones a little too red, so I subtract three

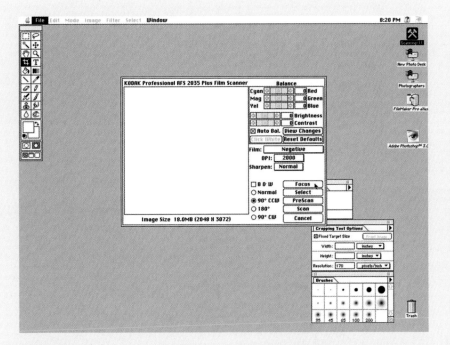

FIGURE 3.8

A computer screen showing the menu for the Kodak Professional RFS 2035 Plus film scanner.

units of Red using the Balance slider in the upper right corner of the window. It is possible to see the results of these corrections by clicking the View Changes button.

When the color balance of an initial scan is bad, use the Click White button. Click on the Click White button, and it changes to Click Now. Find a white area in the photo, place the cursor on it, and click.

Check the color balance of the image by using the RGB—red, green, and blue—numbers that appear whenever the cursor touches the photo. Place the cursor on a neutral area, such as the subject's white jacket. The numbers indicate there is a little too much blue and green (cyan) in the whites. In order to subtract cyan, add red, which will adversely affect the skin tones. In many cases you will not be able to fine-tune the color on the prescan. That is okay, as long as you make the im-

age as close to perfect as possible on the prescan.

I try to compose my photos in the viewfinder, before I expose the film, so they fill the entire 35mm frame. Occasionally, the best composition doesn't lend itself to the 35mm format, so it becomes necessary to crop the image in the computer. Use the cursor for cropping images in the prescan. Put the cursor near a corner of your crop, click on the mouse, and drag the cursor to the opposite corner of your crop (Figure 3.9). By pressing the Command key you can grab the crop box and make finer adjustments to your crop.

The last thing to check is the Image Size, located at the bottom of the window. Remember, a scanned image is made up of a finite amount of digital information called pixels (Figure 3.10). If it is reproduced as a very large photo and there isn't enough information for the size, the image will degrade and fall apart—it will look fuzzy and grainy (Figure 3.11). Therefore it is important to make the file size of the image large enough for quality reproduction

but not so large that it takes forever to move or make corrections.

At the *News* the file size for the average lede photo is in the range of six to seven megabytes.* If the photo runs larger, for example, all the way across the page, the file size must be as large as possible. To change the file size of a photo, change the DPI—dots per inch. This number works in conjunction with the crop. The more a negative is cropped, the smaller the maximum file size can be.

Now click on the Scan button. When the scanned image comes up, the smart thing to do is immediately save a copy of this raw unprocessed image on the hard drive. You do this so that if disaster strikes—the computer crashes or the power goes out, for example—you won't have to waste time rescanning the image. Better safe than sorry.

One of the first things I do to my scanned image is make the final crop. I do this so I don't waste any time or effort correcting areas of the photo that I will crop out later. Use the cropping tool and make sure the Width and Height boxes are empty, unless you have a preset size and the Resolution box is set for the proper output. The output numbers vary depending on the reproduction system for which the image is intended.

After cropping, move to color correction. Go into the Image menu and pull down to Adjust. You will see another pull-down menu that contains three main methods to adjust the color: Levels, Curves, and Color Balance. There are different schools of thought on which method is best. I prefer Curves because it gives me a graphic representation of the image and my changes (Figure 3.12).

*Lede is a spelling peculiar to journalism and means "main."

Using Curves, the first thing you can do is use the Black Eye Dropper to set the black point. You do this to make sure you have the blackest black you can get. This black will have no detail, so make sure you do not put it on an area where you want detail. When you click on the Black Eye Dropper, the frame around it turns black. Move the cursor to an appropriate area. Click on that area, and if the scan didn't make that area black before, it will now change to black. *Warning:* This will also affect similar dark areas in your photo, so be careful. You don't want to lose precious detail.

You can also set the white area where you want the whitest white with detail by using the White Eye Dropper. Follow the directions outlined earlier.

An important option to be aware of when dealing with any of the color adjusting menus is the option key. Holding down the Option key changes the Cancel button on the various color correction menus to Reset. This allows you to return to the original unaltered scan without having to cancel the corrections menu and then reopen it.

Another useful tool for color correction is the Info window. These numbers display the

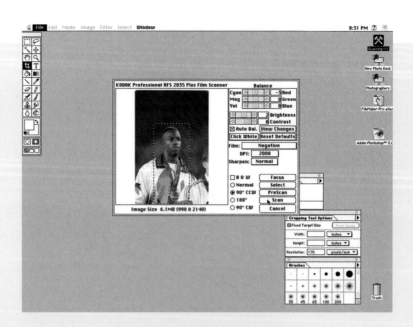

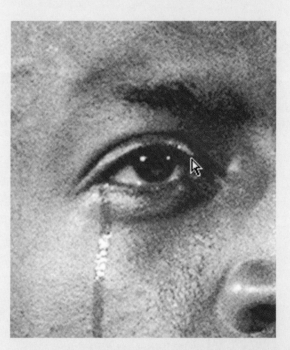

FIGURE 3.9

The RFS 2035 menu showing the adjusted prescanned image and crop marks ready for scanning.

FIGURE 3.10

An extreme magnification of Michael Johnson's eye showing the pixels that make up the image.

FIGURE 3.11

A low-resolution photo reproduced too large, resulting in degraded image of poor quality.

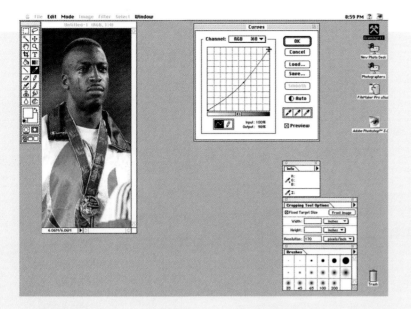

FIGURE 3.12

A computer screen displaying the scanned photo, the Curves window, the Info box, the Cropping Tools Options box, and the Brush sizes.

FIGURE 3.13

When the overall density of an image is too light, the highlights (note Johnson's warm-up jacket) lack usable detail.

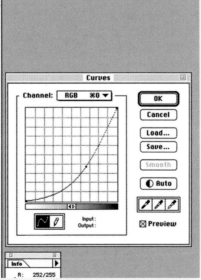

amounts of red, green, and blue in any selected area of the photo. Because it is often difficult to know the exact combination of these three colors that make up a particular color, it is easiest to check a neutral or shade of gray. When checking neutral areas, the numbers for each color should be roughly the same because neutral colors should have no predominant color. This information can be a tremendous help when you can't decide which color is too strong—in other words, when your eyes are tired and you can't tell whether the color you're see-

ing is magenta or its close relative, red.

Setting the black point up in the top of the photo darkens Johnson's face a little, so lighten the midtones by clicking on a midpoint in the curve and pulling it down, all the time keeping an eye on the highlights in the jacket. If you make the overall density too light, you will lose the detail in the jacket's highlights. You don't want to see the highest number—255—because it indicates that there is no detail, and therefore no information, in the white (Figure 3.13).

Johnson's face is still a little red, so go into the Channel section of the Curves menu, and pull down until you can select the Red channel. Click on a point in the middle of the graph, and push it up slightly (Figure 3.14). This removes the red from the photo. If you moved the curve in the opposite direction, you would be adding red to the photo.

Removing red causes the flesh tones to darken and the overall contrast to increase slightly. Go back into the Channel menu and return to RGB. Pull down (lighten) the midtones again. Then click on the black endpoint (upper right corner), and pull it down slightly to lower the contrast (Figure 3.15).

The overall image now looks satisfactory, so click OK. Because the face and the gold medal are still slightly dark, those areas are adjusted next.

Because I want to change only the color and density of the subject's face, I will use the Lasso tool to draw an outline around the subject's face, thus selecting that area (Figure 3.16). As long as the outline remains around the image, any exposure or color adjustment will affect only this selected area. To make drawing the outline around the subject's face easier, I

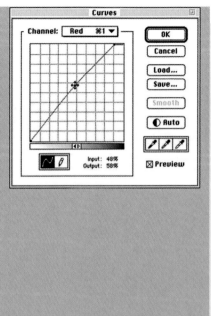

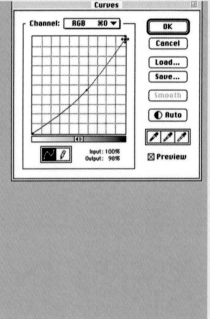

FIGURE 3.14

Pulling up on the Red channel removes some of the cyan cast from the image.

FIGURE 3.15

Pulling down on the RGB channel lightens the image.

the face click on a point in the midtones and pull down the curve to lighten the subject's face. When the face reaches the desired density, click OK.

To lighten the gold medal I repeat the process of selecting the area, feathering it, and then lightening it.

Next I move to Johnson's eyes. The shadows are too dense and harsh, and by dodging I can soften the shadows. *Dodging* is a term carried over from the traditional darkroom. If a certain area of a print is too dark, you hold back—or dodge—some of the light to keep the area from getting too much exposure and becoming too dark (Figure 3.17). Conversely, if an area of a print is too light, you can burn in the area on the print by adding exposure only to that area. In the computer I use the Dodging tool to decrease the density in and around Johnson's eyes. Clicking and holding the mouse while moving over the pertinent area will dodge the image. There is also a Burning tool if an area is too light.

Until now I have ignored the two boxes in the lower right of the screen. One is the Options box, which changes depending on which tool is selected in the Tool box. The Options box is different from the Options key—the box displays the "options" available for the tool selected in the Tool box. The other is the Brushes box. The Brushes box displays the size, in pixels, of the Toning tools—in

increase the size of the image by pressing the Command and plus (+) keys at the same time. Then I click on the Lasso tool and draw around the subject's face.

I don't want the border between the face, where the changes are made, and the background to be strongly defined, so I go into the Select menu and pull down to Feather. This feature softens the edge between the se-

lected area and the nonselected area. The Feather Radius is the width, in pixels, of the border. So instead of having a hard fine border between the changed and unchanged areas, the border is larger and softer. When I adjust large areas like this face, I prefer 11 or 12 pixels. After entering the radius size, click OK.

Now, with the face selected, reopen the Curves menu. To lighten

FIGURE 3.16

You select Johnson's face by drawing an outline around it with the Lasso tool. Now any density or color changes will affect only Johnson's face, not the entire photo.

FIGURE 3.17

Johnson's eyes are lightened with the Dodging tool from the Tool box.

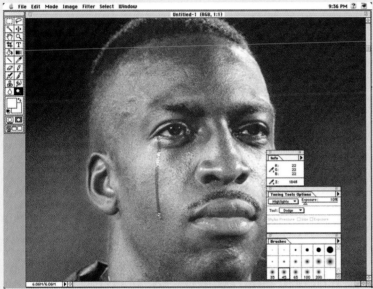

your progress each time you release the mouse. Pressing the Command and Z keys at the same time undoes the dodge and returns to the original version. Pressing the Command and Z keys again returns you to the dodged version. Going back and forth between the dodged and original versions makes it easier to evaluate the dodge. In this case I dodge only the highlights, using an exposure of 9 percent, a number not small enough to take forever to complete the dodge nor high enough to be uncontrollable. I also enlarge the image so I have more control over the dodging.

The last thing to do to the photo is to rid it of dust spots, a process called *spotting*. To spot a photo digitally use the Rubber Stamp tool to clone, or copy, a piece of the photograph near the offending spot and cover it with the cloned material. It's easier to locate and spot the dust when you enlarge the photograph as I did earlier, using the Command and the plus (+) keys. When you locate the offensive mark—the dust—(Figure 3.18) go to the Tool bar and click on the Rubber Stamp tool. You will notice the Options box has changed and now says Rubber Stamp Options. For spotting you should choose normal, Opacity: 100%, and Option—Clone (aligned).

this case the Dodging tool—and whether the tool is hard edged or soft edged. The relative size of the Dodging tool appears as a circle on the screen.

For the Dodging tool the Options box changes to Toning Tools Options. The Toning Tools Options allows me to choose between the Dodging tool or Burning tool. The menu also allows me to choose which areas I want to affect—highlights, midtones, or shadows—and what percentage of the exposure I want to affect with the Dodging tool. One hundred percent would completely erase the image and 1 percent would barely affect it.

One key to effectively using the Dodging—or Burning—tool is to build up the effect gradually. Don't use a high percentage and attempt to do everything with one pass. Use a smaller percentage and go over the area several times. Also, it is important to remember that each time you take your finger off the mouse, you have finished a dodge. When you click the mouse again, you begin again, so it's important to check

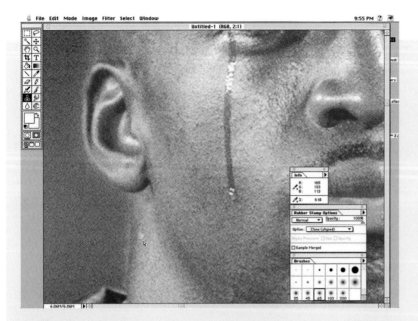

FIGURE 3.18

The arrow points to the dust spot on the photo that will be removed—spotted—with the Rubber Stamp tool from the Tool box.

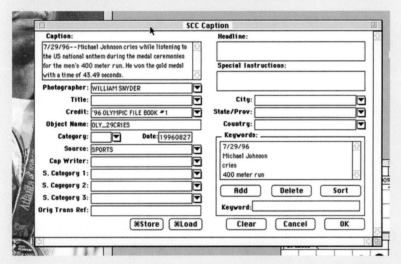

FIGURE 3.19

The SCC caption menu.

are printed on a laser printer, and the photo is compressed and saved. The *News* uses a plug-in program for Photoshop called Software Construction Company SCC Caption. You get to the plug-in by going into the Filter menu of Photoshop and pulling down to Caption. In the Caption area I put the date at the beginning and then write a caption that includes all the who-what-where information that makes for a good caption (Figure 3.19). Good captions do not merely echo the photograph, they add information.

Next, I fill in the photographer's name. At the *News* the Credit box is used for the negative file number. In this case the Olympics photos go into special file books. The Object Name is a slug, or title, used to identify each photo. It also helps us track the photo through the digital world. The first two or three letters are abbreviations for the newspaper section for which the photo was shot. In this case Olympics is a special section. The number is the day of the month, and the last letters are the title of the photo. The Source is the department for which the assignment was shot. In the Keywords section I add those words or information from the caption that will help the library track down a particular photo in the future if it's needed again.

When I finish the captioning, I click OK, which electronically attaches the caption to the photo.

Pick an appropriate brush size from the Brushes box. Now select the area from which you will clone the spotting material. To do this, move the cursor/brush to an area that is similar in density and color to the spotting area. Press and hold down the Option key, and note that the cursor/brush has changed into something that looks like a cross inside a circle. Now click the Mouse. You have selected the area from which the cloning material will come.

Now, when clicking the mouse, you see the brush/cursor and a crosshair. That crosshair indicates the area that is being cloned. If

it's coming from an area that doesn't look like the area you want to spot, reselect another area with the Option—Click. The crosshairs move with the brush/cursor as you keep your mouse depressed. Each time you click your mouse, you are starting the process again, like dodging. Remember, if you don't like the effect, press Command Z to undo the spotting. Once the spotting is finished, the image processing is finished.

At the *News* there are three more steps before the assignment is completely finished. The photo must be captioned, hard copies

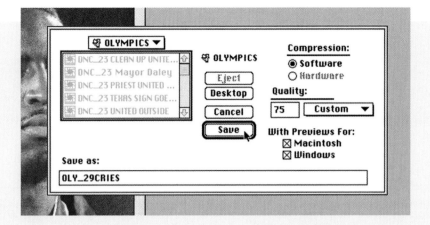

FIGURE 3.20
The Save menu.

Now I compress and save the image.

If photos aren't compressed, an incredible amount of space is required to save the thousands of images produced by the *News* staff. Using the JPEG compression format on a Quality setting of Custom-75, I compressed a 6mb photo down to about 750kb—about an 85 percent reduction. To save the photo go back into the File menu, pull down to Export, and go to SCC JPEG Export. The slug typed on the caption automatically appears in the Save As box.

Check the Quality settings, and make sure to save the image in the proper file. Now it's ready to save (Figure 3.20). Hit Save.

The last item is to make laser copies of the photo, complete with caption. Pull down the File menu again to Export until SCC Proofer appears. *News* photographers must print out two copies, one for the photo desk and one for the section editors. Many *News* photographers print another copy to keep for themselves so they have a record of their work for personal review or contest preparation. This is the final form of the image given to the editors (Figure 3.21).

When everything is finished, images are stored on magnetic optical drives in the *News* library, using a fraction of the space of hard prints. If a hard copy is needed, another laser print can be made, or a digital print from the scan can be made from a high-quality digital printer. And of course a print can be made from the original negative.

Traveling Equipment When *News* photographers travel to assignments around the country and around the world, we use a system similar to our office system. Instead of using large desktop Apple Macintoshes, we use Apple Macintosh PowerBooks. We also use a lightweight Nikon Super CoolScan LS-1000. To send the digital information over the phone lines we use Hayes 28.8, V.34 modems. The entire kit fits in a case about the size of a small suitcase. These outfits are powerful, versatile, lightweight, and relatively inexpensive. The proliferation of one-hour photo stores around the world means we can shoot film without having to carry or worry about processing materials. For assignments in war-torn areas or countries with terrible phone lines we use a portable satellite phone in addition to our transmit kit. To cover the Summer Olympics in Atlanta the *News* sent a little more equipment than for a normal out-of-town trip.

We packed seventeen cases of equipment that included two Apple Macintosh PowerBook 5300ce's, one Apple Power Mac 7600 desktop PC with a 17-inch Radius Precision View monitor, four Nikon Super CoolScans film scanners (an extra in case one broke), three PCMCIA card readers for downloading images from three Canon EOS DCS 3 digital cameras, and two 100mb Zip drives for storage. We also had a Fuji minilab film processor installed in our office space.

All the computers were connected in a network so that images and information could be passed back and forth between them. The Atlanta computer network was connected to the computer network in Dallas with a special phone line, called an ISDN line. Think of phone lines as pipes; the larger the pipe, the more information they can carry. ISDN lines are larger pipes than normal phone lines. To send photographs back to Dallas I merely had to grab a photo in the folder in Atlanta and drag it to the Olympics folder in Dallas. It took about 30 seconds to transmit a 700-kilobyte compressed photo.

Most photographs in Atlanta were made on film, scanned into the Power Mac using the Nikon Scanners, corrected with Photoshop, captioned, and sent to Dallas.

Digital Cameras As I said at the beginning, we used digital cameras, the Canon EOS DCS 3, for the Opening Ceremonies. Let's pause a moment to talk about major differences between digital cameras and film cameras. [At the *News* we now use the Kodak DCS520.]

Digital cameras are physically larger but weigh about the same as conventional cameras. Although the actual focal lengths and

FIGURE 3.21

Two copies of this laser print were delivered to *The Dallas Morning News* photo desk. One is for the photo desk files, and the other goes to the appropriate section editor.

apertures of lenses remain the same, the recorded image area is only 16.4mm × 20.5mm instead of the standard 24mm × 36mm. Therefore when you look through a 400mm f/2.8, it will become approximately a 600mm f/2.8. There is a frame etched into the focusing screen so you can see the proper area.

Digital cameras used at the *News* use 170mb PCMCIA cards to store images. The PCMCIA cards, called *PC cards* (remember those?), are small removable hard disks and hold 123 images. The images can be downloaded or deleted so the PC cards can be used again and again. Because there is no film to scan in a digital camera, you must "acquire" the image from the PC card. You acquire the images through Photoshop by using a plug-in for Photoshop provided with the Canon EOS DCS 3. The computer operator brings up a grid displaying all the photographs on the PC card, selects the desired images, and clicks the Acquire button (Figure 3.22).

Once the images are acquired, or downloaded into the Mac, they are handled exactly like scanned images, with one exception. A special filter can be added to Photoshop to eliminate some of the digital image's noise and make the image look more like a film image. Although the quality of digital images is not quite the same as that of film images, they are close and getting closer.

Unlike film cameras, you can change the exposure index on

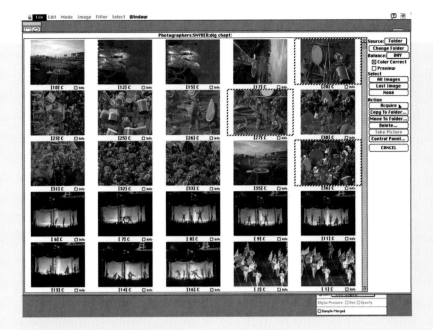

FIGURE 3.22

The Acquire module grid for the Canon EOS DCS 3 camera with three images selected.

each frame in a digital camera. Like transparency film, there's very little exposure latitude, and overexposure is anathema to the image. Highlights disappear and colors lose their intensity. Unlike transparency film, color balance is not a problem; filters built into the acquiring program help correct color casts (Figures 3.23 and 3.24).

With digital cameras you cannot shoot more than a seven-frame burst at any one time. When the shutter is released, the sensor records the image into a buffer and then downloads the image onto the PCMCIA card/hard drive. The cameras are not yet equipped with enough RAM to temporarily store the large number of images that would allow the rapid firing common to film cameras with motor drives.

Olympics Opening Ceremonies For the Opening Ceremonies we moved the faster, more powerful Power Mac 7600 and high-resolution monitor into the hotel across the street from the Olympic stadium. We added a PC card reader and connected the whole system to the hotel phone through a high-speed modem.

The night before the Opening Ceremonies two of us had gone to the dress rehearsal, so we had a good idea of what photographs we wanted to make. There were several aspects of the ceremony the Atlanta Committee for the Olympic Games chose not to reveal during the dress rehearsal in order to increase the excitement, so we had to stay on our toes.

One of the main differences from dress rehearsal night was the heightened security. President Clinton was attending the ceremonies, so we would not be able to enter and exit the stadium easily. We also discovered, much to our consternation, that a gate we had used to get to the hotel from the stadium was locked. We talked with the U.S. Secret Service agent in charge of the street corner between the stadium and our hotel. After he checked our credentials, he gave us the permission we needed to get the PC cards to the hotel.

With an assortment of lenses ranging from 14mm to 600mm, and the digital cameras, the three of us took our positions around the stadium. For the first 45 minutes of the ceremonies we shot photographs. Then one of us picked up all the PC cards, left the stadium through the security entrance, and went to the hotel to edit and transmit.

As we got closer and closer to deadline, we began running disks from the stadium to the hotel with more frequency. The ceremony ended in a hail of fireworks around 11:45 p.m. Dallas time.

We rushed the last disk down the four flights of stairs, out the door, and were promptly stopped by an Olympic committee security guard. The side street we had been using all night was now closed. Some fast talk and stubbornness got us up the side street, but then the street between the stadium and the hotel was closed. The president's departure meant even stiffer security measures. The Atlanta police officer who stopped us from crossing the street wanted us to leave, and our Secret Service agent was a hundred yards away, having a small meeting—he wasn't available to help us!

Meanwhile the clock was moving inexorably toward our deadline, while the other photographer anxiously watched us from across the street, behind the 10-foot storm fence. More fast talking and frantic arm waving eventually attracted the attention of our Secret Service agent. Finished with his meeting, he came over to see why we were causing all the commotion. When we asked if we could cross the street and toss the last two disks of the night to our photographer, he shrugged his shoulders. "Sorry. You can't go into the street. It's closed," he replied.

He didn't walk away, so we stood on the corner, weighing our

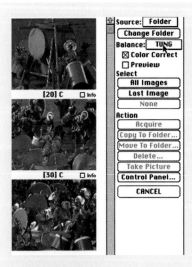

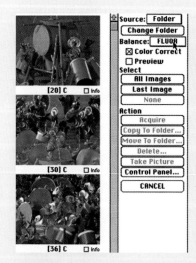

FIGURE 3.23

The DCS 3 Acquire module set for tungsten lighting.

FIGURE 3.24

The DCS 3 Acquire module set for fluorescent lighting.

dwindling options. Deciding we had nothing to lose, we asked if he would be willing to take the disks across the street for us.

Without a word he held out his hand. Solemnly, we handed him the disks. He sauntered over to our anxious coworker and tossed them over the fence. No problem.

Ten minutes later the last image of fireworks majestically mushrooming over a packed Olympic stadium (Figure 3.25) was back in Dallas, moments before deadline. In all we sent 17 images to Dallas before deadline. Digital technology had paid off.

But then the editors decided to stick with a photograph from the beginning of the ceremony that had moved two hours earlier. Some things you just can't fix with computers.

Author's note: William Snyder now is the photo assignments editor of *The Dallas Morning News*.

FIGURE 3.25

Fireworks signal the end of the Opening Ceremonies of the Atlanta Olympic Games.

Final Thoughts

You are studying photojournalism in one of the most—if not the most—exciting times since photography became a practical reality back in 1839. The digitalization of photojournalism has freed you from the confines of the dim, yellow-lighted chemical-optical darkroom and propelled you into the white light of the newsroom, along with reporters and editors. On the picture-taking front, two choices await you: film in black-and-white and color, and a digital recording medium. Some assignments you will have undoubtedly will lend themselves best to one kind of film or the other—the story can better be told with film. With digital cameras, you not only completely get out of the chemical arena but you can bring to readers a heightened sense of immediacy—assignments can be covered much closer to deadlines. This is because photojournalists using digital cameras quickly and easily can process their pictures in portable electronic darkrooms at the coverage scene and quickly transmit them from the scene to their organizations' computers. Lengthy travel time to reach a chemical darkroom and lengthy time working in it is not needed. Assignments also can be covered longer, thus likely resulting in better coverage being presented to readers and, also, more assignments can be covered, thus bringing more varied visual information to readers. Digital picture-taking pretty much is a win-win situation.

With all the advantages of 21st century technology, never forget, however, that the tools of photojournalism, while important and mightily helpful, are there only to assist you in your quest to better communicate with your readers.

Composition Broadly Construed

Starting out as a novice journalistic photographer, you most likely will encounter many events you have not previously photographed. They will be fresh to you and you easily will bring a fresh approach to picturing them. But after you have covered the same events many times, you will undoubtedly need to delve deeply into your creative self to present to your readers an intriguing but nonetheless truthful view of what occurred. One experienced photographer took his readers to a graduation at the Massachusetts Maritime Academy through this eye-catching image.
Steve Heaslip/© Cape Cod Times

Overview

Composition is an integral part of the fabric of images; it is not just a veneer. Composition helps convey messages and becomes part of them. In fact, with a few images composition is the message. Composition also significantly affects how closely photographs approach or deviate from real life. At a minimum composition is the putting together of two or more elements of a scene so that the resulting photograph becomes more than a sum of its parts; it is also the meshing of the parts so that they support each other, thereby enhancing the message.

However, composition is more complex than this narrow physical minimum. *Composition*, as used here, means using all available techniques in pursuit of storytelling images that conform with the photographer's fundamental approach. The resulting photographs must convey the photographer's message in an unmistakably truthful and fair way, and must encourage readers to view them.[1]

Contemporary ideas about desirable composition techniques in photography harken to the 15th century when painters embraced what now is called *central perspective*. This approach to painting yields an image similar to an adult's mental perception.[2] Figure 4.1 illustrates the concept of central perspective. Educator and writer Rudolf Arnheim describes central perspective as what results from positioning a piece of glass between the viewer and subject and faithfully tracing the subject on the glass.[3]

Author Pierre Descargues explains it another way: "Perspective is a way of thinking about observation, a method that harnesses and organizes space. It is a fundamentally practical technique: given two dimensions, it computes the third and, conversely, permits three dimensions to be projected on two."[4] The composition concept of parallel lines—such as railroad tracks—that join and become one as the distance from the viewer increases is an example of a contemporary linear perspective technique that originated in the central perspective movement.

Photojournalists must be lookers. Before they can put an image together, they must know what there is to put together. This is the ability to recognize that which others often miss, commonly termed *photographic seeing*. Fundamentally, photographic seeing is a keen awareness of a scene's constituent parts, including small and detailed aspects. It also is the ability to visualize them, and the overall scene, as different camera lenses will record them. Photographer Bill Brandt got it right when he wrote:

> It is part of the photographer's job to *see* more intensely than most people do. He must have and keep in him something of the receptiveness of the child who looks at the world for the first time or of the traveller who enters a strange country.[5]

Photojournalists must constantly look at things far away, close up, and in the middle distance. Photographers must be aware of the way light strikes subjects, the way it rounds or flattens them, enhances or diminishes them. They must study shadows—the way

FIGURE 4.1

Artist using central perspective.
CULVER PICTURES, INC.

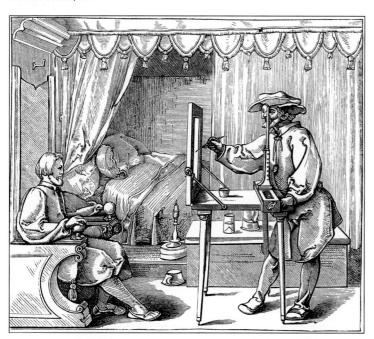

they fall and the way they relate to the light that helped create them. Photojournalists must know how colors change from early morning to late evening. Photographer Henri Cartier-Bresson maintained that "the photographer's eye is perpetually evaluating."[6]

Photographic seeing—keen looking with intensity and purpose—must be a way of life for photojournalists. It is the unceasing visual exploration of human life—of the human condition—and everything affecting it (Figure 4.2).

Photographic seeing has one additional aspect: interpretation. Keen looking with intensity and purpose gains little unless the photographer can recognize and understand the most appropriate truth—sometimes underlying, sometimes hidden—through accurate interpretation. Why is Subject X crossing his legs? What is Subject Y thinking when she yawns? What is going on when Subject Z holds his forehead? Do these nonverbal actions carry hidden or disguised meanings that photojournalists must understand to better communicate to readers? Possibly so. But be careful about interpreting nonverbal communication. Interpretations that are wrong or that reflect on people adversely can lead to embarrassment and lawsuits. You must take great care in the interpretive arena.

A great people-watcher is *LIFE* photographer Carl Mydans. Here is his take on viewing people's nonverbal behavior:

> From my earliest years I have been fascinated by human behavior. By the time I used a camera seriously I had become an obsessive people-watcher, observing mannerisms and body postures, the slants and curves of mouths, the falseness of smiles, the directness or evasion of eyes. When I learned to understand these signals and interpret them, I had found a source of stories as wide and as varied and as captivating as the human race.[7]

As an aspiring photojournalist you are well placed to begin being an informed people-watcher. Many colleges

and universities offer at least one course in what is called nonverbal communication; maybe it is in psychology, sociology, social psychology, or communications. Wherever it may be, taking the course will allow you to explore this subject much more in depth since space here does not allow more than a cursory look at nonverbal communication; the goal here merely is to acquaint you with this important subject. Every aspiring photojournalist should seriously consider becoming intimately familiar with sophisticated and interpretive people-watching by taking a course in nonverbal communication.

Entwined with the concept of composition is the concept of creativity. Some people have it, some people don't. Creativity has been widely investigated, but remains an enigma. Even so, there are some solid hints about its nature. Let's start with *The Random House Dictionary of the English Language.* One definition of creativity from

FIGURE 4.3

In the broadest sense all photographs convey information—they are informational images. Some clearly informative images convey more information than others and in a more stunning way. This is the case here. The propane tank at a mobile home has exploded, and a neighbor atop his home recoils from the blast. The heat of a California wildfire caused the explosion. This image would not exist except for a persistent and alert photographer who reacted quickly. Christopher Assaf waited three hours for the fire to come his way, got no visually compelling picture, and went back to the paper. Then he headed out again and got this moment. Eye-catching and storytelling images can be the reward for a persistent photojournalist who is prepared to grasp the moment when it presents itself.

CHRISTOPHER T. ASSAF/ DAILY PILOT, COSTA MESA, NEWPORT BEACH, CORONA DEL MAR, CALIF.

this source is "the ability to transcend traditional ideas, rules, patterns, relationships, or the like, and to create meaningful new ideas, forms, methods, interpretations . . .." Perhaps another way to put it is to be different and to make that difference count by producing out-of-the-ordinary eye-catching, truthful images.

It is clear that whatever creativity is, people who are blessed with creativity—or who learn it—tend to have some common attributes. A thread that weaves through the literature about creativity is that people who love what they are doing are likely to be more creative than those who are neutral about it or dislike it. Scholar Frank Barron provides this view of the creative person:

It is in personal style, an aspect of selfhood, that I find the ingredients of creativity. Openness to new ways of seeing, intuition, alertness to op-

Photojournalism: An Introduction

portunity, a liking for complexity as a challenge to find simplicity, independence of judgment that questions assumptions, willingness to take risks, unconventionality of thought that allows odd connections to be made, keen attention, and a drive to find pattern and meaning—these, coupled with the motive and the courage to create, gives us a picture of the creative self.[8]

Creativity through composition based on the journalistic bedrock of truthful and fair communication leads to informative photographs that urge readers to carefully view them; this is one of the keys to success in contemporary photojournalism. Try to keep in mind the concept of creativity as you become familiar with the 27 compositional techniques that soon follow.

Journalistic organizations, particularly newspapers and magazines, serve two fundamental editorial purposes: to inform and entertain. Informational images convey hard-core facts, and their form and substance may not be pleasing. Entertaining images amuse or distract readers, and their form and substance typically are pleasing.

Composition, with its underlying creativity, helps photographers convey information, clarifying and emphasizing so that readers can understand the messages intended—whether they are meant to appeal to intellect, emotion, or a combination. Composition techniques, applied creatively, are essential for entertainment photographs. Entertainment images typically carry no inherent news interest that helps to convey their message. Although creative composition techniques often are part of informational images, they are critically important parts of entertainment images. Journalistic photographs often serve both information and

FIGURE 4.5

Mixing information and entertainment often is a good way to get across relatively serious points that time-pressured readers might otherwise skip. This humorous scene of a monkey cooling off on a block of ice visually portrays a heat wave.

JOHN MORAN/*GAINESVILLE* (FLA.) *SUN*

entertainment functions. These images are deemed to be of "mixed" subject matter. The essence of mixed images conveys factual information but also substantially entertains or vice versa; both form and substance are likely to be pleasing (Figures 4.3–4.5).

Techniques

Composition techniques tend to overlap; one way to discuss composition techniques is to divide them into categories that correspond to or approximate their origin: photographer-based, equipment-based, and subject-based.

One important consideration requires special mention: nuance. It is an overarching key to successful photographic communication; overstating its value is difficult. Successful application of composition technique often turns on nuance—a millimeter more here, an inch less there.

Photographers must always consider nuance. They must remember that little things, such as moving to the left or right, bending down or stretching up, waiting a moment more or moving ahead, make the difference between superb images and mediocre ones.

Two composition techniques are so important and so detailed that they have their own chapter, "Light and Color"; it follows. The 27 techniques considered here are not the only composition techniques. However, they will take an aspiring photojournalist well down the composition road.

Photographer-Based Techniques

Approach Once photojournalists are covering an event, they may use two fundamental approaches. The first is the "overt approach"—photographers record the easily viewed physical reality without concern for hidden meaning and without particular concern for the most appropriate truth fairly represented. The second approach is "truthful essence." This approach puts great responsibility on photographers. They must be knowledgeable and savvy enough to picture the most appropriate truth and in a fair way.

One way for photographers to approach truthful essence is to avoid interjecting themselves into situations. In his introduction to *Photographs by Cartier-Bresson* Lincoln Kirstein describes Henri Cartier-Bresson's pictures and gives insight into the photographer's approach:

> His best pictures have a secret atmosphere of the invisible eavesdropper who watches people at their most private preoccupations, as if the mirrors they searched for their most intimate answers photographed them in the act of questioning.[9]

A second way to approach truthful essence is to be so knowledgeable of human behavior and so good at making people feel comfortable that they ignore the photographer. This greatly increases the probability that their external behavior is a true representation of their inner attitude or belief and greatly increases the probability that the photograph communicates the most appropriate truth fairly represented.

The truthful essence approach does not allow photographers or management to disclaim responsibility for misleading readers based on having presented physical reality. The truthful essence approach rests on the assumption that readers trust—or at least are willing to be convinced they should trust—photojournalists to make judgments about truthful essence. It also assumes that photojournalists are well prepared—or are willing to make themselves well prepared—to make such judgments repeatedly and with great accuracy.

It is likely that sometimes—perhaps even more than sometimes—the overt approach results in the most appropriate truth fairly

FIGURE 4.6

Photojournalism communicates little if readers are not drawn to images. A key way to get readers' attention—and visually portray elements of a scene difficult or impossible to portray in an eye-level picture—is by using a high view. Photographers get such views by, for example, holding their cameras above their heads, standing on step ladders, or using helicopters or airplanes as high-level vantage points. This overhead view of J.J., a gray whale found stranded in the surf and near death, on its way to be released in the Pacific Ocean after being cared for at Sea World in San Diego is a good example of a high-level view that conveys information difficult or impossible to capture from a lower view.
NANCEE E. LEWIS/*THE SAN DIEGO UNION-TRIBUNE*

FIGURE 4.7

Like high-view images, low views can tell the story well and capture readers' attention, as this one of then-governor Bill Clinton on the presidential campaign trail does with riveting precision. Because low and high views do not always work out, photojournalists should ensure they get a usable picture by also recording more conventional views.
WIN MCNAMEE/REUTERS/ ARCHIVE PHOTOS

represented being presented to readers. It also is likely that sometimes the truthful essence approach results in less than the most appropriate truth fairly represented being presented to readers. But on balance, the author of this book subscribes to the truthful essence approach as the one that over the long haul probably will most appropriately inform readers. There are land mines in both approaches; as a thinking person you should consider both, debate them with your collegagues, and settle on the one—or some modification of one— that you believe is most desirable.

Distance   Photographers must always select the distance from the main subject that best tells the story. It generally is a good idea to photograph from three distances—far, close, and in between—

because looking at the finished photographs may tell you which distance is best.

Photographers should cover situations progressively because they do not know what may be available as they get closer to the subject. An example is covering a big building fire. Photographers should take pictures from a far distance of the smoke billowing and then move closer to record specifics, such as the building's sign going up in flames, firefighters battling the blaze and rescuing people, and onlookers watching.

Position   Photojournalism is full of images taken from unusual positions. Photographers cherish high and low positions (Figures 4.6 and 4.7) as eye-catching, intriguing, and exciting. Because they love an unusual perspective,

FIGURE 4.8

There is a fine line between space that distracts from story-telling and space that is an important —maybe even key— aspect of the scene. Evaluating space and discarding or including it demands that photojournalists always be keenly attuned to relationships and to the thrust of the situations they are covering. The short but important distance in this image of an unhappy boy parting with his toy soldier costume is a physical representation of what the youngster must be thinking. Always carrying a wide angle and a short telephoto lens, or an equivalent zoom lens, gives you versatility in recording unexpected but important space.
Jeff Horner/Walla Walla (Wash.) Union-Bulletin

photographers often become giraffes and worms. Climbing ladders and hugging the ground give photographers versatility in conveying messages when they need an alternative to the common position of the standing adult.

Space   Space is a valuable commodity in journalism; so much is happening and the newshole—the amount of space available for editorial material in an issue—is finite. Photographs that contain wasted or unnecessary space waste space in the publication—which may push additional photographs out of the story or exclude images of other stories. Photographs should use every bit of their photographic space productively to support the message their photographers want to convey. This does not mean that empty space necessarily is wasted space; it may be highly desirable—a strong and telling ingredient (Figure 4.8).

In the broadest sense photographers must decide what space to include in their pictures and then work within that environment. They then further winnow the space within the frame. If they decide to include a particular space, they fill it or leave it empty. However photographers resolve the issue of space, their photographs must not lack the overall context they need to best convey their message, nor should they include material that is extraneous to the message.

In a physical sense one or more subjects occupy space as the main subject(s) and/or in support of the main subject(s); space itself may be one or more of these subjects.

View   View is the umbrella concept that incorporates all the photographer-based techniques discussed thus far. Let's deal with two types of views: *common* and *uncommon*. A common view is one or more aspects of a scene on which a visually untrained person focuses from an uninvolved vantage point. An uncommon view is one or more aspects of a scene on which a visually trained person focuses in looking for one or more eye-catching, visually intriguing aspects. Presentation of truthful reality—the most appropriate truth—in a different or unusual way is highly desirable for gaining readers' attention, so long as the approach is fair. Visual intrigue captures readers' attention (Figures 4.9–4.11). As desirable as an uncommon view is, photojournalists must make sure that it is not so unusual that readers do not get the message, thus turning different or unusual into a journalistic albatross. They also must make sure that the most appropriate truth is not sacrificed on the altar of an eye-catching view.

Equipment-Based Techniques

Angle   Photojournalists have access to a vast array of lenses with different angles of view—from one with such a

FIGURE 4.9

The ability to see through other than your own eyes will help you to be a successful photojournalist. This is a skill—an art—that you hone by practicing. Just like regularly looking at light to see how it molds and changes reality, you should regularly visualize the world around you from the perspective of others. An intriguing example of this is this image of U.S. Senatorial candidates getting instructions before a TV appearance.
PATRICK DAVISON/*THE DALLAS MORNING NEWS*

FIGURE 4.10

Maybe you've never planted squash in South Carolina, but can't you feel your back hurting just a little and your hand gripping the spade? The state Department of Juvenile Justice horticulture-class student in the background makes it clear that more than one person is working in the field. This photograph gave readers an interesting, involving image that avoided showing the faces of incarcerated juveniles.
JAMIE FRANCIS/*THE STATE*, COLUMBIA, S.C.

FIGURE 4.11

**Difficult as it is, conveying for the reader a
sense of personal involvement—that the
reader is the subject and is doing what the
subject is doing, feeling what the subject is
feeling, and viewing what the subject is viewing—is a hallmark of the photojournalist who
uses view to better communicate with readers.
Here a brave—some might say foolhardy—
soul "runs with the bulls" in Pamplona, Spain.
Do you feel like you are in his shoes or at
least at his side? Do you feel the sharp and
deadly horns bearing down?**

JOHN KIMMICH/© JOHN KIMMICH PHOTO

wide view that it sees behind itself to
one with such a narrow view that it
records only a tiny amount of what is in
front of it. Although they typically limit
themselves to less extreme lenses, photojournalists still have great leeway in
their choices. Most photojournalists
regularly carry in their cars a 20mm or
24mm wide angle; a 180mm, 200mm, or
300mm telephoto lens; and several
lenses with intermediate angles or some
of these and one or two zoom lenses.[10]
Photographers can shoot many journalistic situations with lenses ranging from
wide angles to telephotos. (See Figure
4.12, which shows the same subject
photographed with a 20mm wide angle
and a 200mm telephoto.) Which lens to
use for any specific
situation is a deci-
sion that photojour-
nalists must make
regularly. This deci-
sion alters the reality
presented to read-
ers and therefore it
is particularly impor-
tant to remember
that journalistic con-
cern is for the most
appropriate truth
fairly represented.

In addition to providing a wide geographic view, wide-angle lenses can give
readers a sense of participation and
intimate involvement with subjects;

FIGURE 4.12

Two photographs of the same scene, one (left) made using a 20mm lens, the other (right) using a 200mm lens. Both are taken from the same spot about 10 feet from the subject. Using the 20mm lens, a wide scene is shown and objects near and far are in focus, while with the 200mm lens the field of view narrows to just the area around the subject's head, and the area of the picture that is in focus is quite narrow.

PHOTOGRAPHS BY THOMAS GRAVES

creative use of wide-angle lenses close-up is a sign of a photographer who probably interacts well with subjects and makes them feel comfortable. The normal lens for a 35mm camera is 40 to 50 millimeters; in practice most often 50mm. Photojournalists seldom use a normal lens because its normal adult perspective offers little inherent visual intrigue. However, especially in some low-light situations, it is valuable as a fast inexpensive lens.

Narrow-angle lenses, commonly called *telephotos,* are as indispensable to photojournalists as wide-angle lenses. Telephoto lenses allow photographers to get close without actually being there. They often overcome denied or unavailable access. In addition, they are an important creative tool in photographers' arsenals. Often the photographer can picture the same scene with any of several lenses. Telephotos may help photographers convey meaning more effectively than wide-angle or normal lenses. No matter how close they are to subjects, photographers must always ask themselves whether a telephoto will communicate better.

Focus   Focus refers to the area that the photographer chooses to make tack sharp, with all other areas less distinct to one degree or the other. Focus is a

major tool for emphasizing or isolating parts of scenes. The creative use of focus can convey to readers different messages from the same scene. Although this technique is effective with wide-angle lenses, it is particularly effective with telephoto lenses.

Frame Location   No matter what camera they use—photojournalists typically use the 35mm—they must shoehorn the scene into the frame of the camera. The location of the ingredients of the image in the frame can help or hurt the message the photographer is trying to convey. Several important frame location possibilities are considered here.

Visualize a two-dimensional space as divided top to bottom and side to side into thirds. The four points at which lines intersect are the points at which readers likely are comfortable with main subjects. The Rule of Thirds, shown in Figure 4.13, mandates that main subjects not be in the center of images and ensures that they are not near or on the edges. As with other composition techniques you should follow this rule only when it produces the most effective and appropriate image.

Although they sometimes can intrigue you (Figure 4.14), main subjects in the middle of frames usually are static and therefore boring. Middle-of-the-frame main subjects typically offer no implication of movement, forcing viewers to search all sides to know what is going on there.

Lines, objects, space, animals, or people can act as signposts, guiding readers toward main subjects, and often are effective composition techniques. Depending on the position of the main subject on it, the *S curve* can be one such line. The eye follows the curve, ultimately reaching the main subject. Incidentally, the S curve as itself the main subject is one of the most pleasing composition forms used in photojournalism (Figure 4.15).

Support for main subjects usually appears in front or in back of them but may be found on either side. Back and front support typically gives an impression of depth, thereby increasing the sense of realism (Figures 4.16–4.18). Support may also be substantive, explaining and enlarging the meaning of main subjects.

Using juxtaposition—combining two or more main subjects in a scene so that the resulting message differs from one conveyed by each alone—can be a highly effective composition technique when used discriminatingly. Juxtaposition, however, is highly risky; the synergistic message must be accurate, truthful, and crystal clear or disaster awaits. (See Figure 4.19 for an effective example of juxtaposition.)

Singularity is the opposite of juxtaposition. The message is conveyed by one dominant subject, supported (if at all) by one or more relatively minor secondary subjects (Figure 4.20).

Movement All still photography is done in tiny slices of time. A 30th of a second is a long time in photojournalism, a 500th of a second a short time (but not nearly as short as the 8000th of a second on many photojournalists' cameras). As with lens choice, time choice is a valuable tool in the photographer's creative arsenal. A scene photographed using an extremely short exposure and stopping all movement conveys a different message from the

same scene recorded with a long exposure time, which shows movement.

Subjects can be tack sharp from a focus standpoint, but they may appear unsharp if the subject or the camera or both moved. If your only concern is to stop movement, you should use a shutter speed that lets light strike the film for the shortest time possible. But other factors often come into play that result in an exposure time longer than the shortest time possible; two examples are an urgent need to use a smaller f-stop to gain more depth of field and a

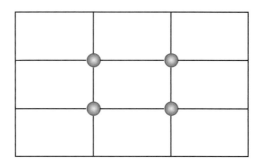

FIGURE 4.13

According to the Rule of Thirds, a main subject can be located at any one of the intersecting lines marked with a circle. Although doing so may result in a visually satisfactory image, photojournalists should never allow themselves to be told that they must approach a journalistic situation in only one way compositionally. ILLUSTRATION BY ILLUSTRATED ARTS (U.K.)

FIGURE 4.14

What's the old saying? The exception proves the rule? This centered image of a vegetable vendor in old Rome's Campo de' Fiori market makes just that point. Although knowing what seems to work most of the time and how to toe the composition line is important, equally important is being able to break out of the straightjacket of conformity to pursue more eye-catching but still truthful images. FRANCESCO ZIZOLA/CONTRASTO/MATRIX

FIGURE 4.15

The S curve is a leading line and more. There is something satisfying and complete about the S curve and something pleasantly intriguing. S curves are everywhere, not just in winding roads. Photojournalists must be on the alert for this often useful and usually visually intriguing shape. MICHAEL GALLACHER/ *MISSOULIAN*, MISSOULA, MONT.

FIGURE 4.16

A couple, victims of a flood, hug as a helicopter lands to pick them up. Crop out the helicopter with your hand; clearly, deleting the helicopter diminishes the storytelling support it provides. The best journalistic photographers look for supporting elements that help communicate more to readers while enhancing their portrayal of the most appropriate truth of the situation. Always remember, however, that more support in an image does not necessarily enhance the most appropriate truth fairly represented. Sometimes less is more. CHAD SURMICK/*THE PRESS DEMOCRAT*, SANTA ROSA, CALIF.

FIGURE 4.17

Imagine this scene without the unsmiling woman. The main subject of this picture is a Croatian city in ruins because of civil war. But the woman in the foreground supports the main subject, devastation, and adds an important humanizing aspect. Photojournalists must see relationships and interactions others tend to miss.

KARIM DAHER/LIAISON AGENCY

FIGURE 4.18

Blot out the 70 in the background and you still have an insightful picture of Mark McGwire rounding the bases on his way to home plate and a home run, his 70th of a season in which he broke Roger Maris' long-standing record of 61 homers in one season. Now put the 70 back in. Is the meaning and message clearer? If you are not knowledgeable about baseball, does the 70 add confusion to the picture? Would a headline, caption, or the lead of an accompanying story negate any confusion? Whatever the case, the photographer put together two storytelling elements—McGwire's smiling face and the 70 sign—something not easy to do in a situation like this one.

AMY SANCETTA/AP/WIDE WORLD PHOTOS

FIGURE 4.19

Photojournalists must never get so carried away with interesting juxtapositions that they pervert—or fail to report—the most appropriate truth. This London image of a mentally ill man in front of a theater advertisement for the play *Les Miserables* is a juxtaposition that rings true. Good photographers always carry at least one camera, even when they are not working; photographic moments can present themselves without warning.

ERICA BERGER

FIGURE 4.20

Whether you view—*read,* in some photographers' parlance—this image of morning horseshoe players as a single subject or as a main subject (the player in the foreground) supported by a secondary subject (the other player), this photograph drives home the communicative power of the concept of singularity.

GREG LOVETT / *THE PALM BEACH POST*

lighting-film combination that mandates a longer exposure (Figure 4.21).

Because of slight subject movement and the inability of any photographer to hold a camera rock steady—particularly the single-lens reflex, which has considerable inherent movement—the entire image may be unsharp unless the photographer uses a shutter speed of 1/250 of a second or shorter. This relatively long exposure time assumes subjects are essentially stationary. However, experienced photographers regularly use shutter speeds longer than 1/250 of a second while hand-holding cameras in low-level light—1/30 of a second is common and even longer shutter speeds are sometimes used. Typically, long exposure times are used in low-level light situations so that photographer-supplied light is unnecessary, thus preserving the original lighting ambiance. Photographers often hold their breaths and lean against nearby stationary objects, such as walls, during these long exposures to decrease camera movement, which can result in unsharp pictures. Unless subject movement is desired, or the technique of panning is used, subjects must be stationary.

Panning (Figure 4.22) is a particularly useful technique that photographers use to imply movement. Typically, photographers try to coordinate the movement of the camera, set at a relatively long exposure time, with the movement of the main subject. Success, which often depends on successive tries, yields a relatively sharp main subject with other areas being unsharp and implying sweeping movement.

Another way to imply movement while keeping the main subject sharp is for photographer and camera to move at the same speed and in the same direction as the main subject. If all goes well, this technique yields a sharp main subject and an ambiance of sweeping movement in other areas.

Illusion of movement in still photographs often is an extremely effective conveyor of messages. Because luck is involved, photographers should be careful to shoot some conventional images as well.

FIGURE 4.21

Stopping an instant in time in a quickly moving situation is one of the technical and visual glories of photography. But doing this well, including getting the subject sharp, is not the easiest thing in photojournalism. Christopher Record used a 180mm lens to bring this visually captivating kneeboarder image to readers. Unless a fast moving subject is pretty much coming directly toward your camera, expect that a shutter speed of 1/1000 or shorter will be needed to stop most or all movement.
CHRISTOPHER A. RECORD/
THE CHARLOTTE OBSERVER

Perspective   Many people familiar with the lenses and techniques of contemporary photojournalists will agree that many journalistic photographs differ from the reality most adults see. Photojournalists seldom use normal lenses, which portray scenes as adults perceive them. In addition, photojournalists typically use unusual angles. This is why most photographs published in newspapers and magazines do not portray reality as uninvolved spectators perceive it. This is not an indictment of the journalistic approach. In fact, to portray reality as uninvolved spectators view it tends to result in boring images that probably don't tell the story as well as more unusual ones. Figures 4.23 through 4.26 show different ways to picture scenes.

However, one subject that you usually should picture as realistically as possible is a building. Some published images of buildings as main subjects make the structures appear to be falling backward. This usually is a sign of unwillingness by photographers or their supervisors or both to spend the modest additional time needed to portray buildings properly, not having the

FIGURE 4.22

specialty lens that fits on a 35mm camera or, alternatively, a view camera, either of which allows for correction of
the problem, a lack of awareness of the
problem, or some combination of one
or more of these (Figure 4.27).

Nonetheless, sometimes photographers find it impractical—and unnecessary or even counterproductive—to
correct a building's verticals, particularly when the structure is not the main
subject (Figure 4.28). And you occasionally can use the vertical perspective
problem intentionally as a composition
tool, so that buildings appear to be
falling backward, without misleading
readers and with considerable visual
effect.

Typically, journalistic photographs
make clear the proportions of their subjects, whether shown as lifesize or otherwise (Figures 4.29 and 4.30). Photojournalists must always keep proportion
in mind. Failure to do so can deceive
readers.

Recording Material   On whatever
film or digital camera they record as-

signments, photojournalists must remember that the medium is part of the
message. They tactfully should tell editors, who decide whether to publish in
black and white or color, which
medium better conveys the message.

Recording Technique   Still photography is a paradox: on the one hand, it is
superb at isolating the telling moment
of an ongoing situation; on the other
hand, its limitations are great. It typically seizes upon one instant, excluding
all others, and presents it in lieu of the
whole.

Even the most technically talented
and intellectually prepared photographer often finds it difficult to condense
so much time into one picture. Yet the
single photograph is the staple of photojournalism, particularly in newspapers and at the wire services that serve
them (Figure 4.31). In a business in
which space equals money, the single
image is already ahead of its multiple-
image competitors.

With multiframe imaging the photographer records two or more instants

FIGURE 4.23
Choosing the lens that establishes the most appropriate ambiance and using it with a skill that makes readers want to view the picture are marks of a successful photojournalist. The photographer got up close and personal by using a wide-angle lens to picture jubilant San Francisco 49ers celebrating their Super Bowl XXIX victory. This could not have been easy in such a crowded, chaotic atmosphere. SUSAN WALSH/AP/WIDE WORLD PHOTOS

FIGURE 4.24
Photographers typically record athletes in action with telephoto lenses, as with this up-close view of tennis star Pete Sampras on Wimbledon's Center Court. Telephoto lenses typically yield little depth of field compared to wide-angle lenses. Note the indistinct background, which makes Sampras stand out. All other things being equal, a less extreme telephoto lens would have yielded more depth of field, a more extreme telephoto lens, less depth of field. RUI VIEIRA/AP/WIDE WORLD PHOTOS

FIGURE 4.25

This image captures steeplechase runners with an extreme wide-angle lens—a 16mm fisheye (fisheye because it looks, and bulges out, like a fish's eye). Photojournalists seem to increasingly favor extreme wide-angle lenses—20mm and wider. Improved optics have diminished, but not completely eliminated, the distortion of light rays entering these lenses, thus decreasing distortion of the image. Even so, remember that things in or near the center of the frame will be far less distorted— if at all—than those closer to the picture's edges.

JOHN MORAN/*GAINESVILLE* (FLA.) *SUN*

FIGURE 4.26

A specialty camera that yields very wide-angle images was used to catch this high-stakes bingo establishment in action.

Librado Romero/The New York Times Pictures

FIGURE 4.27

These two photographs illustrate the problem of how buildings appear to lean away from the photographer, particularly when using wide-angle lenses. The photo at left shows a building "leaning away" from the photographer and was made with a 28mm lens. The photo at right was made with a "perspective control" 28mm lens, which allows the front elements of the lens to be repositioned so the building appears straighter.

Photographs by Thomas Graves

FIGURE 4.28

Buildings in lower Manhattan slant in support of the main subject—picture-taking tourists on a double-decker sightseeing bus. Correcting the buildings would have been unreasonably difficult in this situation—and probably counterproductive visually.

DITH PRAN/THE NEW YORK
TIMES PICTURES

of time in separate but related frames. Photographers achieve multiframe imaging in two ways. The first is by using a film-advance device to record scenes in a rapid-fire manner, much faster than photographers can operate cameras manually. The photographer or editor then selects a single frame representing one moment from this series of photos. Or the photographer or editor selects several closely related frames to publish together as a picture sequence or uses all that were taken (Figure 4.32).

The second way to achieve multiframe imaging is by grouping two or more pictures of the same situation, usually taken over a relatively long period of time—minutes, hours, or days rather than seconds—on one or more pages. This grouping typically tells a more in-depth story than does a single frame or several frames taken in quick succession. This approach can yield picture groups, picture series, picture stories, and photo essays (see Chapter 8).

Another technique is indirect recording of images. Photographers usually record images directly, using light rays that reflect from subject to lens. But sometimes they can communicate the situation better by recording subjects indirectly, when light rays from the subjects reflect off secondary objects, such as mirrors, polished helmets, or the quiet water of ponds, before reaching the camera (Figure 4.33). Photographers must always be alert to images created by light reflected from secondary sources.

Sharpness Sharpness is subjective in photojournalism; it depends on the interpretive skill of viewers. What is tack sharp to inexperienced viewers with no reservoir of photographic knowledge may be much less so to experienced photojournalists.

A photograph may have only one plane—one area—that appears sharp. Most likely this is the result of using a telephoto lens and a large f-stop to picture a subject relatively close to the camera. Or a photograph may have many planes—many areas—that appear sharp. Most likely this is the result of using a wide-angle lens and a small f-stop to picture a subject that is not real close to the camera. What appears sharp or unsharp in a photograph can radically affect the message it conveys to readers. The same scene, the same subject, executed with a different

Truthful images can be misleading if they are not presented in fair proportion. A dollhouse can become a mansion, a small model ship can become a mighty fighting vessel, a huge memorial can become a tabletop sculpture, and a mammoth hot-air balloon being inflated can become a tiny model. With these scenes—the huge South Dakota monument to the Sioux chief Crazy Horse and a mammoth hot-air balloon being inflated—each photographer achieved appropriate proportion by picturing a person with the things. Always keep in mind that your readers are not privy to the real-life scenes like you, the photographer, are. Readers do not have the advantage of seeing the entire scene with its primary and supporting visual and other elements, only that part of it that you show them through your photograph.

CHARLES BENNETT/AP/WIDE WORLD PHOTOS (FIGURE 4.29)
JIM SLOSIAREK/AP/WIDE WORLD PHOTOS (FIGURE 4.30)

FIGURE 4.31

Space is a precious commodity in journalism; a lot of interesting material—text, photographs, and artwork—chases a limited amount of space in newspapers and magazines. The photojournalist who tells the story in one photograph in an interesting and truthful way has a good chance of seeing the picture in print. This image of an Iowa flood victim rescuing his cat after earlier being forced to quickly evacuate and leave him behind after a dike failed was taken by a photographer who clearly is a journalist. It gets across the flood's effect on people and animals while showing the physical scene and does so in a space-saving single picture.

JOHN GAPS III/AP/WIDE WORLD PHOTOS

FIGURE 4.32

Advancing mechanisms—motor drives—that allow a photographer to record many exposures in an extremely short time typically are used for sports action. But they also can be invaluable in helping the photojournalist better communicate other scenes, as illustrated by these motor drive-assisted images of the collapse of a church's fire-ravaged steeple. (If his publication could have published only one frame, the photographer prefers the middle one. Do you agree?) Do not use a motor drive in a quiet environment such as a funeral because its noise will distract and offend.

KEITH HITCHENS/*THE NEWS-SENTINEL*, FORT WAYNE, IND.

Photojournalism: An Introduction

sharpness ambiance can convey different messages (Figure 4.34).

Subject-Based Techniques

Balance   Photojournalists often use
the technique of balance. Balance refers
to equal volume or weight on each side
of the center of the picture; the sides
may be more or less a mirror image of
each other (*symmetry*) or unlike but
equal (*asymmetry*). Whether the photograph is symmetrical (Figure 4.35) or
asymmetrical, whether it shows people
or things, balance gives a sense of reality, a sense of scenes being the way they
ought to be, and thus attracts the
reader's eye.

Expression   Photojournalists should
use captions to clarify the inner feelings
that subjects manifest through their
outward expressions. Photographers
must probe beyond clichés, and not, for
example, assume that crying means
sadness or laughing means joy. Before
reporting inner feelings photojournalists must be certain of what they actually are. Ask. Embarrassment or worse
awaits subjects whose feelings are mis-
reported, and embarrassment and lawsuits await photojournalists (and their

employers) who do the faulty reporting.
    Here are some inner feelings and
how they may be manifested in outward expression:

Joy, happiness, amusement, embarrassment, nervousness, or futility	Laughing
Sadness, joy, or futility	Crying
Disapproval or unhappiness	Scowling
Approval, happiness, amusement, or nervousness	Smiling

FIGURE 4.35

Why balance is such an important photojournalistic tool is not settled. Perhaps it is because people tend to be comfortable with completeness; someone or something unbalanced and alone, without a counterbalancing force, causes discomfort. Do the arms reaching out for the Pope's hands in this image, taken upon the Pontiff's arrival in the United States, give you a sense of balance, a sense of completeness?
KEITH MEYERS/THE NEW YORK TIMES PICTURES

Form   Photographers must always be mindful of the acronym KISS—"Keep it simple, stupid." This does not mean that images may not be complex. It means that photographers should discard everything that does not support the message they want to convey. It also means the messages should be as simple as possible, even if they are complex in form.

In a *unified form* all key aspects work together to convey the message; the picture is synergistic (Figure 4.36). In a *confused form* one or more key aspects conflict with one or more other key aspects or with one or more important secondary aspects. A *minimal form* shows one key aspect without complicating nuances (Figure 4.37). A *complex form* shows more than one key aspect or one key aspect with complicating nuances (Figure 4.38).

Implied Movement   A photograph records only one moment in time. Photographers try to overcome this inherent limitation of the medium by using several techniques, one of which is implying movement. Because of expecta-

tions of human behavior and the concept of gravity a frozen moment can imply movement. Implied movement rests on readers' insight that an image is one small slice of the subject's real-life movement and readers' assumption that additional movement took place after the frozen movement (see Figure 4.39).

Incongruity   With *incongruity* things just do not seem to go together; they are not harmonious. Incongruity is the unusual and sometimes unexpected pairing of two or more subjects (Figure 4.40). Unexpected combinations can make images particularly interesting, if not pleasing.

Interposition   Scenes recorded without significant camera or lens distortion still can yield images that clearly are distorted. These images are truthful representations of reality largely undistorted by the photographic process; however, they do not conform to most adults' reasonable visual expectations. Such images are caused by light rays that bend while passing through, or being re-

FIGURE 4.36

The key aspects of this powerful image—the homeless person, the passersby, and the overall environment—work together to convey the message. Synergism is hard at work. Try to mentally blot out the passersby. Is a different message conveyed? What if the photographer had used a different angle that eliminated much of the background? Would the message be different still? As you make pictures, keep in mind how a scene's different aspects can work together in a synergistic way to present a unified form that better communicates your message.

JIMI LOTT/*THE SEATTLE TIMES*

flected from, one or more intervening objects or substances. An example is the distorted image of a person created when light rays, after being reflected off the person, then bend when passing through water, as shown in Figure 4.41.

Introduction   The two kinds of photographic introduction are framed and open. In a *framed image* the foreground or other secondary subject(s) enrich and enclose the main subject. Framing main subjects is an effective composition tool, but it can be overused. At its most effective it gives an aura of stealth and intimacy; readers feel they are surreptitiously watching real-life scenes (Figure 4.42). Photographers must always think about framing subjects but must never forget the power of straightforward images—of *open images;* these show main subjects devoid of enriching and enclosing foregrounds and secondary subjects (Figure 4.43).

Irony   *Irony* refers to unexpected or unusual results with a dash of humor or low-key sarcasm. Irony is akin to incongruity because it runs counter to the normal and expected. Like incongruity, irony adds an ingredient to photographs that can pique readers' interest. As with incongruity, photographers must be careful to portray only honest irony (Figure 4.44).

Lines, Shapes, and Directions   Lines, shapes, and directions exist in physical reality—roads to the horizon, the circular sun, extended arms implying upwardness—the list is almost endless. Photographers also can use implied

FIGURE 4.37

Can even the most distracted and hurried reader miss the point of this minimal image—a child's face ravaged by war? Powerful images presented straightforwardly and without distractions stand a strong probability of communicating their message to most readers.

GAIL FISHER/*THE LOS ANGELES TIMES*

FIGURE 4.38

Visual depth and subject support make this picture of Walter Mondale, then the nominee for U.S. ambassador to Japan, at his Senate confirmation hearing. Seated in back of the former vice president are his wife, Joan Mondale, and supporter Mike Mansfield, the outgoing ambassador to Japan and former Senate majority leader.

STEPHEN CROWLEY/*THE NEW YORK TIMES PICTURES*

Photojournalism: An Introduction

FIGURE 4.39

Sixteen-year-old American Brooke Bennett is on her way in this image to winning gold in the women's 800-meter freestyle at the 1996 Summer Olympics in Atlanta. Particularly successful implied movement images like this one are difficult to take; a fraction of a second can make the difference between success and failure as can a slightly different angle (of course, this is true with a lot of other types of images photojournalists make). With this picture, is there any doubt in your mind that the teenager has been swimming and will continue to do so?

HANS DERYK/AP/WIDE WORLD PHOTOS

FIGURE 4.40

What to make of this image, incongruous as it seems? Is the woman's putt so important that the burning building is of no interest? Could it be that the woman and her golfing companions already looked at the fire, satisfied whatever curiosity they may have had about it, decided there was nothing they could do about it, and returned to their game? The point is that as a photographer you must never assume something negative about people and ridicule them in print for acting in a way that to you seems unusual. There may be good reason for an incongruous scene. Always seek an explanation from the participants before passing on caption or story information. In fairness to your subjects and out of concern for a lawsuit, never assume anything in the journalism business and report as fact your assumption.

GREG LEHMAN/WALLA WALLA (WASH.) UNION-BULLETIN

Truthful reality or distorted reality? First, because James Granger used a 180mm lens, the youngster is slightly distorted from the compressing effect of a telephoto of that length. But compared to the distortion caused by the water, lens distortion is minuscule. Intervening distortion often yields provocative images, which are truthful for these situations. Do you agree? JAMES GRANGER/LUBBOCK AVALANCHE-JOURNAL

lines, shapes, and directions to infer physical reality. Implications can be as real and meaningful as actual physical realities, and just as truthful. With at least one aspect of lines, shapes, and directions, some photographers and editors are not satisfied with what real-life offers. Apparently in an effort to inject images with a dynamicism that their real-life scenes did not provide and for which there was no real photographic necessity such as being jostled while covering a riot, they embrace the diagonal by slanting in publication what was not slanted in real-life. They typically also do not explain in the caption how the slanting came about. The author of this book does not embrace this technique because of the deviation from truthful reality. On the other hand, however, since this use of the diagonal usually is blatant, it may be that readers understand that the slanting did not exist in real-life and therefore truthful reality is not seriously assaulted.

Here is an outline of five important lines, shapes, and directions and what may occur when you use them:

Vertical	Implies action, conflict
Horizontal	Implies rest, relaxation, serenity
Diagonal	Implies movement, dynamism
Curved	Implies pleasantness, fulfillment
Leading	Actual or implied lines of any direction guide readers to one or more subjects, usually main subjects

The use of lines, shapes, and directions is an important composition technique for emphasizing one or more main subjects or directions and thus communicating more clearly or more surely catching the reader's eye. Figures 4.45 through 4.49 illustrate most of these concepts.

FIGURE 4.42

Never forget that photojournalism requires endless decision making about what events to cover, which lens to use, which moment of time to record and from what angle, whether to frame or not, and so forth. Giving a specific scene better perspective by enclosing it to one degree or the other by another part of the scene may be the better way to tell the story, as here with the funeral service for the musical director of the television show *Mr. Rogers' Neighborhood.* Always remember that visual exploration of a photographic situation may lead to interesting images that also tell the story well.

John Beale/*Pittsburgh Post-Gazette,* © 1999. All Rights Reserved. Reprinted with permission.

FIGURE 4.43

Without diminishing the potential importance of framing, framing may not help inherently interesting subjects. This little girl taking a bow after dancing and jumping from post to post stands as an exemplar of a photographically open introduction.

Peter Monsees/*The Record,* Hackensack, N.J.

FIGURE 4.44

The hound in this blessing of the hounds ceremony, which marks the start of fox-hunting season, is only doing what comes naturally, ironic though it may be.

FRITZ HOFFMANN/NETWORK PHOTOGRAPHERS, LONDON

Meaning and Message   In the hustle and bustle of modern life it is safer for photojournalists to convey only one main subject in their photographs. Everything else in the image, if anything, should support the main subject. The argument against this approach is that even though readers typically spend little time reading, they are reasonably well educated and therefore are likely to understand more complicated images. Also, many readers probably can deal with nuances. Perhaps the best advice is to follow the action. If situations lend themselves to a single main subject, present them that way. Likewise, if situations lend themselves to more complicated treatment, present them that way. If the choice is not clear, go for uncomplicated treatment.

Like meaning, message is a critically important aspect of photojournalism. Single communication with no significant nuance increases the probability that readers will accurately understand what the photographer is trying to convey (Figure 4.50). More complex messages may communicate more in-depth information and in a more finely tuned way (Figure 4.51), but the risk of misinterpretation is greater.

Mood   An important and challenging goal for photojournalists is to portray visually the inner feelings of their subjects. You may glean important clues to the real mood of subjects from their physical environment. It is likely that a baseball fan yelling for her favorite team is in a good mood—assuming the team is winning. An el-derly man sitting on a park bench gazing up at passing clouds may be in a happy mood, may be in a depressed mood, or may just be in a pensive mood. As with other caution-laden techniques in this chapter, take great care to portray only accurate inner feelings.

Repetition   Repetition is an effective composition tool but, like other techniques, should not be overused. Repeating similar elements reinforces their importance and encourages readers to ponder their significance. Repetition typically adds an orderliness and stability to an often chaotic visual world (Figure 4.52).

FIGURE 4.45

Vertical lines and directions can be striking and appealing to readers, as this fly-fishing image surely is.

© GEOFF FORESTER/CONCORD (N.H.) MONITOR

FIGURE 4.46

The opposite of the vertical is the horizontal line or direction; often it is just as appealing or perhaps more so. This image of Rachael Worby, then the First Lady of West Virginia, conducting the Wheeling Symphony Orchestra, makes the point well.

SUZANNE DeCHILLO/THE NEW YORK TIMES PICTURES

FIGURE 4.47

Diagonal lines and directions tend to imply movement and action more than verticals and horizontals do. Does the diagonal formed by Japanese Olympic gold medalist Takafumi Nishitani and his speed-skating competitors do this for you? Always be on the lookout for lines and directions and use them to better catch the reader's attention.
CHANG W. LEE/THE NEW YORK TIMES PICTURES

FIGURE 4.48

How about this idyllic Utah scene punctuated by the curved line of a cave? Pleasant? Little doubt about it. Fulfilling? Probably. Now read the caption accompanying this pictorial-like image. The man is a police investigator with the Navajo Nation. His mission is finding two people who may have killed a police officer in Colorado. The composition technique of the curve is juxtaposed onto societal reality, creating irony that a scene so beautiful can be even indirectly related to a heinous crime. Potential composition techniques should rush through your mind like a hurricane wind, always presenting themselves for use as you, the photographer, deem desirable or necessary.
ERIC DRAPER/AP/WIDE WORLD PHOTOS

Subtlety   Whether with single or multiple subjects, subtlety depends on sophisticated and worldly wise readers recognizing and appreciating indirect or downplayed meaning. Subtle images are effective with some readers and a total loss with others (Figure 4.53).

Tension   Tension is a clashing of wills—physical or psychological—that positions recorded images solidly in anxiety. Tension, like a strained rubber band, anticipates impending action, most likely to the advantage of one participant. Tension ultimately pits one person, one group, one thing, or groups of these against another with the expectation that a winner and loser will emerge (Figure 4.54). Photographers can translate tension to a physical image with a variety of composition techniques. However, tension must be recognized as a technique in its own right before it becomes visual reality through one or more other techniques.

Final Thoughts

Prepared photojournalists have a variety of composition techniques to help them fairly communicate visual messages that are storytelling, eye-catching, and appropriately truthful. A

FIGURE 4.51

Simplicity, although often desirable, is not the only way to get the message across. The picture here does a superb job at communicating in a single image an ambiance of complexity. This photograph does not need its caption to convey victory and defeat at a championship game; however, the caption is needed to convey information not shown.
LUI KIT WONG/*THE NEWS TRIBUNE*, TACOMA, WASH.

FIGURE 4.52

Repetition can be found everywhere—for example, in features, pictorials, sports, and even spot news. This scene shows a mother and her daughter holding oxygen masks after a fire at their apartment. Always be on the lookout for repetition on every assignment you cover—it can add visual interest to your photograph, encouraging readers to view it.
GREG LOVETT/*THE PALM BEACH POST*

Photojournalism: An Introduction

FIGURE 4.53

Talented photojournalists make connections others miss; this is especially true with nuance-rich subtleties. This image of a parade balloon vendor and his balloon is a good example of subtlety that entertains as well as informs. Do you think most readers would recognize the juxtaposed subtlety and appreciate it?

BRYAN GRIGSBY

number of them are noted in this chapter. Photographers should not use these composition techniques slavishly but carefully and sensitively. Photojournalists must constantly search for the best techniques to apply to particular situations, realizing that they always have more than one composition choice for getting the message across. Creative photojournalists visualize ordinary subjects in extraordinary ways without sacrificing their real meaning.

NOTES

[1] Whether a photograph's subject matter is pleasing to viewers is an entirely different question. This is a critically important distinction. It means, for example, that the image elements of someone committing suicide by jumping from a bridge may be pleasing to viewers, but the subject of the photograph—the person jumping and the act of suicide—may be most displeasing.

[2] The camera obscura was invented during this period to aid artists in their quest for accurate representations of reality.

[3] Rudolf Arnheim, *Art and Visual Perception: A Psychology of the Creative Eye* (Berkeley and Los Angeles: University of California Press, 1974), p. 284.

[4] *Perspective*, Introduction and Commentary by Pierre Descargues, trans. I Mark Paris (New York: Harry N. Abrams, 1977), p. 9.

[5] Bill Brandt, *Camera In London* (London and New York: The Focal Press, 1948), p. 14.

[6] Henri Cartier-Bresson, *The Decisive Moment: Photography by Henri Cartier-Bresson* (New York: Simon and Schuster

FIGURE 4.54

Greco-Roman wrestling, super-heavyweights, tension epitomized at the 1996 Summer
Olympics in Atlanta—that's this image. Is there any doubt in your mind that these massive
men—Russia's Alexander Karelin, who won a gold medal by winning this match, and the
United States's Matt Ghaffari—are involved in a clashing of wills? The photographer used
a 400mm telephoto lens and took advantage of a plain background to bring to readers an
up-close, visually compelling, tension-laden moment in this not-so-visually exciting sport.
KENNETH JARECKE/CONTACT PRESS IMAGES

in collaboration with Editions VERVE of Paris, 1952).

7 CarI Mydans, *Carl Mydans, Photojournalist* (New York: Harry N. Abrams, 1985).

8 Frank Barron, "Putting Creativity to Work," in *The Nature of Creativity: Contemporary Psychological Perspectives,* ed. Robert J. Sternberg (Cambridge and New York, Cambridge University Press, 1988), p. 95.

9 Lincoln Kirstein, "Henri Cartier-Bresson by Lincoln Kirstein," An intro-duction to *Photographs by Cartier-Bresson* (New York: Grossman, 1963).

10 For beginning students whose pur-chase of 35mm equipment is con-strained by small budgets, a relatively slow—perhaps f/2-50mm lens does nicely. However, you should buy a fast moderate wide-angle and a fast short telephoto, or an equivalent zoom, as soon as possible.

Light and Color

Q&A: Life at a Small Circulation Newspaper

Charlie Riedel—photo editor, *The Hays* (Kan.) *Daily News*

Light bathes Match of Champions riders as they are introduced at a bull riding competition. If the light was coming from behind the photographer toward the competitors' backs, the scene would have an entirely different ambiance—probably the image would be much less effective, much less eye-catching.
TOM PENNINGTON/*ARLINGTON* (TEXAS) *STAR-TELEGRAM*

Overview

Without light, photography is not possible; it is a key and fundamental ingredient of picture taking. It also is a key ingredient in shaping reality—how readers will perceive a person or thing, both in form and color. The importance of a basic understanding of light and how to use it is difficult to overstate.

Photography requires light both because of its inherent illuminating capability and because of the colors it allows us to perceive. Photojournalists must constantly—every day, every waking hour—look at light and color. You should pay special attention to the way light forms and molds reality in the areas it illuminates, the shadows it helps create, and the way it creates psychological ambiance—a mood (Figure 5.1).

Light is a major composition tool of photojournalists. It places emphasis,

FIGURE 5.1

Light truly is a blessing for photographers. Besides allowing photographs to be made, it allows perceptive photographers to record their vision of the most appropriate truth in a creative way that all but makes readers view their images, thus becoming better informed. This photograph is a good example. Note the light areas—the highlights—and the dark areas—the shadows—and how they work together to sculpt this shadow-boxing Philadelphian. Light is one of the most powerful, if not the most powerful, composition tools available for your use; use it prudently and well.

GERARD LODRIGUSS/THE PHILADELPHIA INQUIRER

Photojournalism: An Introduction

creates an ambiance, and determines reality (Figure 5.2).

The prominent documentary photographer Laura Gilpin put it this way: "Light is our paint brush and it is a most willing tool in the hands of the one who studies it with sufficient care."[1] Light is a key factor in creating real-life truths. Every photojournalist who hopes to convey to readers the most appropriate truth of situations must be intimately familiar with light (and its colors) and keenly aware of the differing messages it can create in the same situation at the same time.

Fundamentals of Light and Color

Light is a small portion of the electromagnetic spectrum. Simplified, it is electromagnetic waves that the human eye can see. It is a fundamental force of the universe that adds luster and excitement to human existence for those who, by intuition or training, recognize and appreciate its many facets.

Electromagnetic waves that people cannot see include the gamma rays used in treating cancer, microwaves used in cooking food and transmitting signals, and radio frequency waves used to bring voices and pictures from far away.

Our concern here is with only a few waves in the spectrum—those that people see, the visible spectrum. These few waves allow photographs to be made and people to see them.

The three fundamental colors of light are on the spectrum between 400 and 700 nanometers (nm—a nanometer is one billionth of a meter). Figure 5.3 shows these colors—the extremes are violet at 400nm and red at 700nm—in relation to the entire spectrum. These are the colors of light that people with normal vision perceive.

The world is full of color. Color distinguishes one thing from another and influences human feelings.[2] Color results when some wavelengths of the visual spectrum are missing; white results when all are present, black when none is present.

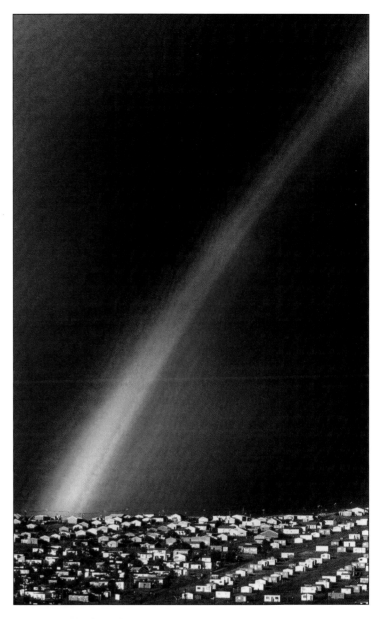

FIGURE 5.2

While some photography is better done in black and white, the realistic beauty of color is never to be underestimated. Without diminishing the overall beauty of this South African rainbow as it arches over a township, look at the individual colors that compromise it. Just as closely and carefully as hopefully you are looking at these colors, always try to closely and carefully look at all light and color before you. Look just before sunrise, at sunrise, in the early morning, in the late morning, at noon, in the early afternoon, in the late afternoon, just before sunset, at sunset, and just after sunset. But don't stop here. Look at how moonlight helps make reality and how artificial light does also. As with everything else around you, always be looking at light and its color.

ODD ANDERSON/AGENCE FRANCE-PRESSE

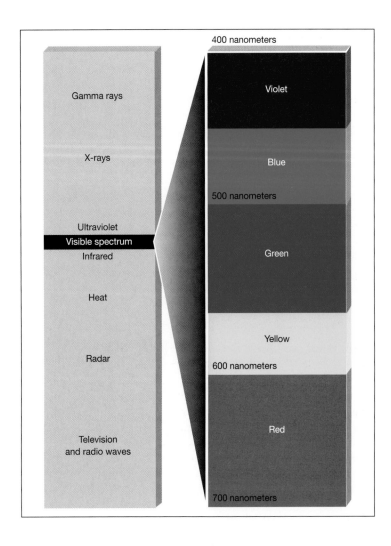

FIGURE 5.3

The Electromagnetic Spectrum.
ADAPTED FROM *PHOTOGRAPHY* BY B. WARREN.
P. 17. ©1993. REPRINTED WITH THE PERMISSION OF
DELMAR PUBLISHERS, A DIVISION OF THOMSON LEARNING.
ILLUSTRATION BY ILLUSTRATED ARTS (UK).

Objects appear colorful, or white or black, because they are reflecting only some of the wavelengths that are striking them, reflecting all the wavelengths striking them, or reflecting none of the wavelengths. Black, white, and colors affect people emotionally. For example, white tends to be neutral, red exciting, and blue calming.

Color is described in three ways: by its hue, value, and saturation (Figure 5.4). *Hue* is the psychological reaction that humans as a group have to particular wavelengths of light; for example, the hue of an apple is red or green; the hue of ocean water is blue or green. *Value* is luminance, how much a color reflects light, particularly compared to colors of similar hue. For example, a red object may appear particularly dull, whereas another of the same hue and similar saturation may appear particularly bright. *Saturation* is the degree of purity of a color, how free it is of diluting influences. For example, a pure deep red is said to be highly saturated, whereas a red considerably diluted with white is said to be of low saturation.

At first glance the world of color seems without organization. Not so. Color is organized as a dichotomy: one extreme is violet, the other red. All other colors fall between the extremes as Figure 5.3 shows.

Color is also organized according to the three primary colors and three so-called subtractive primaries. When added together the primary colors produce almost all other colors. The subtractive primaries, or secondary colors, form other colors by deleting one or more colors. The three primary colors—red, green, and blue—mix in different combinations and shades in the additive method. For example, red and blue yield magenta; red and green yield yellow; blue and green yield cyan. The three primary colors combined in equal parts create white.

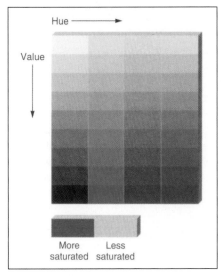

FIGURE 5.4

Hue, Saturation, and Brightness.
FROM *PHOTOGRAPHY* BY B. WARREN. P. 365. ©1993.
REPRINTED WITH THE PERMISSION OF DELMAR
PUBLISHERS, A DIVISION OF THOMSON LEARNING.

The three subtractive primaries, or secondary colors—magenta (red and blue), cyan (blue and green), and yellow (red and green)—begin with white light and remove from it different combinations and shades in the subtractive method. Filters or dyes of these colors remove one primary color or in combination remove more than one. Combining the subtractive primaries blocks all visible wavelengths, and the resulting image is black.

Although creating colors by using the additive method is straightforward, creating colors with the subtractive method is somewhat complicated because white light strikes only the first filter. Other filters behind the first receive only the light transmitted by the filters in front of them. The term *selective absorption* refers to a filter or other medium that absorbs light from part of the visual spectrum while allowing other visible waves to pass. Using the additive method forms images on positive, or transparency, color film; using the subtractive method forms negative color film images.

For humans color is primarily a phenomenon of bright light. Unlike the color-sensitive cones of the eye, which primarily operate in bright light conditions, the rods of the eye, which take over in dim lighting conditions, do not distinguish color.

Photographic color film, on the other hand, distinguishes color in both bright and dim light, a technical property that allows photographers to record colors in dim light. This accounts for photographs that present dimly lit scenes as more colorful than what the eyes of the photographer or other viewers could perceive.

Different kinds of light can also affect color. The same outdoor scene in the early morning conveys different coloration at noon and still different coloration late in the afternoon. The same scene appears to have different colors on a cloudy day at noon than on a clear sunny day at noon. The light of a 100-watt household (incandescent/tungsten) bulb is different from the light of a quartz lamp. The light from a candle is different still. These differences are of little concern in black-and-white photography but take on important meaning when you are using color film.

Fundamental to understanding these differences is Kelvin temperature. The Kelvin temperature system originated with W. T. (Lord) Kelvin, a British physicist. It assigns temperatures to various light sources, including sunlight at different times of the day and under different weather conditions. The Kelvin temperature of light indicates only its color. It does not address the specific electromagnetic waves that comprise the light. This means that light from two sources can be the same color but react to film and filtration differently.

Author Ellis Herwig tells us in his book, *The Handbook of Color Photography* that:

> Color temperature was first determined by heating a piece of iron until it became incandescent. As the temperature rose, the color of the incandescence changed. At relatively low temperatures, the color was reddish. It got more and more blue at progressively higher temperatures. The result was that any color could be expressed in terms of the temperature necessary to reproduce it in hot iron.[3]

A Kelvin (K) temperature of 2,000 degrees is said in photographic parlance to be very low; 16,000 degrees is very high. A temperature of 2,000 K translates to a very red light, 16,000 K to a very blue light. The higher the temperature, the more blue wavelengths are present, many of which we cannot see. These descriptions of Kelvin temperatures come from the art world; admittedly, they seem upside down. The temperature of blue is referred to as *cooler,* even with its higher relative temperature; likewise, red is said to be *warmer,* even with its lower relative temperature. People see a 50-degree Kelvin temperature difference as warmer or cooler. See Table 5.1 for Kelvin temperatures of familiar light sources.

Daylight color film is made so that exposure to 5,500 K sunlight—light close to that at noon on a bright, clear, sunny day with some white clouds —

TABLE 5.1

Approximate Kelvin Temperatures of Selected Lighting Conditions/Light Sources

Clear blue sky	16,000
Lightly overcast sky	7,500
Heavily overcast sky	6,800
Bright, clear sunny day at noon, some white clouds	6,000
Light haze	5,800
Electronic flash	5,600
Quartz lamp	3,200
100-watt household bulb	2,860

creates neither a red nor blue cast. This Kelvin temperature also is close to that of the light produced by electronic flash.

Daylight film exposed at other times and under other lighting conditions will contain a cast, either red or blue; the lower the Kelvin temperature, the redder the cast; the higher the temperature, the bluer the cast. If a cast is deemed undesirable—some can be highly desirable such as the warm ambiance of a late afternoon sun—using one or more filters will remove it.

Using Light

Whatever the situations being photographed, whether in color or black and white, the way photographers use light to a great extent sculpts the messages they convey to readers. Photographers have a much easier time controlling light when they are not covering breaking news events. But even in these situations photographers can partially control light—if by doing nothing more than using electronic flash to soften shadows created by a photographically unsympathetic sun.

Light and the way it strikes subjects—creating highlights and shadows, emphasizing or minimizing, creating an ambiance of tenseness or relaxation—is an aspect of composition that every photojournalist must study at home, at work, at play. Heightened sensitivity to light

and its interaction with subjects comes with practice—looking for light and shadows and color.

Picture-Taking Considerations

Point Source Light

Light emanating from one primary source is termed *point source* light; Figure 5.5 illustrates point source light. Lighting of subjects by direct and relatively intense point source light—the sun, for example—can be described in relation to the position of the camera: front, side, back, and top.

Front Light Front light strikes the main aspect of the subject from in front of or from behind the photographer. Light coming from in front of the photographer probably will be from the photographer's electronic flash. Most likely light coming from behind the photographer will be from the sun.

Plain vanilla describes front light. It typically is not visually exciting, offering an untextured "flat" image where shadows, particularly on faces, are visually dull or largely non-existent because the straight-on light (in relation to the photographer) pushed them backwards into empty space (Figure 5.6). Any three dimensional aspect of the subject is de-emphasized.

Side Light Side light is created when light strikes the subject from only one side and at about 90 degrees to the camera, typically leaving the other side of the subject dark. Side light is visually intriguing, dramatic (Figure 5.7). It tends to create a sense of realness and mystery. Side light also brings out texture in a person's face as well as in other subjects such as a plastered wall.

Side lighted images created using photographer-supplied artificial light of course can be made anytime. Side lighted images created by the sun are most easily made in early-to-mid-morning and mid-to-late afternoon when the sun is relatively close to the horizon.

FIGURE 5.5

Winter point source light rivets on skaters in Boston like an arrow heading for its target. Had the photographer pictured the skaters with the sun at his back, this image would have conveyed a very different ambiance. How would you have approached the scene photographically?
Steven Senne/AP/
Wide World Photos

As a general rule, in a side lighted scene you should expose for the lighted—the "highlighted"—area of the subject. If you expose for the dark area the lighted area will lose most or all its detail—it will "wash out" in photographic parlance.

Back light Back light is the opposite of front light. It comes toward the photographer from behind the main subject. Properly exposed back light tends to create a sense of depth, and with subjects that lend themselves to it, a sense of beauty (Figure 5.8 and the first photo of this chapter).

Photographers commonly expose for the light area of the scene and then lighten with fill light—direct or reflected electronic flash or reflected natural light —what otherwise would be an unacceptably dark area of the subject facing the cameras—typically one or more faces.

Top Light Top light comes from above the main subject (and the photographer), striking it from its top down. Photojournalists regularly use top lighting, primarily from fluorescent lamps near or in a ceiling that illuminate large areas such as a room (Figure 5.9). Expect to find fluorescent lamps on almost every ceiling of every commercial building in the country. When this downward-directed light passes through a translucent medium—most likely a sheet attached to the light fixture—the light rightly can be described as diffused (see next section). Whether diffused or not, top light creates troublesome shadows on subjects' faces, particularly their eyes. Adding a dab of fill light directly from an electronic flash or reflected from white or light-colored nearby walls often solves the problem. Photographers using color film should take care that the camera lens or flash

FIGURE 5.6

Front light comes straight in toward the subject from in front or behind the photographer. Front light is visually dull, because shadows on faces and contours are pushed straight back, thus de-emphasizing the three-dimensionality of the scene. Here, the front lighting comes from an electronic flash fired from the same position as the photographer.

PHOTOGRAPH BY THOMAS GRAVES

FIGURE 5.7

When light strikes a subject from one side only, the effect produced is to leave that one side lit and the other in shadow. Side light is usually considered more dramatic and interesting than front light, because it brings out texture and contours in faces and objects. Here, an electronic flash was positioned outside the window to create this natural-looking side light, a technique sometimes used by photographers on assignment.

PHOTOGRAPH BY THOMAS GRAVES

FIGURE 5.8

When using backlighting, photographers must decide whether subjects are to be silhouetted as in Figure 5.12 or are to show detail, as in this image of people at a wine and food festival in Vermont. Skillful use of a light meter is helpful in obtaining detail. Take care to measure only the important area of the main subject that is not directly lit. If time or circumstances do not permit you to use a light meter, the general rule is to increase your exposure by two stops more than what you would need for main subject areas hit directly by point source light. When they want detail in both highlight and darker areas, photographers often expose for the highlight area and lighten the darker area—backlit faces, for example—with fill light from an electronic flash, sunlight, or other existing light reflected from a permanent surface or from one provided by the photographer.

PAUL O. BOISVERT/THE NEW YORK TIMES PICTURES

lens, or both, have appropriate filtration to ensure that the subject is not bathed with one or more undesirable casts. Top light also can be specialty direction lighting, such as light illuminating a pool table (Figure 5.10). Rarely do photographers create top light, except when they are bouncing electronic flash off ceilings to simulate and intensify existing room light.

Diffused Light

Photographers refer to light that reflects off one or more secondary objects or passes through a material that diverts and scatters it before it strikes the main subject as diffused; diffused light typically yields an overall soft lighting ambiance. (Figure 5.11). Although this lighting lacks the cutting edge of side lighting and the visual

FIGURE 5.9

In the typical office building most light comes from fluorescent lamps set in ceiling fixtures. While these provide uniformity of light over a given area, their top-down direction can be unflattering and uninteresting.
PHOTOGRAPH BY THOMAS GRAVES

separation of backlighting, it creates a mood of its own—peaceful and non-confrontational. It can be an effective composition tool, both in black and white and color.

Silhouettes and Shadows

Photographers use directional light from point sources with great effect in two other ways: silhouettes and shad-ows. Silhouettes (Figure 5.12) are the epitome of understated main subject lighting. They emphasize form rather than detail. They often interact with well-lit backgrounds that support and embellish their messages.

Shadows (Figure 5.13) convey mes-sages in a clear and eye-catching way. They are representations of subjects that block light rays; these rays strike

FIGURE 5.10

Preserving the lighting ambiance of an indoor scene has long been a popular approach in photojournalism. Sometimes the existing light is a particularly strong composition aspect of the scene, as here. Imagine what a single electronic flash, straight on and near the camera, would have done to the pool hall ambiance.

Thomas J. Ondrey/*The Times*, Kettering and Oakwood, Ohio

the side of a subject that is opposite its shadow. Much as black-and-white photography can eliminate distracting color, shadows can eliminate distracting whites and shades of gray from black-and-white images. Shadows also can effectively communicate in color. Areas in color surrounding the shadow are particularly important when shadows are recorded on color film.

Intensity

Until 1988, when exceptionally light-sensitive films—one black and white and one color—became available, light intensity was a particularly important concern to photojournalists. These films also changed the composition as-

pects of coverage; for example, photojournalists can shoot moderately lit night high school football games with existing light rather than with photographer-imported light. This changed the ambiance of pictures that fans see and allowed photojournalists to record more telling aspects. The limitations of electronic flash often no longer are deciding factors in covering the games.

Photojournalism has no generally accepted photojournalistic definitions of high- and low-light intensity. The practical definition used here is based on shutter speeds, aperture size (f-stops), and film speed. When photojournalists need a shutter speed and f-stop combination of 1/60 or longer at f/8 (or its

FIGURE 5.11

Light and how photo-journalists use it significantly affects what they convey to readers. This image of a bride-to-be brushing her teeth before the marriage ceremony eschews the harshness of strong point source lighting; instead, it conveys the nonconfrontational ambiance of diffused lighting.

STEVE HEALEY/*THE JOHNSON COUNTY DAILY JOURNAL*, FRANKLIN, IND.

equivalent) using film rated at ISO 400, the light intensity is deemed to be low. When they use a shutter speed shorter than 1/60 at f/8 (or its equivalent) with film rated at ISO 400, the light intensity is deemed to be high.[4]

High Key and Low Key

If light tones predominate to create a photograph's ambiance, photographers term the picture *high key*. Conversely, if the tones are predominantly dark, they refer to the picture as *low key*. The concept of key is not of great importance to photojournalists, particularly those working for newspapers and wire services. These photographers seldom can control key, and even if they can the limitations of press reproduction often make their

efforts moot. Exceptions do arise, however; acquaintance with key can be useful, even for newspaper and wire service photographers.

Ratio

The last major picture-taking consideration is ratio. *Ratio* is a fraction whose numerator reflects the brightest-lit area and whose denominator reflects the dimmest-lit area. For example, a person's face lighted in high ratio might be 18 to 1, which would probably represent intense side lighting. Typically, ratio is a measurement of the light intensity that is falling on a subject rather than of the light reflected from it. With most subjects this ratio is about the same as that for the reflected light; however, makeup and complexion of

FIGURE 5.12

Dispensing with potentially confusing detail, silhouettes like this one of youngsters on swings at a county fair primarily depend on form to convey their messages. Exposing for front lighting when the subject essentially is back lit produces an image with little or no detail in the part of the subject that is toward the camera. Unless you want a star effect, take care not to aim the lens directly toward the light source. Doing so likely will produce light flare that interferes with the desired image.

DON SHRUBSHELL/*HUTCHINSON* (KAN.) *NEWS*

subjects can significantly alter the ratio, and photographers should be alert to this (Figure 5.14).

Lighting ratios are important in expressing composition lighting ambiances and in serving as indicators of what images will look like when reproduced. For example, some publications have technical problems in reproducing color photographs with high lighting ratios. Technical reproduction limitations always are a concern to photojournalists. After all, what matters is not what computer images or photographic prints look like—it is what mass-reproduced facsimiles look like in publication.

Major Aspects in Brief

Table 5.2 summarizes major aspects of light that photojournalists regularly encounter.

Final Thoughts

Light is a major part of photojournalism—of all photography. Photographers who want to convey their sense of reality fairly represented will have a lifelong friendship with light. They will have an intimate acquaintance that allows them to recognize and appropriately modify all the forms and colors of light and use it to more truthfully inform.

FIGURE 5.13

Similar in lack of detail to silhouettes, shadows are not recordings of real subjects but representations of them, often distorted. Real subjects—such as American Michael Chang playing in the Australian Open Tennis Championships—create shadows by blocking a point source of light. Exposure should be of highlighted areas around shadows. This makes the shadows dark and obvious. RICK RYCROFT/AP/WIDE WORLD PHOTOS

Photojournalism: An Introduction

FIGURE 5.14

This image of people at the dedication of the Philadelphia Vietnam Veterans Memorial is a good example of creative use of high ratio lighting to catch the viewer's eye. Are you intrigued by the lighting into closely examining—reading—the image?
BRYAN GRIGSBY

NOTES

1   Brooks Johnson, ed., *Photography Speaks* (Norfolk and New York: Aperture/Chrysler Museum, 1989), p. 46.

2   Faber Birren, *Color & Human Response: Aspects of Light and Color Bearing on the Reactions of Living Things and the Welfare of Human Beings* (New York: Van Nostrand Reinhold, 1978), p. 24.

3   Ellis Herwig, *The Handbook of Color Photography* (New York: Amphoto, 1982), p. 32.

4   These combinations are likely to be cause for debate, but at least they should give aspiring photojournalists a starting point for deciding what is high- and low-intensity lighting to them.

TABLE 5.2

Major Aspects of Light

- **Natural** — Emanates from the sun or reflected from the moon.

- **Artificial** — Emanates from manufactured source.

- **Mixed type** — Combines natural and artificial.

- **Existing** — Present at scene without photographer supplying.

- **Imported** — Derives from one or more sources supplied by photographers or at their direction.

- **Mixed availability** — Combines existing and imported.

- **Point source** — Emanates from one primary source.

- **Front** — Originates in front or in back of the photographer and strikes the main aspect of the main subject.

- **Side** — Originates at about 90 degrees to the camera and strikes the main aspect of the main subject from only one side.

- **Back** — Originates in back of the main aspect of the main subject and strikes the camera lens.

- **Top** — Originates above the main aspect of the main subject (and the photographer) and strikes it from its top down.

- **Diffused** — Reflects off one or more secondary objects or passes through a material that diverts and scatters it before it strikes the main subject; yields an overall soft lighting ambiance.

- **Silhouette** — Produced by little or no light striking the main subject; the background of the scene is well lit.

- **Shadow** — Image formed in the shape of the person or thing which blocks the strong directional light that strikes the subject on the side opposite the shadow.

- **High intensity** — Enough light for an exposure shorter than 1/60 at f/8 (or an equivalent) using ISO 400 film or a digital equivalent.

- **Low intensity** — Absence of enough light to allow an exposure shorter than 1/60 at f/8 (or an equivalent) using ISO 400 film or a digital equivalent.

- **High key** — Predominantly light tones, few shadows.

- **Low key** — Predominantly dark tones.

- **High ratio** — The brightest-lit area of a subject is at least 12 times more intense than the dimmest-lit area.

- **Medium ratio** — The brightest-lit area of a subject is about six times more intense than the dimmest-lit area.

- **Low ratio** — The brightest-lit area of a subject is only about three times more intense than the dimmest-lit area.

Life at a Small Circulation Newspaper

Charlie Riedel—photo editor, *The Hays* (Kan.) *Daily News,* circulation 13,000

Q: *Why did you decide to work for the* Daily News?
A: *The Hays Daily News* was then and is still a good place for a photographer to work. The paper plays pictures big and reproduces them well in print. At the *Daily News,* I have a lot of control over what I photograph and how my photos are presented in print. I have input in the design of page one and photo packages. In general, the *Daily News* is a very satisfying place for a photographer to work.

Q: *Tell me a little about your paper. For example, what is its coverage area, how many staffers does it have, and when does it publish?*
A: We are part of a small family-owned newspaper group with a long tradition of journalistic excellence. We cover about 15 counties in northwest Kansas with a staff of seven reporters and three photographers, including me and an intern. We publish Monday through Friday afternoons and Sunday mornings.

Q: *What are your job duties?*
A: My job is loosely defined. I spend a lot of time talking to reporters and editors about stories they are working on to insure we have local photo coverage in the newspaper. I determine what stories we cover photographically and assign them to photographers (including myself) based on their abilities, interests, or time they have available. In addition, I shoot a couple of photo assignments a day, assist editors in selecting wire photos, order supplies, keep our film processor and photo computers running properly. The other photographers and I also are responsible for preparing wire photos for pagination. I also occasionally produce informational graphics that usually deal with local issues of interest.

Q: *What equipment do you use for picture taking and picture processing?*
A: I use Nikon 35mm cameras with a wide variety of lenses ranging from a 16mm fish-eye to a 300mm telephoto. All my equipment is personally owned but the *Daily News* provides a monthly camera allowance to help cover my costs. To process film, we use an automatic film processor much like those in many one-hour photo labs.

Q: *Hays' population is about 20,000. Tell me about small-town newspaper photojournalism. What's good and what's not so good about it?*
A: The best part about working in a small community is that people are familiar with me and my work. They appreciate the work that I produce and they communicate that to me often. I get lots of feedback. Because they know me, people also are very trusting of me and are willing to share their lives with me. The downside of working in a small community is that people are familiar with me and often engage in conversations with me addressing me by name. I find this awkward because I often don't remember their names, having met them only once when I may have shot their photo five or ten years ago. Aside from that, the only other drawback is that everything is at a pretty slow pace. Changes don't occur often and it is easy to become too familiar with the surroundings and not notice any more what is unique.

Q: *Do you compete with another newspaper? If not, does the lack of competition sometimes lull you into complacency?*
A: We really don't have much strong competition. I try to set my own goals and standards to keep from getting complacent. For example, each time I shoot a familiar event I try to photograph it better than before. I also strive to show our readers the ordinary world around them in an unusual way.

Q: *What about the limited number of readers that see your work? You would influence many more people working for a large circulation paper. Any thoughts about this?*
A: I usually reach a broader audience with some of my more popular photos by sharing them through The Associated Press wire, or sometimes they end up in larger papers or magazines on a freelance basis.

Q: *How about having to cover people you know or regularly see. Do you think it is harder to be a photographer in a small town than a large city? Can you aggressively cover news in Hays?*
A: The only disadvantage to taking photos of people I regularly see is when I can't remember their names, which makes getting caption information some-

what awkward. Working with people who are familiar with me is usually very smooth. They know what I am there for and they know the type of photography I produce. It is like having hundreds of people out there looking out for me and letting me know when they think there is something going on that might make a good picture. I don't think it is necessarily harder being a photographer in a small town, just different. We have to be very good at juggling lots of assignments and have a flexible schedule. There is no such thing as working a shift. You work when you need to work and take time off when you can. It usually evens out in the end. As far as covering news, I don't think we pull our punches because we are in a small town, but there usually is not very much news happening.

Q: *Do you get professionally and personally bored in a small town? Do you ever yearn for big city life?*
A: I wouldn't say I get bored here. Sometimes I think it would be great to cover things that were more meaningful on a global scale instead of documenting day-to-day life in small-town America. But then I think that small-town America needs a voice also, and to my readers I serve a purpose. As far as personally, I've sat in enough traffic jams in cities to know that for me the negatives of city life outweigh the positives.

Q: *How closely do you work with reporters? Do they generate most of the assignments you do?*
A: I try to work very closely with the reporters. My desk is in the newsroom and assignments are made by verbally discussing stories with reporters rather than passing slips of paper. This helps me have an un-

derstanding of the story before going out on an assignment. I also try to generate stories. Reporters generate probably a third of what we shoot, the photographers generate probably another third of the assignments, which then go on to be reported on, and the remainder of what we shoot is photographer-generated stand-alone photos.

Q: *Do you do any word reporting? If you do, how about a couple of examples?*
A: No, other than writing captions. The opportunity is there to do my own reporting, but that is not really what I enjoy doing.

Q: *What do you do in a typical workweek?*
A: First of all, there is no typical week. On average I might shoot half a dozen assignments, which can range from environmental portraits to accidents to enterprise features (Figure A). About half of these assignments would be photo combos with two to four photos. I would probably also shoot two or three sports assignments in a week. In addition, I might be working on a photo page or project in whatever spare time I would have. This is just the shooting aspect of my job. I would also help prepare wire photos for publication, supervise and coach the other photographers, meet with editors and reporters, and generally stay on top of whatever other challenges involving the photo department might arise.

Q: *How about describing in detail one of your more-or-less typical workdays?*
A: There is no typical workday. That is one of the things I love about this job. That said, here is my day today: At 7:15 a.m., I go to a local hospital where a visit-

ing famous heart surgeon is conducting a teleconference with his colleagues in Russia. I photograph the event for about an hour and drive five miles across town to the *Daily News* building. I arrive at 8:30 a.m. and meet with one of our two managing editors to find out exactly what is slated for today's paper. Today we are running my coverage of the heart surgeon (this will be a two-photo package) and tornado damage clean-up shot by our intern. I process my film (we primarily use color negative), edit the negatives and scan two photos into our computer. I then computer process these scans. By 11, I have given proofs of these photos to our layout editor who designs the paper. I then go back to my desk, return a couple of phone calls from people requesting reprints, make arrangements with the subject of a photo I need to shoot in Colby (about 100 miles away) tomorrow and file some negatives. By 11:30, I write captions to go with my photos and give the layout editor some input on her page one layout.

With my role in today's paper finished, I check with reporters and editors to see what they are working on for tomorrow. I find out that the only story we are working on that is visual is another follow-up on tornado damage. Around noon, I meet with the other photographer and our intern and we divide up the day's duties. We decide I will shoot the tornado damage, our intern will look for a feature and the other photographer will shoot high school soccer this afternoon. We all will keep on the lookout for features though. I have lunch from about 12:30 p.m. to about 2 p.m. I drive about five miles to a cattle feed-yard, which was hit by a tornado several days earlier. I spend about an hour photographing workers repairing damage. By about 3:30, I am back in Hays and decide to stop by the natural history museum, which is currently being constructed. I have been working on a Sunday piece updating the progress of the museum. I spend about 45 minutes photographing workers on the roof of the building before driving back to the paper. I arrive about 4:20 and start to process the four rolls of color negative film I shot this afternoon. While the film is processing, I check a couple of phone messages, check with editors and reporters to insure plans for tomorrow haven't changed and prepare a couple of wire photos for inside pages. Around 5, I edit my film, and scan in four photos of tornado clean-up and two photos from the museum. I will leave them as rough scans until tomorrow morning, when I decide exactly what photos will be in the paper. By 5:45 p.m., my scans are saved and my film filed. I decide to call it a day.

Q: *Does the paper send you to do assignments outside the Hays area?*
A: Ninety-nine percent of what I shoot is in Hays or northwest Kansas, but occasionally if I can pitch an idea with a strong enough local tie, we will travel. I have done several political assignments in Washington, D.C.

Q: *Your work has won in photo contests. How do you compete with photographers working at larger circulation papers? Aren't your photographic opportunities much more limited?*
A: I don't really think it matters what size paper you work at for a person to produce award-winning photography. I think the ability to produce good pictures is more an individual trait than a result of where you are. While it is true that opportunities are not as obvious in a small town, they are definitely out there (Figure B and C). The fact that they have to be sought out often makes them more

---

FIGURE A

A farmer passes a multi-colored pile of milo stored on the ground at a grain elevator in Morland, Kansas as he walks back to his truck. The milo, which is a grain sorghum used to feed cattle, was dumped on the ground because of record harvests of the grain and a lack of storage space in elevators. The different colors in the pile result from different varieties of the crop planted by different farmers. I was attracted to this pile by the interesting pattern created by the grain and saw it as an unusual way to illustrate a story about the milo situation. The photo actually spurred the story being written. Probably the most difficult thing for me was simply waiting for someone to walk past the pile to give some scale to the scene. I staked-out this pile for over two hours just waiting for someone to walk past.

CHARLIE RIEDEL/THE HAYS DAILY NEWS

I chased tornadoes for 15 years trying to get one on film before I finally caught up with this tornado-producing storm west of Hays near Yocemento, Kansas. In the span of five minutes I was fortunate to get two tornado photos; the tornadoes, which came and went, traveled 22 miles causing damage to about a dozen farms. I photographed this tornado the way that one shouldn't: I knew it was headed my way, and I headed straight towards the storm. I saw the top of the tornado behind a hill several miles away and knew I needed to find some place to get out of my car and photograph it when it cleared the hill. I also knew I needed to find a spot where I could take cover if it came too close. I knew I had found my spot when I came upon a cluster of newer, sturdy-looking houses. The owner of one

of these was outside watching the storm, so I stopped, introduced myself and asked if I could join him in his basement if need be. He welcomed me, and moments later I was shooting my first tornado photo. The most challenging part of shooting was lack of light. The storm hit after sunset and light was fading fast. With 400 speed film in my camera and no time to change to faster film, I pushed the film two stops and still had to shoot at 1/30th of a second at f/2.8. I had to brace myself against the back of the man's garage to steady myself enough to hand-hold my 80-200 mm zoom lens still to capture the first image. As the tornado popped over the hill behind the house I started shooting, firing off about 20 frames before the winds became too gusty for me to take any more (Figure B, at left). The tornado spared the house in the foreground, but passed about 300 yards from my position at which time I joined the owner in front of his home where his house provided some shelter from the gusty winds. I never felt endangered so I did not go into the basement. Since the tornadoes had gotten close, I had just enough time to run to my car and switch to a 20mm wide angle lens so I could include the human element of the man in the foreground as he watched the tornadoes swirl away from his property (Figure C, below). By the time I took this photo, there were a pair of tornadoes and the light had gotten even dimmer. It was shot at 1/2 second at f/2.8. It took all my effort to hold still enough to capture this image despite continued strong winds. By the time I had finished off a full 36 exposure roll of film, the tornadoes were a couple of miles away and it had gotten too dark to see them.

CHARLIE RIEDEL/THE HAYS DAILY NEWS

rewarding than the more obvious opportunities. There are some advantages to working at a small paper. First, you have a lot of input in which of your photos are selected for publication. In addition, you have a lot of input in how your photos are displayed in the paper. Also, smaller papers oftentimes can have particularly good reproduction.

Q: *Would you advise aspiring photojournalists reading this to go to work for a small circulation newspaper?*

A: Yes, I believe a small paper gives a person more experience in making photos out of life's ordinary experiences. This forces a photographer to work very hard at making something out of what is often commonplace. My theory is that if you can produce exciting photos of visually boring routine events, you should really shine when you get into situations that are inherently visually interesting. I believe that bigger is not always better as a long-term career goal. While photographers at larger papers are generally bet-

ter paid, there are a lot of advantages to working at a small paper. At a small paper, you definitely are a voice in the newsroom and have real impact on what the paper covers and how it is covered. It is possible to really become part of the community and cover community issues with a depth not always possible in a less trusting urban environment.

Author's note: Charlie Riedel now is a photographer with The Associated Press.

Gathering Caption Information

Q&A: The Road to Success
Thomas R. Kennedy—director of photography, Washingtonpost.Newsweek Interactive

Victory champagne did not stop Associated Press photographer Jane Hwang from gathering caption information from a Texas Rangers player in the locker room after the team won an important game.
ANDY SCOTT/THE DALLAS MORNING NEWS

Overview

Captions help put images into perspective and explain details that are not visually obvious or clear. Photographers must gather information about their pictures so captions can be written. For a newspaper or magazine to publish photographs—and a wire service to transmit them—without accompanying words in the form of captions is almost unheard of.

Captions should not duplicate what is visually obvious. Readers' time is too valuable and publication space is too scarce to waste either with extraneous words. The famous French photographer Henri Cartier-Bresson put it this way:

> As for captions, these should be the verbal counterpoint to the pictures, adding what is necessary or establishing them in their context.[1]

It is likely that no daily newspaper or wire service exempts photographers from caption information gathering. Unless appropriate caption information is available in a timely way, it is all but certain that related photographs will not be published. There is no question that photographers must gather appropriate, complete, and accurate caption information.

Although every photographer must be skilled in gathering caption information, who actually writes captions from the information provided by photographers varies by publication. Caption-writing techniques are the same as techniques for writing longer pieces. The caption should present information succinctly and the writer is well advised, when truthfulness allows, to use strong verbs and avoid adjectives. The caption should not repeat visually obvious information and should of course contain only accurate information, preferably that is verifiable. Caption writers should of course ask themselves, "If we knew nothing about this picture, what would we want to know in addition to what we see?"

Always question the accuracy of handouts, whether these are press releases, police reports, program brochures, or some other source. Make every effort to double-check information from events you did not witness and make certain that you put what you did see in fair perspective.

For photojournalists caption information should be as important as pictures. *Life* magazine photographer Larry Burrows took caption information seriously. In *Larry Burrows: Compassionate Photographer,* a book about Burrows and his photography published after he was killed in Vietnam, a senior editor of *Life* writes that Burrows "would come back from weeks in the field by himself with detailed captions for every frame of his still-unprocessed film."[2] Obviously, gathering caption information was a priority for this famous photojournalist.

Categories of Information

Slight modification of the old journalistic standby, the five *Ws*—who, what, when, where, and why—is a good way to discuss caption information gathering. Let's spend a little time with each of these categories and an additional one, "Other Information."

Who

■ Always ask subjects to spell their names as they want them to appear in print. Rick and Jean may turn out to be Rik and Jeanne. Ask subjects to print their names, particularly if the names are unusual or complicated. Misspelling a name is a journalistic sin. Always spell names back to subjects and have them verify the accuracy. If subjects do not object, recording all information they tell you is helpful. Before recording subjects always obtain their permission.

■ Use physical characteristics, distinguishing clothing or other attachments, or other details that guarantee clear and accurate identification of people or things in the photograph. Be sure not to offend someone by using an objectionable description.

■ Obtain subjects' formal titles if these are relevant. Obtaining informal titles they may have is also desirable.

- Always obtain hometowns. Specific street addresses are necessary only if these are relevant to the photograph; many people dislike having their home addresses published because of potential harassment and security problems.
- Always ask for subjects' telephone numbers so someone can obtain additional details at a later time if needed. If you are in a position to do so truthfully, be sure to let subjects know that their telephone numbers will not be published; note this on all information sent to others. As a general rule, telephone numbers should never be published.
- Always get children's ages. Request adults' ages only if they are relevant. Some people are extremely sensitive about being asked their age; tact is essential.
- Obtain any other relevant information, such as the name of the school a child attends if the photograph is related to the school. Be careful not to use information about children that could make them vulnerable to kidnapping, such as home addresses, routes to and from school, and after school schedules.

What

- Always accurately and completely identify the overall event. Get a brief description and the title of the event if it has one. For example, if you are taking pictures of a school's homecoming parade, do not forget to note that it is the Fourth Annual Homecoming Parade or whatever other identifier is accurate.
- Seek detailed information about each individual image—the participants and what they are doing and other information relevant to the scene. Get as much specific information as you can about what is going on in the picture (Figure 6.1).

When

- Note the day, month, and year and the specific time of day if it is relevant,

for example, 10:13 a.m. If a specific time is important, make certain that it is accurate. Never guess. If you have any doubt, use about, approximately, or a spread (for example, 2 to 4 p.m. or late afternoon) make clear that you mean 10:13 a.m., not 10:13 p.m.

Where

- Use formal names first, followed in parentheses by any informal names. For example, "Plaza of the Americas (the Plaza)." Do not depend on common usage to reflect formal names— for example, "city hall" when the real name is "Government Center." People often do not know formal names, including people who have long been associated with a place or structure. Take care to find a person who knows the formal name or to find a sign that conveys it. Caution: Signs do not necessarily convey accurate formal names.
- Be as specific as possible. For example, use "northeast corner of the intersection of North-South Drive and University Avenue," not simply the "intersection of North-South Drive and University Avenue." But give the street address only if it is relevant and clearly needed.
- Never state that a structure is "on" a road, but rather "by" a road, "near" a road, or "off" a road. Sidewalks are rarely, if ever, on streets; rather, they are along them.

Why

- Make sure you get the real why, not what some uninformed or misinformed person proclaims. Always try hard to confirm information with at least one other source.
- This category may or may not be relevant to caption information. It usually is not necessary—or desirable— to go into why the homecoming parade is being held. On the other hand, stating why a fund-raiser is being held probably is necessary—

FIGURE 6.1

The requirement that photojournalists gather caption information is not new—it goes back many years, probably into the 19th century. In this photograph taken in the early 1990s, photographer Larry Steagall of *The Sun* in Bremerton, Washington continues this important part of a journalistic photographer's job. Steagall covered the annual springtime Viking Festival in Poulsbo, Washington. He photographed this Viking Festival Parade participant and then found him after the parade to get caption information.

JOHN FROSCHAUER

and desirable. This is a judgment call. If you have any doubt, get the information.

Other Information

- Always seek any explanatory information that does not readily fit into any of the preceding categories, such as technical information and its lay description.
- Write down or record any informative quotes.

Final Thoughts

Caption information gathering goes with journalistic picture-taking like bacon goes with eggs, like syrup goes with waffles, like lox goes with bagels. It is a fundamentally important part of photojournalistic coverage, something that a journalistic photographer must be as skilled at as photography itself.

When gathering caption information never guess at what is going on or assume it. Ferret out the facts and do your level best to confirm them with at least one other reliable source. Do not assume that what you saw necessarily is the truth of the situation. A participant or someone directing the scene out of view may be trying to make it seem like something that it is not, or your vantage point may distort or limit the real picture. Search out the most appropriate truth taking great care that in doing so you do not yourself garble the true facts. Keep an unbiased, open mind in your search; do not let your personal biases or opinions distort fact finding.

Notes scribbled in haste that later are unintelligible are worthless. Difficult as it may be, careful penmanship is absolutely necessary. Avoid using pens with ink that is easily blurred by liquids, including perspiration. Always type all caption information as soon as possible, preferably on a portable computer at the scene. Dictating information to a portable cassette recorder is a helpful supplement to written notes.

The bottom line is that caption information must be truthful and presented in fair context so that:

1. The publication maintains its credibility.

2. The publication does not unfairly embarrass, hurt, or arouse the anger of its subjects.

3. The publication and its photographers are less likely to be sued.

4. Photographers maintain a good reputation with colleagues.

5. Photographers are less likely to be reprimanded or fired.

Methodical and careful caption information gathering in the pursuit of the most appropriate truth, fairly represented, is a way of life with good photojournalists.

NOTES

[1] Henri Cartier-Bresson, "Preface," in *The World of Henri Cartier-Bresson* (New York: Viking Press, 1968).

[2] Editors of *Life,* "Conflict," in *Larry Burrows: Compassionate Photographer* (New York: Time, 1972).

The Road to Success

Thomas R. Kennedy—director of photography,
Washingtonpost.Newsweek Interactive

Author's note: Kennedy was director of photography at the National Geographic Society, deputy graphics director, assistant graphics director and feature photo editor at *The Philadelphia Inquirer,* and a photographer and director of photography at other newspapers.

Q: *Drawing on your extensive media experience, how do you advise someone to prepare for a career as a photojournalist?*

A: I think it is important to begin by acquainting yourself with the larger world. It is important to acquire an education that goes beyond the technical aspects of photography. Familiarizing yourself with the aesthetics of art, exposing yourself to current imaging technologies, and learning the basics of storytelling are all crucial components of an education. Beyond that, it is important to realize that the essence of photojournalism is covering the story of the human condition, and that means dealing with people. That is a given. You will always be interacting with others and trying to draw them out. To do so effectively, you need to possess strong interpersonal communication skills and be able to develop sensitivity to appropriate behavior in specific situations. You must be comfortable with others, even when unfamiliar cultural norms or language barriers are present. Exuding personal comfort in relating to others helps the subjects of your photographs feel more comfortable with your presence. They then tend to be more willing to trust you and share the deep intimacies of their lives. This is generally when you get photographs and

a story worth telling to a larger audience. A photographer's ego and artistic ambitions should never interfere with establishing authentic rapport with subjects.

It is essential for beginning photographers to understand that the act of photographing a story is a transactional exchange between photographer and subject. Something is given and received by both parties. A photographer invests time and energy in a subject, hoping to come away with a story that reveals something worthwhile about the human condition. The subject opens access to the innermost details of his or her life so that the photographer can reveal it fully and empathetically. This is the transactional equation, and the algebra that links it together is trust. I believe that photographers can produce stories that reveal important essential truths of the human condition and that those stories can be shared with others to heighten communal and individual understanding. However, to reveal such stories, photographers need to spend time observing their subjects, sharing their lives, and learning enough to be discriminating about what moments are worth recording and putting together as a story. All this activity requires concentration, observation, time, and

patience. The photographer must take the time and trouble to understand the subject and communicate empathy in order to gain the subject's full trust. Then, the photographer must also reveal to the subject with clarity the purpose of the photography. It is important that the photographer communicate integrity of intention and clear empathy. It is my experience that such actions will enable the establishment of bonds of trust that give a subject comfort about letting a photographer deeply into his or her life. At that point, meaningful documentation can occur that yields a deep, rich story. A photographer's code of honor should include a commitment to treat all subjects honestly, and with maximum effort. It is also important that a photographer not unfairly harm a subject through the act of telling their story in photographs.

Q: *Let's get specific. Exactly how do you advise someone to do all this?*

A: I think it is important for a photographer to have an understanding of psychology, sociology, and anthropology. These courses teach important lessons about human behavior, including group dynamics that govern cultures and societies. Knowing something about human behavior, and the cultural framework for it, is essential if one is going to relate well to others. Such subjects also provide useful information about understanding the ways various cultures are affected by the presence of certain forces, including media. Such information can be useful for establishing a framework for gauging the effectiveness of one's own photos in portraying subjects from another culture. It is important to know one's own strengths and weaknesses as a communicator as a means of guarding against the injection of culturally biased or distorted reporting, no matter how unwitting or unintentional.

Q: *So you are advocating a strong dose of liberal arts?*
A: I think exposure to certain classical liberal arts subjects is extremely valuable. Most journalism college curriculums make it challenging for students to attain equal balance between journalism and liberal arts courses. There are so many hours of professional course work required at the junior and senior level that little time is left to gain access to liberal arts courses. I find this situation somewhat ironic because college is the one chance many students have to gain access to liberal arts as part of a formal education. With the technical aspects of photography, students can gain meaningful opportunities beyond the classroom by availing themselves of chances to work for student publications or accept professional internships. College is the best place to absorb liberal arts, and I encourage students to make the most of that opportunity.

Q: *Well now what exactly are you saying? Are you saying they shouldn't major in journalism?*
A: No, I'm not saying that as a blanket rule. I just think journalism schools need to realize that they are not molding technicians when they are training journalists. They should have the goal of turning out students who have the basic attributes to make them good journalists: a fundamental sense of curiosity about the world, knowledge of human behavior, the ability to tell stories using a variety of media as "tools," and the ability to draw people out as a means of accessing their stories. While journalism education must invariably emphasize the "how-to-do-it," such education should also emphasize the "why" behind the journalist's actions. One also must understand the ethics underpinning journalistic activity and the code of conduct necessary for effective practice of the profession. I think it is terribly important for graduating students to have a firm philosophical basis for future journalistic activity. One must understand why we

practice journalism and what we are trying to do with journalist skills.

Q: *Should students look to the future or only to their first job?*
A: A student must look to the future—to do less would be unduly shortsighted. At a minimum, one should begin after graduation looking for answers to certain fundamental questions that hover inevitably over a journalism career. Why am I in photography? What do I want to say with my photos? How can I express myself in a way that adds to the body of photojournalism that has gone before me? Do I have the proper perspective on photojournalism's value to society? Do I have my moral imperatives, personal motives, and ego in the right alignment?

Assuming one is beginning a career with these questions firmly in mind, I think it is important that a photographer spend time developing visual techniques, an aesthetic sensibility, and personal storytelling skills that become ultimately a personal vision. Developing such a vision is often very difficult to do in the group editorial process that governs most newspapers and magazines, because personal agendas tend to give way to more important corporate concerns. Nonetheless, it is essential to have the goal of developing a personal vision from the moment one decides to become a professional photojournalist.

It is clear to me that people enter photojournalism for a variety of reasons. Some may be seeking adventure, or a reason to avoid the 9 to 5 office world. Others may be looking to legitimize their curiosity about life and develop a mechanism to satisfy that curiosity fully. Oth-

ers may want to give voice to the unarticulated stories of people who cannot otherwise seem to attain media visibility in the modern world. While motivations may vary, the demands of the business can take a fierce toll on a person's ability to have a long career and a balanced life. To achieve career longevity and to maintain creative growth over a professional lifetime, one's career must be rooted in profound commitment and a strong philosophical base.

Many photojournalists launch a career with the intention of remaining "on the street" for a lifetime. However, career objectives can shift as life circumstances change. Sometimes change comes because of a changed relationship; marriage, children, commitment to another person with a need for more settled life conditions. At other times, the limited routine of newspaper assignments can create a lethal boredom. Magazines may require grueling travel schedules that tax even the most intrepid adventurer. As photographers age, they tend to work smarter and to use the repertoires forged by years of experience as a means to handle difficult situations. However, at a certain point the physical and emotional toll of years of difficult work situations may begin to impact stamina and enthusiasm. If the demands of street photography no longer seem palatable, then one needs to be able to make a career transition smoothly into a related field like photo editing.

Since one can never fully forecast life changes, I think it is dangerous to start out thinking only of the first job, or making the assumption that the career path is preordained for a

lifetime on the basis of the first job.

Q: *How can a person go about doing freelance work for Washingtonpost.Newsweek Interactive?*
A: The first part of the process is to submit a portfolio for evaluation that reflects your best work. In evaluating freelance talent, I am looking for two fundamental things in the portfolio: (1) An extraordinary ability to see aesthetically and to handle the technical aspects of the medium, and (2) an extraordinary storytelling ability drawn from wellsprings of personal passion and commitment.

When I look at a photographer's portfolio, I am looking to see if the person has a finely honed sense of color palette, a gift for seeing and using light to clarify subject matter, and an ability to compose and record moments that allows one to express the subject matter at hand with maximum emotional fidelity and impact. It is important that the photojournalist understand his or her fundamental task is often to take the routine stuff of everyday life and make it into something that is visually arresting. I want to see if the photographer has the visual acuity to capture incisive moments that are truly revealing of underlying emotional truths and specific facts about the subject. I am also looking to see if a photographer can express a sense of narrative order and natural storytelling that reveals the fullest possible truth of the subject in an authentic and engaging manner. Hopefully such a portfolio is filled with photographs that transport me beyond the boundaries of my own life and put me in direct contact with other peoples and situations I may never directly encounter, and yet which may have profound consequences in my life. A specific report on the life of a Thai villager or a Russian peasant farmer struggling to adapt to changing circumstances of the world economy may well be such a case in point. The key test for me is whether the photographs in the portfolio are emotionally and physically truthful and whether a certain consistency is present in their aesthetic construction from photograph to photograph. I want also to see that the photographer has a passion and commitment to the work. This can be perceived from the photographs themselves as well as conversation with the photographer. If a portfolio contains all these elements, then the chances are good that I will be interested in exploring the possibilities of using the photographer's work at Washingtonpost. Newsweek Interactive. Normally, if interested by a portfolio's quality, I look for an assignment that will test the photographer's skills while also giving him or her a chance to become more familiar with our editorial processes and goals.

Q: *Even though a person is an excellent technical and creative photographer, how important are personal interaction skills—tact and diplomacy, for example?*
A: These are absolutely important. I think interpersonal skills are a major key to success or failure. I've seen some great natural talents undermined by rampant egotism or an inability to get along with others. To gain a subject's trust, a photographer has to exercise some personal humility and exhibit a genuine personal interest in him or her. While having confidence in one's skills and techniques is important too, the subject should never be made to feel like an object being manipulated to satisfy the photographer's own artistic ambition or personal ego. The subject's story must always come first as the main point of the photojournalist's activity.

I have seen rampant egotism and self-centeredness of colleagues act as a barrier to effective personal relations and communication. Temper tantrums and mean-spirited putdowns are never pretty to witness or experience. To operate effectively in a bureaucratic editorial setting with the corporate group dynamic at work, one must learn the art of compromise without ever surrendering core beliefs and values.

Major Subjects

Anywhere there is a crowd expect picture taking to be difficult. For example, you may have a hard time getting to where something significant is occurring or your view may be blocked by others. Opponents and proponents of the death penalty and of the State of Texas executing Karla Faye Tucker, the first woman to be put to death by Texas in more than 150 years, gathered outside the prison in which she was to die, creating an almost carnival-like atmosphere. Photographer David Leeson described in the August 1998 issue of *News Photographer* how he recorded one aspect of the scene centering around a portrait of the doomed woman: "I raised a Canon digital camera over my head, took a few deep breaths and allowed my thoughts to soar above the madness and sorrow to reveal the nearly forgotten reason they gathered in the dark. Inside the walls Karla Faye Tucker had just died." Photojournalism can be an emotionally trying, occasionally gut-wrenching undertaking that you as a new practitioner need to deal with. You need to steel yourself against the emotion without becoming so hardened that you lose the sensitivity needed to communicate to your readers truthful and revealing moments of the human condition.

DAVID LEESON/*THE DALLAS MORNING NEWS*

Overview

All journalistic photographs fall into two broad categories: subject and form. While contests are an obvious reason for pigeonholing journalistic photographs into categories, they are not the only users of categories; publications themselves, at least informally, tend to use at least some. As an example, if you go to work for a newspaper expect to become familiar with the plea from a city desk editor, "I need a feature."

This chapter addresses subject categories and uses eight of them: spot news, general news, features, sports action, sports features, portrait/personality, pictorial and illustration. This is not the only category scheme—others use more categories or fewer categories. The eight categories used

here nicely serve this chapter's need by putting reasonable order into what otherwise could be an unwieldy approach to the many photographs found in publications. But there is little etched in granite about these categories; certainly some images reproduced here easily and legitimately could be placed in other categories. With this background let's explore the eight categories.

Spot News

For newspapers, of course, news is the single most important category. Spot news and its less time-oriented companion, general news, are the heart of newspaper and wire service photography. Spot news photographs carry an urgent, unplanned, and often unpleasant or undesirable ambiance. Coverage cannot be scheduled in advance. Spot news images include automobile accidents, airplane crashes, tornadoes, fires, murders, and bank robberies—the myriad acute, interesting, and usually noteworthy occurrences that help characterize life. For a photojournalist immediacy and intrusion are defining

FIGURE 7.1

Your adrenalin is pumping as you arrive at a spot news scene. First you must overcome your natural excitement and then find out what is happening and decide what is most important. In your quest to photograph, never forget the limitations you labor under at such scenes—do not cross police lines, do not interfere with emergency personnel and their equipment, do not needlessly intrude on victims who undoubtedly already are under great stress. Do not just zero in on the obvious—flames at a fire, for example—but seek out human aspects to the tragedy, which the photographer of this scene did. A three-year-old who set fire to a mattress talks to a fire department battalion chief. The family's apartment was destroyed by the fire.

ROBERT COHEN/*THE COMMERCIAL APPEAL*, MEMPHIS, TENN.

aspects of spot news coverage—you must be there when the event is happening and you usually intrude on people in time of stress.

Spot news occurs without notice and often ends quickly, or at least its most newsworthy aspects do. Unless aftermath photos are acceptable, photographers must arrive quickly. However, they must be careful. Breaking traffic laws puts photographers and others at enormous physical risk. Photographers and their organizations court lawsuits, and traffic citations or arrests mean financial loss, potential jail time, and higher insurance rates. No picture is worth risking lives.

As cities become larger and more crowded, spot news coverage becomes more difficult. Many newspaper photographers use police monitors, cellular telephones, and pagers (a few use two-way radios). But even with these, unless a city is geographically compact and has relatively clear driving lanes, or unless the spot news is reasonably close or relatively long lasting, photographers won't arrive in time. The aftermath is all that is left to picture.

The key to successfully covering spot news, once the photographer has arrived, is to quickly ascertain what is going on and decide which aspect is the most important and truthful—which aspect is the most appropriate truth. Then photographers marshal all the technological and creative aspects of photojournalism to inform readers well within applicable legal restraints and ethical limitations (Figures 7.1 and 7.2). Photographers should always record what appears to be the most important aspect first. But photographers should always record several more aspects of a spot news event because unfolding events may yield even more important pictures or may put in different perspective an aspect that has already occurred. Also, editors may want to use more than one picture to tell the story.

Three lenses (or equivalent zooms) are especially useful for spot news cov-

FIGURE 7.2

Ray Hudson anguishes as a friend's mobile home goes up in flames after an earthquake. The mobile home park is in Sylmar, California, a Los Angeles suburb. Hudson's home survived. One thread that runs through the really wrenching spot news images is people—humanity. Difficult as it sometimes may be, both photographically and emotionally, photographers always should "think people."
Douglas Pizac/AP/Wide World Photos

erage: a wide angle such as a 24mm, a short telephoto such as an 85mm, and a long telephoto such as a 300mm. Some photographers prefer to carry the two shorter lenses around their necks, using a short strap for one camera and a longer strap for the second. This location and combination cut down on the cameras banging against each other as the photographer walks, runs, bends, and reclines and makes them quickly and easily available. Photographers usually sling the camera with the long telephoto lens over their shoulders.

The main fodder of spot news is humanity—accident and fire victims, bank robbers, witnesses and onlookers. Photographers covering spot news inevitably intrude on people in extraordinarily stressful times. You must make every reasonable effort to keep this intrusion to a minimum. Photographers should stay physically as far from the action as possible while still satisfactorily covering the event. Telephoto lenses are made to order in this regard. Avoid using intrusive and attention-getting flash unless you have no alternative.

The famous American magazine photojournalist W. Eugene Smith stated his reservations about spot news coverage: "I accept the reporting of tragedy. I admire truly great news photography . . . but I wish the press would not abuse their power or needlessly bruise the already bruised." He added that " . . . if there must be photographs [in tragic situations], here, in decency, is the one irrevocably right time and place to use discretion in a broad sense and available [existing] light in the narrow sense."[1]

Spot news coverage begins as the photographer approaches the scene—a distant view of a fire's smoke, for example. Picture taking continues as the scene gets closer. Do not wait for the ideal picture at a spot news event. You need to take the so-called insurance shots. Coverage includes the essence of what is occurring as well as supporting aspects. Spot news often presents two sides: the hard-core event and secondary but often humanizing aspects. Hard-core news is a must but so are moments that interject a sense of humanity, reminding readers of the brighter—and darker—aspects of the human condition (Figure 7.3).

People at stressful events often do not want to be pictured or do not want even the event pictured. Photographers should intrude as little as possible, always working to avoid confrontation with participants, spectators, police, firefighters, and emergency medical personnel. Sometimes, however, getting the picture means confrontation. Relatives and friends of victims tend to be particularly adversarial. Verbal threats against photojournalists are common, physical assaults possible. Law enforcement officers sometimes—perhaps often—are unhappy to see photojournalists at spot news scenes. Police and other law enforcement people—including media-friendly ones—are charged with objectively investigating vehicular accidents, fires, and robberies, for example, and may fear, probably correctly in at least some cases, that overzealous or insensitive photojournalists will hurt their quest for the facts. This can be done by, for example, trampling evidence. Some law enforcement officials may not like being watched while they work—good faith mistakes may be publicized and mean-spirited ones exposed. Some law enforcement officials simply may view journalism and its practitioners as mercenary leeches, profiting off the misfortune of others. For one or more of these reasons and probably others, law enforcement and journalism sometimes clash; when this happens, the government authority in which law enforcement is wrapped typically means that photographers lose—they can end up in jail. Covering spot news can be dangerous.

Covering spot news is risky in other ways. Downed power lines, chemical spills, fire-released airborne asbestos, explosions, and criminals with guns are examples of life-threatening hazards for photojournalists. Always approach potentially harmful situations with great caution. Although you cannot guarantee you will be safe—unless you stay away from scenes—at the very least you should always check with authorities at a safe distance before blindly blundering into trouble.

If it is important to picture news events as they would have happened without photographers present, the general rule is that photographers should never participate in events being photographed. One possible exception is helping people whose lives are in danger.

Journalistic photographers, particularly newspaper photographers, regularly go to scenes where people are in peril or happen upon them in driving to or from assignments. Alerted primarily by information gleaned from police monitors and cellular telephone communication with their papers and simply because they are on the road so much, photographers sometimes arrive at scenes where people are in peril before police or emergency medical personnel.

Before getting into the pros and cons of helping or not helping, it needs to be made clear that this book is not telling you to help people in peril and is not telling you not to help people in peril. What you do is your decision and your responsibility. However, you should know what to expect legally if you do or do not help someone; that is the purpose of this discussion. In addition, you should know that, depending on the help you render, helping people in peril can put you in great danger. You can be seriously injured, or killed. Exploding gas tanks, severe water currents, noxious chemicals, and downed electrical lines are only a few of the things that can injure or kill a good Samaritan.

In U.S. law the general rule is that no one has a legal obligation to help a person in peril unless the potential helper and the person in peril have a relationship that creates a legal obligation to help or the potential helper has caused, or otherwise is a party to, harm that befalls the victim, with this relationship creating a legal obligation to help. The authors of one law book put it this way: "Absent a special relationship or a causal connection between the bystander and the harm to the victim, courts have not imposed liability on one who could have, but did not, rescue another from peril."[2]

However, three states—Vermont, Minnesota and Rhode Island (and perhaps more by the time you read this)—have statutes that require a person, under limited circumstances, to help someone in peril. Consider this excerpt from the Vermont statute:

> A person who knows that another is exposed to **grave physical harm** shall, to the extent that the same can be rendered without danger or peril to himself or without interference with important duties owed to others, give reasonable assistance to the exposed person unless that assistance or care is being provided by others.[3]

As with all aspects of law, it is critically important that you know the law in the area where you work. Laws are added, repealed, and amended on a regular basis. Your best source of information is an attorney intimately knowledgeable in the laws of your area. You are urged to consult such a person; perhaps your employer has an attorney on staff or on retainer who briefs editorial staffers on the status of the law.

In a more indirect approach many states have enacted what are called *good Samaritan statutes.* These laws try to encourage people to help others in peril by providing limited legal immunity from suit to someone who helps another. The catch to these statutes typically is the necessity that the helper act with reasonable care (or some other similar way) to be cloaked in legal immunity. If you decide to help a person in peril, have you assumed any legal liability you would not otherwise have? According to another law book, "the good Samaritan who tried to help may find himself mulcted in damages, while the priest and the Levite who pass by on the other side go on their cheerful way rejoicingly."[4]

Once you take on the good Samaritan role, you must act with due care—reasonable care. Exactly what *due care* and *reasonable care* mean in a specific situation most likely will be decided by a judge or jury, if the matter is turned into a lawsuit and not settled before trial.

In deciding whether to help you probably will want to consider the availability of competent medical aid. Almost any place in the country, no matter how rural, is accessible by medical assistance—by ambulance or medical aircraft. On the other hand, if someone is trapped underwater in a car and about to drown, even the nearest medical aid may be too far away to save the person.

When you and the person in peril have a relationship that legally obligates you to help, you must render assistance if you are to avoid legal liability for not helping. You must do what you reasonably can or face the legal consequences. What you "reasonably can" may be calling on your cellular telephone for medical help. You must decide what is reasonable help and hope what you do or do not do and the way you do it is enough to protect you from legal liability. Keep in mind that you can cause a person additional injury far more severe than that already existing—severing the spinal cord by trying to move the victim, thus leaving the person a paraplegic, for example—by trying to physically help when you really do not know what you are doing.

As a photographer or simply a person you must take reasonable care not to prevent the rendering of aid by another to a person in peril. For example, you must not interfere with emergency medical personnel, you must not park on a fire hose so that water is not available to firefighters, you must not park so that emergency vehicles cannot reach the scene, and you must not refuse the use of your cellular telephone (or two-way radio), thus preventing another person from calling for aid.

You must take care not to promise to aid a person in peril and then not do so, for example, by promising to call for emergency medical aid and not doing so. The law appears to be evolving in this area—holding you more and more legally liable if you do not do what you promised to do. It is legally risky for you to breach a promise to aid a person.

If you have been a party to a person's being put in peril, even though the person's injury is not your fault, the law generally requires you to render aid. For example, if while driving your car you are involved in an accident, you have a duty to reasonably aid the occupants of the other vehicle, even though the accident was not your fault. Exactly what "reasonably aid" means depends on the situation; it may mean only telephoning for emergency medical help, or it may mean something more, such as rendering first aid if you can do so without causing further injury. According to one legal text,

> Where the duty to rescue is required, it is agreed that it calls for nothing more than reasonable care under the circumstances. . . . He [the defendant in a lawsuit] will seldom be required to do more than give such first aid as he reasonably can, and take reasonable steps to turn the sick person over to a doctor or to those who will look after him until one can be brought.[5]

While covering spot news (and any other coverage), photographers must respect police lines, crossing them only with official permission. Take great care not to destroy potential evidence—by walking on it, for example. Never stand on emergency vehicles without official permission. Never interfere with emergency personnel. Generally, keep talk to the minimum for gathering pertinent information (Figures 7.4 and 7.5).

FIGURE 7.4

Death—whether accidental, intentional, or natural and whether self-inflicted or inflicted by another—and other distressing things that happen to people are more or less regular events for most general assignment newspaper photographers. You may find these events disturbing, even deeply so. But after awhile, shock or disbelief may tend to be subdued as these unfortunate happenings become a recurring part of your photographic coverage. Just like nicer, more pleasant things you will cover in which people are involved, this side of the human condition presents photographic opportunity that the creative photographer will grasp to tell the story in an intriguing but still truthful way. The subject matter may be exceedingly unpleasant but the photographic approach can be intriguing, as is the case with this eye-catching photograph of a man killed in a fight at a bar being photographed by a police officer. Keep in mind that a newspaper is just that—a NEWSpaper—and spot news in particular often is unpleasant.
EDWARD D. ORNELAS, III/ *SAN ANTONIO EXPRESS*

Press passes or other professional identification may be honored or may not be honored by law enforcement officers. The First Amendment may have real meaning to them or it may be just words on paper, not at all helping the photographer visually cover spot news events. If press passes and other professional identification, and the status the press likes to think it occupies in society, mean nothing to some law enforcement officials, don't be surprised. Photojournalists generally are wrapped in no more legal rights at a news scene than the general public. Tact and good relations with police at a news scene can mean more than volumes of laws, the First Amendment included.

Photojournalism is a people business. Anyone seeking success in it must deal with people, including police officials, in a tactful and understanding way. Where community size allows, friendships with police officials—or at least a passing acquaintance—go a long way in helping spot news coverage. A track record of fair dealing and personal integrity buttresses friendships and acquaintances. Coverage of spot news is one aspect of photojournalism that regularly tests a photojournalist's people skills.

Photojournalism: An Introduction

FIGURE 7.5

An attorney (with hand outstretched), called to the scene by police because he was an acquaintance of the man threatening to jump, tries to talk the man out of leaping from an interstate overpass. Photojournalists should use great restraint in photographing life-and-death situations. Jerry Wolford used a 400mm lens with a 1.4 teleconverter (it attaches to the back of the lens and effectively turns it into a 560mm) and stayed about 130 feet away. "If need be, I would have moved farther away and even left the scene if I felt my presence was going to cause him to take his life," Wolford said. "That's part of my code of ethics. There is no picture worth taking if doing so causes someone to take their life. The older I get, the more I err on the side of humanity instead of the 'get the picture at any price' mentality." With police assistance the attorney succeeded in convincing the man not to jump.

JERRY WOLFORD/*NEWS & RECORD*, GREENSBORO, N.C.

Randy Hayes, *Post Register,* **Idaho Falls, Idaho**

"Engine one, Rescue One, Ambulance One, respond to Highway 20 and St. Leon Road, two-vehicle accident with injuries." It's these words, heard over the emergency scanner, that typically begin spot news coverage.

What is spot news? For me in a small city, it most often is traffic accidents. However, it also can be fires, airplane crashes, bank robberies, train accidents, and drownings—anything newsworthy involving police, firefighters, or emergency medical personnel that isn't on a prethought schedule.

When responding to spot news events, photographers need a sixth sense. It's a feeling you get from the urgency in the voice of the dispatcher directing emergency personnel to the scene. Evaluation of the situation begins before you arrive at the scene. Be alert to the number of emergency personnel and what types of equipment are dispatched, where the action is taking place, and how much communication there is between the dispatcher and emergency personnel racing to the scene (lots of communication usually means the event is particularly serious).

Gathering as much information as possible helps you get ready for what lies ahead. After arriving at the scene my first rule is to leave the scanner in the car. Emergency vehicles, particularly police cars and fire trucks, are equipped with loudspeakers so everything emergency personnel do will be heard without drawing attention to me or possibly distracting emergency personnel with my portable scanner. Once on the scene my focus is on what is hap-

pening visually in front of me; I cover the news, not make it. The last thing a photographer wants to do is be injured at a spot news scene. There is danger all around spot news events. Vehicle accidents may involve volatile liquids that could explode or produce noxious gasses. Getting hit by a rubbernecking motorist driving by is a real possibility as is getting attacked by participants or spectators. Fires can produce flying glass, falling walls, downed electrical wires, and noxious gasses. The list of dangers goes on. Spot news events present a real challenge to photojournalists in more ways than one.

Spot news events require a great deal of photographic restraint. I've found most of my better pictures come from analyzing the emergency situation and then waiting for a photographic moment—a moment that is storytelling and visually intriguing. I shoot sparingly. I seldom use an attention-getting motor drive but rather pick and choose from everything that's happening only those moments that communicate the event's essence or important aspects of the essence. This approach allows me to be as inconspicuous as possible while at the same time allowing me to get to the heart of the event. Remember, the more you stay in the background, the less likely it is that confrontations will arise and the less likely it is that people involved in the spot news will be offended. Spot news environments tend to be adrenaline producing—emotions run high.

Photojournalists are bad guys to many people. Many people see

photographers as exploiters, making dramatic pictures only to sell papers. The accident picture (Figure 7.6) happened at the corner of Highway 20 and St. Leon Road and is a perfect example of this. It shows a firefighter looking under the hood of a car with the covered body, except for a hand, of a person killed in the accident.

At the scene I was approached by a fire captain who asked me not to shoot pictures showing sheet-covered dead bodies inside the car. Unless they are enforcing laws such as the prohibition against photographing classified items at the crash of a military airplane, I usually don't feel bound by requests (or orders) of fire, police, and other government officials not to photograph specific scenes at spot news events. But in this case I did not take the picture because I thought it skated too close to sensationalism; it just didn't feel right. But when I walked in front of the car, I knew I had a storytelling image that would communicate the tragic event and hopefully bring home the reality of how dangerous this particular stretch of highway can be. It has road crossings every mile, putting drivers on it and on intersecting roads in constant danger.

The decision to shoot was clear. Whether the picture would be published was another matter; I don't control publication. Spot news photographs that convey death typically are controversial. You don't run into the paper screaming, "Stop the presses, I have a great picture!" and it happens. I knew I was going to have a

FIGURE 7.6

Passing up a view from the car door toward bodies in the front seat, I went with this one. Is it too gory for your taste, or does it acceptably make its point?
RANDY HAYES/*POST REGISTER*

fight getting the image published because our community is very conservative and that impacts on what we publish. But I believed in the picture and was ready to fight for it. In a meeting attended by the senior newsroom editors, our photo editor, and me, we discussed the pros and cons of publishing the picture. The image clearly communicated how dangerous this highway is and that drivers needed to be more careful, particularly since our tourist season was starting. But it was shocking. Even though people regularly see death on television and in the movies, seeing real-life death frozen in time can be unsettling, even traumatic. The decision was to publish but to downplay the picture by running it below the

fold on an inside section front. By not running it out front or above the fold it was hoped readers would think the paper wasn't pushing the picture down their throats.

The paper received calls and letters about this image, most condemning us for being insensitive to the family of the victims. But there also was support, telling us that the picture sensitized them to an unsafe highway.

When making pictures at spot news events, I travel light. I wear a photographic vest or a coat with lots of pockets that allows me to carry film and different lenses. We are a color newspaper so I typically have three different ISO color films with me suited for different light levels. I carry two

Nikon cameras, one with a very wide-angle lens, the other with a long telephoto. I also carry a moderate wide-angle and a short telephoto to give me more flexibility; these I have in my vest or coat.

In Idaho Falls we have a very good working relationship with emergency personnel; they allow us nearly unlimited freedom. This freedom is earned by self-imposed restrictions. For example, I don't get in the way. If I feel uncomfortable about where I am at a scene, usually it means I'm too close and

FIGURE 7.7

These contacts (images the same size as the images on the film) are my coverage of a girl being helped by paramedics after an auto accident. Notice the different views—wide, close, low, high. The enlargement is the picture I like best; it ran in my newspaper.
RANDY HAYES/*POST REGISTER*

Photojournalism: An Introduction

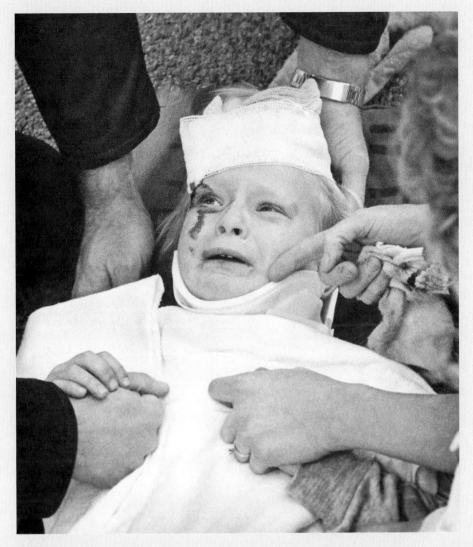

FIGURE 7.8

I chose this image over all others I took at the accident. After closely looking at the contacts, preferably with a loupe (a magnifying glass commonly used in photography), is it the one you would have chosen?

RANDY HAYES/*POST REGISTER*

I move away—I back off and use a longer lens.

When I get to an accident scene, I park far enough away and out of the way of traffic so as not to interfere with emergency vehicles. This sometimes may be a long way, so I always try to wear protective comfortable shoes.

As I approach the scene I first notice the mood. If emergency personnel are working quickly— what one might see as a frantically controlled pace—it means they probably are trying to save a life so the last thing I want is to get in the way. A wide-angle lens

picture might not be the best to shoot at this time. So I'll look for vantage points like a hill, the back of a pickup if the owner does not object or even a sturdy tree to give me a different look at the scene with a longer lens. This keeps me out of the way of emergency personnel. I should add that I like to use a wide-angle lens and do so if interference clearly is not a problem. Even so, I always think of telephoto possibilities.

When photographing a spot news scene, I usually begin by taking a couple of overall establishing pictures. Although I rarely use

these, taking them gives me a chance to survey the scene, get a feel for the mood, and establish a presence. Police and other emergency personnel like to know who they are dealing with. I'll then move closer, staying out of the way but getting close enough to see, for example, at accident scenes the extent of injuries and if I need to concentrate on photographing extrication of victims or am free to look for images such as reactions of relatives or spectators (Figures 7.7 and 7.8). I don't like shooting gore; I think blood for blood's sake is sensationalism.

Major Subjects

My primary goal as a photo-journalist is communicating with readers—letting people who weren't at spot news events and other coverage know what really happened. I'll confess there is an excitement to this. Getting a really good picture is like a big game hunter bagging a prize trophy—it makes the hunt successful and gives the feel of victory (Figure 7.9).

In your community, relations with emergency personnel may not be as easy as they are here in a small Idaho city. However, being straightforward about who you are and having patience, discretion, and tactful persistence should go a long way toward helping you leave an emergency scene with meaningful story-telling images.

FIGURE 7.9

The man in this cab is not the driver of this burning rig but a good Samaritan truck driver who stopped to help. Efforts to separate the cab from the burning trailer were unsuccessful and the cab and trailer ultimately were consumed in flames. The chain at the front of the cab is attached to a truck whose driver tried to help separate the cab from the burning trailer by pulling the cab.

RANDY HAYES/POST REGISTER

Photojournalism: An Introduction

General News

News coverage that is scheduled by journalistic organizations is termed *general,* or *planned, news.* Spot news is always acute, usually directly affecting only a few people or organizations— accident victims or the owner of a fire-gutted store and her insurance company, for example. Covering general news may not have the adrenaline-producing excitement of raging fires, police shootouts, and airplane crashes, but this category regularly offers photojournalists opportunities to inform readers about meaningful happenings (Figures 7.10 and 7.11).

Unlike spot news, general news often gives enterprising photojournalists the opportunity to plan. Planning can mean the difference between adequate and superb coverage, between scooping the competition, including television stations, and following in their reportorial wake.

FIGURE 7.10

Cleveland Indians' pitcher Bob Ojeda wipes tears before the funeral of teammate Tim Crews. Ojeda survived a boating accident that killed Crews and Steve Olin, another teammate. Never wait for the formal event to begin; journalistic storytelling images can happen before and after, and the alert photographer is ready to recognize and record them. SUSAN WALSH/AP/WIDE WORLD PHOTOS

FIGURE 7.11

After all the work, and yes, the good times, it's graduation day. Time to parade in to hear a speaker, hopefully with something interesting to say, and to get your diploma. It's a grand day, no doubt about it. But what about the photographer covering the event for the local newspaper? How to come up with something that will catch the readers' attention? The photographer of this eye-catching moment combined a low camera angle, a wide-angle lens, a late afternoon sun, and a picture-taking mother to show his readers in a creative way a very human moment. SEAN D. ELLIOT/*THE DAY*, NEW LONDON, CONN.

FIGURE 7.12

A runner (far left) in the New York City Marathon makes a wrong turn but recoups to win the race. Never forget the journalism in photojournalism. Photojournalists should always be journalists first, photographers second. This means recognizing and deciding—often quickly—what is really important in a scene. Simply taking a picture is not enough.
KAREN ZOCCOLA/AP/WIDE WORLD PHOTOS

An important aspect of such planning is knowing the story—what it is, where it came from, where it is, and where it probably is headed. If time allows, delve into subjects so you can make informed decisions about coverage and emphasis. This way, you can avoid covering the superficial and obvious, as well as gimmicks set up by publicity-seeking people, and tell the real story.

Because all photojournalists should regularly read in detail the publication for which they work and its competition, many general news assignments will be at least passingly familiar. But this often is not enough. You should also search your organization's library for earlier stories and consult reporters who wrote them. Often, time does not permit more in-depth investigation or even these modest inquiries. But when it does, you should make every reasonable effort to become familiar with the subject.

Familiarity with subjects is only half of what a photojournalist needs; the other half is familiarity with the physical layout of coverage sites and the best way to get to and from them. If subjects of coverage are large scale—massive political rallies, for example—visiting the sites a day or so ahead pays real

dividends at coverage time. Finding the best picture-taking positions and the easiest entry and exit are two obvious payoffs. Eyeballing sites also helps you decide whether coverage requires more than one photographer and how coverage can be coordinated. If subjects of coverage are small scale—the dedication of a monument or a politician announcing for reelection, for example— arriving about 15 minutes early can pay storytelling dividends. Planning to better inform readers pays off. But no matter how much planning you do on a general news event, expect the unexpected. Always be alert to something unplanned or unexpected that gives your readers insight into the event you are covering (Figures 7.12–7.14).

Cooperative reporters from your organization can be a great help to you in your quest to visually inform readers. The best way to ensure that reporters will be a help and not a hindrance is to know them well and appreciate the job they do—the difficulties and pressures they work under. Reporters can provide insight into a story that photojournalists might miss. They can be an extra set of eyes and ears and, if willing, can help with equipment as needed—such as

FIGURE 7.13

A hotel worker brings a flag for the backdrop for U.S. Rep. Todd Tiahrt (R-Kansas) and then Speaker of the House Newt Gingrich. Always be on the lookout for unexpected happenings that tend to put events more into perspective.
STEVE RASMUSSEN/AP/ WIDE WORLD PHOTOS

FIGURE 7.14

Every event you cover involving people offers the possibility to communicate to your readers human emotion as well as what is otherwise happening. Dog—and cat—shows lend themselves to relative closeups of cute or otherwise visually intriguing animals, possibly with winners' ribbons in the foreground or background. AP photographer Mark Lennihan covered the prestigious Westminster Kennel Club 1999 Dog Show in New York City and made this informative, emotion-laden image of John Oulton reacting to his dog's winning "Best in Show." Kirby is a male Papillon whose full name is CH Loteki Supernatural Being.
MARK LENNIHAN/AP/ WIDE WORLD PHOTOS

FIGURE 7.15

Protesting, if not common, certainly is not unusual so expect to cover protests off and on during your photojournalistic career. Some protests are peaceful, some violent. Always be alert for someone trying to harm you. Never get so carried away looking through the camera that you forget to continually scan what's around you. Don't forget also to regularly look in back of you. In this photograph, the people behind the symbolic bamboo partitions are part of a demonstration in Vancouver, British Columbia, Canada at an Asian Pacific Economic Cooperation summit. Their cause is oppressed people and their plight.

Dan Loh/AP/Wide World Photos

holding a second electronic flash in a crowded room. Keep in mind that reporters are people with egos and sensitivities, just like photographers. Just as photographers do not want to be lackeys for reporters, reporters do not want to be seen as water carriers kowtowing to all-important photographers. But cooperation based on mutual respect and appreciation for each other's job requirements leads to readers who are better informed, visually and by the written word. Examples of general news photographs include the dedication of a new hospital wing, an Easter egg hunt, a university homecoming parade, a legislative committee hearing, a politician campaigning for reelection, the performance of a visiting dance troupe, the opening of a new industrial plant, the funeral of a mayor (Figures 7.15 and 7.16).

Incidentally, funeral coverage demands great tact. You need a laid-back unobtrusive approach. Proper dress is necessary. Avoid using flash. Use a telephoto lens unless you get permission from the family beforehand to intrude more blatantly on their grief. In the emotion-charged atmosphere of a funeral never discount the possibility of confrontation, even if you are using a telephoto lens a good way from the gravesite.

A 1995 *New York Times Magazine* story about Robert O'Donnell, the paramedic who snaked himself down a tunnel and freed 18-month-old Jessica McClure, who had got stuck 22 feet underground in an abandoned water well, describes his former wife's reaction to a photographer at O'Donnell's funeral. Apparently unable to adjust to a life of

No matter how large or small your community, things are happening. One way to know about these is to closely read your newspaper every day. Sometimes a tiny blurb about an event can lead to a picture that informs and interests readers. Lou G. Siegel's restaurant in New York City closed and longtime customers got chairs as souvenirs. Photographer Librado Romero captured a nice moment that humanizes the closing. Always be alert for different angles, different views, that will better convey what is happening.

LIBRADO ROMERO/THE NEW YORK TIMES PICTURES

obscurity after being in the national limelight for his heroic deed, the Midland, Texas, man had committed suicide.

As she walked back to her car, Robbie [O'Donnell] noticed a magazine photographer standing a distance away from the gravesite, taking pictures with a zoom lens. "Why do they have to be here now?" she said, loud enough to be heard by the photographer. "That's what started it all for Robert in the first place."

"Ma'am," said the photographer, who was now within arm's distance, "I'm just here doing my job." Then she hitched her camera onto her shoulder, and turned to walk away. With an anger Robbie didn't realize she felt, she shoved the photographer hard enough to make her stumble forward. It felt good, she said.[6]

Features

Strictly speaking, features are images with no news value that do not fit in the other non-news categories used here. In practice, however, "features" is a broad category that includes images with at least some news value and images that may easily fit in one or more other non-news categories.

Feature pictures are generally of two types: light-hearted images that entertain more than inform, and serious images that inform more than entertain and may be connected in some way with news or news-related situations.

Examples of light-hearted feature situations are squirrels chewing on nuts, children playing in large boxes, parents pushing children on swings, and horses being hosed down at a car wash. The list of light-hearted features is almost end-

FIGURE 7.17

A boy delights in a snowy egret's exit with a frozen shrimp. Good lighthearted features are all around—inside and outside; perceptive photographers need only be alert and ready to picture them.

MIKE LANG/*SARASOTA HERALD-TRIBUNE*/SILVER IMAGE

less (Figures 7.17–7.19). Coverage usually is unplanned; photographers often see features as they drive to and from assignments or while looking for them.

Editors tend to use features when space is available and they have no images of a more serious and important nature or when a graphically dull page needs sprucing up. Newspaper photographers quickly learn the importance of regularly submitting light-hearted features.

Today's general interest newspaper needs light-hearted features both for its readers' sake and to smooth the production difficulties of daily publishing. Sometimes layout people do not have enough news material to fill a page or need to balance a page loaded with serious news. Newspapers not only inform. They also entertain.

FIGURE 7.18

Unexpected features are found in unexpected places. M. Jack Luedke was on assignment to photograph people eating lunch under a large and prominent tree in his community. A possum in the tree apparently was dive-bombed by birds so much that it fell to the ground. It started its climb back up the tree but was attacked by the birds—blue jays—at about five feet. Photographer Luedke got about 11 frames of the confrontation before a group of children arrived to have lunch under the tree, and scared the birds away. Always carry two or three lenses with you (or an equivalent zoom) so when happenings come up that you were not expecting you will have the equipment to handle them.

M. Jack Luedke/*The Florida Times-Union*, Jacksonville, Fla.

FIGURE 7.19

Photographer Eric Engman did a good job of using juxtaposition to make an interesting and visually intriguing image of a diver during high school swim team practice. Blot out the divers on the wall mural. Does the picture become more or less interesting? Always remember to look for—and keep an open mind about—combining elements in a scene that together may visually entice readers.

Eric Engman/*Fairbanks* (Alaska) *Daily News-Miner*

Scott Wheeler, *The Ledger*, Lakeland, Fla.

In a perfect world, I would prefer only news photos and photos accompanying stories. The idea of photographers driving around endlessly looking for features would no longer exist. I feel editors become too reliant on this. They put great daily demands on photographers who, despite their best efforts, eventually bring back weaker photos.

With photographers not sent to search for features, I think the product would benefit because editors and reporters would be forced to see more photographic possibilities in their daily stories, thus better meshing words and pictures. This combination, to me, is what photojournalism is, or should be, all about.

However, the world isn't perfect and lighthearted features are demanded. I define lighthearted features as situations found by the photographer that are amusing, funny, or otherwise entertaining. They include images whose reason for existing is the intriguing forms they convey, the so-called pictorial images (Figure 7.20). Lighthearted features are not news and do not fall into any other commonly accepted photo category, except perhaps pictorial. Depending on who's talking, these features are called any number of names—*features, wilds, wild art, stand-alones,* or *CLOs* for "cutlines only." But no matter what the name is, the purposes of lighthearted feature images are always the same: first and hopefully foremost, to show readers the more carefree aspects of their community; second, to balance bad news so newspapers are not so depressing; third, to fill newspaper pages when nothing more meaningful is available and even less meaningful filler would otherwise be used.

FIGURE 7.20

College students kissing in public. Big lake. People in boats passing by. Public walk/bike path nearby. Lots of other people around. This was the larger scene I encountered and shot part of with my 300mm lens from behind the students and without their knowledge. I shot until I was satisfied with what I had and then approached them for caption information. Since *The Ledger* does not use pictures of people featured in photographs without their names in the caption, had they not been cooperative I would have wasted my time. But they did not have a problem with their picture being in the paper and I got a totally natural moment.
SCOTT WHEELER/THE LEDGER

Only lighthearted features that catch the reader's eye in form or his or her heart in emotions should be used. Even when used as filler, they should communicate something to readers, even if it is just to make them smile.

The Ledger and the two newspapers where I interned rely heavily on lighthearted features. I feel this is true of most daily newspapers across the country. Therefore, beginning photojournalists must learn to shoot them. They must prepare themselves to find eye-catching stand-alones to the best of their ability on daily deadlines (Figure 7.21).

Here are a few things that help me in my quest for better features; perhaps they will help you:

- First and foremost I always am on the lookout for a good feature and will stop and shoot it unless I will be late to something important. The best feature pictures always seem to happen when I'm not looking for them. Shooting them, even if I'm not on the clock, saves me the potential frustration of having to come up with one the next day under deadline pressure and maybe a less-quality one at that.
- I read my own newspaper as well as the competition. I find photo ideas here that word-minded editors often don't see.
- For me another good place for ideas is the telephone book. Sometimes names in the telephone book produce photo opportunities. For example, the YMCA might have swim classes going on, the Humane

FIGURE 7.21

I was driving down a quiet street and from a distance saw this 12-year-old-girl reading a book. I pulled over right away and stopped; I wanted to record the moment without her knowing I was photographing her, so I was going to use my 300mm lens. But she saw me before I could take any pictures, so I approached her and told her I worked for *The Ledger* and wanted to shoot some pictures of her. Her mother came out while I was talking to her and I cleared the picture-taking with her and got the caption information. I asked the girl to continue as she was when I first saw her. Had the girl gotten down from the tire as I was driving by, I would have kept driving and found something else. But she stopped in re-action to me pointing a camera at her, so I don't have a problem with telling her what I am doing and asking her to continue as she was when I arrived. I would not ask someone to repeat an act because I missed it. But asking them to continue when my presence caused them to stop, to me is ethically OK.
Scott Wheeler/ *The Ledger*

Society might be washing dogs, or the local library might have a puppet show going on. And if nothing is going on that day, I ask about future events.

■ If I don't have any assignments and can't find anything in the newspaper or phone book, I drive around. If I don't find anything in the usual places like downtown, in parks, or along main arteries of the city, I venture out to roads I have never been on or housing developments I haven't been to. By doing this I learn more about my coverage area and often come back with a photo that is a little different, such as a girl walking her pig along a rural road to exercise it for an upcoming fair.

■ While driving around looking for features, often I see locations that for one reason or another lend themselves to future features. For example, I may see a shadow or reflection in a particular spot that with the right human element would make a good photo. I make note of them. It always is good to have potential future locations and ideas tucked away for the "we need a color feature for 1-A" plea shortly before deadline. Believe me, this happens frequently. Bringing back a nice feature in a short period of time not only makes the paper look good the next day but it makes you look good to your peers.

■ Walking is one thing that keeps me sane when things are slow and I am tired and frustrated with driving around looking for features. It may sound silly, but it produces for me almost every time. By parking the car and walking, whether downtown, in a park, or elsewhere, I always seem to come up with photos that I never would have seen from my car. Also, I feel more in touch with the community when I walk around because I talk with more people. This not only helps me in making better photos but I also dig up an occasional story idea, which I pass along to an editor. And with my 80–200mm zoom lens and my Nikon F5 camera body I use when walking, I travel light while having the equipment I need.

The last thing I want to touch on is approaching subjects. I mostly use telephoto lenses—primarily a conventional 300mm but also an 80–200mm zoom—for shooting features. With this in mind I often shoot before making contact with subjects. This ensures that I get natural unposed moments. I shoot until I am noticed, then I approach the subject for caption information. If the person continues to do what he or she was doing as I begin to walk away, I may shoot more photos if I feel I need to.

There are instances, without question, when I approach the subject first before shooting. For example, when I want to photograph young children, whether on public or private property, I always ask them to get their parents. I ask the parents' permission before photographing. Parents have enough reasons to be nervous. If they see a stranger shooting photos of their kids, they may call the police or, worse, take matters into their own hands.

I also approach adults before shooting if I must go onto private property. This is not out of fear of trespass or intrusion, although that is a consideration but mainly because they notice me more on their own property as contrasted to, say, a park and stop what they are doing before I shoot. In cases like this I will get the caption information first and ask the subjects to continue whatever they were doing before I arrived and to pretend I am not there. Most people seem to forget about me after a few minutes and get back into what they were doing.

I would not ask someone to repeat something that I missed. But when a subject stops to ask what I am doing, I don't have a problem with getting my caption information and asking them to continue what they were doing before I arrived. A lot of times very small fact changes can make a difference on how a photojournalist acts. The situation itself will many times dictate what I do. I would rather shoot first and ask questions, but sometimes that is just not feasible. This seems to be a reasonable compromise that serves the readers well while staying, in my opinion, within the ethical boundaries.

Although I feel newspapers rely too much on stand-alone feature art, lighthearted features (including eye-catching pictorial photos) continue to be a cornerstone of newspaper photojournalism.

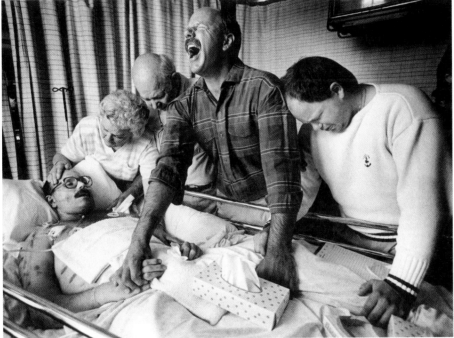

Examples of serious features are the dying AIDS sufferer mounting a valiant fight against the disease, a child violin prodigy destined for fame, a fiercely independent oysterman tonging his way to financial survival, and a volunteer cooking food for homeless people at a local shelter. Serious features typically are planned and often accompany stories. They may be happy or sad or emotionally neutral. Often they convey news overtones or connections, and when they do, they may be better labeled general news or perhaps placed in a hybrid category not used here, news features (Figures 7.22 and 7.23).

Serious features offer photojournalists opportunities to probe the life of their community, to reach toward their subjects' hearts and souls.

Lighthearted and many serious features combine to balance often depressing, sometimes boring, news. They provide alternate reading that at its best helps readers better understand their world. They make readers chuckle, sigh, laugh, and sometimes cry.

You may think features are easy to come by. Sometimes they are and sometimes they will elude you to the point of frustration. An unusual and eye-catching wet weather feature was taken by Charlie Riedel of *The Hays* (Kan.) *Daily News*. His photograph and August 1995 *News Photographer* article, "Eureka!," in which he describes how the photograph came about, are reproduced here (Figure 7.24).

FIGURE 7.24

CHARLIE RIEDEL/*THE HAYS* (KANS.) *DAILY NEWS*

Eureka!

By CHARLIE RIEDEL

Often times, desperation is the mother of invention at the *Hays Daily News* in Hays, Kan. Towards the end of a week of dreary, rainy weather—a condition very unusual in semi-arid western Kansas—unique weather features were getting hard to come by and people were really getting tired of the rain.

I had spent the previous two hours driving around looking for a feature and had no luck at all. Waiting at a stop sign and with a deadline fast approaching, I noticed how the sign appeared in the tiny water droplets on my window.

Presto, I had my feature.

But capturing it on film proved to be far more difficult. First, I had to find a sign with a clean background in a position where I could park my car at the correct angle and distance from the sign.

After finding the right location, I thought the rest would be easy. Wrong! I now had to find a pleasing grouping of raindrops on my windshield, precariously set up a tripod inside my small car, and get the image to stay in focus with my 60mm macro.

This whole process proved very frustrating, because usually by the time I had everything in position, the rain drops would bead up and run down my windshield.

After about an hour, everything came together. I had a photo which summed up public sentiment on the week of continued rain—"Stop Drops".

The photo, four columns on page 1, drew overwhelmingly good response from readers. It was new to our readers and they loved it. A full four months after the photo ran, I still hear comments from readers who liked the photo.

Sports Action

Two local high school football teams are competing—a photographer is there (Figure 7.25). Major league baseball teams in spring training—look for local and national photo coverage. Super Bowl time—expect a convention of photographers.

Obviously, newspaper and magazine sports coverage enjoys a solid and loyal reader following. These readers are deeply interested in the way a baseball player swings his bat or a tennis star her racquet. Many publications put great importance on, and considerable resources into, covering sports events (Figure 7.26).

Sports action images show a baseball player diving for second base, a fullback grinding his way to a touchdown, a tennis star hitting the ball, and a diver cutting the water like a bullet (Figure 7.27). Sports action images also show less mainstream aspects, such as a baseball team manager angry with an umpire

and a pit crew member changing a racing car's tire (Figure 7.28).

Photographing sports action is dangerous. A line drive hit by a baseball player can injure or kill an inattentive photographer. A 130-pound photographer run down by a 240-pound football fullback going full steam will never again forget to pay attention. An errant race car heading for a photographer causes hearts to stop.

Three important ways to minimize your risk in covering sports action and to ensure you record key moments are:

- Knowing how games are played
- Knowing strengths, weaknesses, and preferences of players and coaches
- Constantly being alert to potential as well as actual action

In addition to greatly increasing your chances of successful coverage, alertness goes a long way toward preventing injury or death. The general rule, even

FIGURE 7.25

Players chase the ball during a night high school football game. Depending on the intensity of lighting, covering high school football at night with existing light is fairly easy or all but impossible. This action was taken with a 300mm lens.
CARL D. WALSH/*JOURNAL TRIBUNE*, BIDDEFORD, MAINE

What turned out to be the final play of Super Bowl XXXIV was a cliff hanger, a real nail biter, and a major disappointment for the Tennessee Titans and their fans. Titans wide receiver Kevin Dyson (87), tackled about a yard short of the goal by St. Louis Rams player Mike Jones, made a valiant but unsuccessful effort to get the ball into the end zone for a touchdown. Here is the play taken from two different photographer positions. If you could only use one in your newspaper, which would it be and why? The Rams won 23-16.

MARK HUMPHREY/AP/ WIDE WORLD PHOTOS (TOP) JOHN GAPS III/AP/WIDE WORLD PHOTOS (BOTTOM)

when looking through a lens, is to always keep one eye on the action.

Sports events are competitions of wits. Photographers with intimate knowledge of the game have a far higher probability of safely recording key plays or key events than do their less-informed colleagues. Every photojournalist should know the game being covered, particularly the strategies that make one side or one person a winner and the other a loser. Many university physical education departments offer courses in the fundamentals of major sports—consider enrolling in some.

Knowing the game, the players, and the coaches—their strengths, weaknesses, and preferences—allows photographers to anticipate what will happen and to get into position to photograph it. Where should a photographer be in the following situation?

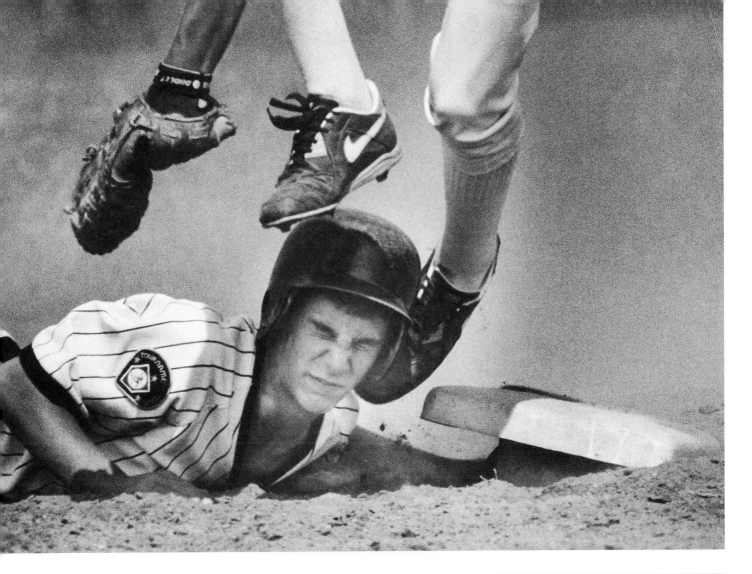

Third quarter of a 21–14 football game.

Third down.

Six yards to go for a first down at the 27-yard line of the team not in possession of the ball.

Team in possession of the ball is losing.

Quarterback of team in possession has good but not great throwing arm.

Kicker of team in possession has mediocre record in longer kicks.

The photographer needs to figure out whether:

The team will run the ball, hoping for a first down but reserving the last down for a pass or field goal attempt.

The quarterback will pass, reserving the last down for another pass or a kick.

Photographers who think a run is imminent may position themselves several yards in front of the line of scrimmage toward the opponent's end zone. Those who think a pass is imminent probably would go behind and more or less to the center of the end zone, assuming the quarterback does not tend to throw to one side.

No set of coverage rules substitutes for really knowing the games, the players, and the coaches. Intimate knowledge of these allows photographers to vicariously enter the minds of the coaches and players—to play the games along with them. This knowledge, combined with superb technical

FIGURE 7.27

Getting really close-up views of baseball action is difficult—the distance photographers typically must stay from the action lends itself to more encompassing coverage. Such images show what occurred but typically do not give a detailed view of a player's expression, as does this one of Pony League tournament action. Photographers should seek to bring their readers facial expressions showing wrenching disappointment, the pleasure of victory, and the strain of the game, difficult as they are to record. At the same time photographers should not forget the storytelling potential of more encompassing views.

©Bill Wade/*The Pittsburgh Press*

FIGURE 7.28

Even a consummate professional like Jack Nicklaus shows emotion while golfing. Here a missed putt causes him to grimace during The Tradition, one of the major tournaments of the Senior PGA Tour. Always look for the human aspect in sports—in anything you cover.
JEFF ROBBINS/AP/WIDE WORLD PHOTOS

proficiency and appropriate equipment, is the best hope for recording key storytelling moments.

Here are a few general guidelines that can help:

1. Telephoto lenses of 180mm and longer are good for sports action coverage. They allow photographers to be "closer" to the action, and these lenses blur foreground and background, thereby emphasizing and highlighting action. High-quality zoom telephoto lenses are particularly useful in sports action when light intensity is not a concern.
2. Motor drives are highly desirable because no photographer can regularly capture the height of action with a single manual exposure.
3. Monopods also are highly desirable when using telephoto lenses be-

cause monopods provide a relatively steady platform.
4. Unless they have a specific reason to do otherwise, photographers should follow the ball in games where a ball is used.
5. Photographers should carry a short telephoto and a wide angle, or a zoom equivalent, while covering action. This allows photographers to record other scenes related to the game, particularly features, as well as action happening close to them.

Just like other coverage, sports demands caption information. If the field or arena has a scoreboard, taking pictures of it immediately after each photographed play is a real help in later zeroing in on when the play occurred. A roster of participants, perhaps in a program, helps identify players. Take care with such lists; they may be outdated or players may change numbers at the last minute. Specially designed forms are helpful in recording information quickly. Avoid using felt pens; liquids, including perspiration, make their ink run.

Photographers at sports events should follow some fundamental rules. The rules help photojournalists avoid unpleasant and unnecessary confrontations with coaches, security guards, and spectators as well as personal injury. Following these rules also helps ensure photographers do not interfere in the games.

Rules for Covering Sports

All Games

Never go onto the playing area.

Kneel as much as possible so as not to block spectators' views.

Never talk with players or otherwise distract them.

Football

Stay within designated photographer areas at college and professional games.

Avoid going in front of players' benches at high school games; never intrude on coaches' "pacing spaces."

Constantly be alert for players running toward you and balls coming at you.

FIGURE 7.29

Basketball

Do not stand or sit directly behind baskets.

Consider taking some pictures from the stands.

Always be alert for players and balls coming at you.

Golf

Never release a camera's shutter, or activate a motor drive, while a player is addressing or hitting the ball.

Never move when a player is hitting the ball.

Never line up directly opposite a player who is putting.

Always be alert for a ball coming at you.

Baseball

Always know the location of the ball—never look through a camera without keeping your other eye on the ball.

Constantly be alert for players running toward you.

Watch out for flying bats.

Back in an earlier era in journalistic photography—say the 1960s—sequence picture-taking of sports action from a high vantage point, probably a photographers' platform on or near the top of the stadium, was common. A photographer using a motor drive would photograph plays that showed potential for intriguing action or the possibility of being a game winner or loser. Actually, it was not uncommon at important football games that every play was photographed from this high vantage point using a motor drive; lots of film was used. Now the trend is toward single moments showing up-close action or emotion. Motor drives still are used because of the difficulty of recording telling moments in the fast-moving world of sports. But instead of three or more images from the same action being used, only one that drives home the key storytelling moment is used; the rest go into a file or are destroyed, never to be seen by the readers. There are

exceptions, but this approach appears to be well established. The photograph here is a good example of the one image approach. Instead of showing the stages of the young pitcher's delivery, only one instant of time is shown. (This image was part of a picture story, a form not being discussed here.) As you read publications—and you should be a regular reader of journalistic publications—be on the lookout for situations where the photographer, or an editor, decided to tell the story in one visually intriguing moment and situations where multiple images taken extremely close together were used to convey the visual information. Try to visualize what you would have done if you were the photographer or editor to even better convey the most appropriate truth of the situations to your readers—eight images, six images, four images, two images, or only one.
© *The Washington Post*. Photo by Khue Bui. Reprinted with permission.

Two important factors separate great sports action photographers from merely satisfactory ones: the ability to anticipate and record key moments and the ability to do so creatively—in a visually intriguing way. One contemporary technique that sports photographers often use is to photograph with a long telephoto lens often from a relatively low vantage point (Figures 7.29 and 7.30). Many proponents believe this emphasizes action, making it more intriguing. In effect, it puts readers in front row seats.

Most technically competent photographers can leave games with decent action pictures. However, great sports photographers record key moments in ways that command readers' attention.

How do you learn to be a great sports photographer? Practicing at Little League and high school daytime games and at nighttime adult softball games is a good way to hone your picture-taking skills. Always remember to ask permission from officials if you want to be near the field. Also, at games involving children it is a particularly good idea to let coaches know who you are, what you want to do, and why.

If you are covering baseball, depending on the size of the diamond, a 200mm or a 300mm lens is good for coverage of second base and home plate from behind first base and also will reach third base, although it is a stretch. An 85mm lens is good for covering first from the same position.

If you are allowed on the field (but of course not the playing part of the field), take great care to watch the ball so it does not strike you. Also, watch for players who are backing up plays because they can run into an inattentive photographer, hurting both themselves and you. Some stadiums have photographer positions on the roofs; be careful not to get so carried away with picture taking that you accidentally step off into space. Bleachers also can be a good place from which to picture baseball.

Different basketball action is hard to come by. But try to avoid humdrum basket-shooting images, typically showcasing players' underarms. Action between players—fighting for the ball, for example—yields interesting and eye-catching images, sometimes with competition-laden facial expressions, and brings home the game's inherent human conflict. Coverage from appropriate floor positions and bleachers near baskets tends to be particularly fruitful. Avoid positioning yourself directly behind the basket so you don't distract players.

FIGURE 7.31

The proud father watches as his daughter nears the finish of a triathlon. Undoubtedly bursting with pride, he joins her, pointing toward the finish line. Unusual? Sure. Unexpected? Little doubt. Very human? Certainly. Moments that define our humanity are all around us. Sometimes they come at unexpected times. You as a journalistic photographer must always be on the lookout for them, and always prepared to record them well. To do this you must be intimately familiar with your photographic equipment and not get so tied up with a gaggle of it that lots of unexpected moments are visually lost forever. At any one time, you should be ready with only the minimum equipment needed to do the job well. This minimalist approach from time to time undoubtedly will cause you to miss important moments but at the same time it should allow you to react quickly and efficiently to record more than you miss.

LANNIS WATERS/*THE PALM BEACH POST*

Whatever the game may be, the keys to getting good sports action are knowing the rules and strategies of the game, using the appropriate photographic equipment, and having the ability to recognize visually interesting or game-determining action and instantly putting the equipment to use (Figure 7.31). Being in the right position at the right time is critical; nothing makes this more possible than knowing the rules and strategies of games so well that you can accurately anticipate coaches' and players' next few moves.

Two great heavyweights going at it in a Las Vegas, Nevada, ring for the World Boxing Association (WBA) heavyweight championship. Excitement singes the air. The fight ends in Round Three. One fighter knocked out or so badly beaten the referee stops the match? No way. The challenger, former WBA heavyweight champion Mike Tyson, is disqualified by the referee for biting both of Evander Holyfield's ears, taking a noticeable chunk out of one of them.

Unexpected development. No doubt about it. Presented here are six images from the ear-biting episode (Figures 7.32–7.37). Envision yourself as one of the photographers ringside. How quickly and well would you have reacted? Instantaneously or delayed. Reaction time in journalistic photography can mean the difference between getting the picture and getting it good or getting a lesser image or no image at all. In photojournalism, always expect the unexpected.

Of these six pictures, if you could only use one in your publication, which would it be? How about two? Three? Overall, how well do you think this episode was covered?

FIGURE 7.32

Tyson bites Holyfield's ear; Holyfield's other ear soon is bitten. Referee Lane is in the background.
Jack Smith/AP/Wide World Photos

FIGURE 7.33

Tyson pushes Holyfield toward his corner after the first biting incident.
Mark J. Terrill/AP/Wide World Photos

The ear that shook the boxing world. Before the fight with Tyson, Holyfield had ear where the hole is.

JED JACOBSOHN/ALLSPORT

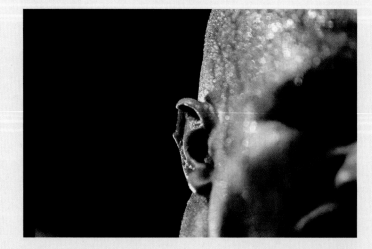

Tyson "emotes" (as they say in sports parlance) after being disqualified for biting Holyfield.

LENNOX MCLENDON/AP/WIDE WORLD PHOTOS

Photojournalism: An Introduction

Sports Features

Although the fundamental purpose of photographic coverage of sports events generally is picturing key moments of action in visually intriguing ways, publications regularly use game-related pictures that do not show game action. Different as they are, these images lumped together are sports features.

Sports feature pictures are the same as features, except they always involve sports. Photographers typically take these pictures immediately before, during, or after sporting events but also may take them at other times. Examples of sports feature pictures are opposing coaches embracing after a hard-fought game, a player on the losing side weep-ing, groundskeepers covering a field from rain, fans cheering or booing, animals running or flying onto the playing field.

Sports Illustrated photographer Heinz Kluetmeier underlines the point that sports images—reaction images, specifically—are important: "So many of the great pictures are not the action itself, but the reaction, be it joy or sad-ness or pathos."[7]

Sports features round out sports events by revealing their off-stage activities. They humanize sports, showing the emotions of players, coaches, and spectators and conveying other game-related activities important but arguably secondary to game play (Figures 7.38–7.43).

FIGURE 7.38

A dejected Temple University basket-ball player, whose team lost to the Uni-versity of North Car-olina (celebrating in the background), sits on the court oozing frustration. Victory and defeat are two important ingredients of the sports features cate-gory.

GERARD LODRIGUSS/*THE PHILADELPHIA INQUIRER*

Victorious, Johnny Tapia does a back flip after defeating his hometown rival, Danny Romero, Jr., in a junior bantam-weight world-title fight in Las Vegas, Nevada. Alertness for the unexpected and the photographic preparedness to record it lead to better informed readers and a more successful career for the photographer.
Michael J. Gallegos/ ©1987 The Albuquerque Tribune

Rain postpones the baseball game you are covering. Time to kick back, put the cameras away, forget the coverage until the game starts? No way. You are there to cover whatever is going on and you can bet that all kinds of things will be going on— fans huddling from the weather, groundskeepers trying to keep the infield dry, striking images of rain against the field's light, and maybe players passing time in an interesting way, like the Fargo Red Hawks doing the limbo during a rain postponement in Duluth, Minnesota.
Elsa Hasch/Allsport

Photojournalism: An Introduction

FIGURE 7.41

Whenever you're covering sports—whenever you're covering any event—always be alert for everything going on around you. Regularly visually scan the area while remaining alert to dangers coming your way—errant baseballs, for example. Associated Press photographer Eric Draper saw St. Louis Cardinal Mark McGwire using a fan to cool off in the dugout and recorded it to give us an intriguing off-the-playing-field image of the man soon to break Roger Maris's home run record.
ERIC DRAPER/AP/WIDE WORLD PHOTOS

FIGURE 7.42

No matter what sport you are covering be alert for sport-related happenings off the playing field. Doing this is easier said than done because you need always to be alert to the sports action that is taking place, or about to take place. *The Dallas Morning News*'s Michael Ainsworth caught this interesting sports feature of spectators protecting themselves from a wayward golf ball at a professional golf tournament.
MICHAEL AINSWORTH/*THE DALLAS MORNING NEWS*

Portrait/Personality

The portrait/personality category holds some of the finest contemporary journalistic photography. But it was not always this way. In the old days of news photography this category usually contained head shots or mug shots. Not now. Usually only by lucky accident did head and mug shots reveal anything about subjects except their physical appearance. The best contemporary images in the portrait/personality category—not all are of faces—offer glimpses into hearts and souls. They come close to transcending the inherent limitations of photography. They let readers walk in the shoes of those pictured. They let readers probe subjects' thoughts and contemplate their values (Figures 7.44–7.48).

Although faces lend themselves to scrutiny of the person within, portrait/personality images need not be facial views to probe for deeper meaning. Back views and body forms can speak volumes.

Good portrait/personality images reveal as much about the photographer as the photographed. Only image makers attuned to nuances of nonverbal behavior and comfortable with personal interaction can consistently visually plumb subjects' inner selves. Only photographers sensitive to and intimately knowledgeable of the human condition can hope to consistently break through the facade that people often present to strangers.

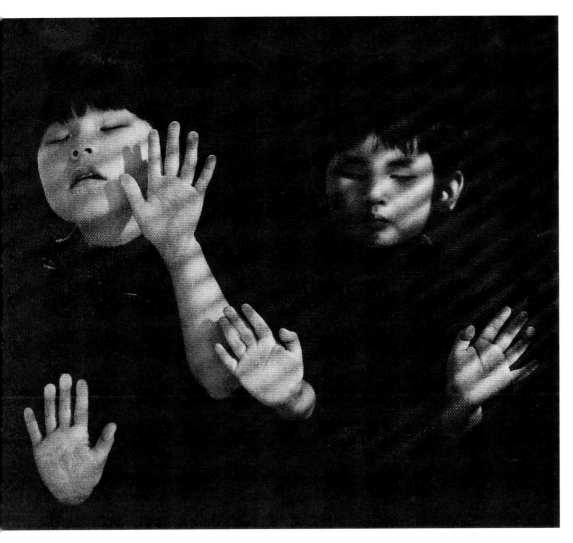

FIGURE 7.45

If communicating the human condition to readers is the most fundamentally important aspect of photojournalism, then human emotion surely is toward the top of the list of visual concerns to photojournalists. Outward expression often is an indicator of inward feeling. What do you think this famous college football coach's expression and tears mean? Does it help to know that Grambling State University's Eddie Robinson is about to coach his last home game after having won more college football games than any other coach?
RUSTY COSTANZA/*THE TIMES-PICAYUNE*, NEW ORLEANS, LA.

FIGURE 7.46

In his waning years how do you picture arguably the greatest professional boxer of all time, ill with a serious neurological disease? A close-up of his face is one possibility. Another is him and his environment. Here Muhammad Ali is shown with memorabilia at his Michigan farm, in the barn where he trained on his way to becoming a boxing icon and a legendary American figure. Photojournalists present to their viewers their vision of the truth. Always take care to be a faithful and good steward of this great responsibility.

©1997 THE WASHINGTON POST. PHOTO BY CAROL GUZY. REPRINTED WITH PERMISSION.

FIGURE 7.47

While many portrait/personality photographs of people are closeups of their faces, more distant views also can effectively communicate information about subjects. This picture of a Central American family on their horse, victims of Hurricane Mitch, is a good example. Does viewing the image leave you with the feeling that you know the people at least a little?

MIKE STOCKER/SUN-SENTINEL, NOW SOUTH FLORIDA SUN-SENTINEL, FORT LAUDERDALE, FLA.

Photojournalism: An Introduction

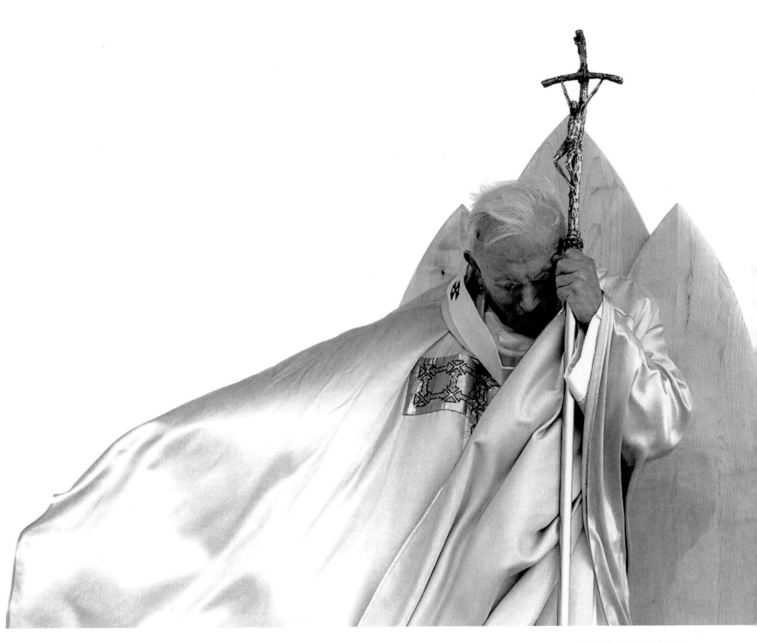

Fred Conrad, *The New York Times*

My specialty at *The New York Times* is portrait/personality photography. I am generally assigned after a reporter has interviewed the subject. If lucky, I get about 30 minutes to do my thing. The challenge is meeting a complete stranger, often in a so-so setting, and coming away with a great portrait. There is no time to reflect—there is only time to react (Figure 7.49).

I seldom get the chance to scout a location beforehand. The big question when I walk through the door is "Where am I going to do this thing?" I try to keep the background simple and uncluttered so as not to detract from the subject. If the background doesn't say something about the subject in a simple and direct way, there is no reason to include it.

The next concern is how to light the subject. For me, simplicity works the best. I generally use only one light source, at most two. I use strobes with an assortment of light banks and gridded reflectors. The choice is whether to light broadly and softly with a large light bank or to use grids to light more dramatically. The story, the subject's face, and the setting dictate how to light. The next important decision is what camera to use. I use a Rollei 6008 for most of my work. Its large negative and square format have worked well for me. Lately, though, I've been playing around with 4 × 5 and 8 × 10 view cameras.

The advantages of using medium and large format cameras are twofold. Most notable is the quality. Reproduction in the newspaper looks great even if the pictures are used large. They also

stand out because most of the other photos in the paper were made with 35mm cameras. The other great advantage to using a larger format is that it slows down the process. It enables both me and the subject to concentrate on one thing, creating a distinctive portrait.

Establishing a rapport with the subjects is important. I talk with them while I am setting up my lights and camera. Mostly, I look for body language. What do they do with their hands? How do they stand or sit? Are they self-con-

FIGURE 7.49

I took this picture of author Harold Brodsky at the offices of *The New Yorker.* **The offices are ugly and very spartan. I decided to focus more on his face rather than the rooms so I chose to use a grid reflector on my strobe head and just light him. He felt uneasy at first as many people do when having their portrait taken. Normally I would talk to him and try to make him more comfortable but I decided not to because I liked the intensity of his gaze. It worked for me.**
Fred Conrad/The New York Times Pictures

scious? Often, after I've shot a couple of rolls and am reloading, I'll notice a completely different body posture or expression. They've let their guard down and have shown me something about themselves that I can use to make a better portrait.

There is one thing that I am always aware of: great pictures are not taken, they are given. Having your picture taken can be an intimidating experience. What worries most people is that they are no longer in control of their self-image. Many of the people that I've photographed are quite concerned about the image that they project. They are powerful people who like to control things, including photographers. I react by telling them what I'm trying to do and explaining how it's done photographically. Once you demystify all the gadgets, the walls come down a bit. Many of my more successful portraits show people looking toward the camera. I think eye contact between the reader and the subject is powerful. It draws the reader's attention to the photograph and the story that it illustrates.

The head-on portrait is an indication of a mutual respect and participation between the sitter and the photographer. When subjects are given the opportunity to project their self-images they often reveal more than they would if their photographs were taken candidly (Figure 7.50).

I recently photographed a retired college professor who is also a well-known feminist writer. She greeted me at the door, saying, "I'm just a grey-haired grandmother, don't make me do anything silly." She went on to explain

FIGURE 7.50

This picture of photographer Herb Ritts was taken at a Soho gallery in New York City where his work was being featured. I used an 8 × 10 view camera. I decided not to include his photographs in the background because they would be distracting. It was his idea to cover his eye when I asked which eye he shot with; he said it was always with his left eye. The effect created by covering one eye is a photo where there is "eye contact" no matter from which direction you view the image.

FRED CONRAD/THE NEW YORK TIMES PICTURES

how the last person to photograph her had asked her to disrobe, wrap herself in a sheet, and stand on her bed with a staff. The photographer apparently thought this would convey the professor's feminist position. I reassured her that I would treat her with respect. Our time together was very productive and a respectful picture later appeared in *The Times*.

Different things work for different photographers. There is nothing wrong with silly, it's just that silly doesn't work for me. What works for me is an attitude of respect. I treat a homeless person the same way I treat a bank president.

Pictorial

Outstanding images in the pictorial category showcase the artistic side of photojournalism. Pictorials typically depend on light and form and their interaction. These images make readers pause, perhaps to reminisce about pleasant and similar experiences, or just to feel a little better, a little brighter (Figures 7.51–7.55).

Pictorials by their nature typically entertain more than inform. They are one extreme of the photojournalism dichotomy (the other is spot news). A photojournalist who recognizes these "pretty scenes" is likely to be a well-rounded photographer. Being able to recognize a pictorial scene also is a sign of visual perceptiveness, undoubtedly an asset in more news-related coverage.

FIGURE 7.51
Good photojournalists always are looking. What's going on at the left out there? What are those people doing, or about to do? What about the ducks in the pond? What is that large glass window reflecting? Denny Simmons clearly was looking when he made this eye-catching pictorial of a college student strolling on a campus walkway in back of windows reflecting trees without leaves at sunset.
DENNY SIMMONS/THE NEWS SUN, WAUKEGAN, ILL.

     Photojournalism: An Introduction

FIGURE 7.52

Sometimes scenes in one or the other news categories, as well as other categories, can rightly be considered pictorials. This news picture of an elderly woman picking her way through massive snow drifts caused by a blizzard is one such scene. If you consider this a pictorial rather than a news picture, then it surely is an atypical pictorial—it informs as well as entertains. Keep in mind that categorizing photographs can be less than a perfect undertaking. News becomes pictorial; feature becomes news; spot news becomes general news and vice versa; portrait/personality becomes feature, and so forth. Try not to get so carried away with pigeonholing an image into one slot or the other that you lose sight of what you really are doing: communicating in a fair way the most appropriate truth as you viewed it to people unable to stand where you stood and view what you viewed.

BILL ALKOFER/*ST. PAUL PIONEER PRESS*

FIGURE 7.53

After arguing that most pictorials are non-news connected pretty pictures, here is another news image that chips away a little more of this assertion. Can there be prettiness—beauty—in a tragic news scene? Hold your book at arm's length and peruse this image of a Los Angeles City Fire Department airplane fighting a Laurel Canyon-area fire by dropping water. Do you see beauty in the tragic scene or just a tragic scene? Do you think this image would be presented in a newspaper as a news picture or as a pictorial? What about in a photography contest?

MIKE MEADOWS/AP/WIDE WORLD PHOTOS

Photojournalism: An Introduction

FIGURE 7.54

Lightning can create a striking pictorial image in the barren desert, in a city of high rises, and over water as is shown here with strikes over the San Francisco-Oakland Bay Bridge. Try to find a man-made or natural structure that will better put lightning strikes in perspective, or perhaps zero in on only the lightning without any props. However you approach photographing lightning, take great care to position yourself so that you are out of the way of the deadly strikes.
JUSTIN SULLIVAN/
AP/WIDE WORLD PHOTOS

FIGURE 7.55

In such a busy world a photograph that communicates serenity, solitude, and quietness can uplift the spirit as undoubtedly does this image of "The Shoals" in the Virginia early morning mist along the New River. Always be alert for the quieter side of life as you deal with spot news and other high intensity assignments.
© SUSIE POST/AURORA AND QUANTA PRODUCTIONS

Illustration

Images in this category visually try to convey ideas and concepts, and products. Both categories demand a particularly high level of technical photographic expertise—either in conventional photography or working with Adobe Photoshop—and keen, incisive minds that can produce images that clearly convey the intended messages while doing so in clever, eye-catching ways.

Conveying ideas and concepts with photography is enormously challenging; editors and photographers work hard to conceive arresting ideas—in a sense, executing these images is akin to editorial cartoonists who comment with visual wit and piercing commentary. If, even after intense brainstorming or just quiet thinking, a photographic illustration does not gel, either as pure photography or as a computer-generated hybrid, it perhaps is best to leave illustrating the story to the graphic artist. Photography simply is too literal a medium to deal easily with the nuances of illustration. But photographers can make terrific photography-oriented illustrations. When they succeed, their images convey messages with striking effectiveness (Figures 7.56–7.59).

FIGURE 7.56

Photographers who can translate a concept like fatigue to a storytelling and eye-catching image like this one add an important dimension to their publications' photographic operations and broaden the communicative value of their publications to readers. They almost certainly make themselves more valuable to the publication for which they work.

GEOFF HINDS/*THE NEWS TRIBUNE*, TACOMA, WASH.

Major Subjects

FIGURE 7.59

The striking contrast between the "Red purse with flowers" and the red ambiance of this photograph with the dark clothing goes a long way toward making this product illustration image visually enticing. If you have any doubt that a picture like this is difficult to create, try doing several. You probably will find that a number of questions present themselves on the road to creating a successful image like this one. In this case, some questions might be: Should the picture be taken in the studio or outside? Should there be an ambiance of red to the overall scene? Should the model's face be shown, partially shown, or not shown at all? How should the purse be held? What color should the background be?

Jean Shifrin/*The Atlanta Journal Constitution*

Final Thoughts

There is nothing magic about these eight subject categories. They offer a simple but sometimes strained framework into which journalistic photographs fit.

Spot news and general news are the categories most important to every general interest newspaper. However, this does not mean that other categories are not important. It does mean that news occupies a place of special importance in publications called newspapers. As you go out on the street to picture the wide-ranging human condition—from the harsh and heartbreaking to the gentle and heartwarming—keep these categories tucked in the back of your mind.

NOTES

[1] Arthur Goldsmith, *The Photography Game: What It Is and How to Play It* (New York: Viking, 1971) p. 131.

[2] James A. Henderson Jr., Richard N. Pearson, and John A. Siliciano, *The Torts Process,* 4th ed. (Boston: Little, Brown, 1994), p. 332.

[3] Vt. Stat. Ann. tit. 12, § 519 (1973).

[4] W. Page Keeton et al., *Prosser and Keeton on the Law of Torts,* 5th ed. With a 1988 Pocket Part by Dan B. Dobbs et al. (St. Paul, Minn: West, 1984) p. 378.

[5] Ibid., p. 377.

[6] Lisa Belkin, "Death on the CNN Curve," *The New York Times Magazine,* 23 July 1995, p. 44.

[7] Cal Olson, "More Than a Photo," *Fifty Years & Counting,* 10th in a series of supplements to *News Photographer,* May 1995

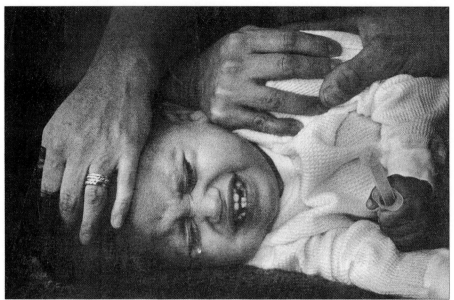

Jon and Alice MacDonough comfort their 3-year-old son, Benjamin, while he gets an injection. Benjamin had to endure semi-weekly shots and 13 hours of daily dialysis because his kidneys were damaged. On Feb. 10, the boy received his father's kidney in a transplant operation.

Saving Benjamin

A father's gift of a kidney helps Golden Gate boy say goodbye to painful medical procedures and have the chance to live a normal life.

Benjamin MacDonough watched from the bottom of the stairs as a man eased his machine out of his room and bumped it slowly down the stairs and out the door.

For the 3-year-old Golden Gate boy, the dialysis machine was simply part of life; as far back as he could remember, he had spent 13 hours a day linked by a foot-long tube running from the apparatus to a port in his abdomen.

Benjamin's mom, Alice, and his dad, Jon, knew the machine kept their son alive by purifying his blood — a normal function of the kidneys. On Feb. 10, four days after Benjamin's third birthday, Jon donated his left kidney to free his child from that machine and to give his boy a chance to be ordinary: to swim, to go to the beach, to spend a weekend at Disney World.

"Kick the machine, Benjamin," said Alice as she walked outside with her son, a month after the successful transplant surgery. After it was loaded in a truck,

Benjamin solemnly stared at the machine that had been so pivotal a part of his life.

And the boy started to weep.

＊ ＊ ＊

It has been more than 6 months since father and son underwent surgery.

Watch Benjamin for an hour and you're likely to witness a ball of energy munching handfuls of M&Ms, singing along with Barney or Lion King songs, or splashing in the pool.

"I didn't think I'd be able to watch this in a million years," said Alice, 25, smiling as father and son played in the pool on a Saturday afternoon in June. "It is such a relief that part of our lives is over."

It is only when Jon, 24, and his son step out of the pool and you see the scars — "scratches," Benjamin calls them — that you remember what that boy has endured.

See BENJAMIN, Page 4B

Jon helps Benjamin dress for bed before a night-long session of dialysis. The dialysis machine at the side of his bed purified his blood through a process of osmosis.

Photography by
Lance Murphey

Story by
Teresa Araque
and
Lance Murphey

ABOVE: Helping to relieve the daily monotony of dialysis, Alice gets ready to tickle Benjamin while he lies in bed.

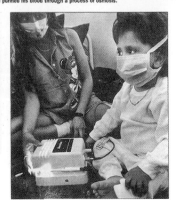

RIGHT: Benjamin helps his mother disconnect his link to the dialysis machine. Benjamin became as involved in his daily care as his parents.

Major Forms

From the picture story, "Saving Benjamin," that appeared in the *Naples* (Fla.) *Daily News*. The child was given a kidney by his father. Photographs by Lance Murphey. Story by Teresa Araque and Lance Murphey. Page design by Lance Murphey. The entire story is reproduced later in this chapter.

Overview

Now that we have covered the broad category of "subjects" in the previous chapter, let's explore the other broad category in which photographs are placed, "forms." For this discussion, let's use six form categories: the single picture, picture groups, picture sequences, picture series, and photo essays and picture stories.

The Single Picture

The basic photographic unit of U.S. newspapers is the single storytelling photograph with accompanying caption. Recognizing and visually composing the storytelling elements of a scene into a single image test journalistic and creative skills. Photojournalists must always scan scenes, particularly news scenes, with a keen and inquiring eye. Look at what first appears to be the most important aspect of the scene. Then look elsewhere to make sure it is what it appears to be. Look all around the main subject for supporting items.

Summing up a scene so that you relate the most appropriately truthful single storytelling image is photographic

FIGURE 8.1

When photographing spot news, you probably will not know how many pictures your publication will want to use. Always make sure that you have one image that sums things up— that tells what happened in one picture. This image is an excellent example of the single storytelling photograph. A pedestrian bridge collapsed at a North Carolina speedway, injuring at least 50 race fans as they left.
TOM COPELAND/*NEWS & RECORD*, GREENSBORO, N.C.

seeing and journalistic reporting at its best (Figure 8.1).

Picture Groups

Although a single picture and its caption is the basic photojournalistic unit, it is not always the best way to communicate visually. Single story-telling images can give an overall sense of what is going on, can communicate a specific detail of the overall scene, and sometimes can do both. But few single images, however well executed, can communicate as much as two or more well-done images (Figure 8.2).

Picture groups—two or more pictures about the same subject published close together—are especially suited to newspapers. Picture groups, if done right, relate considerably more information than a single image. They usually require less space than photo essays and picture stories, an important advantage. Picture groups allow photographers to present abbreviated but fundamentally rounded photographic reports. One possibility, among others, is a relatively distant view anchors the group and puts it in geographic perspective, a medium view sums up details, and a close view shows an important aspect lost in the more distant images. When the situation lends itself to more intense treatment, the picture group can be expanded to a full page and beyond.

Picture groups typically convey more information than their individual pictures can. This synergism works in favor of picture groups, the same as it works for other multi-picture forms and for words and pictures used together.

Picture Sequences

A series of pictures about the same subject taken from the same position within a few seconds is a picture sequence (Figure 8.3). Refinements of battery-powered electric motors that fit on 35mm single-lens reflex cameras popularized picture sequencing in the late 1950s and early 1960s. More reliable drives followed. Now sports action pictures are almost never taken without

FIGURE 8.2

In journalistic publishing, space is money. Even so, newspapers often publish more than one picture of a situation to convey more information to readers about what occurred. The information conveyed to readers—the effect on them—often is greater with picture groups than if the individual pictures within the group were published separately. This synergism is an important reason to publish two or more pictures of the same event together. This two-picture picture group tells about New Mexico inmates being transported by special aircraft to an out-of-state prison. The bottom photo gets across the air transport aspect of the story and the top photo emphasizes the people involved in the move.

ADELE T. CHAVEZ/*THE ALBUQUERQUE TRIBUNE*

1

2

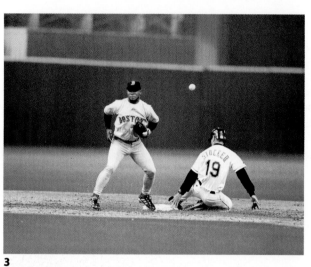

3

4

5

FIGURE 8.3

Tampa Bay Devil Rays' shortstop Kevin Stocker slides into second with a stolen base as Boston Red Sox shortstop Donnie Sadler tries to handle a low throw from the catcher. This sequence, taken in about one second, was shot during a night game in domed Tropicana Field in St. Petersburg, Fla. With Stocker on first base, photographer Al Anderson anticipated action at second base and trained his motor drive-equipped camera and 400mm lens there, prefocused for the appropriate distance. Motor drives quickly advance film, allowing photographers to show their readers closely related action that otherwise would be impossible to photograph with the still camera.

AL ANDERSON/*BRADENTON* (FLA.) *HERALD*

the aid of motor drives. Professional motor drives vary in the number of frames per second that they move, but 6 to 10 is in the ballpark. Motor drives can also help record nonsports action; for example, different facial expressions.

Picture Series

The picture series is a group of pictures about the same subject taken sequentially over a longer period of time than picture sequences and without regard to the photographer's position. A picture series (Figure 8.4) typically tells a broader story than a picture sequence but a more restricted story than a picture group. The picture series also is particularly useful in conveying technical aspects of a story—the various steps in making paint, for example.

Photo Essays and Picture Stories

Photo essays and picture stories are always narratives, whatever form they may follow—chronological order or thematic, for example; they tell stories. Because each format uses multiple images in a relatively encompassing way, its storytelling ability typically is more in-depth than other forms—than the single picture or the picture group, for example.

Photo essays are similar to picture stories, and the terms often are used interchangeably. For those who separate them, essays:

- Tend to have more pictures, often more than 10.
- Usually take a much longer time period to do—weeks, months, or even years.
- Often depict concepts or themes— truth, poverty, illness, or pollution, for example.
- Include the photographer's personal point of view as an integral part of the essay.
- Often are designed for publication by or under the significant influence of the photographer.

FIGURE 8.4

In a broad sense, picture series are picture sequences with a greater time lapse between images. Typically, recording a picture series does not require a motor drive. What the photojournalist does need, however, is a keen sense of what is going on, its importance, and the ability to relate each image to the others accompanying it. This series of Simon de Pury conducting an auction at Sotheby's in New York City is a good example.

Ozier Muhammad/The New York Times Pictures

W. Eugene Smith, the great photo-journalist who specialized in photo essays during and after his tenure with *LIFE* magazine, stressed the importance of the interrelationship of individual pictures:

> You keep working out the relationships between the people, and you look back at the relationships you have established, and you see whether other relationships must be established or strengthened. There should be a coherence between the pictures, which I don't think you find in the usual publication of a group of pictures which are called picture stories.[1]

As you go through this part of the chapter, you will see photo essays and picture stories reproduced as each appeared in its publication. First decide how each appeals to you as a reader. If you particularly like or dislike one, try to decide why. Is it because of the subject matter, the photographer's technique, the design, or a combination of these and perhaps other considerations? If color is used, does it add to the communicative value of the piece, detract from it, or is its use simply neutral? How about the type? Does it help convey the story, help to better communicate it? After you've read the piece by *Dallas Morning News* photo editor Leslie White at the end of this chapter, go back and carefully scrutinize each photo essay and picture story. Does your critical eye tell you the same things about each, or do you now see them in a somewhat different perspective? You surely will want to discuss your ideas with your colleagues and your instructor, not so you may blindly follow what they think but so that you can consider other points of view, some of which you may want to incorporate in your thinking. Your goal in all this, of course, is to draw your own conclusions about what is effective and what is not, about what communicates the message well and what does not. Once you have done this, you should be well on your way to arriving at a personal approach to photographing and laying out—de-signing—photo essays and picture stories.

Whatever conclusions you reach, always remember that in doing photo essays and picture stories, as in doing all forms of photographs, you must be true to your subjects, your readers, and yourself—always laboring to give readers the most appropriate truth fairly represented. You also must work within whatever limitations are imposed on you by your employing organization. U.S. newspapers publish relatively few photo essays, primarily because essays demand considerable photographer time and often considerable page space. Consequently, you will find photo essays mostly in books. But photo essays do appear in newspapers. Reproduced here (see page 227) is a newspaper photo essay. It was published in the *Berkshire Eagle*, Pittsfield, Mass. The commentary by the photographer, Craig Walker, "7 months with AIDS: photos change his life," was published in *News Photographer* magazine.

Books are a main repository for contemporary photo essays. An exemplar of the theme photo essay is the 1975 book *Minamata* by W. Eugene Smith and Aileen Smith.[2] This is the story of the people of a Japanese fishing village on a mercury-polluted bay. Another exemplary theme essay is Donna Ferrato's 1991 book about domestic violence against women, *Living With the Enemy*. Although they only hint at the richness of the entire works, one image from *Minamata* and two from *Living With the Enemy* appear in Figures 8.5 to 8.7. To get the full breadth and depth of these photo essays read the books in their entirety. Figure 8.5 is from *Minamata,* and Figures 8.6 and 8.7 are from *Living With the Enemy.*

Picture stories are photographs—almost always at least four—used together, usually with text blocks or longer word stories. Usually done in a relatively short period of time—a few days or even a few hours—they typically tell about a single subject or some aspect of it. Photographers may do the layouts for picture stories—particularly those of a page or less in length—or the

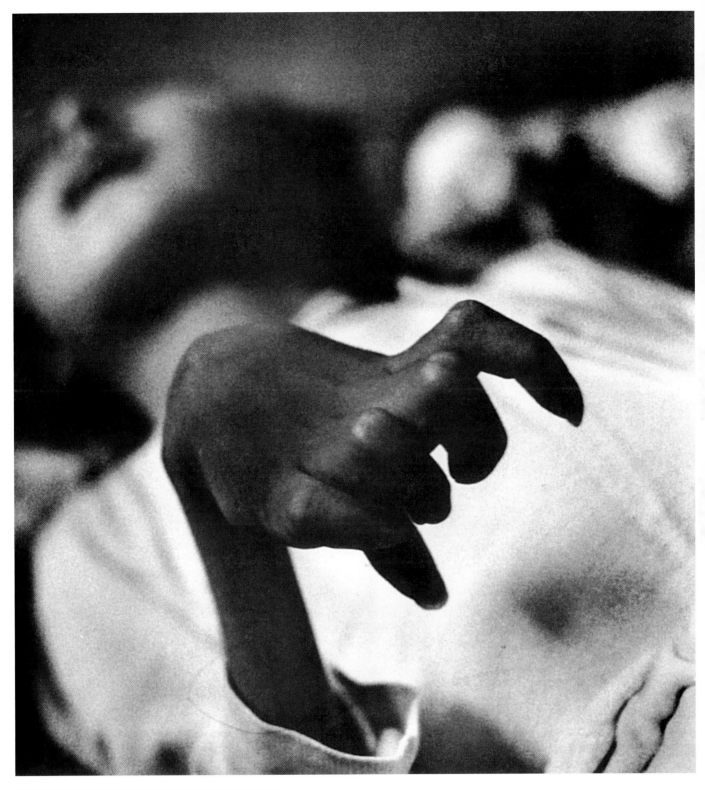

FIGURE 8.6

A woman involved in domestic violence and upset about its effects on her children receives counseling in an impromptu hallway session.

© 1991 Donna Ferrato/Domestic Abuse Awareness, Inc. (NYC)/from the book *Living With the Enemy* (Aperture)

FIGURE 8.7

An eight-year-old boy points and screams at his father as the man is arrested by Minneapolis police for attacking his wife.

© 1991 Donna Ferrato/Domestic Abuse Awarwness, Inc. (NYC)/from the book *Living With the Enemy* (Aperture)

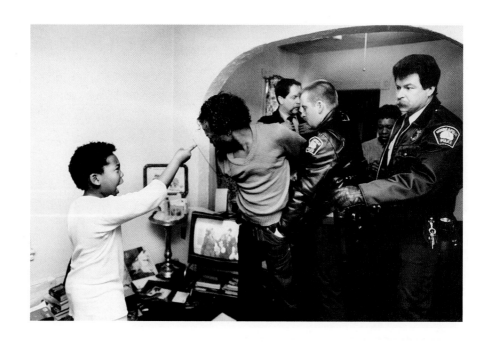

Craig F. Walker

A few weeks ago I stumbled into a casual conversation at work. A reporter asked me, "Has a photo assignment ever changed your life?" I shrugged it off with "Yeah, probably," ducking out of the discussion.

Meanwhile, his off-the-cuff question stirred up thoughts and emotions I thought I had put behind me.

Four years ago our health reporter was doing a profile on a woman who was HIV positive. The woman, Eileen, didn't want to be photographed. After a conversation she agreed to a silhouette. When I met her I expressed that the story would have more impact if there were honest photographs to accompany it. She turned me down cold and I shot the silhouette.

That was the day I decided that I was going to do a photo story on HIV and AIDS in Berkshire County [Massachusetts]. While the stories we had run in the past had been strong and well-written, they lacked the visual contact that draws the reader into the story and molds a relationship with the subject. I began by contacting local support groups in the area and asked them to offer the idea to group members. Not surprisingly, there was no interest. Having worked in small communities for most of my career I've found that people don't always jump up and volunteer when it comes to sharing their private lives. Especially when it comes to an issue as large as AIDS. Over the next few years I would call the group leaders every few months and ask them to bring the topic up again.

The last time I called with the request I hung up the phone and laughed [out of frustration]. Ready to give up, I decided that it was just too small an area and nobody wanted to be put in the spotlight. A week later the phone rang. It was Eileen and she wanted to talk about the possibility of doing a

story. Entering her home the first time, I was taken aback. It frightened me to see how her body had deteriorated since I first met her. The 40-year-old divorced mother was in the final stages of AIDS, bed-ridden and preparing to die.

We met twice before she agreed to the project. She decided

FIGURE 8.8

"A mother fights AIDS," photographs and story by Craig F. Walker, page design by Craig F. Walker and Grier Horner.
THE BERKSHIRE EAGLE, PITTSFIELD, MASS.

to let her story be told because she felt there was a great deal of ignorance about AIDS in the local community. She wanted to help people and hoped that her death might teach others to live. All she asked was that the story not be published until after she died and her two boys Keith, 10, and Ray, 8, had left the area (to live with an aunt).

The next hurdle was selling the idea to the editors. It seemed that there was not a great deal of enthusiasm toward another story about AIDS. After conversation with my photo editor, Charles Bo-

nenti, we made the decision to focus more on the boys and how their mother's dying was affecting them.

I was amazed by how she and her family accepted me. At first I planned on introducing a reporter to do the story, but a month into it Eileen's health took a turn for the worse. Unsure how much longer Eileen would be with us, I realized I would be writing the text myself. I had already established a strong relationship with Eileen and to try to bring in a third party at that point would have been difficult. Fortunately I

had been recording all our conversations and taking notes from the start.

Over the next six months I developed a strong relationship with Eileen and the boys. I also experienced some ups and downs; missing an important picture was sometimes devastating. There were conflicts at times, including one with Eileen's father, who occasionally cared for the boys. The boys, who didn't spend a great deal of time together, were supposed to be doing their homework. With a good bit of hostility the younger, Ray, refused. Ray

FIGURE 8.8 *CONTINUED*

then received a dose of threats and demands from his grandfather. This was the first time I ever saw Keith show concern for his younger brother. He sat Ray down and helped him with his homework so that there would be no reason for the grandfather to follow through with his threats. They worked quietly for a while and I thought this would make a nice moment. This was when I received my own share of threats and demands from Eileen's father. He said that the boys were quiet and if I started taking pictures it would disrupt everything. I disagreed and reminded him that Eileen had given an OK for me to photograph whatever happens. His reply was, "When I'm here I'm in charge." I could see the stress of the ordeal on his face. With Eileen asleep I had nowhere to turn. So I left. That picture wasn't extremely important but the situation made me realize that Eileen needed to explain her wishes to her family again. There were going to be times when Eileen wouldn't be able to speak for herself. While I don't think Eileen's father ever agreed with what I was doing, he eventually understood and we became friends.

My boss gave me as much time as he could, but as is often the case, it never seemed to be enough. I found myself spending a good portion of my free time at their home. I'd often go through a visit without even taking a picture. A lot of time was spent just sitting next to Eileen's bed listening to her talk about her life, her children, her hopes and her prayers.

The final weeks were extremely hard on the family. Most lived out of state and were trying to balance their own family life with being there for Eileen. Stress levels and emotions were running

high. This is when the photography became difficult and I was thankful I had a Leica. [The Leica rangefinder used by Walker is smaller and quieter than a single-lens reflex and therefore less intrusive.] My presence seemed to be hard enough on them; I didn't want my photography to be any more noticeable than was needed.

Eileen was an incredibly strong woman. When it seemed inevitable that she was going to die, she hung on for a few more days. She died on a Thursday when no

family could be there except her father, and then she waited for him to leave the room before passing on.

Then I had to hope that the family would respect Eileen's wishes and let me finish the story. At the wake I only entered the viewing room to pay my respects. I made my picture from the hallway. That evening family and friends seemed a little looser and I was able to move easily through a candlelight vigil. My closing picture was of Ray laughing while

FIGURE 8.8 *CONTINUED*

lifting his older brother over his shoulder during the funeral reception. To me it said that there is hope, and in the long run these two kids will be all right.

After it was all over I was mentally, emotionally and physically drained. When I sat back and thought about what I had just experienced it dawned on me that I now had an incredible responsibility. Eileen had opened up her life to me, she had shown me an amazing story, and now I wanted to turn the last seven months of documenting it into a piece that Eileen could have read and been proud of.

My biggest fear was the text. So before I even thought about picture editing I locked myself in my apartment, with a pen and pad, for three days and wrote the story. I don't do a great deal of writing for the paper so I was surprised at how it just seemed to flow. Being a photographer I wrote in a visual manner, making close observations about the environment, describing with detail the interaction between Eileen and her family and using a lot of quotes to let the subjects tell the story. When I emerged I had more than 100 inches that I was very proud of.

I knew the associate editor, Grier Horner, liked it when he suggested turning it into a two-part series that started on page 1 and jumped inside to two open pages both days. Picture editing was basically easy until it got down to the final 20 but decisions had to be made and everything fell into place. Sixteen pictures ran in all. When laying out the pages I ran into an interesting conflict. As is often the case there didn't seem to be enough space. This is when I would usually say cut the text, only I wrote it.

At publication I was pretty nervous about reader reaction.

FIGURE 8.8 *CONTINUED*

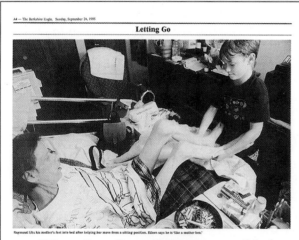

I've found that, for the most part, the people who don't like a story are the ones who call and let you know. Happily surprised, I received countless positive comments from readers and co-workers and a good number of letters to the editor from people who appreciated the story and looked at it as a learning tool. In fact, I never heard a single negative comment.

Overall, it was incredibly painful to watch the boys cope with the fact that their mother was dying. Yet at the same time it was inspiring to watch an 80-pound, bed-ridden woman keep control of herself and her family.

Besides the massive amount of information that I absorbed about HIV and AIDS, I also learned a great deal about what a family is and what it means to live and what it means to die. I've been for-tunate that I've yet to experience a death in my own family. I think my time with Eileen may have given me an idea about what to expect.

So in answer to that reporter's question, yes, there was a photo assignment that changed my life.

Craig F. Walker, "7 months with AIDS: photos change his life," *News Photographer*, February 1996, pp. 41, 44–45.

Author's note: Craig Walker now is a photographer with *The Denver Post.*

---

layouts may be done by picture editors or full-time designers. If the photographer who took the pictures is not doing the layout, the photographer may participate in the process, with the final say most likely resting with the picture editor or designer.

Picture stories in newspapers appear in the regular paper as well as in special sections and in newspapers' Sunday magazines. A selection of four picture stories of varying lengths appears here (Figures 8.9 to 8.12). Whether a page or multiple pages, each in its own way communicates more than a single picture and almost always more than a picture group. Taken as a whole, each picture story says more than its individual pictures viewed separately.

Every serious-minded photojournalist should tactfully encourage editors and photo managers to embrace the picture story form; when a subject demands photo essay treatment—and this is not often—you should tactfully encourage management to give you a commitment for the time and resources you need to follow this intriguing and challenging form.

Picture taking is immensely satisfying. But even more satisfying is creating the entire communications package. Usually, the nature of journalism does not allow photographers to take pictures, write the accompanying text, and weave both into a design seen by readers. The picture story page is a glorious exception at some newspapers.

A lot of information chases after a small amount of newspaper space. If you can, make an early arrangement with the appropriate editor for space in a good place on a good day—the beginning of a section in a Sunday paper, for instance. Your excitement and enthusiasm about your story will help others feel the same way and can lead to better placement.

In picture stories—and their more lengthy kin, photo essays—the relationship of words and pictures is critically important. Successful communication depends on everything working together: all the photos must relate to each other, the text, and the page design, including unused space, which can be at least as important as space that is filled.

Picture stories are everywhere. Ideas for them come from:

- Personal knowledge
- Minor and major stories in newspapers and magazines
- Press releases sent to newspapers and magazines
- Television, Internet, and radio reports
- Friends, relatives, and acquaintances
- Other staff members

One advantage of being a good reporter and writer in addition to being a photographer is that you are able to write the text for a picture story. This helps ensure precise communication to readers. Sharing a picture story with another person means turning over to someone else significant control of

FIGURE 8.9

"The longest days."
PHOTOGRAPHS BY DAVID
LANE/*THE PALM BEACH
POST*

Rob Brown pulls a handcart up a hill.

Water from a Martin County fire truck provides relief from the heat.

Marquelle Watson wipes away sweat as she and Mila Possobon rest by a wagon. Several babies were born and died during the trek in 1847; Watson's doll represents one of those babies.

The longest days

Teens get a taste of pioneer hardships on Mormon pilgrimage

Photos by DAVID LANE
Palm Beach Post Staff Photographer
Story by SALLY D. SWARTZ
Palm Beach Post Staff Writer

The 70 Mormon teens were up at dawn, carrying their heavy sandbag "babies," and pushing their homemade handcarts along the sandy forest trails in the DuPuis Reserve near Indiantown.

"It was hot," said Bethany Rane, "really, really hot."

But the sunburn and mosquito bites, the fatigue and the blisters of a two-day, 16-mile hike gave the teenagers a taste of what their religion's early faithful experienced on a 1,300-mile pilgrimage to Utah 150 years ago.

An equal number of adults helped with the trek, putting on skits and reading from real accounts of the hardships the pioneers encountered. The modern day trekkers had the benefit of plenty of water, prepared meals and games before they bedded down in tents at night.

The "babies," made of three eggs nestled in 10-lb. bags of sand, were assigned to a "mother" in each group. The teens took turns carrying the "baby," and if the eggs broke, burial services were held. Four of seven survived the trip.

"I could really feel for those women who had to bury their babies along the way and just keep walking," Rane said. The trip ended in a cool cloudburst, and the 14- to 18-year-olds returned to their homes in Palm Beach, Martin, St. Lucie and Indian River counties.

Rane's father Blake said the trek was a success. "We wanted to take history and make it come alive," he said. "I think we did that."

After an exhausting day on the trail, David Beers, Ian Nipper and Andrew Young (above) seek rest in hammocks.

Flashlights and lanterns light the many tents (left) as campers prepare for sleep.

FIGURE 8.10

"The Livin' Is Easy."
PHOTOGRAPHS BY ERIC ALBRECHT/THE COLUMBUS (OHIO) DISPATCH. REPRINTED WITH PERMISSION FROM THE COLUMBUS DISPATCH.

Page 6C · Saturday, July 22, 1995

The Columbus Dispatch / **METRO**

THE LIVIN' IS EASY

Story by Francisco Duque
Dispatch Staff Reporter

Photos by Eric Albrecht
Dispatch Staff Photographer

Taylor Mooney searches for tadpoles and other pond inhabitants.

Ashley boys fond of Grandma's pond

ASHLEY, Ohio — For Brandon and Taylor Mooney, visiting Grandma's on hot summer days is a splash.

The children, usually with friends, make a habit of riding over on bicycles and cooling off in the pond that sits about 50 yards from Sarah Bennett's home.

"They're out here every day," said Bennett, 59, who has lived at 6172 Rt. 229 for 32 years.

The spring-fed, 1-acre pond was dug out 26 years ago, Bennett said. Today, willow trees shade part of the shore.

Swimming is allowed only when Bennett is home. On a recent afternoon, she sat near the steel-blue water and watched the children play.

Brandon, 14, went home early, leaving behind Taylor, 12, and friends Steven Bennett, 13; Jeff Bennett, 10; Jason Mathews, 15; and Eli Harper, 14.

Sarah Bennett's German shepherd, Brie, playfully chased the boys as they swung from ropes and hit the water.

Along the sandy shore underneath a willow tree, the boys dug out a 1-foot hole where water had seeped. They dipped their feet into the muddy water and took time to admire the results.

Soon they returned to the swings. One, a single rope, suspends from a tree branch; the other is attached to a metal frame that rises above the water's edge. Daniel Bennett, Bennett's son and Taylor and Brandon's uncle, installed the contraptions.

After an hour of swimming and playing, Taylor had a minor complaint: "The water cools you off almost too much."

The boys later chased a turtle they spotted on the far shore.

Taylor has a penchant for catching animals — especially snakes — and keeping them. To discourage the boy from bringing too many "pets" into the house, his father built a clubhouse in their backyard where his son stores the creatures.

Bennett's husband, Joe, died in 1978. He was a former fire chief in Ashley.

Her property covers 10.5 acres, but "I mow 3 acres," she said. The rest she rents as farmland.

For the children, the pond is the property's prize.

They watched as their friend Eli swung from the rope, flew briefly in the summer air, then belly-flopped into the water.

With his friend Eli Harper keeping watch onshore, Brandon Mooney lets loose at his grandmother's pond in Ashley, Ohio. Grandma is Sarah Bennett of 6172 Rt. 229.

Taylor's catch of the day

ABOVE: Steven Bennett, a friend of the Mooney brothers and no relation to their grandma, positions himself to swing from a tree into the pond.
LEFT: Steven gets airborne.

THE CHILDREN, usually with friends, make a habit of riding over on bicycles and cooling off in the pond that sits about 50 yards from Sarah Bennett's home.

what readers get from the story. If you must share the story with a reporter or writer, make a great effort to see that this person shares your approach.

Whether you are working with a reporter or alone, you should be familiar with the subject before you leave the office. If the subject is a person, consult the clips (previously published stories). Pick the minds of reporters who have covered the person. When setting up an appointment in person or by telephone, try in a low-key way to find out a little more about the person—perhaps his interests and monthly activities. If the subject is a thing—a factory, for example—try to have at least a passing familiarity with the way it works, how its product is produced, and its importance to society,

particularly the economy. Take great care to ensure the subject or your contact knows how much time you need for the story. Stories typically require at least a day to shoot; often you need more time. Expect subjects to be surprised at this and perhaps unwilling to give so much time. Explain why you need the time—the story is serious, and complete coverage demands time to do things right. You should also seek appropriate time from the photo department head.

If you can determine the overall story approach before photographing and reporting, you can save time. If the subject is inherently visually exciting, perhaps you need only a short text block and captions. If the subject is not visually exciting or does not lend itself to visual treatment, perhaps a long story with accompanying pictures is the way to go. The subject may be appropriate for a question-and-answer format.

You must also select the most appropriate medium—all black and white, all color, or a mixture. This is a critical decision. The same subject portrayed in color communicates differently to readers than it does in black and white or a mixture. The subject and the nature of the story should be significant determining factors in your decision. Always consult with the editor running the story to make sure she is in agreement with your proposed approach.

If you are not writing the story, work closely with the writer. After you finish photographing consider giving the writer a memo about how you see the story. You probably will want to discuss what you see as key photographs and to include any important text-related information you obtained. Rather than doing a memo, you may prefer to talk with the writer.

Use no more equipment than you need to do the story. Two or three cameras with no more than four lenses (or equivalent zooms)—a wide-angle, short telephoto, medium-long telephoto, and a close-up lens—ought to get the job done without interfering with it. However, always have other lenses available—a super wide-angle and a long telephoto for example—in case the

FIGURE 8.11

"Saving Benjamin."

Photographs by Lance Murphey, story by Teresa Araque and Lance Murphey, page design by Lance Murphey/*Naples* (Fla.) *Daily News*

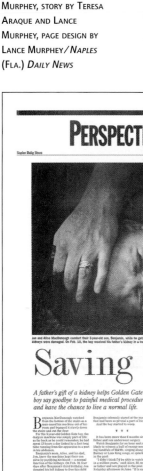

story demands their use. A small notebook, a ballpoint pen and a tape recorder with two 90-minute tapes typically are enough to gather information. Be sure to ask the subject's permission to tape record, both as a courtesy to the subject and to avoid running afoul of laws against surreptitious tape recording. If you want to record over the telephone, be sure to ask permission to avoid violating state and federal wiretapping laws. Clearly label each tape with the subject's name and the time and date of the recording. Take notes that are legible back at the office.

Approach picture stories from a situational point of view, not individual pic-

tures. Doing this helps assure balanced coverage. It also means that when it is time to design the page, the designer has images available that let the story flow in a logical and orderly way. It is easy to get carried away with portraying one visually exciting situation to the exclusion of other storytelling situations; you must avoid this.

Subjects unaccustomed to photojournalists often are leery and uncertain of themselves; they may retreat to a formal mode that can disguise who they really are and how they may really feel. The photojournalist's job is to remove this mask by making the subject feel comfortable. Hotshot photojournalists

FIGURE 8.11 *CONTINUED*

full of self-importance stand little chance of penetrating this barrier. A laid-back attitude of "you're important, and I am here to listen to you, to find out about you and what you do" can help. Genuine interest in the subject is essential to successfully acting as a conduit through which truthful information fairly represented passes to readers. Here is where the importance of planning the logistics before your appointment becomes evident. A rushed pho-

FIGURE 8.12

"Remarried . . . with children."

PHOTOGRAPHS BY APRIL SAUL/THE INQUIRER MAGAZINE, THE PHILADELPHIA INQUIRER

Remarried...
with children

On a visit, Craig and Keith bombard their father (above left), and get in a little Nintendo (above right). The boys haven't warmed quickly to their stepparents, but Diana, playing with Keith, says, "It's got to be natural, not forced." For July Fourth fireworks (below), Frank's two kids (right) trekked down from North Jersey.

At Nicole's elementary-school graduation, Frank ran the camera while Mari-Lynn and Alan chatted. The two men get along quite well — Alan had even asked Frank to be his best man. Frank declined, however, because Mari-Lynn and Diana don't speak.

FIGURE 8.12 *CONTINUED*

tojournalist stands little chance of making a subject feel comfortable and getting through to who the person really is.

If you have only a day to do the complete picture story—gather information for the text and captions and take the photographs—here is how it might go.

When you first arrive, the so-called walk-around is important. Forget about taking pictures for now. Let people talk about themselves and show what they do—a painter her paintings, an industrialist his factory, a banker her bank, a farmer his field. This is a good time to record what subjects are saying if they have no objection to being taped. You may want to explain that the tape recorder is an electronic pencil and that you use it to ensure accuracy and completeness. Offering to give a copy of the tape to people who balk at being taped may remove their reservations. After all, you cannot tape without the subject's cooperation. If taping is out of the question, take notes. The walk-around also offers the opportunity for the sub-

ject to become familiar with you.

The walk-around is a good time to get what journalists call *color*—what the subject and the place look like, smell like, act like. The walk-around is also useful for finding specific picture situations.

Remain laid-back after the walk-around. Perhaps now is a good time to suggest a break, but do not request anything more elaborate than a glass of water; asking for a soft drink or anything else is impolite—wait till someone offers. If you are taping and the person does not object, put the machine near the person to ensure optimum sound. Use care not to turn the volume up so high that background noise drowns out the subject.

After the break is a good time to talk in-depth with the subject. Although basic facts are important, always be alert for little tidbits that will allow you to tell a story that readers can become involved in. Through the words and pictures readers need to see what you saw, feel what you felt, learn what you learned.

When you are ready to take pictures, keep in mind the page design of the story; shoot horizontals and verticals of the same scene so that page design is not limited before it begins. Be sure to record an establishing image, one that shows geographically what the story is about—for example, the never-ending spread of a Western ranch. Include long, medium, and close images. Record small details with a close-up lens. Decide the images you want to capture before you activate the camera. What the photographer sees in the camera's viewfinder an instant before the scene is recorded is what readers should see; cropping of photographs should be done before they are taken, if at all possible. Realistically, however, you will find it is sometimes impossible to avoid cropping after taking the picture. For example, perhaps you could not get as close to the subject as you would have liked and even your longest telephoto lens could not get you there.

How-to aspects of stories—the steps in the making of a product, for example—often can be told well through picture series treatment. Although the how-to of industrial stories is important, emotions can humanize these stories as they do all stories. Excitement and involvement exist in an industrial story as well as in those about personalities. Whatever your subject, budget your picture-taking time. Do not spend so much time on one situation that you cannot cover others adequately. Spend a little time toward the end of the day methodically going through the situations to be sure you have not missed any. Budget an hour at the end of the shoot to recoup missed images or to picture unanticipated situations. Also allow at least 30 minutes to finish caption information gathering. Complete and in-depth caption information is a must. This also is a good time to get information the subject may have—handouts, family pictures, previous articles—that helps in preparing the story.

Subjects often say something particularly meaningful or colorful—a good quote—during picture taking. Interrupt your shooting and record the information, either on tape or paper.

Once you have completed the fieldwork, transcribe your tapes as soon as possible, preferably within a few days. Although someone else could do the transcription, doing it yourself helps ensure accuracy in difficult-to-understand statements and helps ensure everything is in perspective. You should also enter written notes into the computer while they are fresh in your mind. Next, view all images from each situation together and choose images you want to offer for use. Choose enough photos to make page design easier, and try to choose both horizontals and verticals. Always remember that a picture story's fundamental value is in what it communicates as a package.

When photographs and text are ready, page design can begin. Overdesigning is as bad or worse than underdesigning. The goal in page design is to arrange all the elements to support and enhance each other to best tell the story. The reader should be able to follow the story without interference from the design. The page must communicate the story with ease and grace.

Contemporary one-page newspaper picture stories tend to follow a clear design pattern: One picture, typically of the main subject, played large and toward the middle of the page, with other pictures played smaller. The largest photograph may show human emotion or may be a key storytelling image. Captions appear beneath each picture or in one or more groups near their related images. White space, which is an area of the page without design elements, is a design element in its own right. However, too much white space detracts from communication or can become dead space, detracting from the story.

Picture stories and their much longer and more involved kin, photo essays, allow photojournalists to get beyond the usual picture fare of daily newspapers. These forms give photographers an opportunity to explore in depth the "why" in a story as well as convey the "what" and "where." They offer photojournalists a chance to plumb life as deeply as contemporary newspapers and magazines allow.

W. Eugene Smith's "Spanish Village" is reproduced here as readers saw it in the April 9, 1951, issue of *LIFE,* which described it as a "pictorial essay" (Figure 8.13). Whatever name you give it—photo essay, picture story, or pictorial essay—it is superb coverage of the old village of Deleitosa. According to the text, Smith "found that its ways had advanced little since medieval times."[3]

As you look closely at "Spanish Village," note how the photographs interplay with each other and the text. The first image is a full page, the last is two pages, and at the beginning of the story is a relatively small image that gives an overall idea of what the village looks like. Note the placement of captions in relation to the images, and how the design uses empty—white—space, and how the white space relates to other elements of the layout. If you were laying out "Spanish Village," how would you do it? Do large pictures represent more important situations, or are they particularly eye-catching, or both? Would it make sense to put the funeral photograph that closes the essay at the beginning? What—and how good—is Smith's picture-taking technique?

After you finish with "Spanish Village," let's spend some time exploring in-depth the design of one-page picture stories. Leslie White is a photo editor for *The Dallas Morning News* who has been nationally recognized for her picture story designs. Here she shares her approach and technical design techniques. All the design examples presented in her piece are hers.

ON THE OUTSKIRTS
At midmorning the sun beats down on clustered stone houses. In the distance is belfry of Deleitosa's church.

Spanish Village

IT LIVES IN ANCIENT POVERTY AND FAITH

The village of Deleitosa, a place of about 2,300 peasant people, sits on the high, dry, western Spanish tableland called Estremadura, about halfway between Madrid and the border of Portugal. Its name means "delightful," which it no longer is, and its origins are obscure, though they may go back a thousand years to Spain's Moorish period. In any event it is very old and LIFE Photographer Eugene Smith, wandering off the main road into the village, found that its ways had advanced little since medieval times.

Many Deleitosans have never seen a railroad because the nearest one is 25 miles away. The Madrid-Sevilla highway passes Deleitosa seven miles to the north, so almost the only automobiles it sees are a dilapidated sedan and an old station wagon, for hire at prices few villagers can afford. Mail comes in by burro. The nearest telephone is 12½ miles away in another town. Deleitosa's water system still consists of the sort of aqueducts and open wells from which villagers have drawn their water for centuries. Except for the local doctor's portable tin bathtub there is no trace of any modern sanitation, and the streets smell strongly of the villagers' donkeys and pigs.

There are a few signs of the encroachment of the 20th Century in Deleitosa. In the city hall, which is run by political subordinates of the provincial governor, one typewriter clatters. A handful of villagers, including the mayor, own their own small radio sets. About half of the 800 homes of the village are dimly lighted after dark by weak electric-light bulbs which dangle from ancient ceilings. And a small movie theater, which shows some American films, sits among the sprinkling of little shops near the main square. But the village scene is dominated now as always by the high, brown structure of the 16th Century church, the center of society in Catholic Deleitosa. And the lives of the villagers are dominated as always by the bare and brutal problems of subsistence. For Deleitosa, barren of history, unfavored by nature, reduced by wars, lives in poverty—a poverty shared by nearly all and relieved only by the seasonal work of the soil, and the faith that sustains most Deleitosans from the hour of First Communion (*opposite page*) until the simple funeral (*pp. 128, 129*) that marks one's end.

FIRST COMMUNION DRESS
Lorenza Curiel, 7, is a right for her young neighbors as she waits for her mother to lock door, take her to church.

PHOTOGRAPHED FOR LIFE BY W. EUGENE SMITH

120

FIGURE 8.13 *CONTINUED*

FIGURE 8.13 *CONTINUED*

Leslie White, photo editor, *The Dallas Morning News*

Editing and designing a picture story can be one of the most rewarding enterprises in newspaper photojournalism. It is one of the last bastions of near total control of picture size and selection by the photo department in the modern newspaper.

Picture stories, whether designed by a photo editor, a photographer or as a joint effort between the two, allow the photojournalist dominion over the picture selection as the method to tell the story.

General Aspects of Picture Selection   The first step in a successful picture story design is understanding the story the photographer intends to tell. Ideally, the photo editor as designer must do his or her best to protect the vision of the photographer. That happens best when the two discuss the story from the outset and work together as a team.

Working together from the beginning gives both the designer/photo editor and the photographer an equal stake in the outcome of the picture story. Once the photographer has completed the shooting phase of the story, the editing process begins in earnest. The photo editor and the photographer should begin by completely revisiting the entire shoot. Going over the film in detail will gel the idea of what the most important aspects of the story are. At this point in the process, the edit will most often be narrowed down to a somewhat still generous number of photos, anywhere from 7 to 12 images for a single-page story. Although it is a virtual certainty that all of the

images will not make the final edit, it will be helpful in that process to have either prints or digital images to select from. The result of this extra work will be worth it in the telling of the story.

The photo editor and the photographer have now reached one of the most critical points in the evolution of their picture story. Now the photo editor/designer takes on the majority of the responsibility as the story gets closer to publication. A good photographer will make it difficult for the photo editor to choose between images. A good editor knows that it must be done. In the case of a story, it is important not only to choose the best images but also images that work together to tell the story.

Choosing a Lede   Choosing the correct lede photo is the logical first step and the most important one in a successful picture story. The lede photo must serve as the signature photo of the story. In most cases it should be an "eye burner" and in all cases it should serve as a strong entry point that brings the reader into the page. Lede is a spelling specific to journalists as a label for the first paragraph of a story or the largest image on a page.

General rules for a lede photo will differ between the three different photo story types: news, sports, and feature. For example, in a news page, the lede is most often an informational photo that should include a strong dramatic or emotional aspect. In a sports page, it can be an image of an important turning point in the game, or just as often it includes power-

ful emotions such as jubilation or defeat.

The feature story has much more latitude in the selection of a lede, which has both advantages and disadvantages for the photo editor/designer. One advantage is the chance for more creativity in telling the story, but there are dangers as well especially when compared with a news or sports story. The latter types have a sort of "reader saturation" advantage. That is, when the reader gets inside the paper to the news or sports picture page, he or she usually knows from other media the outcome of the big game or of the tragic losses in a fire, for example. The prior knowledge of the event helps the reader enter the subject with a degree of familiarity and interest. In the feature story, selection of the lede is critically important to attract readers.

The best tip in choosing a lede for a feature story is to go for the most storytelling photo available, which ideally contains an emotion-provoking element. And although it may be tempting to choose a tight well-lit dramatic portrait as a lede, it is better to stay away from it. Very few faces are interesting enough to tell a subject's whole story. Portraits work best in picture stories as complementary photos. It is important to remember that the page is being designed for the reader's comprehension and viewing pleasure.

By the time the photo editor/designer and the photographer choose a lede, they have probably looked through the images many times. Perceptions of the story—especially on the part of the photographer—can be clouded by how difficult certain images were to get. Each should try to bring a fresh eye toward the story and select with that in mind.

Narrowing Down the Selections Just as in the process of choosing a lede photo, there are general rules of thumb for complementary photos (generally, the other three to five images on a page that are not the lede but help tell the story). Keep in mind that it is difficult, if not impossible, to get more than six photos attractively on a page. In fact, it is more usual to use four to five images. It is at this stage of the selection process that the "rules" specific to picture stories come into play.

The first rule is that picture stories must have a beginning, a middle, and an end. All successful picture pages hold true to the rule. However, photo editors and designers who practice sophisticated photo usage know that they need not take the rule literally. Often, the geographical placement of photographs on the page can add to readers' perception of "beginning and end" with the beginning at the top and the end at the bottom of the page. The lede photo most often serves as one of the "middle" photos.

The beginning photo is informational and straightforward in nature. Its purpose is to add information not included in the eye-burner lede photo. Adding to its traditional position in the "timeline" of the story, the image was logically made before the peak action occurred. In feature stories about an individual, it may often be a tight portrait. It is currently in vogue to use it cleverly played off of a styled headline treatment (Figure 8.14, *The First 24 Hours*, and Figure 8.15, *Uganda: The Faces of AIDS* and *Mud, Sweat & Cheers*).

The middle photos make up the meat of the story. The bulk of the images in a picture story usually fall into this category. These photos can contain any and every type of image known in photojournalism. The only rule is that they must add dimension to the story.

The ender, as it is commonly known, brings the story to a logical stopping place, the end of the story. The reader should feel a sense of completion or the end of a cycle or an event. Try to stay away from the obvious (sunsets, and the like) if possible. Go for the thought provoking.

Another common rule in picture stories is to vary lens selection in your choice of photographs. The rule should also include varying the content as well. Don't be literal when selecting the support photos, feeling you have to include a wide angle shot, a telephoto, and the like. Include the photos that best tell the

George W. Bush's first hours on the job Tuesday as Texas' 46th governor were filled with ceremony. After the inauguration event in Austin came celebrations with family, friends and supporters. Morning brought his first full day in the office.

Uganda
THE FACES OF AIDS
MUD, SWEAT & CHEERS

Participants celebrate the successful crossing of Lake Peten Itza in northern Guatemala.

Daphne Green of the U.S. team continued despite a badly sprained ankle.

FIGURE 8.15

Beginning Photopackaging.
UGANDA PHOTOGRAPH BY WILLIAM SNYDER; GUATEMALA PHOTOGRAPHS BY ERICH SCHLEGEL; DESIGN BY LESLIE WHITE *THE DALLAS MORNING NEWS*

story. But never, never have two photographs on the page "say" the same thing, in matters of literal or emotional content. A good writer would never include two separate paragraphs in a story that provide the same information because he or she thought of another clever way to write it. As photojournalists, we must hold ourselves to the same strict standard. The edit should be tight with an eye toward variety and information in the images.

There is also a rule commonly held that a detail shot (a tight close-up of an object or a body part, such as face or hands) is required in picture stories. Include a detail shot only if it is worthy on its own merit and germane to the story.

Let's take an in-depth look at *Jenny's Story* (Figure 8.16) and *Scenes from a Revolution* (Figure 8.17).

Jenny is a little girl with cancer, struggling to deal with both her adolescence and her illness. Figure 8.16A is a quiet moment captured by the photographer in one of the rare times she goes without a bandana to hide her baldness. Figure 8.16B is of Jenny at school. Figure 8.16C is of Jenny on her way out of the hospital carrying her younger brother after completing one of her treatments.

The best choice for a lede of the three images is of Jenny at school. It tells us that Jenny is both ill (most young girls would not wear a bandana to school) and that she feels isolated from her peers by the physical distance she puts between them. It is also very horizontal and needs the larger size to "read" well on the page (readability in photographs relates to how much information is included in an image—the more detail an image has, the more size it needs to visually communicate its information). The other two photos work better as support photos. The portrait would be a nice "beginning" photo, introducing us to Jenny. Figure 8.16C would work wonderfully as an "ender." The view of the hospital in the background reminds the reader of her illness; the fact that Jenny is strong enough to carry her brother on her back ends the story with a feeling of hope (Figure 8.16D).

Scenes from a Revolution (Figure 8.17) documents the lives of the farmers in Chiapas, Mexico immediately after a 1994 skirmish between rebel forces and the Mexican army. Figure 8.17A does

an excellent job of portraying civilian reaction to the occupation of a farming town by the Mexican Army. Figure 8.17B is a group of women crying as a baby lays dying after the mother gave birth

FIGURE 8.16

Jenny's Story.
PHOTOGRAPHS BY ARIANE KADOCH, DESIGN BY LESLIE WHITE, *THE DALLAS MORNING NEWS*

A

B

C

D

prematurely due to the stress of avoiding the fighting. Figure 8.17C is a portrait of a girl made while her parents were deciding whether to evacuate their home to avoid further chances of conflict.

Figure 8.17B would make the strongest lede photo for the page for several reasons (Figure 8.17D). It is an extremely emotional photo that would make an incredible impact on the feelings of the readers. It calls attention to the fact that not only the rebel forces and the Mexican army are dying for a cause; innocents are dying too. The photo also needs to be large to "read," to have impact on the page.

Figure 8.17A would work best as the "beginning" photo by placing the reader in the middle of the conflict. While the soldiers take the foreground, the farmer in the background hints at how the lives of the civilians are suddenly

A

B

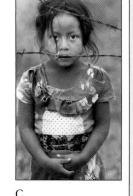

C

FIGURE 8.17

Scenes From a Revolution.
PHOTOGRAPHS BY PAT DAVISON, DESIGN BY LESLIE WHITE, *THE DALLAS MORNING NEWS*

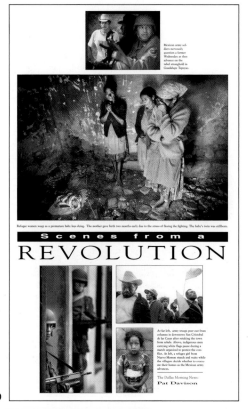

D

overtaken in a practical way by the opposing forces. Figure 8.17C works best as a support photo. The child's contemplative, serious expression hints at the stress that has run through her community. This photo also could be an effective ender.

General Aspects of Design

In picture story design, the number one rule should be less is more. The good photo editor/designer will build an uncluttered "clean" page that adds to the storyline and features solid photojournalism, never his or her own cleverness.

At this point in the process, the designer should have a clear vision of the effect each selected photo will have in telling the story. The designer should have also come to an understanding with the photographer regarding why certain pictures will be used and how.

The lede photo is the anchor of the page. It should be placed first with maximum effect and display in mind. It should clearly be the largest image on the page. The most common position for the lede is in the middle area of the page, although the top is also customary. It would be unusual for the lede to be at the bottom, but not necessarily incorrect. In that situation, the lede should probably be the "ender" photo.

All the complementary photos should be built around the lede image—the dominant picture on the page. The most important factors to keep in mind about the placement of complementary photos are the sizes they need to be to "read" and their logical positions in the timeline of the story.

Often the designer will have to adjust his or her perception of the design in favor of the natural telling of the story. Make no mistake—in the design of the picture story, the photographs come first, the layout second. This means that no matter the design concern, the ender must be at the logical end of the story and must have the size it needs to read well.

Basic Design Rules and The Picture Story

There are many approaches to picture story design and all have their merits. Modular layout is used in most newspaper section fronts and easily applicable to picture page design. Modular design can provide a framework for attractive photo placement. Basically, modular layout requires elements to be squared-off and rectangular with uniform spaces between columns. This method seems to allow the reader's eye to go from image to image with little effort. The layout is clean, simple, and as pleasing to the eye of the designer as to the reader.

Constructive use of white space (a place on the page with no photos, text, or design elements

---

FIGURE 8.18

Modular Design and Constructive Use of White Space. Note that it is possible to draw horizontal lines through sections of each layout—that is the meaning of *modular*. Also note the use of white space in the corners of all the layouts and how they balance from right side to left and sometimes diagonally.

PHOTOGRAPHS (A) BY ERICH SCHLEGEL, (B) BY JUDY WALGREN, (C) BY DAVID LEESON, (D) BY JUDY WALGREN; DESIGN BY LESLIE WHITE, *THE DALLAS MORNING NEWS*

A

B

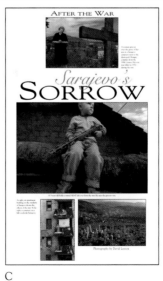

C

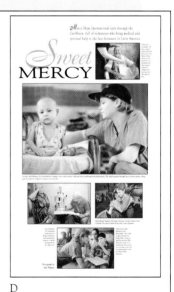

D

of any kind) is a useful tool of the picture page designer. The first and foremost rule is never trap white space (when an area of white space is caught between elements on the page). White space always must be at the outside of the design elements. It should be balanced and planned on the page (Figure 8.18A–D).

Rule lines (black lines near or against the edges of a photograph) should be narrow (.5 to 1 point). Using rules to border photographs and the page itself works as an attractive design element that adds emphasis to the images and shapes on the page. Otherwise, use them only when needed to separate elements. Remember, keep it simple.

Whether the page is color or black and white will largely fall outside the photo editor/designer's sphere of influence. If the photographer and the designer agree that the use of color is warranted by the subject matter and photos, the matter should be dis-

cussed with the editor. Often, it comes down to money; color is more expensive. It is best for a designer who works for a largely color-front newspaper to be prepared for both possibilities because things can change quickly on deadline in a newspaper environment. For example, the picture page is scheduled to run in black and white when a color advertisement is added on deadline that allows for color on an inside page. The editor normally will order color for the picture page since the advertiser in effect is paying for it. Printing or scanning color images on a deadline is a hectic and time-consuming chore. A little preparation can be its own reward in an ever-changing newsroom.

Spot color (color used on a page other than to create a full-color photograph) should be avoided on pages with black-and-white images because its effect is gimmicky.

General Type Every newspaper has a style (either written or unwritten) that dictates the different styles of type that can be used in the publication. It is for purposes of continuity that the rules exist, and they should be adhered to. Thankfully, modern

newspapers have relaxed the stricter guidelines of the past to accommodate feature and specialty pages (non-hard-news pages). That is good news for the picture page designer. So long as designers remain true to the family or families of type, they are allowed a wide latitude in styling them. For example, let us assume that a newspaper uses 9 pt. Goudy justified for body copy type throughout the newspaper in various column widths on the front page and all news pages. The feature page designer and the picture page designer are allowed to increase the size and leading (spacing between lines) of the type and create their own column widths to fit within the framework of their pages. Often, the type is used unjustified (ragged right, for example) for a less rigid look (Figure 8.19).

These specialized type treatments give readers the idea that they are looking at something out of the ordinary.

Designers typically also have liberal use of other design elements such as drop caps (a large initial letter that begins the story) and take-out quotes (a meaningful quote taken from the story and used in larger type on the page to

FIGURE 8.19

Samples of specialized type treatments.

PHOTOGRAPHS (LEFT) BY ARIANE KADOCH, (RIGHT) BY CAROLYN HERTER

Jenny Keenan was 8 years old when she was found to have cancer of the lymph nodes.
Now at 10, she is a normal child in many ways, from romping with her brothers to swinging from a rope on a tree in her Hannibal, Mo., back yard. But she has already faced a most adult reality — her own mortality. She has just completed one-and-a-half years of chemotherapy to treat grade 4 lymphoma. The cancer is in remission, but it has taken a toll on Jenny's family. Her father, a surgical technician, works 18-hour shifts three days a week so he can spend as much time with his daughter as possible. Family life revolves around Jenny because of the cancer. If she becomes ill, everything comes to a halt so she can be helped. In the words of Jenny's mother, Jerilyn, "It's either cope or collapse."

In an attempt to relive the experiences of the old West, a group of 30 cowboys herded 250 head of longhorn steers from Fort Worth to Miles City, Mont. The drive took six months and reached Miles City a few weeks ago.

draw reader interest). Another clever way to make body copy look a little more special is the use of photos partially or entirely inset into the copy. The advent of computer design has made the type styling much easier for the designer.

Caption Style Captions are another area where the picture story designer has room to bend the rules where a regular news page designer cannot. The first option the picture story designer has relates to type changes. Choices such as bold, italic, or normal type within the font family used would not be out of the question, along with slight size variations. A little larger than "style" (the size usually used on regular news pages) type may look better (.5 to 2 pt. depending on the starting size). It is a good

idea as a starting point to try a sort of reverse on the "normal" style used for captions. For example, if the captions on the news pages are in bold type, try roman type. It adds to the overall presentation that the reader is getting something special from the page.

The most common rule bent for captions on picture pages is the use of the caption block; that is, picture story designers are not required to place captions directly under each individual photo as on most regular news pages. They have the discretion to create a group caption that contains information for more than one photograph. The rule is that the caption block (group caption) should be near the images it relates to and contain directional references (i.e., above, at left) to aid the reader in quickly finding the photo they correspond to.

Photo Credits Simplicity can also make a strong statement in photo credits. Because most picture pages are the work of a single photographer, the designer has the option of doing a more sophisticated credit. The geographical placement of the credit on the page is often dictated by the style of the design.

The first rule to follow in placement is to worry about it last. No photographer, no matter how talented, should have his or her work designed around a credit. It is for that reason that photo credits usually appear at the bottom of the page. However, that is not a bad thing considering the options

FIGURE 8.20

Example of Caption and Photo Credit Style.

PHOTOGRAPHS BY ERICH SCHLEGEL, DESIGN BY LESLIE WHITE, *THE DALLAS MORNING NEWS*

This summer 40 amateur adventurers from 20 countries went to Central America to compete for the Camel Trophy, also known as the "Olympics of Four-Wheel Drive," sponsored by Land Rover. Participants crossed areas in five countries that were once part of the Mayan civilization. The purpose of the event is to test each driver's abilities as well as the vehicles'.

Two Land Rover Discoveries (above) get swallowed up by the Mopan River in Belize. At right, jungle camp is set up at dusk after a trip down the old Spanish conquistadors trail in Guatemala.

Miguel Woolmington (above) of the Canary Islands strains for a breath during the challenge on the Mopan River.

Photography by Erich Schlegel

available to the designer. Placing the credit below the photos on the bottom of the page gives the designer room for "spread-out" credit. Because type size should never be more than 14 point, the designer has the option to "track" the type (spread it out over a designated area) to draw more attention to it. Often, a .5 to 1 pt. rule line between the photos and the credit will add an element of attraction to the type that will draw the reader's eye.

Credit for designers on a page has only recently become a matter of discussion among professionals. Most newspapers choose not to do this with anything other than special sections that were unusually time intensive. (Figure 8.20 shows the use of caption style and photo credit.)

Headline Styling and Packaging

The picture page designer can show the most creativity in styling the headlines. The rest of the page is devoted to the proper display of photographs, which calls more for logic and editing than creativity on the part of the designer. Headline styling calls for inventiveness in many ways. The

FIGURE 8.21

Headline Styling and Packaging.
Photographs by Erich Schlegal, design by Leslie White, *The Dallas Morning News*

lede photo and the headline on a picture page are the two most critical elements in pulling the reader into the subject.

Designers have two options in the literal creation of the headline: write it themselves or ask a copy editor to do it. It cannot be stated strongly enough just how important the headline can be on the picture page. Sometimes, it may be the only text except for the captions. It must count. By writing the headline himself or herself, the designer can ultimately control the tone of the story and be sure it supports the photographs.

In sophisticated headline styling, especially using computers, the designer has the opportunity to personalize the treatment that the picture story gets on the page by using words and type to greatest advantage. The headline must hold the pictures together firmly and finally. As with caption and body type, the designer will likely face a few restrictions on which type can be used. However, computers and software can do amazing things with type and turn the most traditional, overused type into an elegant expression (Figure 8.21).

You can mix type in certain configurations for added emphasis. Mixing serif and sans serif type can produce a nice effect. Reversals of type (white type on black)

and shading black to gray are other options.

Packaging a headline with the beginning photo is common and is often an effective treatment (Figures 8.14, 8.15, and 8.21). With the tremendous type manipulating potential of computers, it is important to mention that it is possible to go too far. Always remember that the goal of the designer is to support the photos, not overwhelm them. The computer is merely a tool.

Computers in General Both Macintosh and PC platforms offer a selection of hardware and software that allows for sophisticated picture story design. Newspaper editors can select many options in hardware and software to customize their graphics systems for the specific needs of their publications.

Whatever the platform, computers offer the picture story designer many advantages in the construction of the page. Gone is the cropping wheel and the pencil-to-paper. Instead, the designer pulls a digital photograph directly into the blank computerized page layout. Designers can view the page exactly as it will appear, with all of the images sized correctly on the page rather than imagining them while looking at blank boxes drawn on

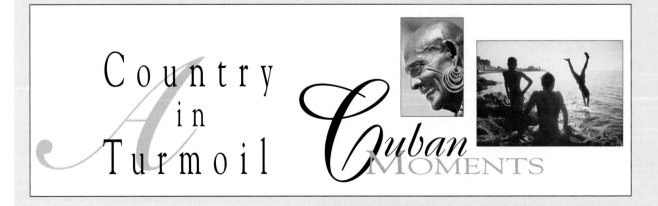

paper. The aid in picture usage decisions is immeasurable. Time-consuming operations such as laying down a rule line on a page or on the edges of a photo are now taken care of in a couple of brief keystrokes. Body copy and headlines can be runaround pictures and styled for impact with an almost ridiculous ease compared to production methods of the past.

The main advantage of using a computer is that all of the graphic elements on the page are brought together in one place and viewed in a state of completion at any point in the process.

One Newspaper's System

The Dallas Morning News's designed pages (color feature section fronts designed by professionals in the news art department) are created on Macintosh computers using the software program Quark™ (one of many page design programs available). Photographs are digitally scanned into computers using desktop film scanners or transferred from digital cameras. Adobe® Photoshop® is used to process the images.

Analyzing a Page from Top to Bottom

The page *Life on the Great American Cattle Drive* (Figure 8.22) is a good example of the design principles and recommendations for photo selection to which I referred earlier. It was chosen for its simplicity in both the photography and the design.

Choosing a Lede and Support Photos

For the sake of simplifying the discussion, let's assume that the edit has already been narrowed down to the five photographs published on the page. The edit has provided for differences in subject content and visual variety. Next, start the selection process by considering the nature of the story. It is a cattle drive, which would obviously include both the animals and cowboys to herd them.

Three photos on this page have enough information in them to legitimately consider them for the lede photo position. They are the longhorn cattle at the top, the man washing, and the men laughing. All are nice, well-composed images that could benefit from the larger size. Because this is a feature page, one photograph doesn't have any more news value than the other; it is strictly an editing choice.

Because we have three photos to choose from, try to consider the images from a reader's standpoint. The reader has probably seen many images of cattle being herded and cowboys shooting the

LIFE ON THE

GREAT AMERICAN

CATTLE DRIVE

Gordon James (above) finds a secluded place away from cow camp to take a "bucket bath" using his horse's feed bucket after a sweaty day in Oklahoma. Showers are hard to come by on the cattle drive. At top, the cowboys herd longhorn steers near Watonga, Okla., on the long drive to auction in Montana.

In an attempt to relive the experiences of the old West, a group of 30 cowboys herded 250 head of longhorn steers from Fort Worth to Miles City, Mont. The drive took six months and reached Miles City a few weeks ago.

Above, Mike Garrison takes tobacco for the drive. At right, wranglers herd the remuda across the plains of Kansas under the morning sky.

Above, drinking beer and telling stories lead to laughter after a long day of herding for the cowboys.

Photography by Carolyn A. Herter

FIGURE 8.22

Analyzing a Page from Top to Bottom.

PHOTOGRAPHS BY CAROLYN A. HERTER, DESIGN BY LESLIE WHITE, *THE DALLAS MORNING NEWS*

breeze many times in the media (newspapers, television, movies). How about trying to give them a little something that they haven't seen before? The image of the cowboy taking an impromptu, almost fully clothed bath is certainly an unusual one, an excellent choice for the lede.

The beginning photo is a little easier. The story is about a cattle drive. By positioning the image of the herd being moved along a dusty trail at the top of the page, the reader is quickly clued into the subject of the story. The portrait of the cowboy could also be argued for, but it says "cowboy" more than "cattle."

The ender photo is a toss-up. The photo of the horses walking into the page with the dramatic sky gives an idea of the ongoing nature of the story. An argument could be made for the picture of the cowboys gathered at the end of the day, but it probably works better as a support photo.

The cowboy "taking tobacco" photo functions somewhere between a portrait and a detail shot. It is wrapped by the slight bit of copy on the page to call attention to the action of putting the chew in the mouth. There are probably those who would object to the overly close cropping of the man's face, but this photo is intended to be more about cowboys in general than one specific man.

The Design   The design of the page is simple and appropriate to the subject. The layout is modular (horizontal lines could be drawn between the elements on the page from left to right). The white space is balanced in the corners. Only one rule line is used on the whole page to help create a more squared off illusion between the "Great American" and the ascender type C & D on "Cattle Drive."

Headlines, Type, Photo Credits, and Captions   The choice of headline type is entirely controlled by the subject matter. A cattle drive is a rather simple, unencumbered event and the type should reflect that. The font used is Goudy Old Style (the font used throughout *The Dallas Morning News*), slightly horizontally stretched (tracked) in Quark™ and then spaced slightly apart. The headline is split into three decks (three separate lines of type) for two reasons: the length of it and to help package the "beginning" photo with the type. The third line "Cattle Drive" is given extra importance by its much larger size.

The body copy exists on this page as a little extra information on the nature and length of the trip. It is a slightly larger size than the caption type size to differentiate between the two different kinds of type. It has a large drop cap and is wrapped around a photo to add interest to the text area.

The photo credit is placed inconspicuously at the bottom right of the page, a few picas below a caption to separate it. It is 12 pt. type, slightly vertically stretched (tracked) to an appearance of 14 pt. type. The vertical tracking gives the type a little different shape from the other type on the page.

The captions are standard fare for feature designs at *The News*. They are Goudy Old Style type changed from the bold used on news page layouts to a more elegant, less bulky version. The captions are placed in three different areas on the page: under the lede photo and on each side of the ender photo. One unusual caption choice was made for this design: the "beginning" photo does not have a caption. The image is self-explanatory and contained with

the headline, which more than adequately explains its content, so a decision was made not to repeat the obvious.

What Now?   This brief visit with the picture story and design should get you started. But more is needed. You need a real interest in the form. You need to invest more time in design education. You need a love of photojournalism.

You may want to take a design course at your school. You will certainly want to look through newspapers and professional photojournalism publications for well-designed pages, photographed and put together by seasoned professionals; these are a tremendous resource. Once you work at a newspaper, a good place to sharpen your design skills is in the art department. The talented artists and page designers will be more up-to-date on trends in software, computers, and design than any other group in the newspaper. Often, a photographer will find kindred souls in the art department willing to help out a fellow creative journalist with a little instruction and a hint or two. Just looking over their shoulders as they work will give you most of the information you need. The rest is up to practice and you.

If you run into any trouble at any point in the process, ask for help. Often, a fresh eye can go a long way in helping to solve design quandaries. Before offering your design for publication, always show it to someone you trust with a design or layout background. Sometimes a page design can be significantly improved with the smallest tweaking. Trust others to help you mature as a designer.

Final Thoughts

The single storytelling picture and accompanying caption is the fundamental photographic unit of newspapers. But other forms are available that tell a more detailed and rounded visual story. Photojournalists must always be alert for the single image that conveys the event being covered. At the same time they must look for multiple image possibilities that can convey more information to readers, that can better inform them.

NOTES

1   Paul Hill and Thomas Cooper, *Dialogue with Photography* (New York: Farrar, Straus, and Giroux, 1979), p. 266.

2   For a magazine version of the *Minamata* essay, see W. Eugene and Aileen Smith, "Death-Flow from a Pipe," *LIFE*, 2 June 1972, pp. 74–81.

3   "Spanish Village: It Lives in Ancient Poverty and Faith," *LIFE*, 9 April 1951, p. 121.

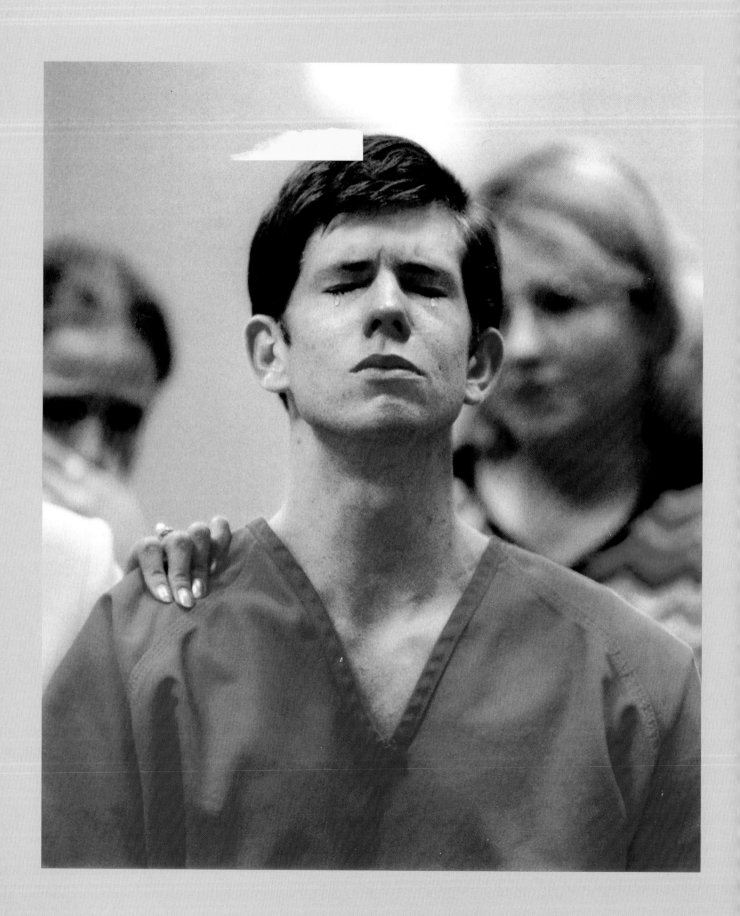

Law

Tears trickle from this 20-year-old's eyes
during sentencing proceedings in a Florida
trial court in connection with the deaths of
three young men, who were killed after they
drove into an intersection where a stop sign
had been removed, allegedly by this defendant
and two others. His and the two others' 1997
convictions on three counts of manslaughter
were overturned by a Florida appellate court
in early 2001. The prosecutor's office may
decide to try the defendants again on the
manslaughter charges or may decide to drop
the matter, options given to it by the
appellate court.
TONY LOPEZ/ST. PETERSBURG TIMES

Overview

Anyone taking or using pictures for publication must have at least a passing familiarity with applicable law. This chapter addresses several legal areas likely to be of concern to photojournalists. Never forget that the law is always evolving; what is law one day may change the next. However, some areas of law are considered settled; that is, they are unlikely to change in the foreseeable future.

This chapter is a general guide, not the final word, about selected areas of the law photojournalists are reasonably likely to encounter. Nothing in this chapter, or elsewhere in this book, should be construed as legal advice. You are urged to consult an attorney if you have concern about a specific legally-related journalistic matter.

What is law and where does it come from? Law is a body of formal enforceable rules that apply to everyone in the same or similar circumstances. U.S. law traces its heritage to England.

The two basic kinds of law are statutory and case. State legislatures and the U.S. Congress make statutory law. Judges make case law; court decisions in particular cases serve, to one degree or the other, as precedent for similar cases in the future.

Courts have varying degrees of authority or influence and not all similar cases are equal. U.S. Supreme Court decisions are the law of the land—the law for every state and every community in every state unless a lower court is convinced that the facts in a similar case before the lower court are different enough to remove the case from being controlled by the U.S. Supreme Court's decision. It is possible that this decision by a lower court could make its way through the appellate process, ultimately being decided by the U.S. Supreme Court. All state courts and other federal courts rank below the U.S. Supreme Court. Lower court decisions hold sway only in the geographic area served by the court that published the ruling, although judges' findings may influence other courts considering similar matters. In general, the hierarchy of influence in the federal system in descending degree of importance is the U.S. Supreme Court, U.S. Courts of Appeals, and U.S. District Courts. Likewise, state courts have a high tribunal, often known as the supreme court of the state, appellate courts, and trial courts. States' top courts sometimes have a different name; for example, in New York the Supreme Court is a lower court—the state's highest court is the Court of Appeals.

Five noteworthy aspects of law for photojournalists are: access, privacy, libel, procedure, and copyright.

Access

No law gives journalists unfettered access to wherever they want to go. It is well established that photojournalists have limited access; indeed, they generally enjoy no greater legal access than do individual citizens.

Trespass

Trespass is one problem photojournalists are likely to encounter on a regular basis. Trespass is a noncriminal legal violation involving private parties. Simplified, trespass is physically being on property without appropriate authorization. Take care that you do not enter onto land that is fenced or marked against trespassing and that you immediately leave any land after being told to do so by a person who has the authority to order you off. If you do not do this, you may find yourself charged with the crime of criminal trespass.[1]

Law professors James A. Henderson Jr., Richard N. Pearson, and John Siliciano begin discussion of trespass in their law book in this way:

> Most nonlawyers associate the word "trespass" with a deliberate intrusion upon another's land by someone "up to no good." Trespassers tend to be thought of as fence-breaking, chicken-stealing no-accounts. However, the legal concept of trespass is much broader, more technical, and largely devoid of moralistic overtones.[2]

Generally, photojournalists only can legally enter private property that is open to the public and can enter only for the purpose(s) for which the property is open to the public. This includes museums, hospitals, restaurants, stores, nursing homes, sports arenas, concert halls, and shopping malls, among others. The U.S. Supreme Court addressed this matter in a 1972 case involving a shopping center. Although the case did not involve photojournalists, it generally applies to them.

LLOYD CORPORATION, LTD. v. TANNER
U.S. Supreme Court, 1972
404 U.S. 1037

Facts An Oregon shopping center had a strict policy that prohibited the distribution of handbills. Nevertheless, members of a group were inside the center when they distributed handbill invitations to a meeting of the "Resistance Community" to protest the draft and the Vietnam War. The group was asked to leave to avoid being arrested and did so.

Analysis The group sued, claiming the shopping center had violated its First Amendment rights of free speech. The U.S. Supreme Court found that property does not lose its private character merely because the public is invited to use it for designated purposes. In this case the public was invited to do business with the shopping center's tenants; the shopping center did not invite the public to use the center for any and all purposes. This concept extends to any number of facilities that serve the public for commercial purposes and applies to photojournalists who want to photograph on such property.

U.S. Supreme Court decisions are the law of the land. However, based on attorney arguments that try to distinguish the facts in a later case from a similar U.S. Supreme Court case, it is not unusual for a lower court to hold that in its jurisdiction a U.S. Supreme Court decision does not control because the facts of the case before the lower court make

the U.S. Supreme Court decision inapplicable. One example is the following case in which the Supreme Court of New Jersey came to a different conclusion about malls than did the U.S. Supreme Court. The New Jersey case is the law in that state until it is overturned by a higher court. This is an example of the complicated nature of U.S. law and why it is critically important for you to seek an attorney's advice in any situation in which you have a legal problem or otherwise need to know the law at the time.

NEW JERSEY COALITION AGAINST WAR v. J.M.B. REALTY CORP.
Supreme Court of New Jersey, 1994
650 A.2d 757

Facts A citizen's group opposed to U.S. military intervention in the Persian Gulf decided in late 1990 to conduct a massive leafleting campaign at several large regional and community shopping malls. Its leaflets urged the public to contact members of Congress to vote against intervention. Some malls denied group members access to their property.

Analysis The group sued, and the New Jersey Supreme Court decided in 1994 that such regional and community shopping malls must allow the distribution of leaflets on political issues by individuals or groups because this is a form of free speech protected under the state constitution. The court based its decision on the mammoth size of these centers, which makes them the functional equivalent of downtown business districts. The court noted that when downtown business districts flourished, people traditionally gathered there to exercise their free speech rights. The New Jersey court briefly mentioned the 1972 Supreme Court case in its analysis, noting that access had been denied at the Oregon shopping center. But in reaching its decision the New Jersey tribunal found significance in the recent evolution of malls as a key gathering place in a community.

Attorney Theresa W. Parrish prepared all case summaries in this chapter.

What about journalists—including photojournalists—accompanying government agents—law enforcement officials and firefighters, for example— onto private property when the agents have the legal right to be on the property and have invited the journalists?

Whenever you accompany government officials onto private property in pursuit of a story, you are risking a lawsuit from the property owner or occupier, or both, against your organization and yourself for trespass, among other claims. Other claims might allege that you violated the owner or occupier's Fourth Amendment rights protecting against unreasonable searches and seizures and that you intentionally inflicted emotional distress. Of course, you also are open to trespass and other claims if you venture alone onto private property in pursuit of a story and go beyond the scope of your permission to be on the land, if indeed you obtained it.

In the past, lower courts have been divided about whether it is legally permissible for law enforcement officials to bring journalists with them onto private property when conducting official business. Now it has been clarified that government agents run great legal risk if they bring journalists along when they enter private property. *Wilson v. Layne*, decided by the U.S. Supreme Court in 1999 and summarized here, is the leading case about this.

WILSON v. LAYNE
U.S. Supreme Court
526 U.S. 603 (1999)

Facts   Deputy federal marshals and local sheriff's deputies in Rockville, Maryland, invited a newspaper reporter and a newspaper photographer to accompany them when they executed an arrest warrant for a fugitive. In the early morning they entered the home of the fugitive's parents but the fugitive was not there. The reporter observed and the photographer took pictures of the action, but the newspaper never published any of these photographs. The parents sued the law enforcement officials, asserting that their Fourth Amendment rights to be free from unreasonable searches and seizures had been violated when the officials brought along members of the media to observe and photograph the attempted execution of the arrest warrant. The parents did not sue the newspaper.

Analysis   The Court decided that a homeowner's Fourth Amendment rights are violated when law enforcement officials bring members of the media into the home during the execution of a warrant when the presence of the media is not in aid of the warrant's execution. The Court rejected arguments that the media's presence served legitimate law enforcement purposes such as publicizing the government's efforts to fight crime, allowing accurate reporting on law enforcement activities, and minimizing police abuses and protecting suspects and the officers. Although the officers were entitled to enter the home because of the warrant, they were not entitled to bring along the media because their presence was not related to the objectives of the authorized search and seizure.

However, the Court held the officers involved were entitled to qualified immunity protecting them from the parents' claim because at the time of this intrusion they could not have anticipated that their actions were illegal since media ride-alongs had become a common police practice. The federal marshal's office even had a ride-along policy that explicitly contemplated the media accompanying its officers and offered tips on what the media would find interesting.

The U.S. Supreme Court decision that government agents are now not immune from suit by private parties who are aggrieved that the media was brought into their homes almost certainly will have an extremely chilling effect on what apparently has been the fairly wide practice of government agents allowing journalists, including photojournalists, to accompany them onto private property while they are discharging official business. Considering the enormous liability government agents now face from private suits, it is unlikely that the media will be nearly as welcome to go with agents onto private property as they have been in the past, thus denying an important access to journalists.

Government

Government officials—national, state, and local—can be a major source of access problems for photojournalists. The limits set by government officials often are justified, representing balancing acts between unfettered journalistic access and the right of government to limit that access in the public's interest. As a photojournalist, expect to deal in the access arena to one degree or the other with people working for all kinds of government entities. Let's take a look at seven of these. They are: Civilian Law Enforcement; Civilian Agencies Other Than Law Enforcement; Public Schools;

Fire Departments; U.S. Postal Service; Courts; and The Military.

Civilian Law Enforcement Civilian law enforcement is an important concern to every photojournalist—ask any photojournalist who has had a run-in with police, particularly those who were charged with crimes in their attempts to cover stories. By its nature journalism demands coverage of events that attract the attention of law enforcement officers. An unfortunate fact, at least from a journalist's vantage point, is that duties and responsibilities of law enforcement officers often conflict with those of photojournalists (Figure 9.1). When the clash occurs, as it occasionally does, expect law enforcement to win, at least initially. The law clearly tilts in its favor.

Because photojournalists face an uphill battle, their best assets in successfully dealing with police and other law enforcement officers are a talent for tactful persuasion and a knowledgeable and pleasant businesslike attitude.

But what can you expect when these do not work. At very least photojournalists should expect a mild to severe

FIGURE 9.1

Carol Guzy, three-time Pulitzer Prize-winning photographer with *The Washington Post*, is arrested about 6:30 p.m. April 15, 2000 by District of Columbia Metropolitan Police. Guzy was covering the mass arrest in downtown Washington, D.C. of demonstrators against the World Bank and the International Monetary Fund. She was charged by police with marching without a permit even though she was wearing press credentials and carrying cameras. Guzy was held by police until about 12:30 a.m. the next day. In an article for *The Post* about her arrest, she wrote: "I got out earlier than most, with a little help from *The Post*. Six hours after my arrest, an officer came with a handful of paperwork dropping the charges and declaring me a victim of circumstances. By then, it was too late to use most of the film I'd shot that day."
Kamenko Pajic/AP/Wide World Photos

tongue-lashing and perhaps threats of arrest. At worst harsh physical treatment, criminal charges, and jail await those who defy law enforcement orders. Although they usually lose in the heat of the moment, photojournalists may win in court. Two court cases, involving a newspaper staff photographer in New Jersey and a television photographer in Wisconsin, are illuminating.

STATE v. LASHINSKY
Supreme Court of New Jersey, 1979
404 A.2d 1121

Facts   A New Jersey court convicted newspaper photographer Harvey I. Lashinsky as a disorderly person for failure to heed a police officer's order to move back from the immediate vicinity of a gory, fatal automobile accident on the Garden State Parkway. He appealed his conviction, contending that he did not intend to interfere with the officer and that he enjoyed special access to such sites because he was a journalist.

Analysis   The New Jersey Supreme Court rejected both arguments, finding that the order was reasonable and that, even if the photographer did not intend to interfere, his actions resulted in interference. The court also found the photographer was not entitled to special access. The court did add that "an officer should, if made aware of the identity and status of an individual as a newsperson engaged in gathering news, be mindful that such an individual has a legitimate and proper reason to be where he is and, if possible, this important interest should be accommodated."

CITY OF OAK CREEK v. KING
Supreme Court of Wisconsin, 1989
436 N.W.2d 285

Facts   In Oak Creek, Wisconsin, television photographer Peter A. H. King was arrested and tried on a charge of disorderly conduct. He had penetrated a police roadblock and a boundary line of a county-owned nonpublic area in order to obtain pictures of an airplane crash site, disobeying a police officer's order to remain off the site. King appealed his conviction on the grounds that his conduct was not disorderly and that he had a First Amendment right of access to the scene beyond that of the general public's.

Analysis   The Wisconsin Supreme Court affirmed the photographer's conviction. The court found that King's conduct fell within the parameters of disorderly conduct because he had deliberately refused to obey the reasonable order of a police officer who was trying to maintain crowd control and because King had disobeyed the order in plain view of a crowd, which tended to disrupt "good order" at the scene. The court also rejected King's argument that the First Amendment and a similar provision of the state constitution gave him greater access rights as a newsgatherer than those of the general public, noting that the U.S. Supreme Court has rejected such an argument.

Civilian Agencies Other Than Law Enforcement   Photojournalists are likely to want to photograph people, places, and things under the control of government agencies and the independent but quasi-government U.S. Postal Service. Here is a brief look at four of these: the U.S. General Services Administration, public schools, fire departments, and the U.S. Postal Service.

General Services Administration   The General Services Administration (GSA) is the organization with legal control of many federal buildings; it is the federal government's housekeeper.

In areas of federally owned or controlled buildings under GSA authority (assuming no court order or security regulation prohibits photography), photojournalists may take pictures for news purposes in common areas such as lobbies, hallways, and auditoriums in which public meetings are being held; they do not need specific permission from GSA officials unless they previously have been informed that an area typically open for photography is off-limits.

Photographing in a GSA-managed building in space occupied or controlled by a tenant—the Internal Revenue Service, for example—requires only permission from the tenant, again assuming no court order or security regulation prohibits photography.[3]

Public Schools   Sooner or later every photojournalist will want to photograph on property owned or controlled by a local school board. Perhaps the assignment is elementary school children on the first day of classes, the newly elected senior class president, cheerleaders, football players at practice, some misadventure, students in the classroom, or other activities and events occurring on public school grounds.

Does the photographer face any legal problems? Of course. Many states have one or more criminal laws prohibiting "wrongful use of public property," including public school grounds. Some states have statutes directly pertaining to trespassing on public school property.

You may find school officials have a sensitivity—or even a prohibition— against photographing children, particularly young children, unless permission from parents has been obtained. Parents can be extremely protective of their children and photographing them without parental permission opens you, your organization, and the school officials who allowed the picture-taking to lawsuits. It also can result in you and your editor being confronted by irate parents.

Fire Departments   Photojournalists should expect regular contact with fire department personnel at fires as well as automobile accidents and other news events to which fire departments respond with firefighters or paramedics, or both (Figure 9.2).

Just about every community has some law, either local or state, making it a crime to "willfully and maliciously" meddle with any equipment related to fire fighting or to interfere with personnel fighting fires or fire paramedics tending the injured.

Unless picture-taking circumstances prohibit using a telephoto lens or using it would significantly diminish visual or storytelling value, photojournalists must try to use telephotos when covering events involving firefighters, paramedics, and other emergency personnel at work. Telephotos usually yield satisfactory coverage while allowing photographers to physically stay away from the most emotional and busy areas. This can reduce photographers' interference, reduce the possibility of criminal charges against photographers and reduce the possibility that participants or onlookers will assault photographers. When circumstances cry out for a wide-angle lens, be careful not to interfere with medical, fire, and other emergency personnel or to further and unnecessarily traumatize those who are already traumatized.

U.S. Postal Service   Photographing in a Postal Service facility without specific permission is limited. The *Postal Operations Manual* states that, "Photographs for news purposes may be taken in entrances, lobbies, foyers, corridors, or auditoriums when used for public meetings, except as prohibited by official signs, the directions of postal police officers, other authorized personnel, or a federal court order or rule. Other photographs may be taken only with the permission of the local postmaster or installation head."[4]

Even when you do not need permission, and time and coverage circumstances permit, it is courteous and thoughtful to let a senior postal official know you plan to take pictures in the facility. After identifying yourself and the publication for which you work, saying something like, "I'd like to take some pictures in the lobby for a holiday rush story," may go a long way toward building goodwill that pays handsome dividends when you need permission to photograph.

The Postal Service does not want the addresses on mail in its custody disclosed to people unauthorized to receive it, including photojournalists and their readers. Therefore expect postal

employees not to show you the address part of mail you may be allowed to photograph. Photojournalists should be sensitive themselves to this restriction, and go out of their way not to take pictures of the address on mail if it accidentally is shown to them or at least make sure that the writing is so small that an address clearly is unreadable in the photograph.

It is illegal to reproduce images of U.S. and foreign government stamps in

Photojournalism: An Introduction

other than a permissible way. While postage stamps may be photographed and reproduced in color, uncancelled postage stamps "shall be of a size less than three-fourths or more than one and one-half, in linear dimension, of each part…".[5] Incidentally, this size requirement also applies to all U.S. money. U.S. money, however, may only be reproduced in black and white unless the current U.S. Secretary of the Treasury has decided that color reproduction is permissible for a particular purpose. The prudent photojournalist only will photograph and reproduce money in black and white (and definitely within the size restrictions noted above). Other U.S. and foreign government and certain private entity documents also carry reproduction restrictions. The wise photojournalist will take a cautious approach when dealing with formal documents—money, stamps, notes, bonds, whatever—of the U.S. government and of foreign governments and of private entities such as banks. While remembering that you are responsible for the actions you commit and cannot transfer criminal liability to others, it probably is desirable for you to check with a ranking editor or manager at your publication, or with the publication's attorney, before possibly getting yourself into trouble with federal law enforcement agents for violating federal law by photographing or publishing in the wrong way, or at all, documents federal law restricts.

Courts

Cameras in the courtroom is a subject that over the years has evoked passion on both sides of the debate. A number of states now permit judges to allow cameras in their courtrooms, and the federal judiciary has opened some of its appellate courts to cameras.[6] At one time the saying "anything goes" pretty much applied to cameras in the courtroom. As far as the American Bar Association (ABA) was concerned, the mat-ter was brought to a head by the outrageous behavior of photographers covering the 1934 Lindbergh baby kidnapping trial.[7] In 1937 the

ABA made Judicial Canon 35 part of its Canons of Judicial Ethics. The canon, titled "Improper Publicizing of Court Proceedings" (amended in 1952), outlawed still photojournalistic coverage of court proceedings. This canon (or rule) remained the official policy of the ABA until 1982 with relatively minor changes. In 1982 the association changed its position and followed the lead of an influential group, the Conference of State Chief Justices. The conference had considered the matter in 1978 and "approved a resolution to allow the highest court of each state to promulgate standards and guidelines regulating radio, television and other photographic coverage of court proceedings."[8]

As of 2000 many states allow photography in their courtrooms on a permanent basis (Figure 9.3) or are experimenting with it. Strict rules typically control courtroom photography. Photojournalists who photograph in courtrooms and their environs must know applicable picture-taking rules and follow them.

For a long time federal courts stood apart from many state courts and retained the ban on photography except for ceremonial-related matters such as naturalization proceedings. After a three-year pilot project involving civil cases in two federal appellate courts and four trial courts, the door to the federal judiciary is ajar, if only slightly, to photography.

In a close vote in 1996 the Judicial Conference of the United States, which makes policy for almost all federal courts, allowed federal appellate courts to permit—or ban—photographing of oral arguments in civil appeals.[9] The resolution does not apply to the U.S. Supreme Court because the Judicial Conference has no authority over it.

From a media standpoint appellate courts offer little of the visual interest of trial courts; they have no sobbing witnesses and no defendants testifying, only lawyers making their cases to the judges. (Appellate courts consider only the application of the law to facts established during trial.) Because of its unique importance, photojournalists would like picture-taking access to the

FIGURE 9.3

Bailiffs restrain a criminal defendant after the judge ordered the man gagged following an angry outburst in a Florida courtroom.

Sam Cranston/*The News-Journal*, Daytona Beach, Fla.

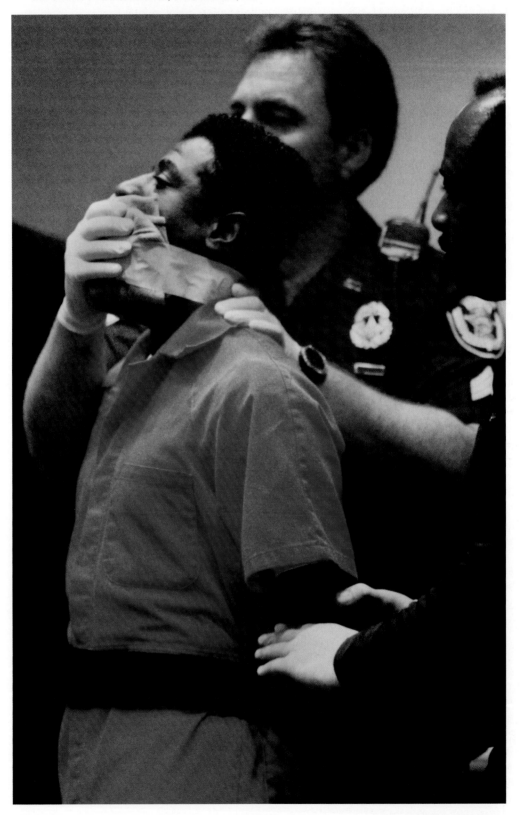

most important federal appellate court in the land, the U.S. Supreme Court. However, at least one justice is adamantly opposed to allowing cameras. Justice David S. Souter told a subcommittee of the U.S. House of Representatives, "I think the case is so strong that I can tell you the day you see a camera come into our courtroom it's going to roll over my dead body."[10]

Also in 1996 the Judicial Conference overwhelmingly voted to "strongly urge" each judicial council to ban still and video photography in U.S. district courts.[11] Almost all these courts already had prohibited photography except for ceremonial-related matters. This prohibition usually extends to the environs of federal district courts, such as halls and foyers and wherever else in or near the courtroom buildings that judges declare to be photography-free. It does not matter that court is not in session.

Each federal judicial district around the country sets its own rules, singularly or in combination with one or more other districts, regarding photography-free areas. Photojournalists should be familiar with these rules, which are available from the various courts.

If you have any doubt about rules governing photography in a state or federal courtroom or in or near the building that houses a courtroom, contact the presiding judge's administrative assistant, secretary, or chief bailiff (if the matter involves a court proceeding) and ask to meet with the judge. For photography-related matters not involving a trial or a particular judge contact the chief judge of the circuit, district, or other judicial jurisdiction.

The Military

Federal law gives military personnel absolute authority to limit physical access of photojournalists and others to military installations, ships, and aircraft; to restrict or prevent picturing of military property and personnel on military installations, ships, and aircraft; and gives limited authority to prevent picturing of installations, ships, aircraft, and personnel from or on civilian property.[12]

The law gives military personnel, including the Coast Guard, the right to decide whether something is sensitive and must not be photographed. This includes military property and military personnel on civilian property. Photojournalists defy military authority at risk to their freedom and pocketbook—and at potential peril to their country. If military personnel confront you, you should never—under any circumstance —do anything more hostile than protest tactfully. Never physically resist or become otherwise abusive. Immediately ask to call your editor, describe the situation, and let the editor take the matter up with higher military authorities. The disagreement will likely be resolved or clarified for the future.

Privacy

As the United States developed technologically in the late 19th century, journalistic enterprises benefited from the innovations that enabled them to reach readers widely and rapidly. This also was the age of yellow journalism. Truth and fairness generally were not prime considerations of the press in this era, which impugned reputations with abandon. The country was ripe for a new law protecting the individual that would provide a right to be left alone.

The birth of a right to privacy was the doing of two lawyers. One, Samuel D. Warren, was a wealthy businessman who had quit his law practice to devote time to a paper-manufacturing business he had inherited; the other, Louis Brandeis, was a practicing attorney and Warren's former law partner. (Brandeis later became an associate justice of the U.S. Supreme Court.)

According to legal scholar William L. Prosser in his 1960 *California Law Review* article about privacy, Mrs. Samuel D. Warren, the daughter of a senator, "held at her home a series of social entertainments on an elaborate scale." The Boston newspapers covered these gatherings "in highly personal and embarrassing detail." The coverage of the wedding of one Warren daughter broke the Warrens' patience. According to Prosser, "It was an annoyance for which the press, the advertisers and the entertainment industry of America were to pay dearly over the next seventy years."[13]

Warren and Brandeis wrote a groundbreaking 1890 article for the *Harvard Law Review* in which they argued that the common law contained a "right to privacy." They wrote:

> The press is overstepping in every direction the obvious bounds of propriety and of decency. Gossip is no longer the resource of the idle and of the vicious, but has become a trade, which is pursued with industry as well as effrontery. To satisfy a prurient taste the details of sexual relations are spread broadcast in the columns of the daily papers. To occupy the indolent, column upon column is filled with idle gossip, which can only be procured by intrusion upon the domestic circle. The intensity and complexity of life, attendant upon advancing civilization, have rendered necessary some retreat from the world, and man, under the refining influence of culture, has become more sensitive to publicity, so that solitude and privacy have become more essential to the individual; but modern enterprise and invention have, through invasions upon his privacy, subjected him to mental pain and distress, far greater than could be inflicted by mere bodily injury.[14]

Photojournalism received its share of criticism too:

> Instantaneous photographs and newspaper enterprise have invaded the sacred precincts of private and domestic life; and numerous mechanical devices threaten to make good the prediction that "what is whispered in the closet shall be proclaimed from the house-tops." . . . While, for instance, the state of the photographic art was such that one's picture could seldom be taken without his consciously "sitting" for the purpose, the law of contract or of trust might afford the prudent man sufficient safeguards

against the improper circulation of his portrait; but since the latest advances in photographic art have rendered it possible to take pictures surreptitiously, the doctrines of contract and of trust are inadequate to support the required protection, and the law of tort [noncriminal legal violation involving private parties] must be resorted to.[15]

All states and the District of Columbia, either through common law or by statute, now recognize a right to privacy, at least to some degree. Although restrictions probably were inevitable, a backlash against the intrusive reporting of the yellow journalism era yielded the privacy doctrines that provide the underpinning for today's standards.

In his 1960 article Prosser laid out four "legs" upon which the privacy "stool" rests. Now generally accepted by the courts, they are:

- Appropriation
- Intrusion
- Public disclosure of private facts
- False light in the public eye[16]

As a photojournalist you may do a single act that brings into play more than one of these privacy legs. Also, the act you did may trigger one or more causes of action outside the privacy arena— perhaps trespass, defamation, and intentional infliction of emotional distress, or perhaps others. With that bit of happy news let's now turn to Appropriation.

Appropriation Appropriation protects the individual's concern for the uses to which his or her name, personality, and image are put. The law gives people the option to prevent others from trading on their name or likeness or to permit such trading for a price. Although the media engage in a business endeavor, it is settled law that "editorial" publication of information and images about people, animals, and things generally does not constitute appropriation.[17] But this does not mean that photojournalists can legally photograph a person performing in an arena to which an admission is charged and where photography is prohibited, or in other similar circumstances. They cannot—unless they obtain permission.

Another circumstance in which photojournalists and their publications easily can run afoul of appropriation involves pictures taken for editorial purposes but used for some other purpose, regardless of whether they were timely published as editorial material. An example of this is pictures taken by photojournalists as an editorial product but which are used in promotions; for example, an in-house ad extolling the creativity of the newspaper's photo staff. Whenever this is done, an appropriate release should be obtained from each person whose picture appears in the ad. Incidentally, this admonition applies to everyone using the likeness of another for commercial gain, whether in the news business or otherwise (more about releases shortly).

A third circumstance in which photojournalists and their publications easily can run afoul of appropriation involves "manufacturing" a photograph that otherwise did not exist; in the 21st century this easily, quickly, and believably can be done with the computer and photo processing software (Figure 9.4). Prominently noting "Photo Illustration" on or near your creation probably will keep you out of the ethical doghouse, but it well may not do a thing for you when an offended and embarrassed person who was made to look bad by your illustrative creativity and the magic of your computer files an invasion of privacy appropriation suit against you and your publication. You should exercise great caution when deciding to change any image from its truthful and fair representation of reality to something else. Dustin Hoffman, the prominent actor, is one who took offense when this happened to him. Learn about Hoffman's federal lawsuit in the summary that follows, but keep in mind that the information is from a trial court. The decision may be appealed and if so may stand or be overturned. An appellate review would make it at least a little more likely that the court's ruling would apply to a similar suit in which you may become embroiled.

HOFFMAN v. CAPITAL CITIES/ABC, INC.
U.S. District Court, Central District of California, 1999
33 F. Supp.2d 867

Facts Actor Dustin Hoffman sued the publisher of *Los Angeles Magazine* after it used computer technology to merge still photographs of famous actors/actresses from classic films with photographs of body models wearing clothing from spring designer collections. The magazine published a photograph of Hoffman as he appeared in the successful 1982 motion picture *Tootsie,* and through a process of technology employing computer imaging software manipulated and altered the photograph to make it appear that Hoffman was wearing a contemporary designer gown and shoes. Hoffman, who has received numerous acting honors during his film career, does not knowingly permit commercial uses of his identity. The magazine did not seek or obtain permission from Hoffman to use his name or likeness. It also did not seek or obtain permission from the company that supplied the photograph from *Tootsie* that was used to create the computer-manipulated image that appeared in the magazine. The magazine made clear in the article that the images were composite computer-generated images. Hoffman sued for violations of his common law and statutory right of publicity and related claims, and sought compensatory and punitive damages.

Analysis The court, after declaring that Hoffman "is truly one of our country's living treasures joining the ranks of an exclusive handful of motion picture talent," found in favor of Hoffman on his claims and awarded $1.5 million in compensatory and $1.5 million in punitive damages. "The photographs were manipulated and cannibalized to such an extent that the celebrities were commercially exploited and were robbed of their dignity, professionalism and talent. To be blunt, the celebrities were violated by technology," the court said.

FIGURE 9.4

Never do something like this with your office computer unless your efforts are for a legitimate illustration for your publication and you have the prior approval of a ranking editor or manager. Your riotously funny creativity easily can turn into a legal disaster for you and your publication if your handiwork sees the light of day, unintentionally or otherwise.

RICH TENNANT/THE 5TH WAVE, WWW.THE5THWAVE.COM

Since releases came up a little earlier, let's visit with them before moving on to intrusion, another aspect of invasion of privacy.

To be on the safe side you should ask anyone you are photographing who is not "newsworthy" to sign an appropriate release. However, as a practical matter newspapers and wire services seldom send their photojournalists out with reams of releases and pockets full of dollar bills to proffer to feature subjects. Doing so is impracticable because of the time constraints under which news organizations labor and the low probability of plaintiffs' being successful for more than minor monetary judgments in lawsuits. This is particularly the case if plaintiffs legally are adults, knew of the photography and the photographer's affiliation, did not object to the picture taking, were in a public place, and their images were presented in a truthful and fair context.

When photojournalists find themselves in situations where releases seem particularly desirable, or where they feel more comfortable having them, they should ask subjects to sign. At least one, preferably two, uninvolved people should witness subjects' signatures. Keep in mind that minors—people who have not yet reached the legal age—do not have the legal capacity to enter into legally binding agreements. The legal age varies from state to state so you are well advised to find out what it is where you work.

If photographs are to be used in a nonjournalistic publication or in some other nonjournalistic way that will allow someone other than the photographer and the subject to see them, the photographer should obtain releases before taking pictures. Applicable situations include, but are not be limited to, photographs that appear in company publications, public displays such as in bank lobbies, and advertising. Releases should be in writing. Oral releases are dangerous. They may not offer protection because of state law, good-faith disagreement about what was agreed to, or the dishonesty of one or more parties.

Releases are legally structured in two ways. If the only concern is with invasion of privacy, releases that are nothing more than consents probably offer adequate protection, particularly if they are tailored to particular situations. Consent is a defense against invasion of privacy claims. An important limitation that may cause a problem after picture taking but before publication is that a person may withdraw consent. Because of this possibility the safer route is to enter into a contract with the person. One party usually cannot legally unilaterally breach an appropriate legally drawn and executed contract without being liable for damages.

If other potential legal problems such as amount of remuneration or publication rights are a concern, the second type of release, a contract, is the better choice. A contract always has three fundamental elements: offer, acceptance, and consideration. What photographers or their organizations are doing is offering a valuable consideration to subjects in return for the subjects' permission to take their photographs and to use resulting images in particular ways and for particular purposes. The "valuable consideration" usually is money but can be anything else of value.

Standardized release forms of both types are available, but using them is relatively risky. Because they typically do not address specific situations, they tend to be broad and general—and could well prove worthless. The rule is that the broader and more general a release, the less protection it probably offers; likewise, the more specific the release, the more protection it probably offers. If you need a contract specific to the situation, an attorney, preferably an expert in contracts and media law, should write it. The lawyer must know exactly what the circumstances are, both with respect to picture taking and use of the pictures. It is critically important to take and use the photographs covered by a release only in the way for which the subject has given permission. Use of the pictures in any other way opens photographers, their employers, and any other people and organizations involved with the pictures to the risk of a successful lawsuit.

Intrusion Simply put, you commit intrusion when you intentionally invade another's seclusion, either physically or in other ways including by photography, and the person has a reasonable expectation that the seclusion will not be breached and the intrusion "would be offensive or objectionable to a reasonable person…".[18] Photojournalistic intrusion most likely will occur on or into private property, but may also be committed on or into public property where a person has the reasonable expectation that the media's prying eye will not wander. For example, you almost certainly have the legal right to photograph a person involved in an automobile accident, the accident being on public property normally open to the general public. But as the 1998 Supreme Court of California case, *Shulman v. Group W Productions, Inc.,* instructs, you take a grave legal risk when you climb into the ambulance at the scene and take pictures of the injured person.[19] Most likely the injured person has the reasonable expectation of privacy in the ambulance and you may be on your way to being a party to an intrusion lawsuit. Incidentally, the owner of the ambulance may take great offense at your aggressiveness and present you and your publication with a trespass lawsuit. There need not be publication for you to commit intrusion; the tort—the unlawful action—is accomplished when you do the deed. The authors of *Mass Communication Law in a Nutshell* tell us that, "The intrusion may or may not also constitute the tort of trespass. Often the intrusion itself is not physical but consists of eavesdropping with telephoto lenses or electronic listening devices in areas private to aggrieved individuals such as their homes or offices."[20]

The California case (*Shulman v. Group W Productions, Inc.*) cited above does a good job of spelling out what intrusion is and putting it in its "privacy" perspective:

Of the four privacy torts identified by Prosser [William Prosser, the author of the famous *California Law Review* article on privacy], the tort of intrusion into private places, conversations or matters is perhaps the one that best captures the common understanding of an "invasion of privacy." It encompasses unconsented-to physical intrusion into the home, hospital room or other place the privacy of which is legally recognized, as well as unwarranted sensory intrusions such as eavesdropping, wiretapping, and visual or photographic spying.[21]

Intrusion is also closely related in some respects to nuisance law, especially when it comes to reporting by surveillance. The *conduct* of a journalist in obtaining information may be so beyond the pale that a court might punish the behavior. In such cases offensive reporting techniques are objectionable in much the same way that a neighbor's extremely loud noises or decision to start a hog farm with its accompanying odor is objectionable.

A clear case of intrusion occurred when a *Life* magazine reporter and photographer gained access to a healer's home by pretending to be the friends of a friend, then surreptitiously took pictures, and relayed tape recordings to law enforcement officials waiting outside while the subject of their investigation examined one of them for breast cancer. In ruling against the magazine the court in *Dietemann v. Time, Inc.* commented, "The First Amendment is not a license to trespass, to steal, or to intrude by electronic means into the precincts of another's home or office. It does not become such a license simply because the person subjected to the intrusion is reasonably suspected of committing a crime."[22]

Public Disclosure of Private Facts

One law book, *Restatement of the Law*, deems this privacy leg "Publicity Given to Private Life," and makes clear that for this leg of privacy to be considered an invasion of privacy, that which is publicized about a person's private life must meet the following basic requirements. Here is how the book puts it:

> One who gives publicity to a matter concerning the private life of another is subject to liability to the other for invasion of his privacy, if the matter publicized is of a kind that
>
> (a) would be highly offensive to a reasonable person, and
> (b) is not of legitimate concern to the public.[23]

It is important that you understand that your reporting the truth does not shield you from a sucessful "public disclosure of private facts" lawsuit. A photograph you make and a word report you do in the form of a caption or story can relate the truth in every respect and still be a "Private-Facts" invasion of privacy.

While the legal jurisdiction in which you and your publication are defending a "Private Facts" lawsuit may in effect allow your publication to determine what is of "legitimate public concern," you cannot depend on this happening. The conservative approach—the prudent approach—is to assume that a judge or jury will decide if the two basic requirements noted above—the offensiveness of what the defendants did and the concern to the public—apply so that the defendants are successful in defeating the lawsuit. There is no way with certainty to know ahead of a decision how a judge or jury will decide.

A woman who was the main subject of a photograph made at an Alabama fair by a newspaper photographer took offense at the paper publishing the picture, which showed her as a jet of air from a fair attraction blew her dress up, and sued. She won her "Private Facts" invasion of privacy lawsuit against the newspaper. The case, *Daily Times Democrat v. Graham*, is summarized below.

DAILY TIMES DEMOCRAT v. GRAHAM
Supreme Court of Alabama, 1964
162 So.2d 474

Facts A married mother of two children visited a county fair "Fun House" where her picture was taken by a newspaper photographer on a platform just as jets of air blew her dress up around her, exposing her from the waist down except for that portion of her body covered by her panties. She did not know she was being photographed. The newspaper published the picture on the front page. While her back was largely towards the camera, her sons were in the picture and she was recognized by others who saw the picture and commented on it to her. She sued for an invasion of privacy claiming public disclosure of private facts, and prevailed at trial.

Analysis The newspaper claimed the photograph was a matter of legitimate news in connection with a story about the county fair. The appellate court disagreed, finding that the photograph disclosed "nothing as to which the public is entitled to be informed." The woman involuntarily caught in an embarrassing pose did not forfeit her right to privacy simply because she happened to be part of a public scene, the court said.

False Light in the Public Eye If an important goal for you is reporting the truth in fair context, this privacy leg should not present much trouble. Nevertheless, let's briefly visit with it. Here is the thrust of False Light in the Public Eye from *Restatement of Torts*, which terms it "Publicly Placing Person in False Light."

> One who gives publicity to a matter concerning another that places the other before the public in a false light is subject to liability to the other for invasion of his privacy, if
> (a) the false light in which the other was placed would be highly offensive to a reasonable person, and
> (b) the actor [the person committing the wrong] had knowledge of or acted in reckless disregard as to the falsity of the publicized matter and the false light in which the other would be placed.[24]

Using this definition journalists and their organizations have a great deal of protection from a successful false light suit because the journalist [the actor] either had to know about the falsity at issue or had to have acted in "reckless disregard" regarding the falsity and "the false light in which the other would be placed." The U.S. Supreme Court has made clear that the "reckless disregard" standard applies to people who are public officials or public figures but has left the door open for a private plaintiff—someone who is not a public official or a public figure—to need only to prove negligence, a lesser standard that puts journalists and their organizations more at risk. While every journalist, including photojournalists, should try hard never to give a person a legitimate false light claim, it is conservative—it is prudent—to assume that all a plaintiff need prove is the lesser standard of "negligence." To put it another way, as a photojournalist you should hold yourself to a tougher standard than "reckless disregard."

To give you an idea of the significant differences between "reckless disregard" and "negligence," here are their definitions from *Black's Law Dictionary*:

> Reckless disregard. **1.** Conscious indifference to the consequences (of an act).[25]

> Negligence, n. **1.** The failure to excercise the standard of care that a reasonably prudent person would have exercised in a similar situation; any conduct that falls below the legal standard established to protect others against unreasonable risk of harm, except for conduct that is intentionally, wantonly, or willfully disregardful of others' rights.[26]

Before ending our short visit with False Light in the Public Eye with a summary of a relevant case, *Leverton v. Curtis Pub. Co.*, here are two False Light in the Public Eye examples from *Prosser and Keeton on the Law of Torts*:

> [One] form in which [false light in the public eye] frequently appears is the use of the plaintiff's picture to

illustrate a book or an article with which he has no reasonable connection, with the implication that such a connection exists—as where, for example, the face of an honest taxi driver is used to ornament a story about the cheating propensities of taxi drivers in the city. Still another is the inclusion of the plaintiff's name, photograph or fingerprints in a public "rogue's gallery" of convicted criminals, when he has not in fact been convicted of any crime.[27]

LEVERTON v. CURTIS PUBLISHING CO.
U.S. Court of Appeals, 3rd Circuit, 1951
192 F.2d 974

Facts A newspaper published a picture of a pedestrian child injured when an automobile struck her. Twenty months later the picture was used by The Saturday Evening Post magazine to illustrate a story entitled "They Ask to Be Killed" that included in a box beside the title the statement "Do you invite massacre by your own carelessness? Here's how thousands have committed suicide by scorning laws that were passed to keep them alive." However, the child had not been careless at the time of the accident; rather the motorist was. A jury found against the magazine on an invasion of privacy false light claim and awarded damages.

Analysis The federal appellate court affirmed the damages award. The photograph when first taken and published by a newspaper was not an actionable invasion of the child's privacy because it was coverage of a news story of legitimate public interest. However, the later use of the picture by a magazine was not protected because of the way it was used. The child was portrayed erroneously as having "narrowly escaped death because of her own carelessness" which presented her in false light. The court affirmed the jury verdict and noted that the child, who once was a legitimate subject for publicity in connection with the accident, later had become "a pictorial, frightful example of pedestrian carelessness."

Libel

Libel is particularly difficult to get a specific handle on in a brief discussion like this. An important reason is that the definition of this private wrong—what constitutes libel—varies from legal jurisdiction to legal jurisdiction. For example, in some jurisdictions slander is not broken out as a separate legal wrong, in other jurisdictions it is. In some jurisdictions, libel itself means one thing, in other jurisdictions something else. Libel is no exception when it comes to your knowing the law related to photography where you photograph and where your organization publishes; since it is so jurisdictionally sensitive, libel may be the first among equals in this regard.

With this background, let's try at least to get you in the libel ballpark.[28]

The Associated Press Stylebook and Libel Manual tells us that "At its most basic, libel means injury to reputation."[29] Reputation is what others think of a person, not what the person thinks of herself. *Black's Law Dictionary* defines reputation as "The esteem in which a person is held by others."[30]

Since slander is part of libel in some legal jurisdictions, it is important for you to know the distinction: simplified, slander is injury to reputation done orally, libel is injury to reputation done by print. *Prosser and Keeton on the Law of Torts* adds some flesh to these barebones simplified definitions:

The distinction itself between libel and slander is not free from difficulty and uncertainty. As it took form in the seventeenth century, it was one between written and oral words. But later on libel was extended to include pictures, signs, statues, motion pictures, and even conduct carrying a defamatory imputation, such as hanging the plaintiff in effigy, erecting a gallows before his door, dishonoring his valid check drawn upon the defendant's bank, or even, in one Wisconsin case, following him over a considerable period in a conspicuous manner. From this it has been concluded that libel is that which is communicated by the sense of sight, or perhaps also by touch or smell, while slander is that which is conveyed by the sense of hearing. But this certainly does not fit all of the cases, since it seems to be agreed that defamatory gestures or the signals of a deaf-mute are to be regarded as slander only, while matter communicated by sound to be reduced to writing afterwards, as in the case of a telegraph message, or dictation to a stenographer, or even an interview given to a reporter, is considered libel. Furthermore, it is generally held that it is a publication of a libel to read a defamatory writing aloud.[31]

How might one legal jurisdiction that does not distinguish between libel and slander define libel?

The *Associated Press Stylebook and Libel Manual* tells us that the state of Illinois is one such jurisdiction, and that:

> In Illinois, libel is defined as 'the publication of anything injurious to the good name or reputation of another, or which tends to bring him into disrepute.'[32]

On the other hand, the *Stylebook and Libel Manual* tells us that the state of California is a jurisdiction that separates libel and slander, and that in the Golden State:

> Libel is a *false* and *unprivileged* publication by writing, printing, picture, effigy or other fixed representation which exposes any person to hatred, contempt, ridicule or obloquy, or which causes him to be shunned or avoided or which injures him in his occupation.[33]

A photojournalist—any journalist—must be careful about printing or saying anything about a person that is anything but provably truthful. Otherwise, do not be surprised if the person hires an attorney, locates people who will swear that what was printed or said about the person hurt his name and reputation in their minds, and

otherwise injured him in the libel or slander arena.

Private figures in most legal jurisdictions must prove only negligence to win a libel suit. The *Stylebook and Libel Manual* tells us that "Negligence is difficult to define. As a rule of thumb, a careless error on the part of the journalist could be found to constitute negligence."[34] *Black's Law Dictionary* defines negligence as: "The failure to exercise the standard of care that a reasonably prudent person would have exercised in a similar situation. . .".[35]

As a general rule, public officials, public figures, and private individuals who project themselves into public arenas by becoming involved in matters of public concern must meet a higher standard of proof than private individuals to maintain a successful libel suit. These people must prove "actual malice." *Black's Law Dictionary* defines actual malice as it relates to "Defamation," which is the umbrella term encompassing slander and libel, as: "Knowledge (by the person who utters or publishes a defamatory statement) that a statement is false, or reckless disregard about whether the statement is true."[36]

Are there any defenses to libel that may keep you and your organization from being successfully sued? The answer is yes, but none that are simple and ironclad, not even communicating the truth. For example, if you accurately print the truth of a libelous statement you obtained from a source, either orally or in writing, you open yourself and your organization to a libel suit. To add to the complexity of libel, what may be a good defense in one jurisdiction may not help you in another.

In the course of your work and from time-to-time you probably will find yourself dealing with less than truthful people who want to use you to hurt others—perhaps as a payback for some previous actual or perceived wrong done to them. They will tell you things with all the sincerity of a minister delivering a Sunday sermon; some or all of it libelous, and if you repeat it in print expect a lawsuit. Also be alert to people playing practical jokes on others; libel suits lurk in this arena also. While you probably will find most people you deal with are upfront and honest—upfront and honest at least in the sense of lacking a sense of malice in their dealings with you—be alert to those who are not.

Beside reporting the truth (with its limited protection in the libel arena), what else might a photojournalist do to keep out of court, or out of the legal settlement process? Actually, even with its limitations, truth is the single best arrow you can carry in your anti-libel quiver. As a practical matter, as a photojournalist you probably will gather much information—most likely much of it for captions—that will never cause you or your organization libel-related problems. But being alert for information that may is a big step in avoiding libel lawsuits. Always bring such information to the attention of a ranking editor or manager *before* you submit it for publication. Objectively explain all the details of how you came to have the information and why you think it is suspect.

While always being alert not to report words that libel someone, you also must always be alert not to make photographs that libel someone. Some examples of potentially libelous photographs are: a telephoto lens so compresses the illusion of space that in some way libel is created; the juxtaposition of a thing or of another person with your subject causes libel; a moment taken out of context and published without adequate textual explanation causes libel; using computer processing to create an image that never existed—replacing a subject's head with another, for example—and by accident or design allowing the fake image to be published causes libel. Always—with every photograph you submit for publication—stand back and take as objective a look at it as you can. Ask yourself if there is anything you see in the photograph that seems questionable. Ask yourself if there is anything in the photograph that a person with reasonable sensibilities may be upset about. If your answer is yes to either of these questions, your wise course is to

bring your concern to the attention of a ranking editor or manager before submitting the picture for publication. Incidentally, never play around with a photograph. Never do anything in the course of your work to a photograph using the computer or otherwise that you think is cute, funny, amusing, or ironic or that is otherwise out of the ordinary and usual professional way in which your publication deals with photographs. Doing so courts a libel suit.

Three Procedural Areas

Photojournalists are likely to become involved in the following three areas of legal procedure. They are subpoenas, depositions, and arrests.

Subpoenas

Photojournalists probably will be served with at least several subpoenas during their careers; every photojournalist should have some idea of what subpoenas are and what to do about them.

A subpoena is a legally binding document issued by a private or government attorney or a legal entity such as a grand jury or a legislative body. Subpoenas require a person to bear witness under oath orally or by producing physical material such as photographs, or both, at a designated time and place. The recipient of a subpoena who does not conform to its requirements or who does not convince a court of law to withdraw the subpoena risks being held in contempt of court. A person who lies in connection with a subpoena risks being charged with perjury. Contempt and perjury convictions may result in jail time.

The usual reasons for issuing subpoenas to photojournalists are (1) to try to force them to produce "outtakes," pictures taken but not published; (2) to try to force them to testify in a deposition, in a trial, or both, about events that occurred and that they witnessed; (3) to get them to confirm that pictures they took are truthful and fair representations of real-life scenes as they viewed them.

Many courts generally support limited protection for the media against forced testimony. At the same time the courts try to ensure that litigants can obtain information that only journalists possess if the information is crucial to one side or the other in a lawsuit. You should become familiar with the court decisions and statutory law in the area where you work so you will know how much protection, if any, you have.

Some publications try to solve the outtake problem by instituting a policy of destroying all unpublished negatives, prints, and computerized images *before* they receive a subpoena; it is a crime to destroy any that are the subject of a subpoena after the subpoena is legally served. One problem with this approach is the loss of potentially historically important pictures.

The other reasons that photojournalists are subpoenaed are not as easy to deal with. If a judge orders journalists to reveal their sources and they refuse, the judge almost certainly will hold them in contempt of court and fine or jail them, or both. Contempt of court in this circumstance is a criminal offense.[37]

Being served with a subpoena is a sobering experience. But being served does not necessarily mean that you must produce what the subpoena demands; your attorney may be successful at legally giving you the right not to conform to the demands of the subpoena. Most likely the journalistic organization for which you work will provide you with an attorney or you may engage one yourself to represent you. You should give a subpoena serious and immediate attention. A subpoena contains a deadline for either producing materials or appearing to testify, or both. Photojournalists served with subpoenas should immediately report to their supervisor or the newspaper executive who has the authority to contact the newspaper's attorney. Never ignore a subpoena because you could find yourself in contempt of court.

Never respond to a subpoena without consulting management. A subpoena also is a management matter, and the newspaper may decide to contest the subpoena—to seek to have it "quashed"—for any number of reasons. The photojournalist probably will be asked about the underlying facts so that management can evaluate issues about compliance and better advise the photojournalist who received the subpoena about the best course of action. Wherever advice comes from, the person who receives a subpoena is ultimately responsible for complying with it.

Sometimes the issuer voluntarily withdraws a subpoena once the newspaper's lawyer becomes involved. Sometimes a judge holds a hearing to decide whether to enforce a subpoena. In any event, you must take a subpoena seriously.

Depositions

Depositions allow attorneys from either side to orally interrogate a person about a matter, to look at documents that bear on the matter, or both. A deposition is taken under oath and has the same legal standing and potential for perjury as does testimony given in court during a trial. Photojournalists must take depositions seriously.

Photojournalists must let no one influence them to testify in a deposition —or in court—to anything other than truthful facts as they know them. Anyone who tries or who in fact does exert such influence commits a crime.

The wise photojournalist will consult an attorney before testifying at a deposition and will have an attorney present to give him or her legal advice during the deposition.

Arrests

Law enforcement officers, including those serving in police departments, regularly deal with situations so dangerous that they could die before their shifts end. This knowledge, along with a tendency to favor law-and-order over media concerns, can lead law enforcement officers to have an attitude of neutrality toward the media at best, animosity at worst. Add abrasive, pushy photojournalists desperately wanting to get pictures at a news event and the scene is set for confrontation. In fact, even laid back, tactful photojournalists can find themselves in confrontations with law enforcement officers but they are less probable to have police problems than their hard-charging colleagues. Some law enforcement officers are sympathetic to the needs of the media, just as some photojournalists are sensitive to law enforcement needs. When these people interact, things tend to go well.

Whenever photojournalists respond to fires, automobile accidents, public suicides, bank robberies, or the myriad of other activities in which people involve themselves and that demand law enforcement attention, photographers run the risk of being arrested, jailed, and standing trial. If you can do so legally, it is best to avoid being arrested; rarely is a photograph worth it.[38]

Law enforcement officers sometimes have good reasons to arrest photojournalists. Law enforcement officers are charged under oath to protect the public welfare and safety. They must preserve scenes to permit a thorough investigation that leads to arrest and conviction of those who committed crimes or to a determination that no crimes were involved. (Figure 9.5). They must accurately and fairly investigate such matters as automobile accidents and homicides and present their findings so that all participants are treated fairly. Police can and do arrest photojournalists who interfere with these important duties.

If you are arrested it usually is wise to plead guilty only upon the advice of an attorney—your employer probably will involve the organization's attorney if you have been arrested. After discussing the case with you, the lawyer may advise pleading guilty, may try to negotiate a lesser charge with the prosecutor assigned to the case in return for a guilty plea, or may advise you to plead not guilty and fight the charge in court.

No matter how it goes, you will be saddled with an arrest record (unless your attorney is able to have it expunged if you are found not guilty or the charges are withdrawn), will endure what surely is an unpleasant experience, and probably will be unable to work full time—it is difficult to cover assignments when in jail, in conference with an attorney, and during trial. In addition, if you are found guilty or plead guilty the conviction almost certainly will follow you the rest of your life.

Copyright

One long-standing policy of the federal government has been to encourage creativity in various fields, including photojournalism. The U.S. Constitution, in Article I, Section 8, addresses the subject: "The Congress shall have Power . . . To promote the Progress of Science and useful Arts, by securing for limited Times to Authors and Inventors the exclusive Right to their respective Writings and Discoveries...." This exclusivity, with the implied potential for economic gain, is known as *copyright*.[39]

The address of the Copyright Office is: U.S. Copyright Office, Library of Congress, 101 Independence Ave., S.E., Washington, DC 20559-6000. A faster way to get forms, information, and answers to questions is to call (202) 707–3000. Information specialists in the Copyright Office's Public Information Office are available weekdays during business hours. Or you can contact the Copyright Office at *http://www.lcweb.loc.gov/copyright/*.

Under current copyright law the original owner of a photograph has a copyright on it from the moment it first exists in tangible form. You need not apply to the federal government for this right. However, for complete protection of a copyrighted interest you do need to immediately register the copyright with the Copyright Office. This ensures that you do not lose important legal rights if someone infringes on your copyright; if that happens and you are protected because you hold the copyright and registered it, you may be able to collect more money damages and payment of your legal fees from the infringer.

FIGURE 9.5

Expect that during your photojournalistic career you will cover many spot news events where police and other officials are involved—automobile accidents, murders, and fires for example. You should never interfere with the physical scenes or with officials at the scenes. Sometimes, perhaps often, you will find officials—most likely police or fire personnel—have made the scenes off limits to the public—including photojournalists. One way this is done is by enclosing the areas with a wide, typically yellow tape as this photograph of a Little Rock, Arkansas, fire scene illustrates. You should never enter into areas enclosed by this tape—expect different wording on some tapes than that on the tape in this photograph—without the specific permission of a police officer, or a firefighter if it is a fire department tape, and should go only where the official says you may go. Sometimes you may find yourself at spot news events before law enforcement or fire officials arrive. Whether you arrive before officials or not, take great care not to disturb the scene. Watch where you walk; thoughtless walking can destroy important evidence such as footprints. Never touch anything; the physical placement of an item can be critical evidence, and a fingerprint smudged by you may let a guilty person go unpunished. Consider using a telephoto lens at some distance from the scene so that you increase the probability that you do not inappropriately intrude while still covering the event.

MIKE WINTROATH/AP/WIDE WORLD PHOTOS

Copyright disputes can end up in court just like a lot of other disagreements. In one case ultimately decided by the U.S. Supreme Court, *Community for Creative Non-Violence v. Reid,* an artist and the organization that hired him to produce a sculpture contested the ownership of the copyright to that work.[40] The dispute focused on the "work-made-for-hire" provision of the Copyright Act of 1976. A work is made for hire when it is prepared by an employee in the scope of that person's employment. Normally, the author of a work is the person who actually creates it by translating an idea into a fixed tangible expression entitled to copyright protection. If it is a work made for hire, the employer or other person for whom it was made is considered the author and owns the copyright under the law.

The sculptor, James Earl Reid, who created the work in this case, was an independent contractor, not an employee, and accordingly was the author and owned the copyright, the U.S. Supreme Court ruled in 1989. Although the organization that commissioned the work told the sculptor what it wanted, the sculptor supplied his own tools, worked in his own studio, worked for just a few months on the project, and was paid a lump sum. This did not create the employer-employee relationship necessary for a work made for hire.

Final Thoughts

Sometimes legal problems are the result of arrogance on both sides. A little courtesy and empathy often go a long way toward diminishing or eliminating legal problems that take photojournalists from the newsroom to the courtroom.

Without diminishing the importance of a solid general knowledge of applicable law and with the realization that easy-to-remember non-inclusive lists are risky in the legal arena, here are some brief guidelines that photojournalists should keep in mind. They may bring to mind more in-depth aspects of law that affect photojournalists and serve as a reminder that many legal re-

strictions exist. They also may remind you that you need to become familiar with the laws where you will be working.

As you read them, keep in mind that with some of them appropriate permission from appropriate individuals can change what otherwise is legally impermissable to legally permissible. Here are the guidelines:

- Tact often yields more access than law.
- Picture taking on public property available for general use by the general public usually is permissible.
- Picture taking from public property of scenes on private property clearly visible to the general public from the same vantage point usually is permissable.
- Picture taking using a telephoto lens from public property of scenes on private property not reasonably visible to the general public from the photographer's position and with the public using only normal vision—no binoculars, for example—is legally dangerous.
- Picture taking on private property and on public or private property open to the general public only for one or more specific reasons, none of which is journalistic picture taking—for example, a department store, a hospital, or a museum—is legally dangerous. Accompanying law enforcement officials, firefighters, or other government officials by invitation or otherwise onto any such property for journalistic coverage reasons generally affords the photojournalist no legal protection.
- Picture taking at a concert or other performance where the audience is not allowed to take pictures is legally dangerous.
- Picture taking of people who intentionally or otherwise are in the public eye is legally permissible so long as the photography pertains to the reason they are in the public eye, they are on public property open to the public for general use and they have no reasonable expectation of privacy.

- Entering military property is illegal.
- Photographing military property and personnel on military property is illegal even if the photographer is on civilian property.
- Photographing classified items or information on or off military property is illegal.
- If you want to photograph on military property—a base, an airplane, or a ship, for example—contact the appropriate Public Affairs Officer or Commanding Officer. Explain who you work for, what you want to do, why you want to do it, and when you want to do it. Expect that sometimes your request will be granted, sometimes not.
- Be cautious when photographing, reproducing, and publishing government and private entity documents. Don't forget the size and color restrictions placed by federal law on the reproduction of money and the size restrictions placed by federal law on the reproduction of stamps.
- Crossing law enforcement, fire, or other such government lines is illegal.
- Entering a courtroom with cameras is legally dangerous. Picture taking in a courtroom is legally dangerous. Picture taking in or near the building housing a courthouse is legally dangerous.
- Dealing with subpoenas immediately is prudent; report every subpoena you receive to management but remember that you alone are responsible for subpoenas issued to you. You are wise to consult an attorney before responding to a subpoena.
- When testifying at depositions and trials you must tell the truth; not doing so opens you to criminal penalties. You are wise to consult an attorney before giving a deposition and before testifying at a trial, and to have an attorney representing you at the deposition and at the trial.
- Immediately report legal problems, whether with authorities or private individuals, to management.
- Absent agreement to the contrary, exposed film, digital camera images, prints, and their computer-generated counterparts, are the property of a photojournalist's employer if they are done in the course of employment with the employer.
- Immense legal liability can flow to photojournalists and their employers if photojournalists violate traffic laws when trying to reach news scenes or other assignments quickly.
- Captions or accompanying stories should contain only truthful words in fair context. Unless you have clear legal privilege to do so, take care not to report defamatory information from a source. Defamation opens photojournalists and their employers to legal liability.
- Photojournalists, particularly those covering news events attended by law enforcement officials, run the risk of being arrested and charged with a crime even if doing nothing illegal or inappropriate. Civil suits can flow out of such coverage, most likely brought by participants or spectators but possibly also by law enforcement officials. Arrests and civil lawsuits can flow from photojournalistic coverage of non-news events. Journalistic photography is a legally risk–laden undertaking.
- Legality of an act does not necessarily make it advisable; ethics or taste may demand it be left undone.
- Laws vary from legal jurisdiction to legal jurisdiction and they can vary in the same jurisdiction at different times. You are well-advised to become intimately acquainted with the laws where you work that relate to journalism.

NOTES

[1] Bryan A. Gardner, ed. in chief, *Black's Law Dictionary,* 7th ed. (St. Paul, Minn.: West Group, 1999), pp. 1508–09.

[2] James A. Henderson, Jr., Richard N. Pearson, and John A. Siliciano, *The Torts Process,* 4th ed. (Boston: Little, Brown, 1994), p. 497.

[3] Public Contracts and Property Management, 41 Code of Federal Regulations, (C.F.R.) § 101–20.310 (1999).

[4] Postal Operations Manual—Contents, POM Issue 8, July 16, 1998, Updated with Postal Bulletin Revisions Through October 19, 2000, 124.58 Photographs for News, Advertising, or Commercial Purposes, p. 25

[5] Crimes and Criminal Procedure, 18 U.S.C. §§ 471–699 (1976); printing and filming of United States and foreign obligations and securities, 18 U.S.C. § 504 (1976) as revised by the 105th Congress, Second Session (1998).

[6] Photojournalists are well advised to err on the conservative side when photographing in a courtroom. Aggressive journalists stretching the rules governing their behavior invite a contempt of court citation and give ammunition to those who would again ban them from taking pictures in courtrooms.

[7] The Lindbergh case has not been the only court case to make a strong statement against photography in the courtroom. Two other famous cases in this regard are *Estes v. State of Texas*, 381 U.S. 632 (1965), and *Sheppard v. Maxwell*, 384 U.S. 333 (1966).

[8] The recommendations of the American Bar Association and the Conference of State Chief Justices are not binding on any state. What a state adopts is solely the decision of the state's highest court.

[9] "A Repeat Performance–Judicial Conference allows cameras back in appeals courts," *ABA JOURNAL* May 1996, p.38.

[10] The Associated Press, "On Cameras in Supreme Court, Souter Declares an Adamant 'No,' " *The New York Times*, 30 March 1996, p. 9.

[11] Administrative Office of the U.S. Courts, "News Release," 12 March 1996, p. 1.

[12] Crimes and Criminal Procedure, 18 U.S.C. § 700–1080 (1976); Gathering, Transmitting, or Losing Defense Information, 18 U.S.C. § 793; Photographing and Sketching Defense Installations 18 U.S.C. § 795; Use of Aircraft for Photographing Defense Installations 18 U.S.C. § 796; Publication and Sale of Photographs of Defense Installations, 18 U.S.C. § 797; Disclosure of Classified Information, 18 U.S.C. § 798.

[13] William L. Prosser, "Privacy," *California Law Review* (August 1960): 383. As with photographing in courtrooms, photojournalists must consider the potential consequences of aggressive behavior. The irritation that the press caused the Warrens is a classic example of press excess that led to considerably more—and earlier—control than might otherwise have been the case.

[14] Samuel D. Warren and Louis D. Brandeis, "The Right to Privacy," *Harvard Law Review* (December 15, 1890): 196.

[15] Ibid., pp. 195, 211.

[16] Prosser, "Privacy," p. 389.

[17] T. Barton Carter et al., *Mass Communications Law in a Nutshell*, 4th ed. (St. Paul, Minn.: West, 1994), pp. 120–22. A long but interesting West Virginia case about appropriation and false light in the public eye, *Crump v. Beckley Newspaper, Inc.*, 320 S.E.2d 70 (1984), involves a female coal miner.

[18] W. Page Keeton et al. *Prosser and Keeton on the Law of Torts*, 5th ed., with a 1988 Pocket Part by Dan B. Dobbs et al. (St. Paul, Minn.: West, 1984), p. 855.

[19] *Shulman v. Group W Productions, Inc., et al.*, 955 P.2d 469 (Cal. 1998), pp. 490–91, 494.

[20] Carter et al., *Mass Communications Law in a Nutshell*, p. 123.

[21] *Shulman v. Group W Productions, Inc., et al.*, p. 489.

[22] *Dietemann v. Time, Inc.*, 449 F.2d 245, 249 (9th Cir. 1971).

[23] *Restatement (Second) of Torts* § 652D.

[24] Ibid., § 652E.

[25] Gardner, ed. *Black's Law Dictionary*, p.1276.

[26] Ibid., p.1056.

[27] W. Page Keeton et al., *Prosser and Keeton on the Law of Torts*, pp. 863–64.

[28] For a particularly interesting libel case involving a prominent Palm Beach socialite and heir to a major tire and rubber company fortune, see *Time, Inc. v. Firestone*, 424 U.S. 448 (1976).

[29] Norm Goldstein, ed., *The Associated Press Stylebook and Libel Manual*, 34th ed. (New York: The Associated Press, 1999), p. 336.

30 Gardner, ed. *Black's Law Dictionary,* p. 1307.

31 Keeton et al., *Prosser and Keeton on the Law of Torts,* p. 786

32 Goldstein, ed. *The Associated Press Stylebook and Libel Manual,* p. 336.

33 Ibid.

34 Ibid., p. 353.

35 Gardner, ed. *Black's Law Dictionary,* p. 1056.

36 Ibid., p. 968.

37 Photojournalists are subpoenaed to testify about events they witnessed while acting as journalists. For an interesting case in this regard involving a drug bust at Miami International Airport, see *Miami Herald Publishing Company v. Morejon,* 561 So. 2d 577 (1990).

38 Publications occasionally want to test a law by intentionally violating it. This is a decision that belongs to management and the photojournalist; photojournalists should never make this decision on their own. But photojournalists should never allow themselves to be coerced by management into breaking the law.

39 For a copyright case involving photographs of the assassination of President Kennedy, see *Time, Inc. v. Bernard Geis Associations,* 293 F. Supp. 130 (S.D.N.Y., 1968).

40 *Community for Creative Non-Violence v. Reid,* 490 U.S. 730 (1989).

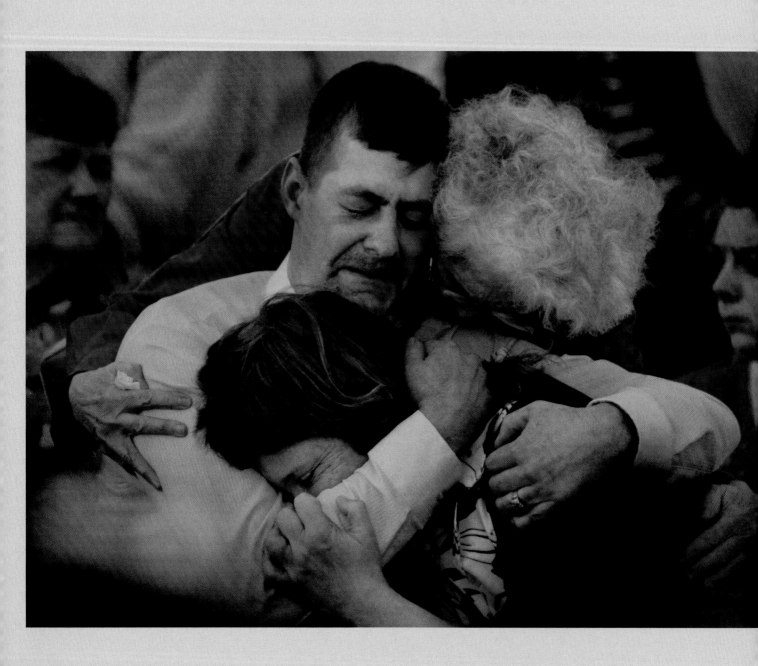

Ethics and Taste

**Parents grieve at the funeral of their
slain 8-year-old daughter.**
ROBERT COHEN/*THE COMMERCIAL APPEAL*, MEMPHIS, TENN.

Overview

Ethics is the prime structure that, through institutional and individual implementation, determines the moralistic ambiance of editorial activity of journalistic organizations, significantly impacting the information—words and pictures—made available to readers. Ethics also is a major factor in determining acceptable behavior of photojournalists. Taste, while undoubtedly having some impact on what is made available to readers, is considerably less influential and important than ethics. Taste, while having some influence in determining acceptable behavior of photojournalists, surely takes a distant second to ethics in this regard.

Ethics

The fundamental purpose here is to whet your appetite and increase your sensitivity to the subject of ethics and ethical considerations that you undoubtedly will face during your career. The goal is to help you build a solid foundation in the ethical arena that will make it easier to deal with ethical questions and will serve as the basis for more in-depth study. But why, you may ask, is an ethical arena desirable? Why not just allow each person to do his or her thing or, alternatively, have a plethora of laws covering every conceivable human activity? Here is philosopher William K. Frankena's view:

> . . . why should society adopt such an institution as morality? Why should it foster such a system for the guidance of conduct in addition to convention, law, and prudence? To this the answer seems clear. The conditions of a satisfactory human life for people living in groups could hardly obtain otherwise. The alternatives would seem to be either a state of nature in which all or most of us would be worse off than we are, even if Hobbes is wrong in thinking that life in such a state would be "solitary, poor, nasty, brutish, and short"; or a leviathan civil state more totalitarian than any yet dreamed of, one in which the laws would cover all aspects of life and every possible deviation by the individual would be closed off by an effective threat of force.[1]

Where to Look

Photojournalists regularly confront questions for which the law provides little or no guidance. Because society has left many aspects of human behavior untouched by these formal rules, photojournalists—indeed all journalists—must look elsewhere for guidance about appropriate behavior. An important place to find this guidance is under the broad conceptual umbrella that covers various ideas about right and wrong, known as morality or ethics.

Philosophers for more than 2,000 years have grappled with questions of self-imposed restriction.[2] In doing so they helped establish the branch of philosophy known as *ethics*. What is ethics? For the purpose of this book ethics is a system of control free of government intervention that is dependent on good faith reasoning, which results in actions that are "right" because they are supported by the best reasons. Ethics guides people toward doing what they "should" and what is "right." Sanctions for straying from expected behavior usually fall short of physical force but nevertheless are real and highly effective in castigating deviants and forcing them to return to the ethical norm.

Photographic Examples

Here is a selection of photographs that your author believes reasonably can be said to be in the ethical arena in one way or the other (Figures 10.1–10.9). (In a strict sense every journalistic photograph ever taken is in this arena in one way or the other.) Carefully look at these photographs—read them. Ask yourself if any should not have been taken. Ask yourself if any should not have been published. Decide if any in your opinion reasonably should not be in the ethical arena with the rest. Think about how you would feel if you or your relatives or close friends were the subjects. Think also about the readers who

FIGURE 10.1

A boy anguishes over his dog, mortally injured by a car. When editors learned the dog had died, they decided not to publish the picture. It later ran at the request of the boy, who wanted to encourage drivers to drive with caution.

MIKE STOCKWELL/*THE SUN CHRONICLE*, ATTLEBORO, MASS.

viewed these photographs. What about the readers? Do they have a right to be visually informed? Do you think there is a balance to be drawn between individual privacy and everyone else being privy to what occurred? As you go through these photographs and come to your conclusions, make note of your reasons and share them with your fellow classmates. Flesh out the important question: Why?

Why Is There a Photojournalistic Problem?

Since the advent of photography more than 160 years ago, still photographs in journalism largely have stood as representations of reality. They generally have stood in the place of viewers who are unable to see for themselves the scenes recorded by photographers. This surrogate position was reaffirmed in the early part of the 20th century with the

FIGURE 10.2

A high school baseball player with the visiting team gestures at the hometown crowd after scoring what turned out to be the winning run. Would you publish this image? Does the player's youth influence your decision?

JOHNNY BAILEY/*THE GAINESVILLE* (GA.) *TIMES*

FIGURE 10.3

During a 1987 news conference in his Capitol office the Treasurer of the Commonwealth of Pennsylvania, R. Budd Dwyer, put the barrel of a handgun in his mouth and pulled the gun's trigger, killing himself. The next day he was to be sentenced after having been found guilty of criminal charges, including bribery. At the news conference he strongly maintained his innocence. If you were on duty when these photographs arrived at your newspaper, would you have supported publishing them? What are the pros and cons of using or not using them? Would Dwyer's status as a high-level state official who had been convicted of crimes have affected your decision? What about the very public forum in which he killed himself? Are these photographs simply too shocking to be published?

PAUL VATHIS/AP/WIDE WORLD PHOTOS

FIGURE 10.4

A drowned child's body is recovered from a lake. If you think that publishing this photograph poses an ethical problem, would you feel differently if the child's face were not visible?

JOHN PINEDA/MIAMI HERALD

FIGURE 10.5

One of the important missions of photojournalism is to communicate to readers the human condition, to show people as they really are. The ethical question then is: How far is this mission to be taken? Without doubt, reputable U.S. journalism has drawn an ethical line that is not to be crossed. A problem with this line is that the closer it gets to allowing pictures to be published, the fuzzier it tends to get. Call this a gray area where one person acting in good faith will publish, another acting likewise will not. What about this photograph of the mother of a 20-month-old who just found out the child died in an apartment fire. If there is any question about publishing this picture, what reason or reasons may be put forth to deny readers seeing this slice of the human condition? The author of this book believes that there always is a balance that should be drawn between informing readers and encroaching on the grief of people. Whether the drawing of this balance tips the decision toward voluntary censorship or toward publication should in your author's view first turn on one or more applicable core rules—maxims—with consideration if need be for the particular situation and its nuances (discussed later in the chapter).

ETHAN MILLER/LAS VEGAS SUN

FIGURE 10.6

Should—or is—the ethical-related decision to publish a photograph based on, or influenced by, how close or far away the event shown in the photograph happened from a paper's circulation area. Consider this image from Acapulco, Mexico. Floods and landslides caused by a hurricane killed 120 people in the resort city. Here a soldier digs out the body of a child, one of the hurricane's victims. Since the child's face is not visible, is this a picture you would publish without hesitation even if the scene were from your city? If the face were visible, would this make a difference to you in publishing the photograph if it were from your city or from a foreign country where it is less likely that relatives would see it in your publication? How much consideration in publishing photographs of news events should be given to the feelings of relatives and friends of a victim, or to the victim if he or she is alive?

JOSE LUIS MAGANA/AP/WIDE WORLD PHOTOS

FIGURE 10.8

Does whether a scene is portrayed in black and white or in color make a difference in the
truthfulness that is conveyed? Is it more "appropriate" to picture some scenes in black and
white, others in color? What about these images of professional cyclist Fabio Casartelli of
Italy lying mortally hurt after he fell during a race? Is there any ethical question about publishing either of these photographs? Does it make any ethical—or taste—difference that the
man was participating in a public event? That he was a professional?

PASCAL PAVANI/AP/WIDE WORLD PHOTOS

Photojournalism: An Introduction

A firefighter carries a mortally wounded child after the bombing of the Alfred P. Murrah Federal Building in Oklahoma City. Newspaper readers' reaction to this image was mixed—some were critical of its being published, some supportive. Amateur photographer Charles Porter IV, who took the picture, won the 1996 Pulitzer Prize for spot news photography.

CHARLES H. PORTER IV/CORBIS SYGMA

"candid" technique. In recent times the still photograph's position as a truthful surrogate for real life was seriously examined beginning about 1970 when the U.S. photojournalistic community turned a particularly critical eye toward the truthfulness and fairness of what it was producing. Photographs could lie and mislead by accident or intention; serious introspection was called for and constant vigilance needed (Figure 10.10).

The intensity of this concern significantly increased in the late 1980s and early 1990s with the mainstreaming of the electronic darkroom and its processing of photographs in the computer. Almost unbelievable changes could be made in an image with, for all practical purposes, no telltale evidence that the original image had been changed. Now with the electronic darkroom firmly established and digital picture taking on its way to being mainstream in photojournalism, photojournalists and their editors and managers continue their intense well-founded interest in ethics and ethical behavior. The literature is full of the subject. It is discussed at workshops and seminars. Photo department and general editorial meetings are arenas for discussion of photo-related ethics matters. The subject clearly is on the front burner, stoked by easy and untraceable digital manipulation and by concern for journalistic practices generally.

But why all this concern about ethics? As a practical matter, if photojournalists do not act in a way perceived to be ethically correct, they easily can find themselves recipients of the wrath of outraged subjects and readers. Also, they may be castigated by their journalistic peers or even fired by their bosses. Ethics and ethical theory are important to photojournalists in down-to-earth, practical ways.

Ethical Theory

Making ethical judgments is simplified and more dependable when it is based on a conceptual framework that orders and guides the myriad individual journalistic situations that demand ethical consideration. Ethical theory is that framework. Ethical theory offers the potential for simplifying diverse situations so that deciding what to do is easier. The alternative is dealing with every situation without a consistent guidepost.

What Is Ethical Theory and What Drives It?   Different as they may be, all theories about how people should voluntarily conduct their lives fall under the umbrella of philosophy known and studied as ethical theory. Ethical theory can be maddeningly controversial and confusing. One philosopher propounds a theory only to have other philosophers pounce on it, methodically pointing out its shortcomings. However much complexity and controversy may reign in the arena of ethical theory, reason is a unifying factor. An ethical theory does not materialize from thin air. An ethical theory that has the best reasoning behind it is the one that ought to prevail.

Categorizing Ethical Theories

Ethical theories typically fall into one of two broad categories: deontology or teleology. These are fundamental to putting at least some order into the conflicting and sometimes chaotic world of ethical theory. They also are fundamentally important to our quest of arriving at a wise and workable ethical approach.

Deontology A simplified explanation of deontological theories is that their main concern is with a person's actions rather than the result of the actions.

The exemplar full-fledged deontological theory comes from the 18th-century philosopher Immanuel Kant. It commonly is referred to as the *categorical imperative*. Kant postulated that it is the following of rules, rather than the results, that is of primary importance. These are only the rules that a person would want everyone else to follow. Kant wrote, "The goodness of a good will is not derived from the goodness of the results which it produces . . . a good will continues to have its own unique goodness even where, by some misfortune, it is unable to produce the results at which it aims."[3]

Philosopher S. Jack Odell tells us that:

> Some deontological theories ground ethical judgments on reason; others ground them in God's will; some appeal to human decision; others claim that the correctness or incorrectness of an action is to be decided in terms of the conventions of society; some hold that an act is right or wrong depending upon whether or not it has an objective though nonnatural property of being good or bad; others try to ground ethics in nature.[4]

Teleology A simplified explanation of teleological theories is that their main concern is with the results of actions, not the actions themselves.

Odell explains that "a teleological ethical theory is any theory which measures the rightness or the wrongness of an action or set of actions in terms of its/their consequences."[5]

There are two types of teleological theories: altruistic and egoistic. Altruistic theories are concerned with the effect of a person's action on others. Egoistic theories are concerned with the effect of a person's action on that person. Examples of two teleological theories are ethical egoism, which exclusively promotes self-interest, and utilitarianism, which promotes the general good.

Ethical Theories Various ethical theories have been propounded since Aristotle's time (about 350 B.C.). Each has tried to structure human behavior by giving guidance and direction to thinking people in their effort to determine the most appropriate course of action. All have been considered and criticized; most have been discarded or relegated to the periphery of contemporary philosophical thought.

A problem for photojournalists—for a lot of people—is that no single ethical theory appears to be universally accepted in contemporary American society. This does not mean there are no ethical theories popular at the beginning of the 21st century. Two theories dispelling this notion are *utilitarianism* and the *theory of natural law*. According to philosopher William K. Frankena, all utilitarians hold "that what is morally right or wrong is ultimately to be wholly determined by looking to see what promotes the greatest general balance of good over evil."[6]

The theory of natural law is an important theory of Christianity. According to philosopher James Rachels:

> The Theory of Natural Law holds that moral judgments are 'dictates of reason.' The best thing to do, in any circumstance, is whatever course of conduct has the best reasons on its side. Thus the believer and the nonbeliever are in exactly the same position when it comes to making moral judgments. Both are endowed with powers of conscience and reason. For both, making a responsible

moral judgment is a matter of listening to reason and being true to one's conscience. Thus non-believers are able to function as rational beings, even though their lack of faith prevents them from realizing that God is the ultimate author of the rational order in which they participate and which their moral judgments express.[7]

On the Road Toward an Ethical Approach for Photojournalists

Let's take a two-pronged approach on our journey down the toward-an-ethical-approach road. The first prong is knowing the mission of the organization for which you work and how this mission is accomplished. The second prong is deciding whether the deontological or teleological approach or some combination of them is the more likely avenue for accomplishing the mission.

Mission of the Organization   Clearly, it is crucial for concerned photojournalists to understand and accept the mission of the organization for which they labor and the ways this mission is accomplished. The organization's general journalistic mission and its photojournalistic mission and the acceptable ways to accomplish them may be spelled out at hiring. This may be done in a written or oral statement at orientation. If not done at hiring, it likely is done sometime, perhaps in formal meetings, in hallway discussions, or in newsroom debate.

Without doubt, a key mission of every reputable U.S. journalistic organization is to transmit truthful information, and an important goal for photojournalists is to approach their employing organization's mission of truthful reporting as closely as humanly possible. The question then is, what is truth?

Great question, difficult answer.

Because of its difficulty, the discussion here is not about the philosophical aspects of truth; rather, it largely is limited to a practical picture-taking-

oriented approach. If you want to venture into the hard-core philosophical aspect of truth, consider reading literature about the subject; you might even take a course in your school's philosophy department that deals with the subject.

What might be a practical definition of truth for the journalistic photographer? Try this as a starter:

For photojournalistic picture-taking purposes, truth is reality viewed, interpreted, and photographed by photojournalists acting in good faith and in a sense of fairness and objectivity and with the goal of fairly presenting to their readers the most appropriate truth of the reality that was viewed, interpreted, and photographed.

Where are the flaws in this definition? Surely it is not perfect.

One concern is that it does not address the knowledge differences between photographers. Is it reasonable to assume that a photographer who has significant prior knowledge about the subject being viewed—about its history and current state, for example—will, all other things being equal, come to a different conclusion about what is the most appropriate truth than a photographer who knows little or nothing about the subject other than that he has an assignment to photographically cover it? If this is so, does it necessarily mean that the knowledgeable photographer's most appropriate truth will be more accurate, more "good" than his uninformed colleague? Is it possible that ignorance-based "serendipitous discovery" is sometimes a better way to find the most appropriate truth than previously acquired knowledge that may lead to a predisposed inclination that results in less than the best most appropriate truth? This book's author thinks that while serendipitous discovery may sometimes be desirable, that the prior knowledge approach more likely will more consistently lead to the best most appropriate truth being recognized. However, this prior knowledge approach is not without risk. Unless a knowledgeable photographer keeps an open mind to new information, a previously acquired mind-set could result in other than the best most appropriate truth being conveyed to readers. What is this prior knowledge and how does a photographer get it? It is not only knowledge about the immediate subject, but a reservoir of knowledge about different subjects, not the least of which is human behavior and the human condition. Acquiring this kind of knowledge means taking courses in college other than journalism skills. It means having an ongoing commitment to reading wide and deep on your own in college and throughout your working career. It also means seriously reading your publication every day, regularly listening to local and national television news reports, and regularly reading any other publications that deal with your community. In addition, regularly reading *The New York Times* for its broad and in-depth international and national reporting and commentary and, perhaps surprisingly, for its fine photography is highly recommended. On a more specific level, it means learning as much about your subject as reasonably possible. It means seeking out reporters and photographers at your publication who covered the subject and gleaning information—including perspective—from them. It means checking your publication's library for previous stories, and checking other relevant sources. Reason must prevail in all this, however. If you are given an assignment to cover a subject in the next 15 minutes about which you know nothing, it is unreasonable to expect that you can gather much new information about it. But if you have the time, you should try hard to become as informed and updated as reasonably possible. In any case, you should have so prepared yourself in college and in ongoing self-help that you have at least some general knowledge of the subject. The prior knowledge approach means that a good journalistic photographer is far more than someone only highly skilled in the technical aspects of picture taking; it means you are a journalist in the truest sense.

A second concern about this definition of truth is the differing values people have. Social background and education are only two variables that potentially can result in two people having very different values. As an example, it would be surprising if any two people chosen at random in your photojournalism class have exactly the same values. Values—at least some—tend to be modified or otherwise changed as a person grows older—as a person has more and more life experiences. However they come about, individual variations in values can lead to different perceptions of the most appropriate truth. It is possible that two people having fundamentally the same knowledge about the subject and the same time to cover it and both acting in good faith and in a sense of fairness and objectivity will come to different conclusions about the subject's most appropriate truth. In this author's view, this is a truth-finding variable that cannot be conquered, that maybe should not be conquered. The world is probably a more interesting place because of our values differences—as long as photojournalists act in good faith and in a sense of fairness in their effort to ferret out and fairly present to their readers the most appropriate truth of the reality that they viewed, interpreted, and photographed.

Most likely a close reading of the definition of truth presented here—for example, looking closely at each word's meaning and how the words go together to convey meaning—will yield more concerns; you really should give it a go. After you have done this, maybe you and your instructor and your peers can come up with something better, something more practical and helpful in giving guidance to photojournalists trying to search out the most appropriate truth of a situation and to fairly represent it to readers.

Before moving out of the truth arena, let's deal with two last aspects: (1) multiple truths, and (2) time with subjects.

Even the best informed photographer must search for the most appropriate truth from the multitude of truths presented by any subject of photographic coverage. For example, hold an arm in front of you when facing a blazing sun. The side of your arm facing you is not directly lit; it looks very different than the opposite side, which is directly and well lit. Which side of your arm is the most appropriate truth at the moment? The shadow side facing you? The two sides partly lit and partly in shadow? The well lit side? Photojournalists must pay careful attention to the most appropriate truth. All photographic situations present multiple truths; choosing among them affects subjects and readers. Selectivity is as important in ethics as it is in composition and light. Less-than-optimum choices mislead readers just as wrong ones do.

Editors and reporters who force photographers into certain situations can stymie the search for the most appropriate truth. An example is a photographer who is forced to cover a blatantly posed and clearly contrived event, such as a staged check presentation. The most appropriate truth is the human good done by the money donated to the local children's hospital. Admittedly, the photographer covering the check presentation can search for the most appropriate truth of the staged event. But the photographer has no chance to search for the most appropriate truth of the spirit and intent of what is represented by the ceremony; the assignment maker has left the photographer off the true appropriate ethical playing field. In the photojournalistic arena, the search for the most appropriate truth begins with those who make photo assignments; it also includes higher level editors, the publisher, and the owners—anyone in a position to influence the organization's ethical ambiance.

Communicating the most appropriate truth to readers also means that photographers must be given appropriate time with their subjects—in and out in 10 minutes seldom is enough time. Being given—and actually spending— enough time with subjects to gain additional information before and during picture taking is a key in reaching the goal of communicating the most appropriate truth.

One reason time with subjects is particularly important is because of the false or misleading facade, by design or otherwise, that many present when being photographed. These are faces that show people not as they are in real life but as they would like to be or as they think others want or expect them to be. Once subjects become comfortable with photojournalists, they often relax, presenting themselves as they usually are. They thereby give the photojournalist's search for the most appropriate truth a decent chance of succeeding.

The concern with time emphasizes the importance of management in truth seeking. If photojournalists are not allowed adequate time to gather off and on-site information about assignments, even the most diligent search for the most appropriate truth is hobbled or defeated. Editors and managers are key players in photojournalistic truth seeking.

When photojournalists have the freedom to make a reasonable search for the most appropriate truth, how might they go about discovering it? If the goal is to make an image portraying an overall truth rather than one or more component smaller truths, the search obviously must concentrate on overall truth, however it manifests itself. Small truths should be ignored, except as they help form overall truth or modify it. An example is the elephant. The overall truth of this huge mammal is not a hind leg the blindfolded person feels, not the trunk that grabs food, or the tail that holds other tails; the overall truth is the components. All combine to make the one unified whole elephant, the overall truth. Unprepared and unperceptive photojournalists likely will settle for a leg truth, a trunk truth, or a tail truth, misleading readers about the overall truth (Figure 10.11).

This does not mean a distant view of the elephant is the only way to convey overall truth compositionally—quite the contrary. Overall truth may well be conveyed by emphasizing a small truth, perhaps the trunk, and implying the rest. It also may be conveyed by presenting multiple smaller truths together—two, three, or more revealing, different, and important parts of the overall truth conveyed in different photographs. Accompanying these smaller truths for unmistakable clarity may be a single image that presents the overall truth.

If the goal is to make an image that portrays a component smaller truth rather than the overall truth, the search obviously must concentrate on the smaller truth, however it manifests itself. Overall truth can be examined as it helps form the smaller truth or modifies it.

The most appropriate truth may not be one or more obvious physical aspects of a situation but rather tiny physical nuances or even intangible feelings or interactions. If this is so, the goal of photojournalists is to recognize and visually portray these, a task often approaching Herculean proportions. Perhaps a sense of space, which otherwise usually detracts, does it; perhaps a small upward glance of the eyes, or of an eyebrow, does it. Perhaps a slightly furrowed brow or another message conveyed by other body language does it. Only perceptive and sensitive photojournalists are able to detect these in a consistent and dependable way.

Zeroing in: Deontology or Teleology or Both?   Well, what's it going to be? Is it an approach with only a set of well-reasoned rules, well-reasoned principles—call them maxims? Is it an approach with no such maxims and with concern only for the results of actions? Is it an approach that is some combination of the two?

Your author subscribes to the "some combination of the two"; specifically, a deontological approach with the freedom to modify or supersede it if really need be with teleological considerations.

Professor John C. Merrill advocates this approach in *Photojournalism: Principles and Practices*, 2d ed.:

. . . the photojournalist starts with *deontology*—a basic dedication to certain ethical principles or maxims. He feels a 'duty' to conform to them; they are, to a real degree, commandments which he feels are basic to his total ethical stance.[8]

Merrill goes on to argue that photojournalists should be willing under certain circumstances to cast a broader ethical net:

The photojournalist must show a willingness—quite in line with intelligence and basic moral sensitivity—to deviate from such principles when he feels he *should*—when reason dictates another course, when projected or anticipated consequences tend to warrant the desertion of these basic ethical maxims.[9]

The author of this book thinks consequence consideration can be helpful in ultimately "maximizing the good," for ultimately getting the best ethical result. This view assumes that no one is smart enough or clever enough or informed enough to construct a body of maxims that satisfactorily covers all photojournalistic ethically related situations, laden as they often are with nuances. Therefore, you need to consider consequences in an effort to do what is right, to do what you should. When a maxim does not clearly apply without exception, your author believes it is important to use consequence consideration in the photojournalist's quest to arrive at the best ethical result.

FIGURE 10.11

Photographers photographing an elephant. What is the most appropriate truthful image? To arrive at the answer, is it necessary to know why the photographers are photographing what they are photographing?

ILLUSTRATION BY ILLUSTRATED ARTS (UK)

Consequence consideration also can be used to help the photojournalist choose the ethical road that should be traveled when two or more maxims clash; for example, one demands one course of action be taken, another demands a conflicting course of action be taken. Therefore, in your author's view, invoking consideration for consequences comes about in two ways: (1) the most appropriate maxim, if applied without regard to consequences, appears to lead to a less satisfactory ethical result than if consequences are considered; (2) maxims conflict making the best ethical way muddy and assistance is needed. It should be stressed that deviation from the most applicable maxim should only be done for good reason. (The teleological and deontological approaches—and ethics in general—are more complicated and detailed than the abbreviated discussion here; particularly interested readers may want to read, among others, William K. Frankena's *Ethics* and James Rachels' *The Elements of Moral Philosophy*.)

What about maxims? Where do these ethical rules or tenets or principles come from? Over time, reputable U.S. journalism as an institution has developed some; for example, "we only report the truth" and "we do not re-create news events." Interestingly, it may be that some of these institutional maxims were born from consideration of specific acts, a teleological basis for deontological maxims. As far as your personally acquired maxims, you may already feel strongly about certain photojournalistic matters. How did you come to feel this way? Most likely it is from what your parents taught you; what you learned from friends and other people you respect; what you learned from your religion; what you learned in school; what you learned from newspapers, magazines and television; what you learned from people who were critical or complimentary of your photographic work, perhaps during your high school days or now in college. Layered on top of your personal ethical maxims undoubtedly will be the maxims of the journalistic organization that employs you. Some—perhaps most—of these maxims may dovetail with your personal ones; some may conflict.

Photojournalists, particularly newspaper and wire service photographers, live in a fast-moving pressured environment. They simply do not have the luxury while making pictures of going through lengthy, searching, and reasoned mental discourse in deciding what fundamental ethical road they are going to travel to reach a decision about an ethics-related question facing them on an assignment they have begun. Certainly each assignment, each situation, will have its own set of facts, its own nuances, and these must be considered on the spot. But a photojournalist's well-marked ethics map needs to be in place. Deontology—with teleological-based deviation from maxims only when really needed—may be part of that map for you.

The One Just Right Ethical Theory for Photojournalists   Hope you are not disappointed, but your author is not going to venture into this minefield. Rather than advocating for any particular ethical theory, your author is going to take a limited pass, preferring instead to note some requirements he would want in or applied to any ethical theory he embraced. In addition to the deontology-teleology combination discussed above, these include:

- a reason component that leads to the best ethical action based on the best reasons;
- a concern component that advocates truthfully and fairly informing readers while at the same time seriously considering the rights and sensibilities of subjects who are being photographically covered;
- a component that takes into account the values and sensibilities of readers;
- a component that takes into account the values and sensibilities of the photojournalist;
- a component that takes into account the mission and ethical values of the

photojournalist's employing organization;

- a component that takes into account the role of journalism in the country's democracy and the role of the country in the lives of its citizens.

Perhaps you disagree with one or more of these. Perhaps you can think of additional ones that you would want in any ethical theory you adopt. Search your reason and your soul. Consult books dealing with the subject. Take a course about it. Ethical theory is quite an undertaking.

Taste

"It's ethical, but in poor taste" is a refrain photojournalists may hear when their images are under scrutiny. The questions explored here are what is taste and is it a legitimate part of photojournalism?

For an answer to the first question the obvious place to turn is the dictionary. The most relevant definitions of taste from *The Random House Dictionary of the English Language,* 2d ed. unabridged, are:

the sense of what is fitting, harmonious, or beautiful; the perception and enjoyment of what constitutes excellence in the fine arts, literature, fashion, etc. … one's personal attitude or reaction toward an aesthetic phenomenon or social situation, regarded as either good or bad.

Before coming to a conclusion about the legitimacy of taste in photojournalism, you need to know more about it. Two books, *The Encyclopedia of Philosophy* and *Taste and Criticism in the Eighteenth Century,* provide help.[10]

In the world of aesthetic theory, which includes taste, journalistic photographs fall into the category of "useful art." Their primary purpose is not to be viewed aesthetically as in the fine arts but rather to communicate specific messages.[11] Therefore, the worth of journalistic photographs primarily is in the messages they convey, not in their aesthetic value.

In relatively recent history concern for taste flourished in the first half of 18th-century England, where the branch of philosophy termed *aesthetics* began in an organized way about the same time. This concern was a reflection of a newly found concern for the passions in philosophy, as contrasted with concern for reason and understanding.[12] Great interest in the concept of taste occurred from 1710 to 1760. There was an increasing distinction in this era "between man's feeling for beauty and his sense of reason."[13]

Edmund Burke, the British statesman and writer, in his 1759 book, *On Taste,* defined the concept:

I mean by the word 'Taste' no more than that faculty or those faculties of the mind, which are affected with, or which form a judgment of, the works of imagination and the elegant arts.[14]

This background goes a long way toward answering the first question at the beginning of this discussion: What is taste? The other question remains: Is taste a legitimate part of photojournalism? In your author's view, the answer is more no than yes. Why? Isn't an image in good taste always more desirable than one in poor taste? Isn't it better to publish no image than one in poor taste? Why the deemphasis of taste?

First, as Burke made clear in *On Taste,* people's tastes vary with their development in life. Young photojournalists fresh from graduation surely do not perceive things the same way they will in five years. Ten years later their perception almost certainly will differ from what it was five years earlier; the pattern continues until retirement. Burke saw it this way back in 1759:

In the morning of our days, when the senses are unworn and tender, when the whole man is awake in every part, and the gloss of novelty fresh upon all the objects that surround us, how lively at that time are our sensations, but how false and inaccurate the judgments we form of things![15]

FIGURE 10.12

Baseball players spitting. This image has seen its share of good taste–poor taste debate. But why not let the reader decide which? Are readers so tender that doing so will cause them unbearable anguish, unreasonable anguish, or even a tiny bit of anguish?

JOHN MORAN/*GAINESVILLE* (FLA.) *SUN*

The second important brake on liberal use of self-imposed censorship through taste is the number of people at a publication who can modify or kill photographic coverage. These begin with people making the assignment, continue through the photographer and the photo editor, include one or more low- and mid-level general editors, and finish with the chief editor or even perhaps the publisher. There is much opportunity for censorship based on personal and individual subjective judgment.

Judgments of taste clearly are personal affairs (but can be turned into institutional policy), resting on all of a person's life experience. One person's good taste is another person's poor taste. Censorship of photographs based on individual taste raises the real possibility of censorship carried too far. How much better is it to largely limit self-imposed censorship to the sieve of reason manifested through ethical considerations? With few exceptions, it is better to leave the matter of taste to the individuals who are in unique positions to make it with great personal authority: the readers (Figure 10.12). However, as is true with other extraordinary occurrences, photojournalists are well advised to tell their editors or managers of any problem with taste so the matter can be weighed and decided before publication.

Journalism, as a useful art dedicated to fully informing readers, is at best an awkward place for critical taste to flourish. It is not that from time to time the censor of organizational taste does well to impose itself. It is that the risk is too great that personal critical taste will be imposed in less than extreme situations by individuals. Too many variables and too many people are involved; anarchy of taste ultimately ill informs readers.

Your author is not arguing that taste never is to be invoked as the basis for self-censorship. The argument is against an anarchy of taste, a state of affairs where single individuals censor images based on personal taste. In situations where taste must be imposed as the only brake on images deemed to be ethical—but in such poor taste that readers must be protected—such decisions should not usually turn on the taste of a single person. Rather, they should be based on the clearly thought out taste of the organization. There is too much truth in the saying "beauty is in the eye of the beholder" for a multitude of individually applied tastes to withhold photographic information from readers (Figure 10.13).

Final Thoughts

This book's author argues for one ethical approach: deontology modified when really need be by teleological considerations, for consideration for consequences. It is your burden, your responsibility to decide if you embrace this approach, which, as far as the argument made here, is comprised of a set of core maxims based on reason that can be modified as really need be—certainly not willy-nilly—by consideration, in Professor Merrill's words, of the

FIGURE 10.13

"The Critic." Whose taste is better? Beauty really is in the eye of the beholder. Do you agree?

WEEGEE/ICP LIAISON

"projected or anticipated"[16] consequences of following one or more of your maxims in specific photojournalistic situations. This modification—or nullification—can come about when consequence consideration favors one maxim over one or more others or when there is no maxim conflict and the applicable maxim needs to be modified or nullified so that the best ethical result is achieved. Critically considering this approach, discussing it with your instructor and comparing your thoughts with fellow students should go a long way toward helping you adopt it or reject it in favor of something else your reasoning brings you to prefer.

But a word of caution is needed. You are not a photojournalistic island. Your employer undoubtedly will have views about appropriate ethical behavior for photojournalists. Unapproved deviation from these views makes you a prime candidate for discharge. Expect your ethical behavior to be significantly controlled by editors and managers who almost certainly will keep a keen eye focused on what you produce and how you produce it. Being intimately familiar with your employing organization's mission and ethical values and having seriously thought about ethics yourself should go a long way toward helping you successfully deal with the ethical questions that inevitably will confront you. Establishing a reputation with your editors and managers of being a person who follows their ethical—and taste—rules and who communicates truthfully and promptly with them when ethical or taste questions arise should help protect you from getting into serious trouble that could result in your being fired. If you find yourself in meaningful conflict with the organization's ethical or taste rules and tactful persuasion is not successful, perhaps it is time for you to look for another employer whose views more closely parallel yours.

One potential hazard in the search for good ethical results in photojournalism needs to be mentioned before closing out this chapter; you really need to avoid it. That hazard is succumbing to cutting ethical corners in the pursuit of personal and professional success. In the competitive world of photojournalism, trying to get recognized as a really good—even a great—photographer or photo editor by your editors and managers and by other publications' editors and managers who then may want to hire you at a higher salary and perhaps with better working conditions can put enormous pressure on a photojournalist to do what it takes to produce what appear to be extraordinary images or otherwise perform in what appears to be an extraordinary way. Possibilities are: manipulate the scene here; create a scene there; accept a "present" that really is a bribe to tailor your coverage a certain way; skate over the accepted ethical line with computer processing. All these and many more are possible. You must never allow the understandable desire to be thought of as really good to entice you down an unethical road . . . it is indeed a slippery slope that almost certainly will end in professional disaster for you. Skating close to the ethical edge, and undoubtedly crossing it as time progresses, is a poor and personally risky way to try to get ahead.

Like law, ethics does not always lend itself to easy, simplistic, always right, black-and-white solutions. Ethics addresses specific real-life situations that often are wrapped in nuances. Ethics is the rightful arena of critically thinking individuals who understand the ongoing, never-ending quest to get it as right as humanly possible so that readers can be as well informed as possible.

NOTES

[1] William K. Frankena, *Ethics*, 2d ed., Prentice-Hall Foundations of Philosophy Series, eds. Elizabeth and Monroe Beardsley (Englewood Cliffs, N.J.: Prentice-Hall, 1973), p. 114.

[2] For example, see Aristotle, *Nicomachean Ethics*, trans. Martin Ostwald (New York: Bobbs-Merrill, 1962); and Richard Norman, *The Moral Philosophers* (Oxford, England: Clarendon, 1983).

[3] Immanuel Kant, *Groundwork of the Metaphysics of Morals*, trans. H. J. Paton

(New York: Harper & Row, 1964), p. 17.

4 John C. Merrill and S. Jack Odell, *Philosophy and Journalism* (New York: Longman, 1983), p. 79.

5 Ibid.

6 Frankena, *Ethics,* p. 35. See also John Stuart Mill, *Utilitarianism,* ed. Oskar Piest (New York: Macmillan, 1957).

7 James Rachels, *The Elements of Moral Philosophy,* The Heritage Series in Philosophy, ed. Tom Regan (New York: Random House, 1986), p. 45.

8 John C. Merrill, "A Sound Ethics for Photojournalism," in Clifton C. Edom, *Photojournalism: Principles and Practices,* 2d ed., (Dubuque, Iowa: Wm C. Brown Company, 1980), pp. 186–87.

9 Ibid., p. 187.

10 Paul Edwards, ed., *The Encyclopedia of Philosophy,* vol. 1 (New York: Crowell Collier and Macmillan, 1967), pp. 18–56; H. A. Needham, ed., *Taste and Criticism in the Eighteenth Century: A Selection of Texts Illustrating the Evolution of Taste and the Development of Critical Theory* (New York: Barnes & Noble, 1952).

11 Edwards, *The Encyclopedia of Philosophy,* p. 40. Admittedly, some may gravitate over time to become "fine art," but these are minuscule in number compared to the millions of journalistic photographs that appear once in newspapers and magazines and then are never seen again.

12 Needham, *Taste and Criticism in the Eighteenth Century,* pp. 14, 19.

13 Ibid., p. 35.

14 Edmund Burke, *On Taste,* quoted in Needham, *Taste and Criticism in the Eighteenth Century,* p. 118.

15 Ibid., p. 123.

16 Merrill, "A Sound Ethics for Photojournalism," p. 187.

One Woman's Road in Photography

Erica Berger — freelance photographer, New York, New York

Q: *Is there an assignment that stands out where being a female photographer was an advantage?*
A: I think perhaps the year and a half documentary I did on 19 women on Long Island, New York, who were afflicted with breast cancer. By virtue of the disease, the assignment lent itself to many physically intimate situations. The women had to disrobe in doctor's offices, and it is difficult enough to convince doctors to include a photographer in any physical exam, let alone breast exams. This is not to say in any way that a male photographer could not have done the job, but with families dealing with a dying woman, it's very difficult to convince those around them that a camera has a place in their lives, let alone convince a husband whose wife is suffering to allow a man with a camera to view her partially disrobed. It is one more obstacle to place between the photographer and the subject. We are not talking just one woman, where a photographer would have the time to get close enough to the subject where the gender wouldn't necessarily come into play. What photographers hope for in these situations is complete access accompanied by the trust of the subject. I had to quickly gain the trust of 19 women and their families.

Q: *Let's visit with that assignment a little more. But first let's go back to when you first started in photojournalism. After short stints at two dailies in Florida,* you joined the Miami Herald *in 1981.*
A: Yes, the *Herald* was where I always wanted to work. Miami is my hometown, and I grew up reading the paper.

Q: *Tell me about being a female staff photographer for the* Miami Herald.
A: As I recall, women comprised about one-fifth of the photo staff. Management was respectful toward women. There was the usual gossip and sexual innuendo among the photo staff, fairly commonplace at newspapers back then. Of course, now everyone is more careful, though I think there were times, as I grew into the business, that I was careless, and became adept with off-color remarks too!

There was always the undercurrent of women having to prove to themselves and to everyone else that they were not hired just to fill a quota, and I worked very hard to fit into that masculine world. Doors were opening to women in photojournalism in the mid to late 70's a lot quicker due to affirmative action. In that way we had quite an advantage.

Q: *Do you think you were treated any differently at the* Herald *from the male photographers? Do you think you were discriminated against? Do you think you were given privileges your male counterparts were not?*
A: No, I don't think I was. That's not to say that everyone would agree with me on the positive or negative end of that question! I felt that I was working with one of the most talented staffs in the country, and I was lucky to be there. I learned an enormous amount from all of them. It's a grueling business, physically taxing.

There are many more women in the business now, but still fewer than men. Just recently I worked with a male model in his 50's who said he had never worked with a female photographer before me. Early on in my career—I won't tell you which paper—an editor said at the end of my job interview, "Now you're not going to run off and get married are you?" These days it is highly unlikely managers would be unsavvy enough to say something so sexist.

Q: *You left the* Miami Herald *and went to work for* Newsday *in New York City?*
A: Yes, though unfortunately the New York City edition of *Newsday* folded in 1994.

Q: *Any discrimination problems working for* New York Newsday?
A: No.

Q: *Let's talk now about the problems you have had that you don't think your male counterparts have had.*
A: Well, if anything, there have often been situations where I thought it helped to be female. I also worked on a series on abortion. I was able to get into the clinic, speak with the patients, and photographically document an abortion. She was 19 years old. I think it would have been more difficult for a man to go through an abortion with a female stranger, be able to sit in the recovery room with a half-dozen women who've just come through an abortion and make the pictures. I know

this is frustrating for the guys. But I remember a hunting trip that I wanted to cover, and of course they sent a guy with those seven male hunters. There are certain things we cannot change, and if given a choice, I think most editors would prefer not sending a female to share a tent with a bunch of men. When I photographed male prisoners, which was a little risky, I think the response from them was different from the one they would have given one of my male co-workers simply by virtue of the fact that they don't see too many women while sitting in a jail cell. Maybe it makes them happy to see a woman, or angry, or sad. This is why assigning editors are so important. They need to size up an assignment and figure out how best to have it covered.

Q: *Do you think female photographers approach their subjects, generally, from a different perspective than male photographers?*
A: No, I believe that each individual has his or her own approach. Some men have said to me over the years that they felt that being female makes a photographer more sensitive. That has not been my experience. I don't think men are as apt to express that sensitivity outwardly as often, but it certainly shows in their work. I have found editors to be biased in assigning work to me that could just as easily been assigned to a male simply because they didn't want to take a chance on his sensitivity level. People approach assignments according to their personal history, which not only includes gender, but race, politics, background, and family situation. I don't believe in complete objectivity. I used

to get called out on news all the time during the wee hours of the Miami mornings because I didn't have a family. A parent is not apt to take as many risks.

Q: *Tell me about New York City-based freelancing. What publications do you work for? Any discrimination problems?*
A: There are no obvious discrimination problems. I love freelancing because it is giving me a chance to shape my own life. Trust me, freelancing is really tough. But after 15 years in newspapers I needed to move on. There is a huge market for photography, and finding a niche takes a lot of soul searching. At a newspaper, I had very little control over my schedule—over what I photographed. One day I would shoot food in the afternoon and a basketball game in the evening. With hundreds of magazines to shoot for, I have to target what interests me most, what I want to say with my work, and where I hopefully can beat out all the other photographers competing for the same shoot. It's never a given that one magazine will continue to use me no matter how much I may have worked for them in the past. Photo editors move on, magazines change editors all the time, changing their focus, bringing in new art directors, and then all the contacts I painstakingly made have gone somewhere else, hopefully taking my phone number with them. I've worked for *Life, People, Forbes, Newsweek,* and a slew of business trade publications. Each assignment needs to be treated as if it's my last chance to work for that publication, because frankly, if I do a mediocre job, photo editors need only look at their huge list of photographers

and call the next person who is as hungry for work as I am. When I first went out on my own, I worked on a start-up magazine called *Smart Kid.* It was innovative and exciting, and while photographing kids was not something I'd considered too often, it gave me a chance to do some exciting, different work (Figure A). I quickly acquired wonderful multipage tear sheets, a cover and was able to convince editors that I could bring the same energy to other assignments.

Q: *Give me a detailed look at one of your recent freelance assignments. How did you get and execute it?*
A: I met David Friend, then Director of Photography and New Media at *Life* magazine, at a Halloween party. We stayed in touch, and almost a year later, when I felt I had a decent portfolio to show him, I went into the magazine, met with all the photo editors, and an hour later had my first assignment. Based on that work, I landed an assignment from *Life* to do environmental portraits in North Dakota after a big flood. I visited North Dakota three times for that story, and on the one-year anniversary of the flood, the eight-page story was published. Boy, I remember not wanting to go to that Halloween party. I am sure glad I did. After the breast cancer project, that was my favorite shoot.

Q: *Back to the cancer project, wasn't that published in book form?*
A: Yes, *We're All in this Together: Families Facing Breast Cancer* was published using all the stories and photos from the original series that ran in *Newsday.* It is my most important work,

On assignment for *Smart Kid* magazine to illustrate a story about kids and their pets, I enlisted the aid of my nine-year-old nieces, Mandy and Jamie. The girls agreed to be photographed with mice, which we bought at a pet store. I photographed them at their home in Orlando. Because there was no background suitable for the picture, I used parachute fabric borrowed from their stepfather (my brother) and turned their kitchen into a makeshift studio. I made this photograph with only one strobe, a ring flash, which is a trendy light originally used for copy work. This flash is what created the red, round highlights in their eyes. I wanted a blatantly posed picture because the story was generic (not specifically about any particular children). This picture ran full page in *Smart Kid*, which is now defunct. Having the opportunity to do a wide variety of assignments—for example, one week doing a mainstream documentary-style assignment and the next week doing something that nudges up to art photography like this picture—keeps the work interesting and challenging.

ERICA BERGER

and the photographs are still traveling around the country to various museums and galleries four years later. The work has a life of its own, and that makes me happy. Particularly the essay on the life and death of Sue Rosenbaum, a major activist in the national breast cancer organization called 1 in 9. When I met Sue, I would never have believed she would be gone six months later. I watched her from a distance, her head wrapped in a turban, hunched over a playpen, dropping in the shower gifts for her expected first grandchild. She was shy only at first.

From the very beginning she wanted her story told. Having her agree to our chronicling her life and death was the easy part. She believed everyone could benefit by knowing more about breast cancer, and she was willing to give up her privacy if the information about her disease would encourage more women to become active in their own medical care, from early diagnosis to education about treatment.

Sue knew she was dying, and nothing could really prepare the writer and me for the pain of watching someone so brave confront her mortality. When the cancer was discovered, it was in Stage 4 (advanced metastatic cancer with 6 to 12-month life prognosis). It was inoperable, but she would never stop searching for a new way to fight her illness (Figure B).

We were very conscious from the beginning that while we would be spending a lot of time together, we would observe and not stay in her face every moment. She was not sentimental about her illness and fought it with anger and perseverance. Because her cancer was so advanced, I had no time to get to know her without regard to the disease. I was photographing many other women for an 18-month-long breast cancer series, 19 in all, four of whom died before the project ended. When it became evident that her condition was worsening, I stayed with her family when I could. We knew we wouldn't have as much time with Sue as we originally thought.

The writer, Irene Virag, and I tried to learn of every important day in advance. Before we left their home each day, we would compare notes with Sue and Marc, her husband. Soon our date books held every Rosenbaum birthday, shower, anniversary, wedding, party, and doctor day. Sue spent very little time at the hospital the last five months of her life, so we didn't have to deal with hospital personnel for access. She was tended by a home health aide and a visiting nurse. While it was evident her parents were uncomfortable with the idea of photographs being taken during Sue's final days, they, as well as all her family and friends, gave us complete cooperation.

Our editors at *Newsday* gave us the time to complete Sue's story, holding back some of our deadlines on other stories in the series. Irene and I always went to the Rosenbaum home together. I vividly remember sitting in a dark restaurant one afternoon where we confided to one another how difficult it was to make the trip each day to watch this lovely woman die. We grew to love her family, and there were times when they would want to comfort us. We became friends they could talk to about their pain, frustrations, and fears. They accepted the camera and not once did they ask me to move or leave the room. We would sense when we had stayed long enough. There were days when hours would pass and I would not have shot one frame.

There was never a time when Irene and I did not agree on how to handle a situation, from what to cover to what birthday gift to buy for Jessie, Sue's little girl. We relied on each other to get through the worst of it, and our family and friends, though supportive, always cautioned us on getting too close to our subject. To this day, I believe that had we kept too much professional distance on a story this intimate, we never would have produced a story worthy of its subject.

Q: *Would you encourage a female to become a journalistic photographer?*
A: Before I answer that, let me mention a few things that I think probably would be helpful to someone in school who wants to go into photojournalism. First off, accept that it's going to be tough. Photojournalism is not for a person with a thin skin. Getting an internship is important—it was one of the smartest things I ever did. Also important is working on the student paper. I think learning a foreign language is invaluable, especially if you want to work overseas. Attend photojournalism seminars whenever possible. Interact with working photojournalists at every opportunity. Become familiar

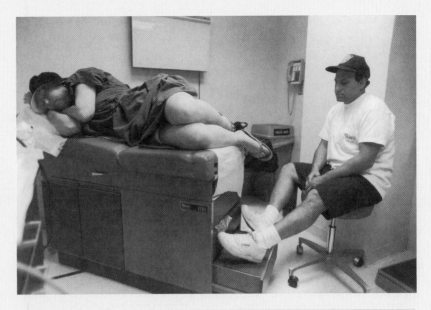

with as many newspapers and magazines as possible. Know how to put together a portfolio.

Enter every contest available to help get your work noticed. If you are interested in freelancing, find out who is in charge of hiring at the publications you are interested in shooting for. Call them and make appointments. You cannot be shy about it. Be aggressive but polite. Ask if there's part-time work. If they tell you they are not hiring, ask if there's internships, or minority programs if they apply. If they tell you they will look at your work but not meet with you, send it in. Don't take rejection personally.

Now, let me answer your question.

I would encourage anyone who really feels a calling to the profession. I witness every sort of emotion in life. That's where my passion lies. Documenting the human drama is so com-

pletely fulfilling that in the first 10 years of shooting, I sometimes felt I was living the lives of everyone else, it was that absorbing. What I didn't realize is that I was emoting through the camera right along with my subjects. What an incredible experience. I couldn't lose. I could feel like I was actually experiencing what the subject was. If they were dancing, I was dancing, or singing, or crying, or laughing. Now I think I have incorporated that passion to witness life, and I have something to say through my work. I have opinions, I am curious. There's wonderful travel, and it's still exciting to meet each new subject. If philosophy, anthropology, sociology, and psychology excite you, photojournalism is a way of communicating that excitement to so many. There is so much self-satisfaction to be had. And it's a great kick to see my work in print.

Chapter 11

19th-Century History

"Train Wreck On The Providence Worcester Railroad Near Pawtucket, Rhode Island," August 12, 1853. This was taken using the daguerreotype process, one of two competing photographic approaches that gave birth to photography in 1839.
ATTRIBUTED TO L. WRIGHT/COURTESY
GEORGE EASTMAN HOUSE

Overview

Time Line
of Pre-20th-Century
Photography

Beginnings

Photography—A
Practical Reality

The Daguerreotype

The Calotype

The Daguerreotype as
News

The Collodion Glass
Wet Plate

The Civil War

The Frontier

Portraits in the Second
Half of the Century

The Photographing of
Movement

The Woodcut

Dry Film

The Halftone

Late 19th-Century
Photojournalism

Documentary
Photography

Social Documentary
Photography

Photography as Art

Final Thoughts

Overview

Every photographer today is building on the rich history of photography. This history is a tapestry of technological developments and extraordinary people who invented or used the technology to create an extraordinary photographic heritage. Contemporary photographers evoke this heritage every time they take a picture.

This chapter briefly explores early photographic and journalistic processes, topics, and personalities. The chapter ends with a brief look at photography as art. Of necessity this chapter—and Chapter 12, about the 20th century—is a condensed and selected history; there is much more. The limited time lines at the beginning of each

Time Line of Pre-20th-Century Photography

ca. 350 B.C.	Aristotle describes the camera obscura, meaning darkened chamber.
1600s	Camera obscura becomes significantly smaller and more portable.
1725	Johann Heinrich Schulze discovers light alone causes silver salts to darken.
1790	Thomas Wedgwood is first to use light to record images on chemically sensitized material.
1819	Sir John Herschel discovers hyposulphite of soda—"hypo"—later used to make images permanent by removing the unexposed silver salts.
ca. 1827	Joseph Nicéphore Niépce takes earliest surviving photograph.
1839	Two competing processes—the daguerreotype by Louis Jacques Mandé Daguerre in France and the calotype by William Henry Fox Talbot in England—make photography a practical reality.
1842	Earliest known news photograph—the ruins of a major fire—is taken in Germany.
1844	Earliest known U.S. news photograph—a daguerreotype of Philadelphia's Girard Bank occupied by military troops because of an uprising—is taken.
1851	Sensitized collodion glass wet plate is introduced, combining the best of the daguerreotype and calotype. Within a decade replaces both, as well as the albumen glass plate (a photographic plate coated with a light-sensitive emulsion, a main ingredient of which was egg whites). Picture taking and developing must be done while emulsion is wet, requiring photographers to have darkrooms available immediately before and after making an exposure.
1854	Small business-card-sized portrait photograph, the "carte-de-visite," is introduced in France and becomes popular in United States by 1860. Ultimately, it supplants the daguerreotype.
	Ambrotype patented in United States.
1855	Photographer Roger Fenton covers the Crimean War.
1856	Stereoscopic pictures become popular and remain so into the 1890s.
1858	Enlargers using sunlight are introduced, but technique and machine do not become popular until more light-sensitive paper is introduced in the 1890s.
	Prolific French photographer Nadar (Gaspard Félix Tournachon) takes the first aerial photograph from a balloon. In personality, style, and selected subject matter, Nadar is a precursor of contemporary photojournalists.
	Oscar G. Rejlander and Henry Peach Robinson lead movement to use photography as art. Julia Margaret Cameron and Lady Clementina Hawarden quickly follow. Peter Henry Emerson, Eugène Atget, Edward Steichen, and Alfred Stieglitz later become prominent.
1861	Tintypes, introduced in 1856, supplant ambrotypes in popularity. They also are called melainotypes and ferrotypes.
1862	Mathew Brady and associates, among others, cover the U.S. Civil War.

FIGURE 11.1

"Girard Bank,"
May 9, 1844.

WILLIAM AND FREDERICK LANGENHEIM/LIBRARY COMPANY OF PHILADEPHIA

chapter hint at the richness of photography's history. In relation to world history photography is an infant or perhaps a toddler. The recording and permanent preservation of real-life images was a long time in coming. But when photography arrived, it leaped to instant prominence, where it remains.

Beginnings

With the technical developments pioneered by Johann Heinrich Schulze, Thomas Wedgwood, and Sir John Herschel photography became a reality in the first half of the 19th century when French inventor Joseph Nicéphore Niépce took the first photograph known to still exist today.

1864	Carbon printing paper is introduced; it yields high-quality prints.
1866	Cabinet photograph is introduced in England, destined to replace the carte-de-visite.
	Sophisticated photographic lenses are developed in Germany and England; the Rapid Rectilinar, an English lens, becomes the lens of choice until 1893.
1867	Photography of the U.S. western frontier undertaken by former Civil War photographers and others.
1871	Richard Leach Maddox introduces state-of-the-art gelatin emulsion, allowing creation of the dry plate. The dry plate becomes widely available in 1878 and by 1881 replaces the wet plate.
1873	New York City paper publishes first U.S. newspaper photograph in a daily newspaper using the halftone process.
1877	Eadweard Muybridge photographs galloping horse, setting the stage for the stopping of action and for motion pictures.
	Photography of medical subjects is common, having begun soon after introduction of the daguerreotype and calotype in 1839.
1878	Light meter is introduced.
1886	News photography is well underway.
1887	Flashpowder, precursor of the flashbulb and the electronic flash (strobe), is invented in Germany.
1888	Jacob A. Riis photographs New York's slums.
	Dry flexible roll film becomes available. The emulsion is on paper and must be removed and put on glass before developing and printing, but this soon changes with the introduction of transparent backing.
	George Eastman's Kodak hand-held camera joins a host of similar cameras; it, and a processing arrangement sold with the camera, become enormously popular.
	The National Geographic Magazine is marketed; later it is renamed *National Geographic.*
1890	Magazines regularly reproduce photographs using the halftone process.
	Frances Benjamin Johnston's photographic career is underway. She is a quasi-journalistic photographer and one of the first editorially-oriented female photographers.
1895	Paper backing added to roll film allowing handling in light.
	Highly light-sensitive printing paper is marketed.
1898	James Henry "Jimmy" Hare covers the Spanish-American War and goes on to photograph many other events as a prominent early photojournalist.

But the first development in the history of photography came much earlier, in the form of the camera obscura.

It had long been known that light passing through a small hole into a darkened room would create a reversed and inverted image of the scene outside. The ancient Greek philosopher Aristotle (384–322 B.C.) had described the optical principle that is the basic ingredient of what became known as the camera obscura—darkened chamber (Figure 11.2).

However, before it became a fundamental aspect of photography, the most important practical application of the camera obscura was as an aid to artists, who traced its images. They then used the tracings as guides in their hand painting. The traced images also were end products, as works of art themselves.

In the 17th century the camera obscura became significantly smaller and portable. It was fitted with a lens that better directed and focused light. People could view its images externally—without actually having to be in a darkened room. Artists well into the 19th century regularly used the portable device in their drawing and painting.

Although the ability to create images by using light in a camera-like device had long been known, making them permanent remained an unsolved problem. In Germany Johann Heinrich Schulze took the first steps toward solving it in 1725 when he discovered that light alone causes silver salts to darken.

About 50 years later Sweden's Carl Wilhelm Scheele and Switzerland's Jean Senebier contributed important related information about wavelengths, silver chloride, turpentine, and light. Photography was about to be born. Thomas Wedgwood, of the china-making Wedgwoods, also had a hand in the development of photography. In the late 1700s, using silver nitrate and the sun, he tried making what today are called *contact prints*. It was a good try, but Wedgwood could not find a way to make these "sun prints" permanent.

In 1819 a major discovery by Sir John Herschel, a prominent English scientist, set the stage for the ultimate success of what was to become known as photography. Herschel found that hyposulphite of soda made an image permanent by removing the unexposed silver salts. After hearing in late 1838 or early 1839 of two men's efforts—Louis Jacques Mandé Daguerre in France and William Henry Fox Talbot in England—in making permanent photographic images, Herschel put his keen mind to work. He applied his 1819 hyposulphite of soda experiments to photographic imaging. Herschel, an unselfish man of broad vision, generously made his discovery public without asking for or receiving financial compensation.

The earliest surviving photograph was taken about 1827. It shows a courtyard containing a pigeon coop, as viewed from the bedroom window of the photographer, Joseph Nicéphore Niépce (Figure 11.3).

FIGURE 11.2

Camera obscura, 1544.

<small>Unidentified artist/ Culver Pictures, Inc.</small>

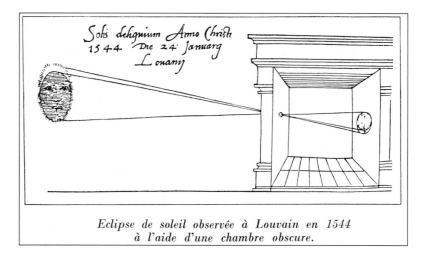

Eclipse de soleil observée à Louvain en 1544 à l'aide d'une chambre obscure.

It seems crude now, but this heliograph (from the Greek *helios* for "sun" and *graphos* for "drawing") had stunning implications. It also was a long time in the making. Niepce tried for years to produce images that did not fade until he hit on a way to preserve them, thus giving the world his courtyard photograph on a pewter-plate backing. Compelling evidence exists—his letters—that makes it certain that this French inventor preserved—made unsensitive to light—photographic images as far back as about 1817.

Photography—A Practical Reality

Competition between the two most important photo trailblazers, Louis Jacques Mandé Daguerre of France and William Henry Fox Talbot of England, was keen. But it was Daguerre, a businessman and promoter in the mode of a P. T. Barnum, who arguably was by a sliver destined to become the single most famous person in the early history of photography with the announcement of his photographic process, the daguerreotype.

Talbot closely followed Daguerre in fame with his calotype, but a third trailblazer of photography was not so fortunate. The scientific establishment ignored Hippolyte Bayard of France. His importance in the development of photography—and his process—has been relegated to an interesting footnote. Shortly after Daguerre's announcement Bayard made public the photographic process he had devised. It was a direct positive made on paper, but an influential and powerful Daguerre supporter saw to it that the French Academy of Sciences ignored Bayard's effort. The daguerreotype became firmly established in France, and Bayard's process did not become popular. However, he

FIGURE 11.3

"View from the window at Le Gras." Niépce's now-famous courtyard photograph; its exposure was about 8 hours, ca. 1827.

JOESPH NICÉPHORE NIÉPCE/GERNSHEIM COLLECTION, HARRY RANSOM HUMANITIES RESEARCH CENTER, THE UNIVERSITY OF TEXAS AT AUSTIN

became a prominent member of the Paris photography world as a user of a process that was competing with the daguerreotype, Talbot's calotype (discussed later).

Interestingly, both Daguerre and Talbot switched to Herschel's hypo (now sodium thiosulphate), and each soon eliminated the problem he had with fading images. Photography was on its way.

The Daguerreotype

Louis Jacques Mandé Daguerre was a painter and the owner of a premier Paris attraction, the Diorama. This exhibit used large translucent panels and shifting lighting effects to amuse and amaze its customers. Daguerre used the camera obscura to help produce Diorama images and developed a burning desire to permanently preserve the actual images made by the camera obscura, thus eliminating the necessity of tracing.

In 1829 he became a business partner of Niépce, who had visited him in Paris after learning of their mutual interest in preserving images made by light. Niépce died three years later, but Daguerre continued on his own, discovering a way to cut photographic exposure time from 8 hours or more to approximately 30 minutes. A way to make the images permanent continued to elude him, however. Then in 1837 he found a way to fix the images with an ordinary salt solution. Because it did not remove all the unexposed silver salts, this was not the ultimate solution. However, it was a minor milestone on the road to the adoption of hyposulphite of soda, which did preserve an image. Although Daguerre had relied largely on the work of his late partner Niépce, the true technical brain behind the daguerreotype, Daguerre named it after himself.

The most famous daguerreotype taken by its namesake shows a Paris boulevard in what was then the entertainment district. Because of the relatively long exposure—at least minutes, although no one knows the exact time—the only recognizable person in the picture is a man having his shoes shined.

All the other people were moving so much that they were not recorded on the plate in one place long enough to be visible.

When his hopes of using the daguerreotype to launch a private commercial venture did not work out, Daguerre sold the process to the French government. He received a life pension, and the French made the process available for the world to use without charge. The one exception to the free use was England and Wales, where because of a patent Daguerre obtained, potential users were forced to buy a franchise. In reply to an inquiry, Daguerre wrote that "the process has been sold, not to the civilized world, but to the Government of France for the benefit of my fellow countryman."[1] He therefore obviously felt free to enforce the patent he received.

The daguerreotype had serious disadvantages. It was physically delicate. It had to be protected by glass from scratching and sealed from the harmful effects of air, which tarnished it. Viewers had to look at it at just the right angle in order to see a positive image. It had the inherent limitation of an image that was unique—it was not possible to make copies directly from it (although it could, of course, be photographed). Despite these problems, the world embraced the daguerreotype, which recorded an image on a highly polished copper plate coated with silver. Nobody was more enthusiastic than the Americans.

The daguerreotype image was extraordinarily sharp, almost to distraction. Exposure times in 1840 varied, depending primarily on the amount of sunlight. In any case, they were long—from 5 to 70 minutes. These incredibly long times by contemporary standards soon shrank to seconds with the introduction of an improved lens, an improved emulsion, and a new and additional heat–chemical processing step.

As chance would have it, a prominent American was in Paris when the daguerreotype was made public. He quickly helped spread the news at home by writing a long letter about the amazing new process to his brother, the editor of the *New York Observer.* The man was a painter who would become famous for the invention of the telegraph. He was Samuel F.B. Morse. Morse was so taken with the daguerreotype that he told his brother that "the exquisite minuteness of the delineation cannot be conceived. No painting or engraving ever approached it."[2] Morse's brother published the letter on April 19, 1839. Samuel Morse returned home an ardent promoter of the daguerreotype.

Although the earliest daguerreotype process was difficult—the exposures were so long that the photographer could not freeze even the slightest movement, the chemicals were unstable, and no one had written a standard instruction manual—it appealed to the Americans. The daguerreotype would be the overwhelmingly popular form of photography for Americans for the next 20 years. Figure 11.4 shows an American-made daguerreotype of a U.S. artist.

The Calotype

The announcement of Daguerre's new process came as an enormous shock to

William Henry Fox Talbot in England. Talbot, an educated gentleman scientist and scholar, had been working since 1834 on a process to record and permanently fix images created by the camera obscura. His early efforts involved the making of what he called "photogenic drawings," images similar to those made earlier by Thomas Wedgwood. Talbot placed various items on sensitized paper and exposed them to light. From these relatively simple pictures he progressed to images created by a camera.

Under pressure from Daguerre's well-publicized success Talbot made his process public only a few weeks later. He ultimately named it *calotype* from the Greek for *kalos* for "beautiful" and *typos* for "impression."

The calotype process was as miraculous as the daguerreotype but quite different. First, it was a negative-positive process that allowed the making of unlimited copies by passing light through the negative. Second, the image was recorded on paper rather than metal. Third, it yielded a slightly unsharp image because of the pattern of the fibers in the paper on which the image rested, as shown in Figure 11.5.

Talbot owned a substantial estate in England, Lacock Abbey, and took many photographs of and around his home.

FIGURE 11.4

Daguerreotype of painter Asher B. Durand, ca. 1855.

UNIDENTIFIED PHOTOGRAPHER/COLLECTION OF THE NEW-YORK HISTORICAL SOCIETY

FIGURE 11.5

"The Misses Binnie and Miss Monroe." A calotype ca. 1845.

DAVID OCTAVIUS HILL AND ROBERT ADAMSON/THE METROPOLITAN MUSEUM OF ART, HARRIS BRISBANE DICK FUND, 1939

Interestingly, it was Talbot's friend Sir John Herschel, of hypo fame, who suggested that Talbot replace photogenic drawing with the term *photography* (light writing). This word comes from the Greek *phos* for "light" and *graphos* for "writing." Talbot also adopted Herschel's suggestion to use the words *negative* and *positive* in place of his terms *re-reversal copy* and *reversal copy*.

Unlike Daguerre, Talbot was possessive of his process, having received no compensation from his government for its use. He charged a fee to anyone who wanted to use the calotype process and was diligent in protecting his copyright. This discouraged would-be calotypists and almost certainly was a reason that the independent-minded Americans so heartily embraced Daguerre's process. Another important reason for lack of interest in the calotype was that many Americans considered the sharp daguerreotype to be technically superior. Although the calotype never caught on in the United States, it was popular in England and Scotland and in certain parts of Europe.

The calotype's life probably was extended by a supplementary process invented in France by Gustave Le Gray. Before applying the emulsion Le Gray waxed the paper on which the light-sensitive emulsion rested. This yielded sharper, more defined images. Although it was secondary to the daguerreotype, the calotype left a meaningful legacy, both in the photographs it produced and as a precursor of the contemporary negative-positive process.

The Daguerreotype as News

Although it was not possible for publications to mass-reproduce photographs directly until nearly the end of the century, photographic coverage of news events occurred early in the history of photography using the daguerreotype process. Although the daguerreotype was far better suited to portraiture, some efforts at covering news are noteworthy. Fires, train wrecks, riots, and even a war were subjects of early photojournalists. These images, through the intervening woodcut process (discussed shortly), found their way into various publications.

Early photojournalists all used large tripod-based cameras with a combination of plates and lenses that required long exposure times. The earliest known news photograph was taken in 1842 in Germany. The earliest known U.S. news photograph was taken in 1844 in Philadelphia (see Figure 11.1). The German photograph shows ruins after a major fire. The U.S. photograph shows the Girard Bank, occupied by military troops because of an uprising. One of the most famous news daguerreotypes of this era shows a raging fire. It was taken in 1853 and appears in Figure 11.6. Another prominent daguerreotype of this era also was taken in 1853; it is a Rhode Island train wreck and appears at the beginning of this chapter.

The Collodion Glass Wet Plate

Following the daguerreotype and the calotype were increasingly improved processes, including the collodion glass wet plate and, much later, dry flexible film. A British sculptor, Frederick Scott Archer, invented the collodion glass wet plate process. It combined the sharpness of the daguerreotype and the reproducibility of the calotype. However, it had to be handled gently (Figure 11.7).

Photographers made enduring images with the collodion glass wet plate process. It required the photographer to coat its glass holder with emulsion immediately before taking the picture and to process it immediately after (Figure 11.8). Roger Fenton, Gaspard Félix Tournachon (Nadar), Mathew Brady, Alexander Gardner, Timothy H. O'Sullivan, William Henry Jackson, Eadweard Muybridge, Carleton E. Watkins, and Francis Frith all used the collodion glass wet plate process. Their names live on as giants of 19th-century picture taking. Many collodion glass wet plate images were mass-reproduced using woodcuts. The image in Figure 11.9 of the hanging of conspirators in the assassination of Abraham Lincoln was made with the collodion glass wet plate process.

FIGURE 11.6
**"Burning Mills, Os-
wego, NY," 1853.
Note that the image
is hand-colored.**
GEORGE BARNARD/COURTESY
GEORGE EASTMAN HOUSE

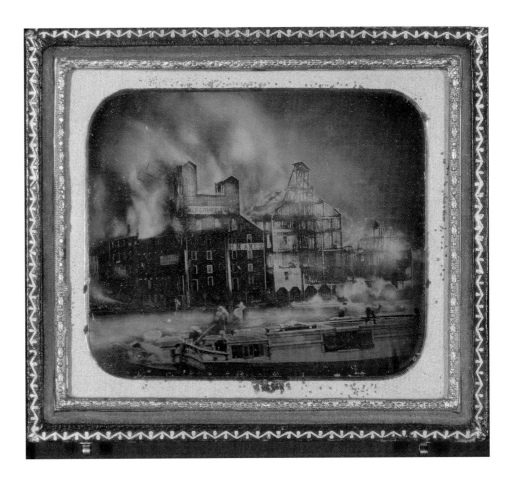

FIGURE 11.7

**Glass wet plates were highly vulnerable to breakage, as demonstrated by this damaged
plate of famed 19th-century American photographer Mathew Brady (seated front row, far
left) and others, 1860.**
UNIDENTIFIED PHOTOGRAPHER/LIBRARY OF CONGRESS

FIGURE 11.8

The necessity of having a complete darkroom on site when a picture was made was an important limitation of the collodion glass wet plate process. For picture-taking in the field, darkrooms and related items were transported by wagons, wheelbarrows, animals, and humans. Shown here in a woodcut (discussed later) is an 1877 human-carried backpack darkroom set up for use. These backpacks were popular in Europe.

Unidentified Photographer and unidentified woodcut artist/Gernsheim Collection, Harry Ransom Humanities Research Center, The University of Texas at Austin

The Civil War

Mathew Brady was one of the most prominent photographers—if not the most prominent—in the United States before the Civil War, photographing and operating galleries in New York City and Washington, D.C.

According to historian E. F. Bleiler, "Brady had become, for all practical purposes, semi-official photographer to the American presidency; and presidents, governors, literary men and millionaires all hung upon his walls."[3]

With his political connections Brady easily got permission from Abraham Lincoln to cover the Union side of the Civil War. He also was friendly with high-ranking Union generals. The way was cleared for him and his associates to travel with the armies, although he had to finance the undertaking himself.

FIGURE 11.9

Four conspirators in President Lincoln's assassination are hanged, 1865.

Alexander Gardner/Library of Congress

Photojournalism: An Introduction

According to photographic historian and author Beaumont Newhall, "Brady's men photographed every phase of the war that their technique could encompass: battlefields, ruins, officers, men, artillery, corpses, ships, railroads"[4] (Figures 11.10 to 11.12). A Brady darkroom wagon was a common sight to Union troops.

Brady employed a number of photographers. In fact, he took relatively few of the Civil War pictures that originally bore his name. "Brady" on a photograph really was more a signature of his organization than an assurance that the picture was taken by the boss. While this was common at the time, the practice was not liked by at least some photographers and it was changed in mid-war; photographers working for Brady henceforth would see their own credit with their images.

Two Brady men who produced striking photographs of the war were Alexander Gardner and Timothy H. O'Sullivan. At the beginning Gardner and O'Sullivan worked for Brady. Because he refused to give Gardner credit for pictures he took and refused to let him keep negatives taken on his own time, Gardner left Brady's employ and took O'Sullivan with him. Both photographed the war until it ended, and then photographed the American frontier.

Selected Civil War pictures, including some taken by Brady himself, were used as guides for creating woodcuts and published in the mass media. Brady and his men were not the only photographers to cover the war from the Union side, and the Confederate side also had its photographers.

The Frontier

After the Civil War the nation's attention turned west (Figure 11.13). Railroad companies started laying track, and geological surveyors began their work. Battle-hardened photographers of the Civil War saw great opportunity out west, and they quickly joined the railroads and the survey teams.

Alexander Gardner photographed construction of part of the Union Pacific Railroad and then photographed parts of the Southwest. Timothy H. O'Sullivan and William Henry Jackson joined a survey team. It was usual for photographers to carry more than one camera in photographing the frontier, some of which were quite large. According to Newhall, "in 1875 Jackson astounded the photographic world by packing a camera for 20 × 24-inch plates up the Rocky Mountains."[5]

In addition to recording construction of the railroads and their environs, photographers pictured Native Americans and the land they lived on. It was not unusual for these images to be sold to the general public, the profits often going to the photographers who took them.

Two other prominent photographers of the western frontier were Eadweard Muybridge, later to become famous for his motion photographs, and Carleton E. Watkins. Both worked out of California and extensively photographed Yosemite Valley. Both used large-format cameras. The West was not the only place where photography was recording new frontiers. Photographers such as Francis Frith, an Englishman who recorded Egypt and the Holy Land, were traveling to the far corners of the world.

Portraits in the Second Half of the Century

Exciting and informative as they were, frontier images were minuscule in number compared to the number of portraits—close up, intermediate, and full length—produced in the second half of the 19th century. Photographers used different processes and styles, including the ambrotype, tintype, carte-de-visite, and cabinet.

The ambrotype was a thin collodion glass wet plate negative juxtaposed against a black background after processing. Typically, the negative and its black background were mounted in a case. It looked very much like a daguerreotype (Figure 11.14).

Although popular in the United States, the ambrotype had a fairly short life, from about 1853 until about 1863. It was replaced by the much more

FIGURE 11.10

**"A Harvest of Death," 1863. Dead soldiers on the Gettysburg bat-
tlefield on a misty morning.**

TIMOTHY H. O'SULLIVAN, PRINTED BY ALEXANDER GARDNER/LIBRARY OF CONGRESS

FIGURE 11.12

**"Ruins of Gallego Flour Mills,
Richmond" [Virginia], ca. 1864.**

MATHEW BRADY (STUDIO OF)/THE MUSEUM
OF MODERN ART, NEW YORK. PURCHASE. COPY
PRINT © 1999 THE MUSEUM OF MODERN ART
NEW YORK

FIGURE 11.11

**Ulysses S. Grant, then a Major General and
later President of the United States, in the
field in Virginia during the Civil War, 1864.**

MATHEW BRADY/CORBIS/HULTON-DEUTSCH COLLECTION

FIGURE 11.13

"North from Berthoud Pass." Taken in the western frontier, 1874.
WILLIAM HENRY JACKSON/COURTESY GEORGE EASTMAN HOUSE

practical tintype, which could be easily carried and was sturdy enough to be mailed.

The tintype—called *melainotype* or *ferrotype* before *tintype* took hold as the most commonly used name for all photographs produced on metal plates by fundamentally the same process—was a thin sheet of "japanned" iron—an iron sheet coated with a high gloss black varnish which then was coated with a light sensitive emulsion (Figure 11.15). Although typically near or at the low end of the technical quality scale when compared to other photographic processes of the time, tintypes were easy, quick, and inexpensive to make. The authors of *The American Tintype* tell us that:

> The tintype, like its predecessors, the daguerreotype and the ambrotype, was an image of the sitter, reversed left-to-right. Produced on sheet iron in production-line fashion with multiple copies per shot, then clipped apart with tin shears at a lower cost than conventional paper prints from a negative, it was clearly a product of the Industrial Revolution.[6]

FIGURE 11.14

The backing of an ambrotype was crucial to viewing the image as a positive. Here the backing is removed from one half of this ca. 1858 portrait, transforming that half into a negative.
UNIDENTIFIED PHOTOGRAPHER/GERNSHEIM COLLECTION, HARRY RANSOM HUMANITIES RESEARCH CENTER, THE UNIVERSITY OF TEXAS AT AUSTIN

FIGURE 11.15

Tintype—more precisely ferrotype—of an unidentified U.S. Civil War soldier on the Union side, ca. 1862.
UNIDENTIFIED PHOTOGRAPHER/CHICAGO HISTORICAL SOCIETY

The tintype's heyday was in the 1860s. But this extremely popular approach to photography for the common person—tintypes were dirt cheap and millions were created—hung on into the early part of the 20th century after having been championed in the United States in the mid 1850s from an early 1850s European idea. According to *The American Tintype*, "in France and England the making of photographs on japanned iron plates became known as 'the American Process.'"[7]

Just as the ambrotype gave way to the tintype, the tintype gave way to the carte-de-visite. Apparently, the idea for the carte-de-visite came from the calling cards commonly used at midcentury by the gentry. The carte-de-visite was patented in 1854, became popular about 1860, and remained so for most of the decade. The carte-de-visite was a small picture, $3^1/_2 \times 2^1/_2$ inches. The photographer used a specially designed camera that allowed the recording of eight images on one piece of film (Figure 11.16). The photographer made a single print, and a low-paid assistant typically cut the eight pictures apart and mounted each on a card.

Families everywhere owned the photo albums made to hold "cartes." Popular as they were, these pictures typically made no effort to delve into the soul of a person photographically; this was left to more serious photographers of the day who worked with large-format cameras and who created some superb images.

First introduced in 1866, the cabinet photograph was one of the more popular forms in which the collodion glass wet plate process was used. A cabinet image was $5^1/_2 \times 4$ inches and was attached to a mount of $6^1/_2 \times 4^1/_2$ inches. A cabinet of the actress Sarah Bernhardt is in Figure 11.17.

The Photographing of Movement

Concern for the photographing of movement goes back to Niépce's courtyard picture (see Figure 11.2), where he obviously chose as his main subject stationary objects. The normal walking movement of people was recorded before the 1860s. Because a person at a distance appears to be moving less than does a person close to the camera who is moving at the same speed, moving subjects usually were photographed at a distance.

The stopping of fast movement—a galloping horse, for example—is associated with a major figure in the history of photography, Eadweard Muybridge. As a California photographer of scenic views, Muybridge attracted the attention of a wealthy former governor of the state, Leland Stanford. Stanford was fond of horse racing and owned a number of horses. He wanted to share with friends in other countries the action of one of his favorite horses, Occident. Muybridge was engaged to do the photography. His studies of animal and human movement were to make him even more famous than his Yosemite Valley pictures.

Muybridge successfully photographed Occident by using a series of ingenious panels and multiple cameras. Later he was to refine this technique by

FIGURE 11.16

"Uncut Carte-De-Viste, Princess Gabriella," ca. 1863.
André Adolphe Eugène Disdéri/Gernsheim Collection, Harry Ransom Humanities Research Center, The University of Texas at Austin

FIGURE 11.17

Cabinet photograph showing actress Sarah Bernhardt in a play's death scene, ca. 1880.

NAPOLEON SARONY/COURTESY GEORGE EASTMAN HOUSE

FIGURE 11.18

"Galloping Horse," ca. 1885. Taken during Muybridge's association with the University of Pennsylvania.

EADWEARD MUYBRIDGE/GERNSHEIM COLLECTION, HARRY RANSOM HUMANITIES RESEARCH CENTER, THE UNIVERSITY OF TEXAS AT AUSTIN

using multiple cameras whose shutters were activated by a series of strings struck by an animal running a predetermined course. In connection with his later association with the University of Pennsylvania, Muybridge would take hundreds of pictures of animals and people in motion. One of his photographs appears in Figure 11.18.

The Woodcut

Until the 1870s technical limitations forced photojournalists to live with a secondary reproduction process if their photographs were to appear in mass circulation publications. There was no method to reproduce both type and literal images of photographs on paper at the same time; photographic images had to go through a major intervening artistic process, the woodcut.

Creating woodcuts was a slow and laborious process of cutting images into wood. An interesting aspect of making woodcuts was parceling the job out, usually when time was critical, to a number of artists. It took so long for a single artist to cut all the lines necessary for a reasonably faithful reproduction of a photograph that the process required 20 or more artisans, each making a small part of the image. The parts were reassembled, much like a jigsaw puzzle, and the combined woodcut was then used to print the image. The artists' skill and creative interpretation often varied considerably. Photographers would have to wait for the invention of the halftone process before their work was liberated from the woodcut process.

Dry Film

In 1871 photographic emulsions moved into the modern era with the publication of a letter in the *British Journal of Photography*. Richard Leach Maddox, a physician, described a process that allowed photographic plates to be coated and dried before being used. Seven years later Charles Harper Bennett made an important improvement when he invented a process that yielded emulsions much more sensitive to light. Bennett made action photography a practical reality.

The first practical dry plates were marketed in 1878; glass was the support on which the emulsion was coated. Sheets of a clear material similar to plastic—celluloid—replaced the glass in 1883. In 1888 a roll of paper marketed by the Eastman Company (today Eastman Kodak Company) replaced the celluloid sheet. The next year, 1889, the company replaced the paper roll with a celluloid roll. In 1895 the Eastman Company added a light-protecting backing of paper to the celluloid roll; this allowed photographers to carry, load, and unload the film in daylight.

Film was becoming standardized. It was sensitive to colors other than blue. Before 1903, when panchromatic film was marketed, photographic film to one degree or the other was not sensitive to certain colors but had a particular tendency toward sensitivity to blue. This is why many early photographs show the sky as white—in photographic parlance it is washed out. The exposure necessary to properly expose other parts of a scene, such as a person's face, let too much light from the sky strike the film, causing overexposure that translated to skies lacking detail in the photographs. Celluloid film was predictable in its sensitivity to light and was much more sensitive to it. It was flexible, transparent, and smaller. Inventors also were making great advancements in lenses and shutters.

George Eastman introduced his box camera, the Kodak, and its accompanying film development scheme in 1888. This was a unique combination that proved an enormous success. (The name Kodak had no separate meaning—Eastman made it up.) The small hand-held Kodak took pictures that were 2.5 inches in diameter. Upon finishing the 100-exposure roll the photographer would send the camera and film to Eastman's processing plant in Rochester, New York, where the film was developed and printed. The company loaded a new roll into the camera and returned everything to the photographer. Eastman and his Kodak appear in Figure 11.19.

The Halftone

About the same time that George Eastman's Kodak was becoming the rage, photojournalism was coming into its own. The reason was the halftone, arguably the most important development in photography's march toward the journalistic prominence that it has achieved. The halftone allowed publishers to reproduce photographs easily and faithfully with text on the same rotary press.

Primarily through the skill of woodcut artists publications had used photographs in modified form with type for many years. In addition to being slow, the woodcut filtered the photograph through the mind of at least one woodcutter before readers saw it. The halftone changed all this, eliminating the artistic go-between and allowing readers to see more accurate representations of photographs—more accurate representations of real life.

On December 2, 1873, *The Daily Graphic* in New York City published the first photograph in a U.S. newspaper using the halftone process. It was an exterior view of Steinway Hall in New York; the paper described the halftone process as "granulated photography." Another famous early halftone image also appeared in *The Daily Graphic.* It

FIGURE 11.19

"George Eastman on board the S.S. Gallia," 1890. Eastman is photographed as he photographs with a Kodak. Note the circular aspect of the picture that is characteristic of this camera.

FREDRICK CHURCH/COURTESY GEORGE EASTMAN HOUSE

FIGURE 11.20

"A Slightly Damaged House, Johnstown, Pa., U.S.A." 1889.

GEORGE BARKER/COURTESY GEORGE EASTMAN HOUSE

was of a New York City shantytown and was captioned "Reproduction direct from nature."

Others—going as far back as Talbot—had tried to find a way to directly mass-reproduce photographs and type. The quest, as with most things photographic, did not involve a single person in one great shining moment of inventiveness; it was a long and complicated journey.

At the close of the 19th century, photography was on the verge of establishing itself as an important aspect of American journalism. Foreign publications such as the English newspaper *The Illustrated London News* and American publications such as the *New York Herald, Frank Leslie's Illustrated Newspaper, The Daily Graphic,* and *Harper's Weekly* were among the first to try to combine photography and journalism. Other U.S. pioneers in the early 1890s were inexpensive mass-circulation magazines such as *McClure's* and *Cosmopolitan* and the hybrid newspaper-magazine *Illustrated American.*

Not every publication of the late 19th century embraced the photograph. Not until the 20th century was photography accepted as a regular and important part of almost every publication.

Late 19th-Century Photojournalism

Photography of news events around the world was well underway before the turn of the century. Two examples of late–19th-century news coverage appear in Figures 11.20 and 11.21, taken in 1889 and in 1895, respectively; the 1889 image (Figure 11.20) is a stereoscopic picture. A stereoscopic picture has two images of the same scene taken from

FIGURE 11.21

"Street Accident in London" [England], 1895.

PAUL MARTIN/GERNSHEIM COLLECTION, HARRY RANSOM HUMANITIES RESEARCH CENTER, THE UNIVERSITY OF TEXAS AT AUSTIN

slightly different angles with a double-lens camera. When the two photographs are viewed together in a special viewer, they create the illusion of a three-dimensional image.

Frances Benjamin Johnston Frances Benjamin Johnston was one of the first female photojournalists in the United States. As an art student in Paris, she was making hand-drawn newspaper illustrations when she began photographing professionally in 1888. She covered various events for publications of the day, photographed extensively at the White House, took portraits, and ended her career by portraying houses in the South. She helped establish that women could be successful in the world of photojournalism. One of her White House pictures appears in Figure 11.22.

James Henry "Jimmy" Hare One of the first full-fledged news photographers of contemporary times was James Henry "Jimmy" Hare.

Hare was English, born in London in October 1856. He worked in his father's camera manufacturing business and was an amateur freelance photographer. He came to the United States and accepted a job in a New York City camera manufacturing concern but resigned when the company was sold. He then began to freelance seriously. In 1895 he became a photographer for the New York-based *Illustrated American*.

Hare resigned after nearly three years with the *Illustrated American*. When the battleship *U.S.S. Maine* blew up in Havana harbor in February 1898, increasing support in the United States for the Spanish-American War that began in April 1898, Hare convinced *Collier's Weekly* to send him to Cuba. Hare went on to photograph many other events (Figures 11.23 and 11.24).

Documentary Photography

Documentary photography is picture-taking done with the sole or primary intention of informing about reality in an objective and truthful way. Documentary photography traces its heritage to Niépce's ca. 1827 courtyard picture.

FIGURE 11.22

Alice Roosevelt, daughter of President Theodore Roosevelt, in the White House wearing her debut gown, 1902.

Frances Benjamin Johnston/Library of Congress

Documentary photography was common in the 19th century. All sorts of subjects were pictured—landscapes, still lifes, architecture, fires, accidents, floods, industrial progress, medical problems, prominent personalities, and wars, for example.

While some documentarians intentionally used intriguing compositional techniques (including lighting) to entice viewers to view their images, the predominant documentary approach, particularly in the United States, was a more straight-forward photographic effort. Visually enticing viewers with creative photographic techniques—unusual angles and eye-catching lighting, for example—was not a high priority for many photographers. Even if a

FIGURE 11.23

**"Carrying Out Wounded During the Fighting at San Juan" [Puerto Rico].
Taken during the Spanish-American War, 1898.**

JAMES "JIMMY" HARE/GERNSHEIM COLLECTION, HARRY RANSOM HUMANITIES RESEARCH CENTER, THE
UNIVERSITY OF TEXAS AT AUSTIN

documentary photographer wanted to use a photographically creative approach, the equipment and processes of the time, at least until late in the century, were formidable obstacles. Tripods, long exposures, limited lens selection, and for some time the need to have fully equipped darkroom close by surely to one degree or the other negatively impacted the 19th century documentary photographers who wanted to be photographically creative. Notwithstanding all the creative-related problems, European photographers, with a long history of painting to draw on, tended to be more creative than many U.S. photographers.

American documentary photographers tended to emphasize people more than their European counterparts who tended to embrace form—the form of a building or of a bridge or of a

FIGURE 11.24

"Aftermath of a Flood in Dayton" [Ohio], 1913.

JAMES "JIMMY" HARE/GERNSHEIM COLLECTION, HARRY RANSOM HUMANITIES RESEARCH CENTER, THE UNIVERSITY OF TEXAS AT AUSTIN

Photojournalism: An Introduction

scenic view, for example (Figure 11.25 and Figure 11.26). However, just as many European documentary photographs contain people, many American documentary photographs are similar in creativity to European-made images; the trend is there but the dividing line is fuzzy. However different the European and American approaches may have been, in general documentary photographers on both sides of the Atlantic fundamentally were dedicated to showing the world as it really was, to being objective, to relating the truth of what was before their lenses.

Social Documentary Photography

A variation of documentary photography—some term it social documentary—also was done in the 19th century.[8] What is social documentary photography?

Social documentary photography is documentary photography done with an end purpose in mind other than to simply objectively and truthfully visually inform, although social documentary photographs may do this. This purpose is

FIGURE 11.25

"Bourbonnais Railway. Roundhouse for 32 Locomotives at Nevers [France], First Interior View," ca. 1862.

A. COLLARD/COURTESY GEORGE EASTMAN HOUSE

FIGURE 11.26

"East and West Shaking Hands at Laying Last Rail at Promontory, Utah." Joining the tracks of the Central Pacific and the Union Pacific Railroads completed the first U.S. transcontinental railroad, 1869.

ANDREW J. RUSSELL/COURTESY OF THE OAKLAND MUSUEM OF CALIFORNIA

FIGURE 11.27

"Flashlight Photograph of One of Four Peddlers Who Slept in Cellar," ca. 1890. "Flashlight" refers to the type of artificial light used to take the picture and is different from the contemporary flashlight.

JACOB RIIS OR UNDER HIS SUPERVISION/MUSEUM OF THE CITY OF NEW YORK

social change, almost always the improvement of living or working conditions of the downtrodden or disadvantaged. However laudatory the ends may be that it champions, social documentary photography typically serves a propagandistic role.

While in your author's view every image ever made—including journalistic images—is subject to questioning about whether it is the most appropriate truth fairly represented, the propagandistic nature of social documentary images makes them a bit more suspect than documentary images or journalistic images. On the other hand, many social ills existing since the beginning of photography were bad enough that photographs could be made that showed the most appropriate truth fairly represented and that also well served the nonphotographic goals of their makers. Because social change was and is the driving force behind social documentary photography does not necessarily mean that all or even most social documentary photographers of the 19th century (and later) were photographically untruthful boosters of their social causes. David Octavius Hill and Robert Adamson, early Scottish calotypists, may have been the first true social documentarians. Photographic

historian and author Naomi Rosenblum relates that:

A consciously conceived effort involving the depiction of working people was undertaken in 1845 by Hill and Adamson. Probably the first photographic project to embrace a socially beneficial purpose, it apparently was suggested that calotypes might serve as a means of raising funds to provide properly decked boats and better fishing tackle that would improve the safety of the fishermen of the village of Newhaven, Scotland.[9]

While social documentary photography was practiced early in the history of photography, it came into its own in the late 19th century. The presentation of social documentary images was important; they typically were shown in groups rather than individually. Major improvement in the mass reproduction of photographs allowed these images to be easily reproduced and widely distributed.

The now-famous U.S. social documentarian, Jacob R. Riis, followed likeminded photographers in England, France, and Germany who yearned to improve the lot of those they perceived as needing help. Riis was a New York City police reporter who had the opportunity to see the city's slums. He developed a desire to do something to help the people who lived in them. Without formal photographic training Riis embraced the camera as an important tool in influencing others to share his social concerns. To this end and with photographic help he made, or supervised the making of, a number of photographs, culminating in the 1890 book *How the Other Half Lives.*

Riis and his photography set the tone for U.S. social documentary photographers of the 20th century. An example of this genre, taken by Riis or under his supervision, appears in Figure 11.27.

In the United States the most prominent social documentary photographer to follow Riis was Lewis Hine, a sociologist. The most prominent social documentary project was the New Deal-era

FIGURE 11.28

**"The Two Ways of Life",
1857.**

OSCAR GUSTAVE REJLANDER/THE
ROYAL PHOTOGRAPHIC SOCIETY
PICTURE LIBRARY, BATH, ENGLAND

Resettlement Administration's (later the Farm Security Administration) picturing of the United States on hard times, particularly in the rural United States because of bad weather and the Great Depression. Chapter 12 further discusses both Hine and the rural America project.

Photography as Art

Many art-oriented people embraced photography as a way to convey their visions to others; however, they took different approaches. Some took a documentary approach, others thought a subjective interpretation of real-life was important, others deviated even further from real-life by, for example, combining different photographs into one and creating allegorical images—putting wings on a child is an example. However they used photography to convey their visualizations, photographers in the 19th century art arena laid the groundwork for the many 20th century people who embraced and expanded photography as art and in doing so created a massive body of work. Hopefully you will be enticed by this brief and selected look at 19th century art photography to explore it much more in depth, and to do the same with 20th century art photography. Perhaps you will want to read one or more books on the subjects; "Selected Readings" at the back of this book is a good place to start. You may even want to take a course in art photography history; consider checking

your school's art department courses. Before moving on to "20th-Century History" and the photojournalistic richness that it contains, here is a brief look at several art photographers and several art photography approaches.

Oscar Rejlander (1813–1875) was a great cut-and-paste photographer. His allegorical picture, "The Two Ways of Life," is made up of about 25 different negatives printed on the same sheet of photographic paper (Figure 11.28).

Julia Margaret Cameron (1815–1879), the wife of a British civil servant, was a well-placed Victorian to whom photography was an agreeable pastime. She took pictures of many prominent English personalities and became famous for her portraits. Her portrait of writer Thomas Carlyle appears in Figure 11.29.

FIGURE 11.29

"Thomas Carlyle," 1867.

JULIA MARGARET
CAMERON/NMPFT/SCIENCE &
SOCIETY PICTURE LIBRARY,
LONDON, ENGLAND

FIGURE 11.30

"The Terminal," New York City, 1892.
Alfred Stieglitz/Gernsheim Collection, Harry Ransom Humanities Research Center, The University of Texas at Austin

She also created allegorical photographs—so-called narrative scenes. An example is a biblical child with wings.

Peter Henry Emerson (1856–1936) was the leader of a rebellion against the combination printing technique used by Rejlander and others. According to photographic historian and author Beaumont Newhall, Emerson "protested with a vehemence that shook the photographic world."[10] Newhall writes that Emerson "held that the artist's task was the imitation of the effects of nature on the eye."[11] A major art photography movement, naturalism, was born in the mid to late 1880s, conceived by Emerson. Emerson argued that realism was not enough, that photographers must mix realistic depiction and their interpretation of truth and feeling.

Eugène Atget (1857–1927) must have seemed a strange figure to the people of Paris around the turn of the century. He was a large man lugging a huge camera and tripod along the boulevards and lanes of the city. In fact, Atget was making a major contribution to what later would be termed documentary photography. In the 1920s another photographer, Bernice

Abbot, discovered Atget's work and energetically promoted it.

Two Americans whose work is heartily embraced by the contemporary art photography world are Alfred Stieglitz (1864–1946) and Edward Steichen (1879–1973). Both were born and began their photography in the 19th century, and both also photographed in the 20th century. Stieglitz in particular did significant work in both centuries; Steichen's significant work largely is in the 20th century. Stieglitz later in his career became a believer in what at the turn of the century had been called *pure photography.* Those who adhered to this style thought that photographers should keep their manipulation to a minimum and that realism was important. Two of Stieglitz's photos appear in Figures 11.30 and 11.31.

Steichen was a pictorialist early in his photographic life. Pictorialism was an important photographic movement from the late 1880s to the beginning of World War I. Photographic historian and author Naomi Rosenblum relates that photographers who embraced pictorialism "regarded the optical sharpness and exact replicative aspects of the medium as limitations inhibiting the

FIGURE 11.31

"Winter on Fifth Avenue," New York City, 1893.

ALFRED STIEGLITZ/GERNSHEIM COLLECTION, HARRY RANSOM HUMANITIES RESEARCH CENTER, THE UNIVERSITY OF TEXAS AT AUSTIN

FIGURE 11.32

"Solitude," 1901.

EDWARD STEICHEN/ THE MUSEUM OF MODERN ART, NEW YORK. COPY PRINT © 1997 THE MUSEUM OF MODERN ART, NEW YORK. GIFT OF THE PHOTOGRAPHER.

expression of individuality and therefore accepted manipulation of the photographic print as an emblem of self-expression."[12] To pictorialists beauty mattered more than literal fact.

Among other photographic endeavors, Steichen took pictures of people, such as the sculptor Auguste Rodin (Figures 11.32 and 11.33). Steichen was a member of a New York City–based photography society formed in 1902 by Stieglitz to promote pictorial expression as fine art. It was called the Photo-Secession—*secession* denoted independence.

Final Thoughts

Just think about it. No photographs. No direct real-life representations of what came before, or of the present. No baby photos. No family photos. No graduation photos. No events photos. No civilian leaders photos. No military leaders photos. No war photos. No peace photos. No photos at all.

Then after a long gestation, photography dramatically bursts onto the scene. With rapid technological advances and enthusiastic practioneers it becomes common, showing life near and far with amazing detail.

The 19th century wrote the early scenes and opened the play that is photography, setting the stage for the many exciting developments and photographs and personalities that would flourish in the 20th century to which we now turn.

FIGURE 11.33

"Rodin and 'The Thinker.'" 1902.

Photojournalism: An Introduction

NOTES

1. Beaumont Newhall, *Latent Image: The Discovery of Photography,* Science Study Series (New York: Anchor Books and Doubleday, 1967), p. 107.

2. Beaumont Newhall, *The History of Photography,* rev. ed. (New York: Museum of Modern Art, 1982), p. 16.

3. E. F. Bleiler, "Introduction to the Dover Edition," in Alexander Gardner, *Photographic Sketch Book of the Civil War* (New York: Dover, 1959).

4. Newhall, *The History of Photography,* p. 89.

5. Ibid., p. 100.

6. Floyd Rinhart, Marion Rinhart and Robert W. Wagner, *The American Tintype* (The Ohio State University, 1999), p. 6.

7. Ibid., p. 7.

8. Naomi Rosenblum, *A World History of Photography,* 3rd ed. (New York: Abbeville Press, 1997), p. 341.

9. Ibid., p. 343.

10. Newhall, *The History of Photography,* p. 141.

11. Ibid.

12. Rosenblum, *A World History of Photography,* p. 297.

20th-Century History

"Dr. Ernest Ceriani Providing Emergency Treatment for Little Girl Kicked by Horse." From the 1948 *LIFE* magazine essay "Country Doctor: His Endless Work Has Its Own Rewards."
W. EUGENE SMITH/© HEIRS OF W. EUGENE SMITH/COURTESY BLACK STAR

Overview

The 20th century had a tough act to follow—all the technological developments and talented photographers of the previous century. But follow it did and in a big way. Cameras and lenses and other hardware continued to improve or to be invented. Film vastly improved but in the early 21st century faces replacement for photojournalistic purposes by an electronic still recording approach, digital imaging. The halftone reproduction process gave way, even in newspapering, to the offset process, giving photographers and their mass circulation publications the means to reproduce high-quality images.

But most of all the 20th century proved to be a time rich with journalis-

Time Line of 20th-Century Photography

1902	Jessie Tarbox Beals arguably becomes first full-fledged woman news photographer.
1903	Graflex camera introduced in the United States.
1906	San Francisco catastrophic fire after earthquake is covered photographically.
	Panchromatic film is available but not widely used until 1928.
1907	The Lumière brothers of France introduce the first practical widely used color process, the Autochrome.
1908	Lewis W. Hine continues fledgling tradition of United States social documentary photography.
1910	Newspaper photography becomes firmly established in the United States.
1922	Flashpowder widely used in the United States after being invented in Germany in 1887.
1923	First photograph transmitted by wire.
1924	Ernemann-Werke A.G. and E. Leitz market the Ernom (later the Ermanox) and Leica "candid" cameras, respectively.
1925	Flashbulb invented in Germany where it is perfected in 1929.
1927	Rolleiflex is marketed.
1929	Speed Graphic, introduced in 1910, replaces the Graflex as the primary camera of U.S. newspapers.
	Heyday of German picture magazines.
1930	Flashbulb introduced in the United States as The Photoflash Lamp.
1931	*The Milwaukee Journal* initiates a daily picture page.
1932	Carl Zeiss of Germany introduces the 35mm Contax I camera; Contax is a worthy competitor of the Leica.
1935	Historical section of the United States Resettlement Administration (later Farm Security Administration) is established.
	The Associated Press establishes wire photo network, followed in 1936 by United Press.
	Black Star picture agency begins.
	Agfacolor Neu (sic) film is marketed.

FIGURE 12.1

San Francisco fire, 1906.
ARNOLD GENTHE/COURTESY GEORGE
EASTMAN HOUSE

tic photographs and the many photographers who created them. These exceptionally talented image makers created a massive body of journalistically oriented work in a relatively short time. This chapter provides a selection of these pictures and a brief look at a few of the people who helped create them. The coverage here gives only a hint of the richness of 20th-century photojournalism. You should seek out the numerous 20th-century picture books and pursue them with a critical eye. This book's *Selected Readings* is a good place to start.

To better put this time period in perspective, here is a limited time line of 20th-century photography relating to journalism.

1936	*LIFE* publishes first issue.
1937	Kodachrome color film becomes available for the 35mm still camera, based on a 1912 invention in Germany; revolutionizes color photography.
	Look publishes first issue.
1941	Portable electronic (stroboscopic) flash becomes practical; in wide use by late 1950s.
1942	Ansco-Color color film introduced as a transparency film that the user can process.
	Kodacolor color film introduced as a negative film that in its early years must be processed by Kodak.
1946	National Press Photographers Association founded.
	Magnum picture agency begins.
1947	Ektachrome color roll film marketed as a transparency film processable by users.
	Polaroid camera invented.
1948	Japanese-made rangefinder Nikon is marketed.
1949	*LIFE* photographer David Douglas Duncan begins to use Japanese-made Nikkor lenses; word of their desirability spreads to the United States.
1954	Tri-X black-and-white film marketed by Kodak.
1959	Japanese-made Nikon F single-lens reflex camera marketed.
1960	35mm cameras—rangefinder and single-lens reflex—gain momentum in replacing the Rolleiflex, Mamiya C3, Yashicamat, and Speed Graphic as the standard for U.S. newspaper and wire service photographers.
1965	35mm single-lens reflex camera with interchangeable lenses becomes camera of choice for U.S. newspaper photographers.
1978	The Associated Press introduces the electronic darkroom.
1982	Digital still camera becomes available.
1985	Reuters and Agence France-Presse begin international wire photo services, including U.S. operations.
1987	Photojournalists adopt automatic cameras and self-focusing lenses.
1988	Kodak introduces T-Max P3200, an extremely light-sensitive 35mm black-and-white film with relatively fine grain and great "pushability."
1991	Electronic darkrooms commonplace at U.S. newspapers.
1993	Zoom lenses with high-quality optics become popular with photojournalists.
1995	Color negative film comes into wide use by newspapers and wire services.
1999	Digital still cameras mainstream at major wire services and a few newspapers; almost certainly soon will be mainstream at most, if not all, newspapers; whether picture agency and magazine photographers embrace digital picture taking is more iffy.

Cameras and Lenses

Although the basic optical principles for photography have not changed over the years, cameras and lenses have come a long way since the 19th century. Equipment that photojournalists use today evolved from bulky manual cameras and slow, imprecise lenses to small automatic cameras and fast, self-focusing lenses.

Over the years manufacturers developed cameras of different designs, some more useful to photojournalism than others. In the 20th century photographers used no single camera type to the exclusion of others (see Figure 12.3). However, some dominated photojournalism at one time or the other.

The Graflex

The Graflex was a bulky handheld camera that was standard equipment for newspaper photographers during the first two decades of the century (Figure 12.2). It was a far cry from the small 35mm equipment of the present day, but it got the job done. From about 1903 until the 4 × 5 Speed Graphic replaced it in the early 1920s, the Graflex was the camera that most newspaper photographers used. They continued to use it, along with the Speed Graphic, for many years; it did not disappear until the 1950s.

The Speed Graphic

From roughly 1929 until about 1960 the Speed Graphic, with its interchangeable lenses and two shutters (one in the lens and one at the back of the camera), was the camera that defined the newspaper photographer in the United States (see Figure 12.14).

At first with flashpowder, then with flashbulbs, and toward the end of its reign with electronic flash, the Speed Graphic was a major factor in the form, and to a limited extent the substance, of what generations of readers saw of the world. The Speed Graphic was a large camera, clearly difficult to conceal. Therefore, newspaper photographers of this era sometimes used smaller cameras to cover assignments where the size of the Speed Graphic was a disadvantage. Examples of these cameras are the 35mm Contax and Leica, and the larger 2 1/4 × 2 1/4 twin-lens reflex, such as the Rolleiflex.

FIGURE 12.2

"News Photographers Covering Dynamite Explosion" with Graflex or similar cameras, Communipaw, New Jersey, 1911.

JAMES "JIMMY" HARE/ PHOTOGRAPHY COLLECTION/ HARRY RANSON HUMANITES RESEARCH CENTER/ THE UNIVERSITY OF TEXAS AT AUSTIN

FIGURE 12.3

At least three types of still cameras were used by photographers to cover the 1958 wedding of actress Jayne Mansfield and Mickey Hargitay, as this photograph illustrates. The predominant still camera appears to have been the large and boxy 4 × 5 press camera—the Speed Graphic or similiar cameras. This camera is in the right foreground and in the left and right background. The smaller format 2 1/4 × 2 1/4 Twin-lens Reflex is being used by the photographer standing high to Mr. Hargitay's left. The even smaller format 35mm is being used by the photographer more-or-less behind Ms. Mansfield. Note the number of electronic flash units being used.
WAYNE MILLER/MAGNUM PHOTOS, INC.

With relatively slow lenses and film, pictures taken with Speed Graphics produced in low-level light generally lacked a candid lighting ambiance. Photographers typically used a single flash. This defined the lighting of the picture and limited the distance of the subject from the camera, thus defining the scene that was recorded.

According to photographer Frank Scherschel and photo editor Stanley E. Kalish, *The Milwaukee Journal* issued its photographers this basic equipment in 1947:

A 4 × 5 Speed Graphic, fitted with an f/4.7 lens, synchronizer, 18 film holders, a No. 1 Crown tripod, a tilting top for angle shots, up to three extensions for side lights and flashbulbs, and an A and a K2 filter and lens shade, a focusing cloth, bulbs,

and a carrying case. (Film and bulbs have never been limited, on the theory that unrationed supplies make for better pictures.)[1]

Supplementary specialized equipment was available from a pool. *Journal* photographers also often used smaller format cameras for special assignments, such as clandestine courtroom photography. They also regularly used telephoto lenses for assignments such as daytime football games.

Some photographers of the Speed Graphic era became experts at using two or more flashbulbs, or multiple electronic flash (strobes), to light a subject. This approach eliminated harsh shadows behind subjects and gave the image an illusion of depth and reality.

In fairness to this camera of the past and the photographers who used it, some played it like a great musician plays a violin. These photographers produced candid, sensitive, storytelling pictures, particularly when unencumbered by the need to use flash. Many photographs of the Speed Graphic era stand as monuments to the talent of their makers.[5]

The 2¹/₄ × 2¹/₄ Twin-lens Reflex

The Speed Graphic held on until the early 1960s, although by that time the 2¹/₄ × 2¹/₄ Rolleiflex (Rollei)—and two other twin-lens reflex cameras, the Yashicamat and the interchangeable lens, Mamiya C3—had become the basic cameras for newspaper and wire service photographers. The Rolleiflex appears in Figure 12.4.

Called the 2¹/₄ × 2¹/₄ because of the size of its frame of film (in inches), this camera served as a bridge between the larger 4 × 5-inch Speed Graphic (and similar cameras made by other manufacturers such as the American-made Burke and James and the German-made Linhof) and the smaller 35mm cameras. For example, for several years beginning in the late 1950s and until about 1965 the basic camera type of The Associated Press was the 2¹/₄ × 2¹/₄, either the Yashicamat or the Mamiya C3.

Because of its small size, 35mm film demanded an exactness in exposure, processing, and handling that escaped many of the old-time newspaper and wire service photographers; they were accustomed to the much larger and technically forgiving 4 × 5-inch negative of the Speed Graphic. A number of these photographers looked upon the 35mm with suspicion, as a toy not to be taken seriously. Although some newspaper photographers used the 35mm camera as an adjunct to the larger format cameras, for most the Rollei and other 2¹/₄ × 2¹/₄ cameras were not such a giant step from the large-format Speed Graphic. By the early 1960s only hard-core 4 × 5 users claimed Speed Graphics and similar 4 × 5 cameras as their cameras of choice.

The Ermanox and a Prominent User

The German-made Ermanox used 4.5 × 6-centimeter glass plates rather than roll film. Its main advantage was an extremely fast lens, allowing photographers to take pictures in relatively low light. Soon after its introduction in 1924 it sported an f/1.5 lens, faster than its original f/2. The Ermanox appears in Figure 12.5.

The Ermanox never caught on in any serious way in the United States. Its brief but important life was limited primarily to Europe. The most prominent user of the Ermanox—he also used the Leica—was German lawyer-turned-photographer Erich Salomon.

Salomon became famous for his candid existing light photographs of European statesmen. He also took the first existing light photograph of a U.S. president in the White House and while in this country photographed newspaper publisher William Randolph Hearst. Salomon's work is closely akin to the existing light style used so much by contemporary photojournalists. Reproduced in Figure 12.6 is a Salomon picture—his image of a European statesman pointing at him as he took the man's picture (see also Figure 12.15, a magazine cover with a Salomon photograph).

The Leica and an Early User

The 35mm camera migrated to the United States from Germany in the 1930s. It quickly became the camera of

FIGURE 12.4

Rolleiflex, 1955.

Courtesy of Rollei Corporation

FIGURE 12.5

Ermanox, with an f/2 Ernostar lens, ca. 1924.

Gersheim Collection/ Harry Ranson Humanities Research Center/ The University of Texas at Austin

Photojournalism: An Introduction

choice for magazine photographers, although they used other cameras, particularly the Rolleiflex. Not until the early 1950s, when the Japanese-made 35mm Nikon rangefinder camera became widely available in the United States, were the popular European-made 35mm cameras, particularly the Leica and its competitive counterpart the Contax, challenged.

Dr. Oskar Barnack invented the Leica in 1913. Photographer and educator Paul Wolff relates that Barnack was fascinated by the newly invented motion picture camera and the world of cinematography. He developed an improved motion picture camera and made movies, becoming enamored with filmmaking. In Barnack's quest to save as much of the expensive film as possible, he developed a small still camera to make test exposures on short lengths of movie film.[2] Thus the forerunner of the contemporary camera that is extraordinarily popular with photojournalists, the 35mm, in the broadest sense was a light meter.

Barnack thought his crude little camera might be transformed into a proper one for taking still photographs. Because World War I intervened, it would be another 11 years—shortly after the Germans marketed the Ermanox in 1924—before a vastly improved version of the Leica was ready (Figure 12.7). It took images meant to be printed and displayed as single pictures.

According to photographic historian and author Naomi Rosenblum, this new camera was:

> Easy to handle, with a fast lens and rapid film-advancement mechanism

FIGURE 12.6

Statesman points at photographer Salomon, 1931. Note the existing light technique—it could be right out of today.
© Berlinische Galerie/bpk Berlin, Erich Salomon Archive

FIGURE 12.7

Leica, 1925.
Leica Camera, Inc.

FIGURE 12.8

"SPAIN," 1933.
HENRI CARTIER-BRESSON/
MAGNUM PHOTOS, INC.

. . . [it] called forth intuitive rather than considered responses and permitted its users to make split-second decisions about exposure and framing, which often imbued the image with a powerful sense of being a slice-of-life excised from a seamless actuality.[3]

The first of the mass-produced versions of this new rangefinder Leica was the F series; other more advanced Leicas followed. An early user of the Leica was a European photographer active from the 1930s, Henri Cartier-Bresson. Cartier-Bresson became famous for his photographic approach of taking pictures at the "decisive moment" and for the photographs he made using this approach, one of which appears in Figure 12.8.

Nikkor Lenses, an Early User, and Early Nikon Cameras

David Douglas Duncan was in occupied Japan in 1949 when he was introduced to Japanese lenses. This *LIFE* staffer, who soon would become a famous war

photographer and who later in his career would focus on other subjects (including Picasso), was instrumental in introducing Nikkor lenses in the United States.

Duncan and a colleague, Horace Bristol, experimented with the lenses and, reports Duncan, "discovered, to our utter amazement, that their [Nippon Optical Co.] three standard lenses for 35mm cameras were far superior, in our opinions, to any standard 35mm lenses available on the open market— British, American or German." Except for wide-angle lenses, and what Duncan termed "extreme telephoto lenses—over 135mm," for which he preferred German-made lenses, he equipped his Leica bodies with Japanese-made lenses.[4]

Word quickly spread to the United States about Duncan and his Leica-Nikkor combination. Nippon Optical Co. (popularly now known as Nikon) introduced its rangefinder camera bodies and lenses in the United States about 1950, and the company soon became the camera manufacturer of choice for many U.S. photojournalists, particularly many working for newspapers. Magazine photographers still tended to prefer their Leica rangefinder cameras.

The competition between Leica and Nikon was great. Photographers who used Leicas swore their German-made equipment was sturdier and technically superior to the Japanese-made Nikon. Nikon users were equally adamant that a combination of quality and price made their equipment the better choice. Then in 1959 Nikon dropped a photographic bombshell when it introduced the Nikon F single-lens reflex (Figure 12.9).

The Nikon F offered a modest price, through-the-lens viewing, quality lenses, and important accessories such as a motor drive, all features that helped establish its manufacturer as an important source of cameras and lenses now used by U.S. photojournalists.

Recent 35mm Cameras and Lenses

In the 1980s other Japanese camera makers began to seriously challenge Nikon's domination of the market. In addition, E. Leitz, the maker of Leica, continued to market excellent equipment, including its rangefinder camera and a single-lens reflex camera introduced in 1964.

Automatic Cameras Photographers for almost 150 years had no choice but to manually adjust their cameras, manipulating the f-stop and shutter-speed scales and focusing the lenses. Then in the early 1980s camera manufacturers started marketing single-lens reflex cameras that determined proper exposure and focused their lenses. Newspaper and wire service photographers and their organizations did not leap to embrace this new technology. Perhaps this was because of their significant investment in more conventional equipment, perhaps because the equipment did not meet their technical and creative standards, perhaps because they were reluctant to allow machines to substitute for human judgment, or some combination of these. Nevertheless, automatic camera bodies and autofocus

FIGURE 12.9

Original Nikon F, 1959.

COURTESY, NIKON CORP., JAPAN

lenses made inroads; improved versions are well established in photojournalism today, although many photographers continue to manually adjust their camera bodies and lenses when they prefer their judgment over that of the equipment.

Digital Cameras In 1982 the Sony Corp. introduced the world's first digital still camera. Since then Sony and other companies, including prominent photojournalistic film camera makers, have marketed ever improving models of digital cameras. Digital cameras are electronics-based and do not use film. Images taken with digital cameras do not need to be chemically developed, a major advantage over film and its cameras. Digital camera images easily and quickly can be put into a publishing company's computer system.

By the mid-1990s it was clear that the preeminence of film seriously was threatened by digital imaging. By the late 1990s major wire services and a few newspapers had replaced their film cameras with digital ones, and many newspapers were selectively using digital cameras. It seems likely that many newspapers in the near future will embrace digital cameras, relegating film cameras to a specialty role if they are used at all. If, and when, picture agency and magazine photographers move from film cameras to digital cameras is more in question.

The birth and refinement of digital still cameras for photojournalistic use is one of the premier—if not the premier—picture-taking technical developments of the 20th-century.

An Autochrome image of Marguerite Lumière, wife of Auguste Lumière, ca. 1907.
UNIDENTIFIED
PHOTOGRAPHER/
LUMIÈRE INSTITUTE

Film

Photography is the recording and preserving of images. Early photographers tried numerous schemes to capture the elusive image, and through the years photographers have used various kinds of recording processes. Except for specialized aspects such as infrared, all recorded the scene either in color or in black and white and shades of gray.

Color

In the 1820s, well before photography became a practical reality in 1839, the trailblazing photographic inventor Joseph Nicéphore Niépce dreamed of recording the world in all its color. However, the first practical color process, named the *Autochrome*, was not marketed for more than 80 years, by the Lumière brothers, Auguste and Louis, in 1907. An example of the

Autochrome, which yielded color transparencies, appears in Figure 12.10.

The road to using color images in photojournalism was rocky until the early 1900s. It was then that newly developed black-and-white panchromatic film emulsions allowed the realistic black-and-white recording of scenes (panchromatic film is sensitive to all visible wavelengths). The development of black-and-white panchromatic emulsion was a major milestone in the development of color picture taking. Panchromatic film allowed photographers to record the three primary colors with reasonable accuracy. They used filters that blocked the wavelengths of the other colors. This process yielded three black-and-white negatives—one for each primary color—and printing plates made from these images. Pressmen applied the appropriate color ink to each plate on the press and configured the presses so that the paper struck each plate individually at exactly the same place. If done with great precision, this process produced a realistic color image that mimicked the scene originally photographed.

Some cameras required only one exposure because they separated the light into the primary colors and directed it to three different pieces of film at the back of the camera. Some U.S. newspapers used this system into the 1950s.

What photojournalism really needed was a truly portable and convenient means of photographing in color—one that did not depend on the external filtration of light to create three black-and-white images. Relief came about 30 years after the introduction of panchromatic black-and-white film.

In the mid-1930s New Yorkers Leopold Godowsky and Leopold Mannes, working with Eastman Kodak Co., created a small, convenient, and practical film that recorded wavelengths of the primary colors. The film was Kodachrome, first sold as movie film but introduced in 1936 as 35mm still film. Kodachrome had three emulsion layers. Unlike most of its predecessors, it required only one exposure instead of three; it was as simple as black-and-white film to expose. Other color films were quick to follow.

A positive film introduced by Kodak in 1946, Ektachrome, went on to become the dominant positive film in the U.S. newspaper world from the 1950s until Fuji's positive film became a serious competitor in the 1970s. Ektachrome could be processed by the user, a local lab, or Kodak.

Today's makers of transparency color film used by photojournalists include, among others, Kodak and Fuji, the Japanese company. Today many newspapers prefer negative film because of its forgiving exposure nature, its ease and speed of processing, and its relatively low cost. Both Kodak and Fuji make negative color film, as do other companies.

Black and White

For photojournalists the single most important contemporary introduction in the black-and-white film arena was Tri-X Pan, marketed in 1954 by Kodak. For many years Tri-X, as it is commonly called, was the clear favorite of American photojournalists. Serious competitors, one of which is a Kodak film introduced in 1986, T-Max 400 Professional, now challenge Tri-X. The British company Ilford markets another black-and-white film used by photojournalists, HP-5 Plus, an ISO 400 film introduced in 1990 as an improved version of HP5, introduced in 1978. Also competing is Fuji's Neopan 400 Professional, introduced in 1987.

Challenging the popularity of all ISO 400 films in low-light situations is an extremely light-sensitive Kodak film, T-Max P3200, introduced in 1988. It is an excellent alternative to "pushing" ISO 400 films. Another excellent alternative is the Fuji-made ISO 1600 film, Neopan 1600 Professional, introduced in 1988.

The Electronic Darkroom

Almost all, if not all, daily newspapers and all major wire services now input, edit, store, and output photographs using electronic darkrooms. If any daily newspaper still has not converted to the electronic darkroom, it is highly likely that it soon will, dispensing with its chemical-optical darkroom. According to Hal Buell, former Associated Press assistant general manager for news photos, "Gone are the days of brown fingernails stained by photographic chemicals, of yellow safelight-illuminated darkrooms with wet sinks, and of conventional photographic prints." Replacing photographers and darkroom technicians who used enlargers and chemical solutions to produce positive paper-based images are editors, photographers, and technicians who use computers and related hardware and software to produce images that do not appear on paper until they are published.

Electronic darkrooms—also called by other names, such as *electronic picture desks, digital darkrooms,* and *imaging darkrooms*—receive pictures from non-digital and digital sources. Non-digital information—film images, for example—must be converted to digital information before entering an electronic darkroom's computer. This conversion in photojournalism typically is done by a desktop film scanner although flatbed print scanners also are used. Digital information—digital camera images or images in another electronic darkroom, for example—go directly into the electronic darkroom's computer; no scanning is needed.

Because of the manipulative potential of an electronic darkroom's computers—major and minor changes easily and quickly can be made to a photograph by a skilled operator so that the changes appear to even a critical viewer to be part of the original image—journalistic organizations, particularly in the early years of the electronic darkroom, grappled with the degree of manipulation—processing—that was ethically acceptable. Now that the dust largely has settled in this arena, it appears that computer processing of photojournalistic images is severely restricted; certainly not anything even halfway close to putting one person's head on the body of another person is allowed by reputable publications. More leeway is given to images that will be labeled and published as "Photo Illustrations," although manipulation is limited with these. Overall, there is little doubt that at least in the early years of electronic darkrooms their manipulative potential was the catalyst for ethical concern to be moved to the front burner, if it already was not there.

Flash Light

One of the fundamental factors limiting photography in its early years was the lack of an effective portable artificial light source. First flashpowder, then flashbulbs, and finally and most satisfactorily electronic flash (strobe) solved this problem.

Flashpowder

Flashpowder, used well into the 20th century after being invented in Germany in 1887, was dangerous to both photographers and subjects. Typically it was poured into a flashpowder pan, a metal trough with a handle.

John Reidy, who began his career in newspaper photojournalism in 1925 at the *Daily Mirror* in New York City, describes the typical method of using flashpowder to take posed pictures:

> It was carried in a 3.5-ounce bottle. Photographers in those days very often would cover an assignment in a group. The photographers would set up their cameras on wooden tripods. One photographer would fire a single flash, calling out, "Open." All the photographers would open and close their shutters.
>
> If the scene was inside a room, only one picture was usually possible because the smoke from the flashpowder would descend from the ceiling and practically obliterate any further idea of taking another picture. But occasionally someone would try to get off a second flash, particularly if he was by himself. If he didn't wait until the left-over hot embers from a previous flash had

cooled, there might be an accident. When powder being poured from the bottle hit a left-over hot ember, it exploded. The bottle he was holding with the remaining powder also exploded. Flashpowder was like holding a hand grenade.

Photographers also had flashpowder pans which they could connect to the shutters of their lenses with cable releases. Photographers usually used these only outside and in candid situations that required mobility. The slightest wind blew a mist of powder out of the gun. If it landed on a hand or arm and the photographer discharged the gun, the explosion was likely to follow the powder, resulting in burned flesh. Photographers typically wore a glove or wrapped a protective handkerchief around the hand firing the flash.

Photographers did not use reflectors inside or out. The ambiance produced without a reflector, particularly inside, was more desirable than with one; also, the flash explosion would instantly burn and darken a reflector. Flashpowder without a reflector yielded an even soft light in a room, much like that yielded by today's bare-bulb strobes. Inconvenient and dangerous as it was, photojournalists in the late 19th-century and well into the 20th-century welcomed flashpowder and found it indispensable.

Flashbulbs

Flashbulbs, introduced in 1925, perfected in 1929, and widely marketed in the U.S. in 1930, were the photojournalist's portable artificial light source of choice into the 1950s (Figure 12.11).

Flashbulbs made life a lot better and easier for photographers when they replaced dangerous flashpowder. Even so, they were not ideal. Some were large, and even those that were smaller were not particularly convenient to carry around. All would burn fingers when unthinking photographers tried to change them too quickly after discharge. And they were not totally reliable. As related by Thomas F. Spidell, supervisor of the public service bureau of the *Milwaukee Journal,* they "had a tendency to fire [at random] because of static electricity or electromagnetic energy."[5]

Even so, flashbulbs were safer and more convenient than flashpowder. What they did not do when used with reflectors and aimed directly at main subjects (and they often were) was preserve the existing light ambiance of scenes or convey a sense of realistic depth. A typical photograph from the heyday of the single-flashbulb-on-the-camera era appears in Figure 12.12, taken in 1942 by New York City police beat photographer Arthur Fellig. Fellig was commonly known as Weegee, a pseudonym that derived from the Ouija board and reflected Fellig's ability to be in the right place at the right time to get pictures.

As flashbulbs gained favor, some photojournalists began to use multiple bulbs off their cameras to overcome the lack of depth perception in images and the problem of subjects that faded into a dark background. Both flaws were common to photographs produced with a single flashbulb on or near the camera.

Electronic Flash (Strobes)

About three decades after photojournalists adopted flashbulbs, a new artificial light source—some portable—became widely available and used. The electronic flash broadened photojournalism by expanding photographers' ability to portray the world, including extraordinarily fast-moving objects (Figure 12.13).

Harold E. Edgerton, a graduate student in electrical engineering at the Massachusetts Institute of Technology (MIT), built on the electric flash developed in the mid 1880s in Germany. Edgerton became interested in stopping motion by using an electric flash device. According to James R. Killian, Jr., a former president of MIT, Edgerton "recognized the opportunity to develop stroboscopes for the purposes of 'stopping motion,' and he proceeded to develop the first modern stroboscope, described in the May 1931 issue of the journal *Electrical Engineering.*"[6] In the early 1930s Edgerton had significant help from two students, Kenneth Germeshausen and Herbert E. Grier, who later became his business partners. Edgerton's shop also developed a portable electronic flash powered by batteries. Eastman Kodak Co., then the exclusive sales agent for the studio version of the electronic flash, distributed a few units of Edgerton's flash in 1941. World War II cut short the production of these portable units, but word of

FIGURE 12.11

Photographers (top center) using flashbulbs with Speed Graphics or similar 4 × 5 cameras to photograph famed aviator Charles Lindbergh during a recess in the 1935 trial of the man accused of kidnapping the Lindbergh baby.

FIGURE 12.12

**"Gunman Killed by
Off Duty Cop at 344
Broome Street,"
1942.**
Weegee/ICP/Liaison
Agency

FIGURE 12.13

**"Antique Gun Firing"
captured using elec-
tronic flash, 1936.**
Dr. Harold E. Edgerton/
© The Harold & Esther
Edgerton Foundation,
1999/Courtesy of Palm
Press, Inc.

their development quickly made its way to Edward Farber, a photographer for *The Milwaukee Journal* who had a scientific bent. Farber took an interest in the concept at the urging of Frank Scherschel, head of the *Journal's* photo department.

Because Farber's work required glass tubes, he enlisted the help of a local glassblower, Egon Grimm. Together they developed a portable unit, refining it so that by late 1941 it weighed only 13.5 pounds; a later non–portable version appears in Figure 12.14.

The *Journal* ran a contest to name the new device, and a college professor won with *stroboflash,* or *strobe,* for short.

Farber, like Edgerton and his colleagues, saw the marketing potential of a portable electronic flash and started a company, Strobo-Research. Again, World War II intervened, but after the war Farber, with the help of others, rejuvenated the company. It later was sold to Graflex, the maker of the Speed Graphic camera and other photographic equipment.

An important advantage of electronic flash over flashbulbs was that photographers could use the same electronic flash unit over and over again. Because of its extraordinarily short flash, it had the added feature of stopping fast movement. This proved to be an important consideration for photojournalists, particularly when covering poorly lit night events where subjects were moving and the photographer needed to provide light.

FIGURE 12.14

Milwaukee Journal **photographers in 1949 look out over a later version of Farber and Grimm's strobe. John Ahlhauser, one of the photographers pictured, reports that the strobes in this photo were not considered portable because they operated only with A.C. electricity and weighed about 35 pounds. The photographers are holding 4 × 5 Speed Graphics except for the woman who is holding a 4 × 5 specialty camera for taking color photographs.** GEORGE KOSHOLLEK/ *MILWAUKEE JOURNAL,* NOW *MILWAUKEE JOURNAL SENTINEL.* PRINT COURTESY OF JOHN AHLHAUSER

The electronic flash continues to be a major tool used by contemporary photojournalists—both as a main light source and as a secondary one. However, as digital still photography cameras mature, photojournalists may have less need for any artificial light source. Digital cameras of the future may allow photographers to record in much dimmer existing light than now is possible.

Magazines

Magazines, many of which were photography oriented, had their heyday during the first 70 years of the 20th century. The picture magazine trend began in Europe and moved to the United States.

European Magazines

Germany, France, and England were hot-beds of avant-garde, large-circulation, picture-oriented magazines in the 1920s and 1930s (Figure 12.15). The *Berliner Illustrierte Zeitung, Munich Illustrierte Zeitung, Vu, Weekly Illustrated,* and *Picture Post* were precursors of the great U.S. general interest picture-oriented magazines, *LIFE, Collier's, The Saturday Evening Post,* and *Look.*

These European magazines, and others like them, employed talented editors sympathetic to the view that photography was an important and effective way to communicate. Editors such as Stefan Lorant and Kurt Korff and photographers such as Eric Salomon, Martin Munkacsi, Wolfgang Weber, Walter Bosshard, and Felix Man are forever engraved in the history of photojournalism as trailblazers of the 1920s and 1930s. These talented people either encouraged a candid multiple-picture approach to magazine photojournalism or actually produced pictures of this genre. It is difficult to overstate their collective influence on photojournalism as later practiced in the United States.

U.S. Magazines

Picture-oriented publishers and editors in the United States generally tended to take their lead from European publications. Four U.S. picture-oriented general interest publications, three weeklies and one twice monthly, ultimately garnered large circulations. The weeklies were: *LIFE, Collier's* and *The Saturday Evening Post;* the twice monthly was *Look.* You may find copies of all four in your school's library. Consider taking a couple of hours, compare them, and come to your own conclusion about the photography they used and how well they used it. Before moving on to "Newspapers and Wire

FIGURE 12.15

Cover of *Berliner Il-
lustrirte Zeitung:*
"Statesmen," 1931,
with a photograph by
Erich Salomon. The
German magazine
was in the forefront
of photojournalism.

© BERLINISCHE GALERIE/BPK
BERLIN, ERICH SALOMON
ARCHIVE

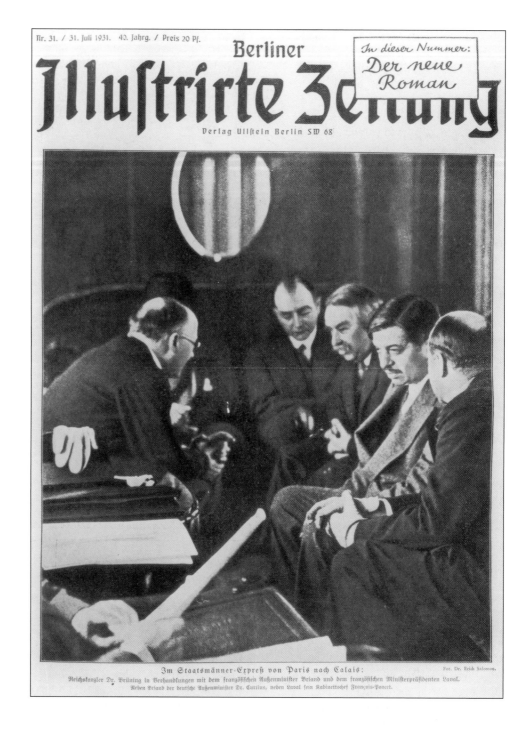

Nr. 31. / 31. Juli 1931.   40. Jahrg. / Preis 20 Pf.

In dieser Nummer:
Der neue
Roman

Berliner
Illustrirte Zeitung

Verlag Ullstein Berlin SW 68

Im Staatsmänner-Expreß von Paris nach Calais:
Reichskanzler Dr. Brüning in Verhandlungen mit dem französischen Außenminister Briand und dem französischen Ministerpräsidenten Laval.
Neben Briand der deutsche Außenminister Dr. Curtius, neben Laval sein Kabinettschef François-Poncet.

Fot. Dr. Erich Salomon.

Services," let's spend a little time with
one of these weeklies, *LIFE,* and with
the twice monthly, *Look.* Let's also do
the same thing with a specialized
magazine of long standing, *National
Geographic.*

LIFE   For more than 35 years (1936–
1972) the weekly magazine *LIFE* was a
premier general interest picture–
oriented magazine in the United States.

LIFE had ambitious goals from the
beginning. Writing in its prospectus under the heading "The Purpose," *LIFE*'s
founder Henry Luce set the tone and
the goals for the magazine with these
words:

To see life; to see the world; to eyewitness great events; to watch the
faces of the poor and the gestures of
the proud; to see strange things—

machines, armies, multitudes, shadows in the jungle and on the moon; to see man's work—his paintings, towers and discoveries; to see things thousands of miles away, things hidden behind walls and within rooms, things dangerous to come to; the women that men love and many children; to see and to take pleasure in seeing; to see and be amazed; to see and\ be instructed; . . . .[7]

LIFE took its lead from the avant-garde picture style and layout of the European magazines. Working for LIFE was the goal of many talented photojournalists, including many working for newspapers. The lure of covering major stories and personalities instead of automobile accidents and local social events, working with some of the best photographers in the world, and the opportunity to influence millions of readers instead of thousands was incredibly strong.

LIFE's original staff photographers were Margaret Bourke-White, Alfred Eisenstaedt, Thomas D. McAvoy, and Peter Stackpole. Bourke-White, formerly an architectural and industrial photographer, had worked for Luce's *Fortune* magazine; she joined LIFE in 1936. Bourke-White took the magazine's first cover photograph (Figure 12.16) and went on to a distinguished globe trotting career (Figure 12.17) before Parkinson's disease forced her to stop taking pictures. She was the author of several books, including an autobiography, *Portrait of Myself*, and *You Have Seen Their Faces*, about the rural South. Her co-author on the latter was her then-husband, the writer Erskine Caldwell.

Margaret Bourke-White is a giant in photojournalism's history. Her stellar picture-taking aside, she helped set the stage for the many women who now are photojournalists. Her equally famous LIFE colleague, Carl Mydans, said about her, "In a man's world, Margaret was one of the great achievers of our time."[8]

It was a sad day when the weekly LIFE followed its former competitor *Look* and ceased publication in 1972. Their demise left a giant gap in

U.S. photojournalism, both for photographers and readers.

Look   *Look* concentrated on in-depth stories related to news and on features (Figure 12.18).

Gardner Cowles, news editor of the *Des Moines Register and Tribune* and a member of the family that owned the newspaper, started *Look* in 1937. Cowles, who was to become editor in chief, later wrote that he was impressed by readers' response to *Register and Tribune* photographs. In particular, he was impressed by "the public interest in stories which allied pictures and text."[9] Cowles engaged a researcher to conduct a poll about this. It supported his impression, and he launched *Look*.

FIGURE 12.17

Mohandas K. Gandhi, a giant in India's struggle for independence from Great Britain, in 1946 with his spinning wheel, his charka. Spinning their own cloth meant that Indians did not have to buy British textiles, a great aid in maintaining their British textiles boycott. The spinning wheel was symbolic of the Indian quest for independence.
MARGARET BOURKE-WHITE/ *LIFE* MAGAZINE © TIME INC.

Cowles had published 903 issues of *Look* when he shut the magazine down in 1971. He wrote that he did so for several reasons, including among others the "soaring costs of paper, printing, distribution, and the staggering increases in postal rates."[10] Another reason, according to Cowles, was the loss to television of revenues from advertising.

Although it took more than a decade for *Look* to evolve into a first-class picture-oriented magazine, it ultimately offered readers superb photography by particularly talented photojournalists. In the magazine's later years *Look* used exceptionally fine paper. *Look*, like *LIFE*, also used the work of freelancers.

National Geographic Ask people on the street to describe a journal and they probably will use the words stodgy and technical. These may fit some journals but definitely not the "Official Journal of the NATIONAL GEOGRAPHIC SOCIETY Washington, D.C."[11] Although *National Geographic* is the official journal of the National Geographic Society, it is much more. It is a world-class publication that exhibits the work of excellent photographers. It long has been a leader in publishing photographs, particularly in color.

Predating *LIFE* and *Look* by almost 50 years, *National Geographic* began in October 1888 as a dull, brown-covered monthly that contained scholarly articles on geographic topics. It used no photographs. The first issue's circulation was 165, and its formal name was *The National Geographic Magazine*.

The contemporary *National Geographic* almost always has a superbly reproduced color photograph on its yellow-bordered cover; it rarely uses a black-and-white image. The magazine is chock full of finely reproduced pictures, almost always in color. It contains articles on geography, some of which interpret the word liberally; typically, *Geographic*'s stories are written in popular style.

In short, *National Geographic* is highly professional and technically superb and has a long history of association with photography—it began emphasizing photography in 1903. The magazine borrowed photographs from the federal government and obtained some from explorers and others. By 1910 it was using black-and-white and color-tinted photographs regularly, hinting at the quality and orientation of the magazine of later years. *National Geographic* published its first color picture, an Autochrome, in 1914. The September 1959 issue marked the beginning of the magazine's regular use of a color photograph on the cover. The first all-color magazine appeared in February 1962.

In its earlier days the magazine's policy was to print "only what is of a kindly nature . . . everything unpleasant or unduly critical being avoided."[12] *National Geographic* abandoned this policy in the 1970s, allowing the magazine to address controversial topics such as chemical pollution and human evolution.

Newspapers and Wire Services

In the early part of the 20th century the large and unwieldy Graflex camera was king. Flashbulbs would not replace flashpowder for about 25 years. Photographers tended to travel to news events in packs and to zealously guard their jobs from the incursions of newcomers.

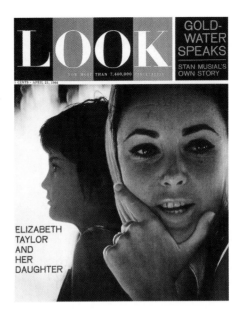

FIGURE 12.18

Cover of *Look*, April 21, 1964, with photograph of Elizabeth Taylor and daughter Liza by Pete Turner. Founded in 1937, the magazine concentrated on in-depth coverage until it ceased publication. COVER PHOTO BY PETE TURNER/ COURTESY OF PETE TURNER STUDIO

Almost all photographers of this era were men.

One early 20th-century photographer, considered by at least one author to have been the first woman news photographer, was Jessie Tarbox Beals. Beals was a restless, brash, and adventurous person who did various kinds of photography professionally, including working from 1902 to 1904 for the *Buffalo Inquirer* and the *Courier*. Her relatively short stint as a newspaper photographer was a precursor of the significant involvement of women in contemporary photojournalism.

Newspaper management in the 1950s began to understand that photography by serious, thoughtful photojournalists was an important communicative tool. This realization was fueled—if not ignited—by the 35mm camera, which allowed photographers to regularly produce candid, storytelling images in existing light. Also, increasing numbers of photojournalists began to earn four-year college degrees and more respect from editors and reporters.

Until about 1960 newspaper and wire service photographers—with notable exceptions—regularly used a flash-on-the-camera approach; the primary style of the time was not candid photography that probed beneath the obvious. Still, they produced many memorable pictures, three of which are reproduced in

FIGURE 12.19

Mayor William J. Gaynor of New York City is shot in an assassination attempt, 1910.

Unidentifed Photographer/ CORBIS-Bettman

Figures 12.19–12.21. Most U.S. newspapers and arguably the most prominent wire service of the time, The Associated Press, would not evolve to the candid, existing light style until the 1960s.

An early successful wire transmission of a photograph, a portrait of the German crown prince, occurred in 1907. *Scientific American* published the transmitted version on its cover.

Transmission of the prince's photograph was made possible by experiments of a professor at the University of Munich, Alfred Korn. Korn's process involved two revolving drums, one hold-ing a 5 × 7-inch transparency and the other a blank piece of film. Light passed through the transparency, struck a selenium photocell, and was translated into electric current. The wire carried the current, and a receiving machine with blank film reconstructed it into black and white and shades of gray. This set the stage for almost instanta-neous visual communications around the world.

In 1935 The Associated Press inaugu-rated the world's first privately owned photographic wire network. The first picture transmitted to 24 participating

FIGURE 12.20

The dirigible Hindenburg burns at its mooring, Lakehurst, New Jersey, 1937.
SAM SHERE/
CORBIS/HULTON DEUTSCH
COLLECTION

members was of a plane crash in New York. Soon other worldwide picture-gathering organizations began, including Soundphoto, owned by Hearst; Wired Photos, started by Wide World Photos but taken over by *The New York Times* and later The Associated Press; NEA-Acme Telephoto, owned by Scripps-Howard; and UPI Telephoto, which incorporated Acme Telephoto and was owned by Scripps-Howard. Much later, in 1985, two worldwide wire service organizations, the British-based Reuters and French-based Agence France-Presse, began U.S. wire service operations for photographs. Incidentally, "wire service" is not to be taken literally. While telephone wire still is used, in the mid-1980s The Associated Press began transmitting photographs by satellite. Now AP and other major wire services transmit, with very limited exceptions, all their photos by satellite.

Lewis Wickes Hine

Lewis Hine probably is the single most famous—and influential—American social documentary photographer of the 20th century.

Sick and near death, George Herman "Babe" Ruth, steadying himself with a baseball bat, says goodbye to New York Yankee fans, and they say goodbye to the baseball legend. It was Babe Ruth day at Yankee Stadium, 1948. This photograph won the 1949 Pulitzer Prize. NAT FEIN/*NEW YORK HERALD TRIBUNE*/THE NAT FEIN COLLECTION, INC.

Hine was from a working-class background. He was educated as a sociologist and had a deep concern for the welfare of others. He involved himself in social documentary photography in the mold of Jacob A. Riis. Hine pictured workers in Pittsburgh, immigrants at Ellis Island, American Red Cross relief efforts in Europe, and the construction of the Empire State Building. He focused his camera on children at work in questionable, even brutal, circumstances. The resulting pictures were a factor in the passage of national child labor laws. Two of Hine's pictures appear in Figures 12.22 and 12.23; both are of working children.

The work of Hine and Riis left a photographic legacy of concern, particularly for the poor and down-trodden. This bequest was an antecedent to arguably the most important social documentary photography ever done in the United States. This was the photographing primarily of rural America on hard

times but which also included other aspects of American life.

The Documentation of Rural America

The U.S. government's documenting primarily of rural life in the 1930s and 1940s is one of the great photographic projects of all time. This project began in 1935 in the New Deal's Resettlement Administration and finished in the Farm Security Administration, a unit of the Department of Agriculture.

In an appointment that proved a non-photographer could manage a major photographic project and its photographers, the Resettlement Administration named Roy Emerson Stryker, an economics professor at Columbia University, chief of its historical section. Photographic historian Beaumont Newhall tells us how Stryker shaped the project:

Photojournalism: An Introduction

The scope of the documentation and its general aim were controlled and guided by Stryker, who briefed the photographers on the sociological and economic backgrounds of their assignments, stimulated their imagination, and encouraged their curiosity.[13]

The pictures' underlying purpose was to help justify President Franklin D. Roosevelt's New Deal programs to aid rural America, which was suffering from adverse weather conditions (the Dust Bowl) and the Depression economy. Toward the end of the project Congress became displeased with the "negative" tone of the photographs, which then took a more positive approach until the project was terminated in 1943.

Stryker's unit took a lot of pictures that had nothing to do with what later would be considered a great social documentary project. Years later Stryker told his coauthor of a book about the project that "most of what the photographers had to do to stay on the payroll was routine stuff showing what a good job the agencies were doing out in the field."[14]

According to Stryker, the photographers had one thing in common: "a deep respect for human beings." Stryker also maintained that "we had no idea that we were doing anything of the importance that later historians have credited us with."[15] Images from the project appear in Figures 12.24–12.26.

Robert Capa: The War Photographer with Pizzazz

Robert Capa was born in Hungary as André Friedmann. He changed his name because he thought "Robert Capa" carried more pizzazz—more

FIGURE 12.25

Oklahoma dust storm, 1936.
ARTHUR ROTHSTEIN/
LIBRARY OF CONGRESS

panache—than "André Friedmann" and would help sell his photographs. Capa became known for his dashing lifestyle as well as for his photographs.

Capa produced two of the most memorable war pictures of all time: the death of a Spanish soldier at the moment he was struck in the head by a bullet and a blurry picture of an American soldier in the surf off Normandy on D-Day. Disaster befell Capa's film of this now-famous World War II landing. A London darkroom technician turned the dryer heater up too high; the emulsion softened and ran on almost all the images. His landing picture, one of the few saved, appears in Figure 12.27. Capa died in 1954 when he stepped on a land mine while covering the war between the French and Vietnamese, the long conflict that was a precursor to the Vietnam War.

World War II

Wars, for whatever reason, attract journalistic photographers. Photographic

FIGURE 12.26

Frozen California crops meant no work for this migrant mother and her family. She is pictured with her children, 1936.

Dorothea Lange/Library of Congress

coverage of war goes back to Roger Fenton's coverage of the Crimean War beginning in 1855, and maybe earlier. Perhaps human conflict is the reason, perhaps it's being at a big event, the possibility of becoming a famous photographer, a desire to inform, or simply being sent by one's employer. Whatever the reasons, talented photographers cover wars.

No war in the 20th century was larger or had more at stake than World War II. Many telling photographic images were produced by the many photographers covering this gut-wrenching event. Reproduced here are three images of World War II (Figures 12.28–12.30; see also W. Eugene Smith's heart-wringing photograph of a U.S. Marine holding a baby on Saipan in Figure 12.31). These photographs provide a glimpse of the photography done about one of the worst wars in human history.

The National Press Photographers Association

The largest national organization of photojournalists in the United States is the National Press Photographers Association (NPPA). Its approximately 9,500 members are primarily newspaper and television photographers. Among the founders of NPPA in 1946 was Joseph "Joe" Costa, then a photographer for the *Daily News* in New York City and president of the New York Press Photographers Association. According to photojournalist and author Claude Cookman, the association's "first and premier purpose" as set forth in its constitution is "the advancement of press photography in all its branches."[16]

From its founding the NPPA has worked pugnaciously for the right of photographers to photograph in the nation's courtrooms. At the state level this battle generally has been won, with the significant help of others. Among the NPPA's key activities today are a "Job Information Bank,"contests for its print and television photographers, educational activities, and publications,

FIGURE 12.27

One of the defining images of World War II and among the few 1944 D-Day landing pictures taken by Robert Capa to survive a darkroom error.

Robert Capa/Magnum Photos, Inc.

FIGURE 12.28

"Three dead American soldiers lying in the sand on shoreline near half sunken landing craft on Buna Beach, New Guinea, 1943."

GEORGE A. STROCK/*LIFE* MAGAZINE © TIME INC.

FIGURE 12.29

Slave laborers in a Nazi concentration camp at the end of World War II, 1945.

UNIDENTIFIED PHOTOGRAPHER/AP/WIDE WORLD PHOTOS

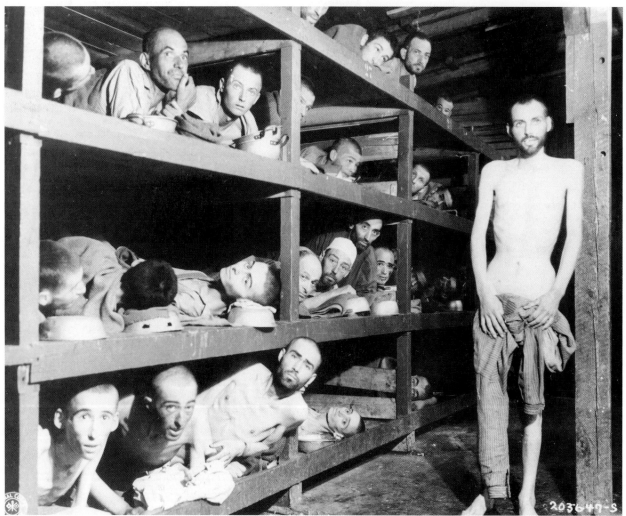

Photojournalism: An Introduction

particularly its fine association-wide magazine, *News Photographer,* edited by former photojournalism professor James "Jim" Gordon.

W. Eugene Smith: A Giant in American Photojournalism

Every aspiring photojournalist with a scintilla of social consciousness and the slightest hint of individuality should become familiar with the photographer who exemplifies the concerned photojournalist. W. Eugene Smith's name is synonymous with the in-depth, sensitive, revealing photographic essay.

Smith began taking pictures full-time in 1937, covered World War II in the Pacific where he was severely wounded, and ended his picture-taking career about 35 years later with a lengthy essay about Japanese fishing people deeply and tragically affected by mercury pollution in their bay. In its book form the essay is titled *Minamata.*

Early in his career Smith worked for *Newsweek,* then freelanced in association with Black Star picture agency. He joined *LIFE,* quit, and worked as a freelance war photographer, then rejoined *LIFE.* From 1955 through *Minamata* (1975) he freelanced. His colleagues revered Smith for his photography and for his insistence that editors use his photographs the way he believed they should be used. He quit *LIFE* for the last time when editors refused to follow his advice in designing his essay on Dr. Albert Schweitzer.

Smith once taught a course that he called "Photography Made Difficult," an insight to his personality and attitude toward photography. Figures 12.31–12.33 present three images by Smith. Also see the opening photograph of this chapter of a country doctor at work. Each hints at the probing humanistic approach of one of the last century's photographic giants.

The Korean War

Less than five years after World War II ended, the United States became involved in another war, officially termed a police action and fought under the flag of the United Nations. Photojournalists—Al Chang, Max Desfor who won the 1951 Pulitzer Prize for one of his Korean War photographs (Figure 12.34), David Douglas Duncan, and Frank "Pappy" Noel, among others—covering this war produced notable pictures. Pappy Noel, an AP photographer who spent three years as a prisoner of North Korea, took exclusive pictures of his fellow prisoners of war.

The 1960s and 1970s

For newspaper and wire service photography the 1960s were a time of flux, both in cameras and photographic style.

Photojournalists still used Speed Graphics occasionally, 2 1/4 × 2 1/4 twin-lens reflexes were not uncommon, and the 35mm rangefinder had pretty much

FIGURE 12.30

"A jubilant American sailor clutching a white-uniformed nurse in a back-bending, passionate kiss as he vents his joy while thousands jam New York City's Times Square to celebrate the long awaited victory over Japan," 1945.

ALFRED EISENSTAEDT/*LIFE* MAGAZINE/© TIME INC.

U.S. Marine holds a fly-covered baby rescued in 1944 from a cave on Saipan during the war in the Pacific. This photograph, which conveys both the Marine's humanity and a feeling of hope in the midst of war, originally was part of a lengthy picture group photographed by W. Eugene Smith and his *Life* colleague Peter Stackpole. The article, entitled "Saipan—Eyewitness Tells of Island Fight," was written by Robert Sherrod.

W. EUGENE SMITH/© HEIRS OF W. EUGENE SMITH/COURTESY BLACK STAR

"Walk to Paradise Garden." W. Eugene Smith photographed his children in 1946 while he recuperated from serious wounds he received while covering U.S. Marines fighting in the Pacific in World War II. The now-famous picture helped Smith get back into photography, something he had wondered whether he ever would do again.

W. EUGENE SMITH/© HEIRS OF W. EUGENE SMITH/COURTESY BLACK STAR

Steelworker tends flaming coal. From the 1958 *Popular Photography Annual 1959* essay "Pittsburgh —W. Eugene Smith's Monumental Poem to a City."

W. EUGENE SMITH/© HEIRS OF W. EUGENE SMITH/COURTESY BLACK STAR

FIGURE 12.34

Refugees "crawl perilously over shattered girders" of Pyongyang, North Korea's bridge over the Taedong River as they flee south in 1950 to escape advancing Chinese Communist troops. This photograph won the 1951 Pulitzer Prize.

MAX DESFOR/AP/WIDE WORLD PHOTOS

given way to the 35mm single-lens reflex.

To the extent that the camera influenced style—and it usually did—candid existing light photographs were gaining ground. Single flash-on-the-camera-aimed-directly-at-the-subject pictures of the 1950s (and before) were well on their way to limited use. The era of the 35mm camera as the overwhelming choice of newspaper and wire service photographers was at hand, about 30 years after it became the camera of choice for European magazine photography.

The 1960s and 1970s were a time of social upheaval (Figure 12.35). The civil rights movement, begun in earnest in the 1950s, moved to the front burner in the 1960s. The Vietnam War reached its zenith in the late 1960s, rising in intensity after the United States became directly involved in the mid-1950s and ending in the mid-1970s.

The 1960s saw candid existing light documentary style photography become solidly established at newspapers and wire services; this popular style continues (Figure 12.36).

The Civil Rights Movement

Many journalistic photographers over approximately 20 years of the civil rights movement covered the efforts of African-Americans to gain equality. While not the only activities that were covered, violence and sorrow arguably were the visually defining ones.

Civil rights demonstrators regularly clashed with police and segregationists. Covering civil rights demonstrations was fraught with danger for photojournalists. While civil rights advocates typically welcomed photographic coverage, police, who invariably became involved, and segregationists tended to look unkindly on photographers and their coverage. In short, photojournalists could get their heads bashed and cameras smashed, and be thrown into jail. Three memorable images from the civil rights movement appear in Figures 12.37–12.39.

The Vietnam War

Talented photographers from all over the world converged on Southeast Asia in the 1960s and 1970s to cover the Vietnam War. At least 14 still photographers were killed in Vietnam or neighboring countries, including one whose work is reproduced here, Larry Burrows

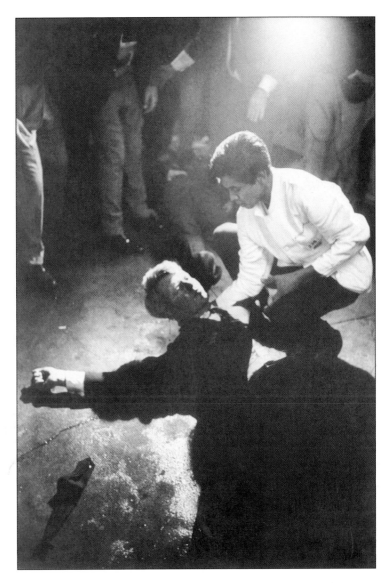

FIGURE 12.35

Robert F. Kennedy lies mortally wounded in 1968 on the floor of a Los Angeles hotel after being shot. Senator Kennedy had just finished thanking supporters in another part of the hotel for their help in winning the California presidential Democratic primary election. Some people at the scene objected to pictures being taken.

BILL EPPRIDGE/*LIFE* MAGAZINE © TIME INC.

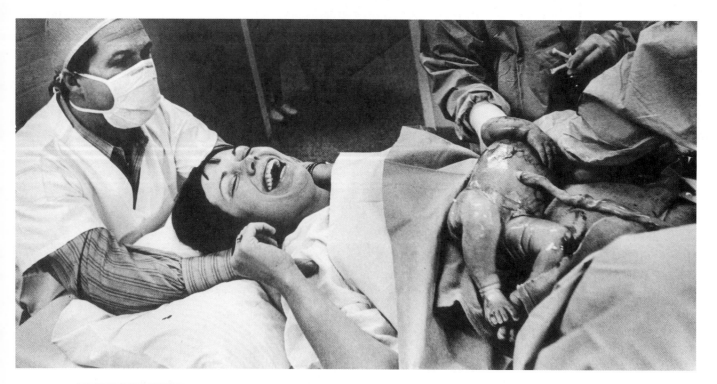

FIGURE 12.36

"Husband and wife experiencing the moment of life by Lamaze method of birth, 1972." This image helped redefine acceptable subject matter in newspapers.
© BRIAN LANKER/*TOPEKA CAPITAL JOURNAL*/ COURTESY BRIAN LANKER STUDIO

of *LIFE*. Four Vietnam War photographs appear in Figures 12.40–12.43.

Burrows, who was British-born, died when the helicopter in which he was riding crashed in Laos after being hit by ground fire. Former *LIFE* associate editor Robert Morse, who worked with Burrows on dozens of assignments, wrote:

> I think what drew people to him was an utterly honest simplicity. He was a man without a touch of pretense. His quiet, quizzical presence belied all the clichés about derring-do photographers.[17]

The 1980s and 1990s

The 1980s ushered in arguably the single most radical technical development of 20th-century photography: digital imaging. Digital processing of images, typically using the desktop film scanner and the desktop computer (the electronic darkroom), was established by the early 1990s and by mid-decade had all but replaced prints made in newspapers' chemical-optical darkrooms.

Having replaced film cameras at the end of the 1990s at major wire services and a few newspapers, digital

cameras—similar in looks to 35mm single lens reflex film cameras—appear to be on the way soon to relegating film cameras to the back burner at most, if not all, newspapers. Whether picture agency and magazine photographers follow suit is more iffy.

In the film arena, negative color film became a major player in the newspaper and wire service worlds.

The 1980s and 1990s saw the continuance of the candid existing light documentary style that had begun in earnest at U.S. newspapers in the 1960s. The relatively limited photographic composition techniques used at many newspapers gave way at some papers to an expanded view of desirable composition. For example, sometimes unused space is useful space; subjects looking at the camera can be a virtue rather than a vice; unnaturally slanted scenes are intriguing; centered subjects help images communicate; unsharp images are acceptable; visually decapitated people are fine.

Overall, this liberalization of picture-taking composition techniques—particularly the more way-out ones—is known in some photojournalistic quarters as the *interpretative approach*. It

FIGURE 12.42

U.S. Marine Lance Corporal James C. Farley, crew chief of the helicopter *Yankee Papa 13*, reacts to the death in the Vietnam War of the copilot of another helicopter, *Yankee Papa 3*. The copilot, Lieutenant James Magel, helped a wounded crewman from his disabled helicopter to *Yankee Papa 13* but was shot just as he reached the rescuing helicopter. Mortally wounded, Lieutenant Magel died despite Farley's first aid. You can find Larry Burrows' coverage of *Yankee Papa 13* in the April 16, 1965 issue of *LIFE* magazine. This photograph was published on the cover.

LARRY BURROWS/*LIFE*/TIMEPIX

FIGURE 12.43

Helped to a helicopter, U.S. Marine Gunnery Sgt. Jeremiah Purdie, wounded by shrapnel in the head and knee, reaches out as he is led past a stricken comrade after a fierce fight for Hill 484 during the Vietnam War, 1966.

LARRY BURROWS/ *LIFE*/TIMEPIX

can be argued, on one hand, that collectively the interpretative approach is an effort to better portray the world within the limitations of the still image. The counterargument is that this approach is largely oriented to the photographer's sense of individual expression to the detriment of readers who are accustomed to viewing the world in journalistic publications in a more traditional fashion. Most likely, there is truth in both arguments to one degree or the other. But there can be little debate that for truthful communication to take place between photojournalists and readers, readers must understand the messages photojournalists are trying to communicate. If readers do not understand these messages, they are poorly served and the composition techniques used are a failure.

These years also saw the management of some papers begin to modify their approach to picture taking. Photographers on these papers enjoyed considerable time to cover assignments, much more than the traditional amount allotted.

A particularly important development in the 1980s and 1990s was the large number of women going into photojournalism, many as newspaper and wire service photographers. Women long were involved in photography, going back almost to when it became a practical reality in 1839. But until about the mid-1980s women in photojournalism were more a fringe than a mainstream force. They now have gained parity on many photo staffs.

Final Thoughts

With the introduction of the electronic darkroom and digital still picture taking, the 20th century has proved almost as exciting in technological development as the century of photography's birth. But it has proved most exciting in the way legions of talented and thoughtful photojournalists used photography. Men and women with great social insight and true human sensitivity superbly used highly developed film, both black and white and color, and in the last part of the century began using the radical new picture-taking process of digital imaging. Their photographs are a legacy that enlightens and enriches contemporary viewers. This rich visual reservoir stands ready to show people of the 21st century and beyond how things were back in the 20th century.

Aspiring photojournalists have the advantage of being able to draw on this vast body of images. Wise practitioners will consider seriously what came before, using it not with slavish emulation but as a guide from which to search for individual photographic style and commitment.

NOTES

[1] Frank Scherschel and Stanley E. Kalish, "News and Press Photography" in Willard D. Morgan and Henry M. Lester, eds., *Graphic Graflex Photography: The Master Book for the Larger Camera* (New York: Morgan & Lester, 1947), p. 254.

[2] Dr. Paul Wolff, *My First Ten Years with the Leica: A Historical Survey over Almost Ten Years of Leica Photography,* trans. H. W. Zieler (New York: B. Westermann Co., n.d.), pp. 9–10.

[3] Naomi Rosenblum, *A World History of Photography,* 3rd ed. (New York: Abbeville Press, 1997), p. 465.

[4] David Douglas Duncan, "Photo Data," in *This Is War!* (Boston: Little, Brown, 1990).

[5] Thomas F. Spidell, ed., "*Journal* Photographers: Pioneers in Their Field," in *Six Decades: The News in Pictures* (Milwaukee: Journal Co., 1976), p. 14.

[6] Harold E. Edgerton and James R. Killian Jr., *Moments Of Vision: The Stroboscopic Revolution in Photography* (Cambridge, Mass.: MIT Press, 1979), p. 3.

[7] Time, Inc., "A Prospectus for a New Magazine," New York City, © 1936, p. 1; see also Loudon Wainwright, *The Great American Magazine: An Inside History of LIFE* (New York: Knopf, 1986), p. 33.

[8] "The Great Achiever," THE PRESS, *Time,* 6 September 1971, p. 46.

[9] Gardner Cowles, "Foreward," in Leo Rosten, ed., *The Look Book* (New York: Harry N. Abrams, 1979), p. 18.

[10] Ibid., p. 17.

[11] *National Geographic,* December 1999, cover.

[12] National Geographic Society, "Evolution of National Geographic Magazine," in *News,* a press release, June 1991, p. 3.

[13] Beaumont Newhall, *The History of Photography,* rev. ed. (New York: Museum of Modern Art, 1982), p. 244.

[14] Roy Emerson Stryker and Nancy Wood, *In This Proud Land: America 1935–1943, as Seen in the FSA Photographs* (Greenwich, Conn.: New York Graphic Society, 1973), p. 14.

[15] Ibid., p. 7.

[16] Claude Cookman, *A Voice Is Born: The Founding and Early Years of the National Press Photographers Association Under the Leadership of Joseph Costa* (Durham, N.C.: National Press Photographers Association, 1985), p. 14.

[17] Robert Morse, "Famous People," Editors of *Life, Larry Burrows: Compassionate Photographer* (New York: Time, 1972).

Tips for Operational Success

1. Keep a camera with a zoom lens and a compact strobe in the front seat area of your car. This outfit is for unexpected situations you will want to photograph. Often there is not time to open your trunk, rummage through your gear and still get the picture. Be sure the outfit is firmly secured so it does not become a dangerous flying missile in a quick stop or accident.

2. Keep a small container on the front seat with change, particularly quarters. The money is for tolls, parking meters, telephones, etc. Keep a brush or comb here also.

3. Carry a company identification card with you; carry business cards with your name and the name, address and telephone number of your newspaper; carry at least one credit card and at least $50.00.

4. Memorize editors' work and home telephone numbers in case contact is needed in an emergency.

5. Keep a portable personal computer in your car. It should use the same—or compatible—software as your photo department computers. If not kept in the trunk, secure it for the reasons in No. 1.

6. Always have a ballpoint pen and notebook handy. Often there is no time to search for these to take caption notes. A hand-held tape recorder can be a good supplement to written notes so consider having one handy also.

7. Keep film in an insulated container; it stays fresh longer.

8. Keep a cotton photo vest and a fanny pack in your car.

9. Never put down your camera bag or other equipment in a public place without constantly watching it.

10. Keep several large and small towels in your car for drying equipment and wiping perspiration. On casual assignments, such as at the beach, a headband is helpful.

11. Dress for the occasion so you blend with your subjects. Be prepared to change clothing on short notice.

12. Keep a change of clothes, including a jacket, a pair of shoes, and a rainsuit in your car.

13. Female photographers should keep well-constructed flat shoes in their cars. All photographers should keep waterproof boots for rainy weather, fires and muddy situations.

14. Keep an emergency stash of film in an insulated container in your car. Be sure to change the film by its expiration date.

15. Keep a totally manually operated camera in your car as a back-up.

16. Keep a roll of duct tape in your car; wrap some around your monopod or a leg of your tripod.

17. Keep a disposable camera in your car. You may need to mix with a crowd without advertising you are the media.

18. Keep a readily accessible thumb-size flashlight and a small screwdriver set for field repairs in your car.

19. Keep city, county and state maps of areas where you work, or are likely to be sent, in your car.

20. Keep small, plastic self-locking bags in your car. These will help when rolls of film need to be separated or sent to your office. Keep a small-end felt-tip pen that marks on most surfaces in your car.

21. Never permanently attach photographic or journalistic identification to your car; it invites thieves.

22. Avoid opening your car trunk, or otherwise showing your equipment, if anyone is nearby.

23. Inform your car insurance company of exactly what you do and that you use your car doing it. You almost certainly will need to carry a business-use rating. This will cost more, but you should never deceive your insurer.

24. Always answer your company's telephone in an informative and courteous manner. Unless otherwise instructed by management, state your department and your name. Make sure this is done in a way that will make callers feel comfortable talking with you.

25. Obtain a passport and keep it up to date. Carry three extra passport photos in case government officials in other countries want them. Know immunizations required to enter countries you likely will visit, and ones needed to return home. Your organization may want to send a photographer out of the country on short notice. The person with a valid passport and proper immunizations has a better chance of going.

Contributors to "Tips for Operational Success" are: Erica Berger, freelance, New York, N.Y.; Bernie Boston, *Los Angeles Times* (retired); Denis Finley, *The Virginian-Pilot,* Norfolk, Vir.; Craig Hartley, freelance, Houston, Texas: Kim Kulish, Saba Press Photos; Mike Pease, *St. Petersburg Times;* Amy Sancetta, The Associated Press; Jack Rowland, *St. Petersburg Times;* Bob Self, *The Florida Times-Union,* Jacksonville, Fla.; Scott Wheeler, *The Ledger,* Lakeland, Fla.; Alan Youngblood, *The Ocala* (Fla.) *Star-Banner;* and the author.

Selected Readings

From the vast reservoir of literature the following are presented as a starting point — only a starting point — for knowledge-hungry students. These readings are divided into categories for easier reference. Because subjects sometimes overlap, the categories are not necessarily mutually exclusive. If a reading is not found in one category, you are encouraged to pursue others.

Since law is ever evolving, it is particularly important for readers to search out the latest editions of legal publications. Books about other subject matter often are reincarnated as revised later editions. With the disclaimer that revisions do not necessarily improve a book and can occasionally weaken it, readers are urged to search out later editions than may be noted here.

Inclusion of a reading in "Selected Readings" does not necessarily mean your author recommends it. You probably will find many of these readings helpful, even excellent. But you are the one who must pass judgment on the worth of any reading.

Table of Contents

1. ABOUT ART

De La Croix, Horst, Richard G. Tansey, and Diane Kirkpatrick. *Gardner's ART—Through the Ages*. 9th ed. Orlando, Fl: Harcourt Brace & Company, 1991.

Gilbert, Rita. *Living With Art*. 5th ed. New York: McGraw-Hill, Inc., 1997.

Ocvirk, Otto G., et al. *Art Fundamentals—Theory & Practice*. 8th ed. New York: McGraw-Hill, 1998.

Sayre, Henry M. *Writing About Art*. 3rd ed. Englewood Cliffs: Prentice Hall, Inc., 1998.

2. COMMENTARY/CRITICISM

Barthes, Roland. *Camera Lucida— Reflections on Photography*. New York: Hill and Wang, 1981.

Goldbert, Vicki, ed. *Photography in Print—Writings from 1816 to the Present*. Albuquerque: University of New Mexico Press, 1981.

Gordon, George N. *The Languages of Communication—A Logical and Psychological Examination*. Studies in Public Communication series. New York: Hastings House, Publishers, 1969.

Gordon, James R., ed. *News Photographer—The magazine of photojournalism*. Bowling Green, Ohio and Durham N.C., National Press Photographers Association.

Gundberg, Andy. *Crisis of the Real—Writings on Photography 1974—1989*. New York: Aperture, 1990.

Hill, Paul and Thomas Cooper, eds. *Dialogue with Photography*. New York: Farrar/Straus/Giroux, 1979.

Jay, Bill. *Occam's Razor—An Outside-In View of Contemporary Photography*. Munich, Germany: Nazraeli Press, 1996.

Johnson, Brooks. *Photography Speaks—66 Photographers on Their Art*. Norfolk and New York: Aperture/The Chrysler Museum, Inc., 1989.

Morris, Wright. *Time Pieces—Photographers, Writing, and Memory*. New York: Aperture, 1989.

Mydans, Carl. "With Mind and Heart and a Magic Box." *Life,* 23 December 1966, 77.

Ritchin, Fred. *In Our Own Image—The Coming Revolution in Photography*. Aperture Writers and Artists on Photography series. New York: Aperture Foundation, Inc., 1990.

Sontag, Susan. *On Photography*. New York: The Noonday Press—Farrar, Straus and Giroux, 1977.

"The Voice of the Photograph." *Life,* 23 December 1966, 74.

3. CREATIVITY/COMPOSITION/VISUAL PERCEPTION

Arnheim, Rudolf. *Art and Visual Perception—A Psychology of the Creative Eye*. Berkely and Los Angeles: University of California Press, 1969.

Arnheim, Rudolf. *Visual Thinking*. Berkeley and Los Angeles: University of California Press, 1972.

Burgoon, Judee K., David B. Buller, and W. Gill Woodall. *Nonverbal Communication—The Unspoken Dialogue*. 2d ed. New York: McGraw-Hill, 1995.

Gilchrist, Margaret. *The Psychology of Creativity*. Carlton, Victoria, Australia: Melbourne University Press, 1972.

Gombrich, E.H. *Art and Illusion—A Study in the Psychology of Pictorial Representation*. 2d ed. rev. The A.W. Mellon Lectures in the Fine Arts 1956, National Gallery of Art, Washington. Princeton, N.J.: Princeton University Press, 1969.

Knapp, Mark L., and Judith A. Hall. *Nonverbal Communication In Human Interaction*. 4th ed. Forth Worth: Harcourt College Publishers. 1997.

Messaris, Paul. *Visual Literacy: Images, Mind, & Reality*. Boulder: Westview Press, 1994.

Perspective. New York: Harry N. Abrams, Inc., Publishers, 1977.

Rothenberg, Albert and Carl R. Hausman, eds. *The Creativity Question*. Durham, N.C.: Duke University Press, 1976.

Sternberg, Robert J., ed. *The Nature of Creativity.* Cambridge: Cambridge University Press, 1988

Stroebel, Leslie, Hollis Todd, and Richard Zakia. *Visual Concepts for Photographers.* London: Focal Press Limited; New York: Focal Press Inc., 1980.

The Art of Seeing—the Kodak Workshop Series. Rochester, N.Y.: Consumer/Professional & Finishing Markets, Eastman Kodak Company, 1984.

Whiting, John R. *Photography Is a Language.* New York: Arno Press, 1979.

Zakia, Richard D. *Perception and Photography.* Englewood Cliffs, New Jersey: Prentice-Hall, Inc., 1975.

4. ETHICS/TASTE

Frankena, William K. *The Elements of Moral Philosophy.* 2d ed. Englewood Cliffs: Prentice-Hall, Inc., 1973.

Kirkham, Richard L. *Theories of Truth—A Critical Introduction.* Cambridge, Mass., and London, England: The MIT Press, 1992.

Lambeth, Edmund B. *Committed Journalism—An Ethic for the Profession.* 2d ed. Bloomington and Indianapolis: Indiana University Press, 1992.

Merrill, John C., and S. Jack Odell. *Philosophy and Journalism.* New York and London: Longman, 1983.

Needham, H.A., ed. *Taste and Criticism in the Eighteenth Century—A Selection of Texts Illustrating the Evolution of Taste and the Development of Critical Theory.* New York: Barnes & Noble, Inc., 1952.

Newman, Jay. *The Journalist in Plato's Cave.* Rutherford, N.J., and London: Fairleigh Dickinson University Press, Associated University Presses, 1989.

Rachels, James. *The Elements of Moral Philosophy.* 2nd ed. New York: McGraw-Hill, 1993.

5. HISTORY: GENERAL

Gernsheim, Helmut and Alison. *A Concise History of Photography.* 3rd rev. ed. New York: Dover Publications, Inc., 1986.

Newhall, Beaumont. *The History of Photography.* Completely Revised and Enlarged Edition. New York: The Museum of Modern Art, 1982.

Pollack, Peter. *The Picture History of Photography—From the Earliest Beginnings to the Present Day.* Revised and enlarged edition. New York: Harry N. Abrams, Inc., Publishers, 1969.

Rosenblum, Naomi. *A World History of Photography.* 3rd ed. New York: Abbeville Press, 1997.

6. HISTORY: TARGETED

Auer, Michael. *The Illustrated History of the Camera—From 1839 to the Present.* Boston: New York Graphic Society, 1975.

Brettell, Richard with Roy Flukinger, Nancy Keeler, and Sydney Kilgore. *Paper and Light—The Calotype in Great Britain and France, 1839—1870.* Boston: David R. Godine, 1984.

Buckland, Gail. *Fox Talbot and the Invention of Photography.* Boston: David R. Godine, 1980.

Buckland, Gail. *Reality Recorded—Early Documentary Photography.* Greenwich, Conn. New York Graphic Society, 1974.

Carlebach, Michael L. *American Photojournalism Comes of Age.* Washington: Smithsonian Institution Press, 1997.

Carlebach, Michael. *The Origins of Photojournalism in America.* Washington and London: Smithsonian Institution Press, 1992.

Early Colour Photography. With an Introduction by Sylvain Roumette. New York: Pantheon, 1986.

Edgerton, Harold E. and James R. Killian, Jr. *Moments of Vision—the Stroboscopic Revolution in Photography.* Cambridge, Mass., and London: The MIT Press, 1979.

Enyeart, James, ed. *Decade by Decade—Twentieth-Century American Photography.* From the collection of the Center for Creative Photography. With Essays by Estelle Jussim, Van Deren Coke, Martha A. Sandweiss, Naomi Rosenblum, Helen Gee, Terence Pitts, Charles Desmarais, and Nathan Lyons. Boston, Toronto, and London: Bulfinch Press, Little, Brown and Company, 1989.

Friedman, Joseph S. *The History of Colour Photography.* London and New York: Focal Press, 1968.

Fulton, Marianne, with contributions by Estelle Jussim, Colin Osman and Sandra S. Phillips, and William Stapp. *Eyes of Time—Photojournalism In America.* Boston: Little, Brown and Company, 1988.

Galassi, Peter. *Before Photography—Painting and the Invention of Photography.* New York: Museum of Modern Art; Boston: Distributed by New York Graphic Society, 1981.

Gernsheim, Helmut. *Creative Photography—Aesthetic Trends 1839—1960.* 1st American Edition. Boston: Boston Book & Art Shop, 1962.

Gernsheim, Helmut. *The Origins of Photography.* With 191 Illustrations. New York: Thames and Hudson, 1982.

Gernsheim, Helmut and Alison. *L.J.M. Daguerre—The History of the Diorama and the Daguerreotype.* 2d rev. ed. New York: Dover Publications, 1968.

Gernsheim, Helmut in collaboration with Alison Gernsheim. *The History of Photography—From the Camera Obscura to the Beginning of the Modern Era.* With 390 photographs and engravings. New York: McGraw-Hill Book Company, 1969.

Gidal, Tim N. *Modern Photojournalism—Origin and Evolution, 1910—1933.* New York: Macmillan Publishing Co., Inc., 1973.

Gover, C. Jan. *The Positive Image—Woman Photographers in Turn-of-the-Century America.* Albany: State University of New York Press, 1988.

Hurley, F. Jack. *Portrait of a Decade—Roy Stryker and the Development of Documentary Photography in the Thirties.* Photographic editing by Robert J. Doherty. Baton Rouge, La.: Louisiana State University Press, 1972.

Kahan, Robert Sidney. "The Antecedents of American Photojournalism." Ph.D. diss., University of Wisconsin, 1969.

Lothrop, Easton S., Jr. *A Century of Cameras—From the Collection of the International Museum of Photography at George Eastman House.* Dobbs Ferry, N.Y.: Morgan & Morgan, Inc., 1973.

Maddow, Ben. *Faces—A Narrative History of the Portrait in Photography.* Photographs compiled and edited by Constance Sullivan. A Chanticleer Press

Photojournalism: An Introduction

edition. Designed and coordinated by Massimo Vignelli and Gudrun Buettner. New York Graphic Society. Boston: Little, Brown and Company, 1977.

Miller, Russell. *Magnum—Fifty Years at the Front Line of History.* New York: Grove Press, 1997.

Neubauer, Hendrik. *Black Star—60 Years of Photojournalism.* Cologne, Germany: Könemann, 1998.

Newhall, Beaumont. *Latent Image—The Discovery of Photography.* Albuquerque: University of New Mexico Press, 1983.

Newhall, Beaumont, ed. *Photography: Essays & Images—Illustrated Readings in the History of Photography.* New York and Boston: The Museum of Modern Art, Distributed by New York Graphic Society, 1980.

Newhall, Beaumont. *The Daguerreotype in America.* 3rd rev. ed. New York: Dover Publications 1976.

Palmquist, Peter E., ed. *Camera Fiends & Kodak Girls—50 Selections By and About Women in Photography, 1840—1930.* Palmquist, Peter E., ed. New York: Midmarch Arts Press, 1989.

Pouncey, Truman. *Photographic Journalism—A Guide for Learning with the Graphic.* Dubuque: Wm C. Brown Company, 1952.

Price, Jack. *News Photography.* New York: Round Table Press, Inc., 1937.

Rinhart, Floyd, and Marion Rinhart. *The American Daguerreotype.* Athens, Ga: The University of Georgia Press, 1981.

Rudisill, Richard. *Mirror Image—The Influence of the Daguerreotype on American Society.* Albuquerque: University of New Mexico Press, 1971.

Smith, Cynthia Zoe. "Emigre Photography in America: Contributions of German Photojournalism from Black Star Picture Agency to 'Life' magazine, 1933–1938." Ph.D. diss., The University of Iowa, 1983.

Taft, Robert. *Photography and the American Scene—A Social History 1839—1889.* New York: Dover Publications, 1964.

Walker Evans. *Photographs for the Farm Security Administration, 1935—1938.* With an Introduction by Jerald C. Maddox. New York: Da Capo, 1975.

Wolf, Dr. Paul. *My First Ten Years With The Leica—A historical survey over almost ten years of Leica photography.* New York: B. Westermann Co., nc., undated.

7. LAW

Gilmor, Donald M., Jerome A. Barron, Todd F. Simon. *Mass Communication Law: Cases and Comment.* 6th ed. Belmont: Wadsworth Publishing Company, 1998.

Middleton, Kent R. and Robert Trager. *The Law of Public Communication.* 5th ed. New York: Addison Wesley Longman, 2000.

Teeter, Dwight L., Jr., Don R. LeDuc, and Bill Loving. *Law of Mass Communications—Freedom and Control of Print and Broadcast Media.* 9th ed. New York: Foundation Press, 1998.

8. LIGHT/LIGHTING/OPTICS/COLOR

Birren, Faber. *Color & Human Response—Aspects of light and color bearing on the reactions of living things and the welfare of human beings.* New York: Van Nostrand Reinhold Company, a division of Litton Educational Publishing, Inc., 1978.

Edgerton, Harold E., and James R. Killian, Jr. *Moments of Vision—the Stroboscopic Revolution in Photography.* Cambridge, Mass., and London: The MIT Press, 1979.

Editors of Eastman Kodak Company. *Using Filters.* The KODAK Workshop Series. Kodak publication KW-13. Rochester, N.Y.: Silver Pixel Press, 1998.

Falk, David, Dieter Brill, and David Stork. *Seeing the Light—Optics in Nature, Photography, Color, Vision, and Holography.* New York: John Wiley & Sons, 1986.

Park, David Allen. *The Fire Within the Eye—A Historical Essay on the Nature and Meaning of Light.* Princeton, N.J.: Princeton University Press, 1997.

Pirenne, M.H. *Optics, Painting & Photography.* Cambridge, England: Cambridge University Press, 1970.

Wilhelm, Henry with contributing author Carol Brower. *The Permanence and Care of Color Photographs: Traditional and Digital Color Prints, Color Negatives,* *Slides, and Motion Pictures.* Grinnell, Iowa: Preservation Publishing Co., 1993.

Williamson, Samuel J., and Herman Z. Cummins. *Light and Color in Nature and Art.* New York: John Wiley and Sons, 1983.

9. PERSONAL DEVELOPMENT/ PEOPLE SKILLS

Kleinke, Chris L. *Meeting & Understanding People—How to develop competence in social situations and expand social skills.* New York: W.H. Freeman and Company, 1986.

Post, Peggy. *Emily Post's Etiquette.* 16th ed. New York: Harper Collins Publishers, 1997. (Particularly these sections: "I. Communications"; "II. Your Professional Life"; "IV. Formalities.")

Verderber, Rudolph F. and Kathleen S. Verderber. Inter-Act Using Interpersonal Communication Skills. Belmont, Calif.: Wadsworth Publishing Co., 1998.

10. PHOTOJOURNALISTS/ PHOTOJOURNALISM

Caputo, Philip. *DelCorso's Gallery.* New York: Holt, Rinehart and Winston, 1983.

Chapnick, Howard. *Truth Needs No Ally—Inside Photojournalism.* Columbia and London: University of Missouri Press, 1994.

Herr, Michael. *Dispatches.* New York: Vintage Books, 1991.

Knightley, Phillip. *The First Casualty—From the Crimea to Vietnam: The War Correspondent as Hero, Propagandist, and Myth Maker.* New York and London: Harcourt Brace Jovanovich, 1975.

Mellow, James R. *Walker Evans.* New York: Basic Books, 1999.

Morris, John G. *Get the Picture—A Personal History of Photojournalism.* New York: Random House, 1998.

Parks Gordon. *A Choice of Weapons.* New York: Harper & Row Publishers, 1966.

11. PICTURE BOOKS (NO PRINCIPAL PHOTOGRAPHER)

Alabiso, Vincent, Kelly Smith Tunney, and Chuck Zoeller, eds. *Flash! The Associated Press Covers the World.* With an introduction by Peter Arnett. New York: The Associated Press in association with Harry N. Abrams, 1998.

Buell, Hal. *Moments—The Pulitzer Prize-Winning Photographs.* New York: Black Dog & Leventhal Publishers, Inc., 1999.

Collins, Charles M., and David Cohen, eds. *The African-Americans.* With a foreword by John Hope Franklin. Text by Cheryl Everette, Susan Wels, and Evelyn C. White. New York: Viking Penguin, 1993.

Faas, Horst and Tim Page, eds. *Requiem—By the Photographers Who Died in Vietnam and Indochina.* With an introduction by David Halberstam. New York: Random House, 1997.

Faber, John. *Great News Photos and the Stories Behind Them.* 2d rev. ed. New York: Dover Publications, Inc., 1978.

Gee, Helen. *Photography of the Fifties—An American Perspective.* Tucson: Center for Creative Photography, 1980.

Great Photographic Essays from LIFE. Commentary by Maintland Edey. Pictures edited by Constance Sullivan. New York Graphic Society. Boston: Little, Brown and Company, 1978.

Images of Our Times—Sixty Years of Photography from the Los Angeles Times. By the staff photographers of the *Los Angeles Times.* Preface by William F. Thomas. With an introduction by Jim Wilson and an afterword by Iris Schneider. New York: Harry N. Abrams, Inc., 1987.

Leekley, Sheryle and John. *Moments—The Pulitzer Prize Photographs.* Updated Edition: 1942–198 New York: Crown Publishers, Inc., 1982.

Life Classic Photographs. With Personal Interpretation by John Loengard. Boston, Toronto, London: New York Graphic Society Books and Little, Brown and Company, 1988.

Loengard, John. *Life Photographers—What They Saw.* A Bulfinch Press book. Boston: Little, Brown and Company, 1998.

Manchester, William. *In Our Time—The World as Seen by Magnum Photographers.* With essays by Jean Lacouture and Fred Ritchin. New York and London: The American Federation of Arts in Association with W.W. Norton & Company, 1989.

Neubauer, Hendrik. *Black Star—60 Years of Photojournalism.* Cologne, Germany: Könemann, 1998.

Newhall, Beaumont, ed. *Photography: Essay & Images*—Illustrated Reading in the History of Photography. New York and Boston: The Museum of Modern Art, Distributed by New York Graphic Society 1980.

Perkes, Dan, project dir. *Moments in Time—50 Years of Associated Press News Photos.* New York: Gallery Books, 1984.

Pfister, Harold Francis. *Facing the Light—Historic American Portrait Daguerreotypes.* Washington, D.C.: Smithsonian Institution Press for the National Portrait Gallery, 1978.

Pictures of the Times—A Century of Photography from the New York Times. With essays by William Safire and Peter Galassi. Related exhibition June 27 – October 8, 1996 organized by Peter Galassi and Susan Kismaric, the Museum of Modern Art. New York: Harry N. Abrams, Inc. 1996.

Rosten, Leo, ed. *The Look Book.* New York: Harry N. Abrams, Inc. Publishers, 1979.

Sobieszek, Robert A. *Masterpieces of Photography from the George Eastman House Collections.* New York: Abbeville Press, Publishers, 1985.

Stryker, Roy Emerson, and Nancy Wood. *In This Proud Land—America 1935—1943 As Seen In the FSA photographs.* Greenwich, Conn.: New York Graphic Society Ltd., 1973.

Szarkowski, John, ed. *From The Picture Press.* New York: The Museum of Modern Art, 1973.

Szarkowski, John. *Looking at Photographs—100 Pictures from the Collection of the Museum of Modern Art.* New York: New York Graphic Society Books and Little, Brown, and Company, 1973.

The American Image—Photographs from the National Archives, 1860—1960. With an introduction by Alan Trachtenberg. New York: Pantheon Books, 1979.

The Family of Man. Created by Edward Steichen for The Museum of Modern Art. With a prologue by Carl Sandburg. New York: The Museum of Modern Art, 1955.

The Fifties—Photographs of America by Eve Arnold, Cornell Capa, Bruce Davidson, Elliott Erwitt, Burt Glinn, Ernst Haas, Erich Hartmann, Bob Henriques, Costa Manos, Wayne Miller, Inge Morath, Dennis Stock of Magnum. With an introduction by John Chancellor. New York: Pantheon Books, 1985.

The World's Great News Photos 1840—1980. Selected and edited by Craig T. Norback and Melvin Gray. New York: Crowns Pubishers, Inc., 1980.

Tucker, Anne, ed. *The Woman's Eye—Selections from the work of Gertrude Kasebier* *Frances Benjamin Johnston *Margaret Bourke-White *Dorothea Lange *Bernice Abbott *Barbara Morgan *Diane Arbus *Alisa Wells *Judy Dater *Bea Nettles.* With an introduction by Anne Tucker. New York: Alfred A. Knopf, 1975.

12. PICTURE BOOKS/ PERSONALITIES (INDIVIDUAL AS MAIN SUBJECT AND/OR PRINCIPAL OR SOLE PHOTOGRAPHER)

ANSEL ADAMS

Adams, Ansel. *Ansel Adams—Images 1923—1974.* With a foreword by Wallace Stegner. Boston: New York Graphic Society, 1974.

Adams, Ansel. *Autobiography.* Boston: Little, Brown and Co, 1985.

Adams, Ansel. *Photographs of the Southwest.* Boston: New York Graphic Society, 1976.

ROBERT ADAMSON
(SEE DAVID OCTAVIUS HILL)

WILLIAM ALBERT ALLARD

Allard, William Albert. *A Time We Knew—Images of Yesterday in the Basque Homeland.* Text by Robert Laxalt. Reno: University of Nevada Press, 1990

Allard, William Albert. *Time at the Lake—A Minnesota Album.* Duluth, Minn.: Pfeifer-Hamilton Publishers, 1997.

Allard, William Albert. *Vanishing Breed—Photographs of the Cowboy and the West.* Boston: A New York Graphic Society Book and Little, Brown and Company, 1982.

Zwingle, Erla, and Russel Hart. *William Albert Allard—The Photographic Essay.* With an introduction by Sean Callahan. American Photographer Master Series, Henry Horenstein, ed. A Bulfinch Press Book, Boston: Little, Brown and Company, 1989.

EUGÈNE ATGET

Abbott, Berenice. *The World of Atget.* New York: Paragon Books, G.P. Putnam's Sons, 1979.

Szarkowski, John, and Maria Morris Hambourg. *The Work of Atget.* 4 vols. New York: The Museum of Modern Art, 1981–85.

RICHARD AVEDON

Avedon: Photographs, 1947—1977. With an essay by Harold Brodkey. New York: Farrar, Straus & Giroux, 1978.

Avedon, Richard. *Evidence— 1944—1994.* New York: Random House, 1994.

Avedon, Richard. *In the American West.* Reissue ed. New York: Harry N. Abrams, 1996.

Avedon, Richard. *Portraits.* With an essay by Harold Rosenberg. New York: Farrar, Straus and Giroux, 1976.

GEORGE N. BARNARD

Barnard, George N. *Photographic Views of Sherman's Campaign.* With a preface by Beaumont Newhall. New York: Dover Publications, Inc., 1977.

JESSE TARBOX BEALS

Alexander, Alland, Sr. *Jessie Tarbox Beals—First Woman News Photographer.* New York: Camera/Graphic Press Ltd., 1978.

ERICA BERGER

Virag, Irene. We're All In This Together—Families Facing Breast Cancer. Photographs by Erica Berger. A *Newsday* Book. Kansas City: Andrews and McMeel, 1995.

MARGARET BOURKE-WHITE

Bourke-White, Margaret. *Portrait of Myself.* New York: Simon and Schuster, 1963.

Bourke-White, Margaret. *Shooting the Russian War.* New York: Simon and Schuster, 1943.

Caldwell, Erskine, and Margaret Bourke-White. *You Have Seen Their Faces.* Photographs by Margaret Bourke-White. Text by Erskine Caldwell. New York: Arno Press, 1975.

Callahan, Sean, ed. *The Photographs of Margaret Bourke-White.* With an introduction by Theodore M. Brown and a foreword by Carl Mydans. Boston: New York Graphic Society, 1972.

Callahan, Sean and Maryann Kornely, eds. *Margaret Bourke-White—Photographer.* A Bulfinch Press book. Boston: Little, Brown and Company, 1998.

Goldberg, Vicki. *Margaret Bourke-White—A Biography.* New York: Harper & Row, Publishers, 1986.

MATHEW BRADY

Horan, James D. *Mathew Brady—Historian With a Camera.* Picture collation by Gertrude Horan. New York: Crown Publishers, Inc., 1955.

Meredith, Roy. *Mr. Lincoln's Camera Man—Mathew B. Brady.* 2nd rev. ed. New York: Dover Publications, Inc., 1974.

BILL BRANDT

Brandt, Bill. *Bill Brandt: Behind the Camera.* With an introduction by Mark Haworth-Booth. With an essay by David Mellor. New York: Aperture, 1985.

Brandt, Bill. *Camera in London.* London and New York: The Focal Press, 1948.

LARRY BURROWS

Larry Burrows—Compassionate Photographer. Time, Inc. 1972.

JULIA MARGARET CAMERON

Gernsheim, Helmut. *Julie Margaret Cameron—Her Life and Photographic Work.* Millerton, N.Y.: Aperture, 1975.

Weaver, Mike. *Julia Margaret Cameron, 1815—1870.* Boston: Little Brown and Company, 1984.

CORNELL CAPA

Capa, Cornell and Richard Whelan, eds. *Cornell Capa—Photographs.* A Bulfinch Press Book. Boston: Little, Brown and Company, 1992.

ROBERT CAPA

Capa, Cornell and Richard Whelan, eds. *Robert Capa Photographs.* New York: Alfred A. Knopf, 1985.

Capa, Robert. *Images of War.* New York: Paragraphic Books, a division of Grossman Publishers, 1964.

Capa, Robert. *Slightly Out of Focus.* New York: H. Holt, 1947.

Heart of Spain—Robert Capa's Photographs of the Spanish Civil War. With historical essays by Juan P. Fusi Aizpurua, Richard Whelan, and Catherine Coleman. From the collection of Museo Nacional Centro de Arte Reina Sofia. New York: Aperture, 1998.

Robert Capa: Photographs. With a foreword by Henri Cartier-Bresson. With a remembrance by Cornell Capa. With an introduction by Richard Whelan. New York: Aperture, 1996.

Whelan, Richard. *Robert Capa: A Biography.* New York: Alford A. Knopf, 1985.

LEWIS CARROLL

Lewis Carroll—victorian photographer. With an introduction by Helmut Gernsheim. London: Thames and Hudson, 1980.

HENRI CARTIER-BRESSON

Cartier-Bresson, Henri. *Henri Cartier-Bresson: Photographer.* With a foreword by Yves Bonnefoy. New York Graphic Society. Boston: Little, Brown and Compnay, 1979.

Cartier-Bresson, Henri. *The Decisive Moment—Photography by Henri Cartier-Bresson.* New York: Simon and Schuster in collaboration with Editions VERVE of Paris, 1952.

Cartier-Bresson, Henri. *The World of Henry Cartier-Bresson.* New York: A Studio Book, The Viking Press, 1968.

Photographs By Cartier-Bresson. With introductions by Lincoln Kirstein and Beaumont Newhall. New York: Grossman Publisher, 1963.

BRUCE DAVIDSON

Davidson, Bruce. *Brooklyn Gang.* Sante Fe, N.M.: Twin Palms Publishers, 1998.

Davidson, Bruce. *Central Park*. With notes by the author. With a preface by Elizabeth Barlow Rogers. With an essay by Marie Winn. New York: Aperture, 1995.

Davidson, Bruce. *East 100th Street*. Cambridge, Mass.: Harvard University Press, 1970.

DAVID DOUGLAS DUNCAN

Duncan, David Douglas. *Goodbye Picasso*. Paris: Stock, 1975.

Duncan, David Douglas. *Picasso Paints a Portrait*. New York: Abrams, 1996.

Duncan, David Douglas. *Self-Portrait: U.S.A.* New York: Harry N. Abrams Inc., 1969.

Duncan, David Douglas. *This Is War!* Boston: Little, Brown and Company, 1990.

Duncan, David Douglas. *War Without Heroes*. New York and Evanston: Harper & Row Publishers, 1970.

Duncan, David Douglas. *Yankee Nomad: a photographic odyssey*. New York: Holt, Rinehart and Winston, 1966.

ALFRED EISENSTAEDT

Eisenstaedt, Alfred. *Eisenstaedt—Remembrances*. A Bullfinch Press Book. Boston: Little Brown, 1990.

Eisenstaedt, Alfred. *The Eye of Eisenstaedt*. New York: Viking Press, 1969.

Eisenstaedt, Alfred. *Witness To Our Times*. With a foreword by Henry R. Luce. Text prepared by Milton Orshefsky and edited by Joseph Kastner. New York: The Viking Press, 1966.

PETER HENRY EMERSON

Newhall, Nancy. *P.H. Emerson—The Fight for Photography as a Fine Art*. An Aperture Monograph. Millerton, N.Y.: Aperture, Inc., 1975.

Turner, Peter and Richard Wood. *P.H. Emerson—Photographer of Norfolk*. Boston: David R. Godine, 1974.

ELLIOTT ERWITT

Erwitt, Elliott. *Personal Exposures*. New York and London: W.W. Norton & Company, 1988.

WALKER EVANS

Agee, James, and Walker Evans. *Let Us Now Praise Famous Men*. Boston: Houghton, Mifflin Company, 1969.

Walker Evans. With an introduction by John Szarkowski. New York: The Museum of Modern Art, 1971.

ROGER FENTON

Roger Fenton—Photographer of the Crimean War. His Photographs and His Letters from The Crimea. With an essay on his life and work by Helmut and Alison Gernsheim. New York: Arno Press, 1973.

Roger Fenton—Photographer of the 1850s. Catalogue for an exhibition organized by Lynne Green and Muriel Walker, Hayward Gallery, London, 4 February to 17 April 1988. London: Yale University Press for the South Bank Board, 1988.

DONNA FERRATO

Ferrato, Donna. *Living with the Enemy*. With an introduction by Ann Jones. New York: Aperture, 1991.

ROBERT FRANK

Frank, Robert. *The Americans*. With an introduction by Jack Kerouac. Millerton, N.Y.: Aperture, 1978.

LEONARD FREED

Photographs 1954—1990—Leonard Freed. With an introduction by Stefanie Rosenkranz. New York & London: W.W. Norton & Company, 1991.

ALEXANDER GARDNER

Gardner, Alexander. *Gardener's Photographic Sketch Book of the Civil War*. New York: Dover Publications, Inc., 1959.

Katz, D. Mark. *Witness to an Era—The Life and Photographs of Alexander Gardner—The Civil War, Lincoln, and the West*. New York: Viking, 1991.

WILLY GEORG

Georg, Willy. *In the Warsaw Ghetto: Summer 1941*. With an afterword by Rafael F. Scharf. New York: Aperture, 1993.

FRITZ GORO

Goro, Fritz. *On the Nature of Things: The Scientific Photography of Fritz Goro*. With an introduction by Stephen Jay Gould. With a biographical essay by Thomas, Peter, and Stefan Goreau. With commentary by Nobel Prize-winning scientists. New York: Aperture, 1993.

PHILIP JONES GRIFFITHS

Griffiths, Philip Jones. *Dark Odyssey*. With a biological profile by Murray Sayle. New York: Aperture, 1996.

JAMES HENRY "JIMMY" HARE

Gould, Lewis L., and Richard Greffe. *Photojournalist—the Career of Jimmy Hare*. Austin and London: University of Texas Press, 1977.

JOSIAH JOHNSON HAWES (SEE ALBERT SANDS SOUTHWORTH)

DAVID OCTAVIUS HILL AND ROBERT ADAMSON

Bruce, David. *Sun Pictures—the Hill-Adamson calotypes*. Greenwich, Conn.: New York Graphic Society Ltd., 1973.

Ford, Colin, ed. *An Early Victorian Album—The Photographic Masterpieces (1843—1847) of David Octavius Hill and Robert Adamson*. With an introduction by Colin Ford and an interpretive essay by Roy Strong. New York: Alfred A. Knopf, 1976.

Ovenden, Graham, ed. *Hill & Adamson Photographs*. With an introduction by Marina Henderson. New York: St. Martin's Press, 1973.

LEWIS W. HINE

America & Lewis Hine—Photographs 1904—1940. With a foreword by Walter Rosenblum and an essay by Alan Trachtenbert. Biographical notes by Naomi Rosenblum. Millerton, N.Y.: Aperture, 1977.

Doherty, Jonathan L., ed. *Women at Work—153 Photographs by Lewis W. Hine*. Rochester, N.Y.: George Eastman House in association with Dover Publications, Inc., New York, 1981.

GRACIELA ITURBIDE

Iturbide, Graciela. *Images of the Spirit*. New York: Aperture, 1996.

Gutman, Judith Mara. *Lewis W. Hine and the American Social Conscience.* New York: Walker and Company, a division of Walker Publishing Company, Inc., 1967.

Hine, Lewis W. *Men at Work—Photographic Studies of Modern Men and Machines.* New York: Dover Publications, Inc.; Rochester: International Museum of Photography at George Eastman House, 1977.

Steinorth, Karl, ed. *Lewis Hine: Passionate Journey, Photographs 1905—1937.* Texts by Anthony Bannon, Marianne Fulton, and Karl Steinorth. Published in association with the International Museum of Photography at George Eastman House. Zurich: Edition Stemmle, 1996.

WILLIAM HENRY JACKSON

Hales, Peter B. *William Henry Jackson and the Transformation of the American Landscape.* Philadelphia: Temple University Press, 1988.

Newhall, Beaumont, and Diana E. Edkins. *William H. Jackson.* The Amon Carter Museum of Western Art. Dobbs Ferry, N.Y.: Morgan & Morgan, Inc., 1974.

FRANCES BENJAMIN JOHNSTON

Daniel, Peter, and Raymond Smock. *A Talent for Detail—The Photographs of Miss Frances Benjamin Johnston 1889—1910.* New York: Harmony Books, 1974.

MARK JURY AND DAN JURY

Jury, Mark and Dan Jury. *Gramp—A man ages and dies. The extraordinary record of one family's encounter with the reality of dying.* Photographs by Mark Jury and Dan Jury. Narrative text by Mark Jury. New York: Penguin Books, 1978.

YOUSUF KARSH

Karsh, Yousuf. *Karsh—A Fifty-Year Retrospective.* A New York Graphic Society Book. Boston: Little, Brown and Company, 1983.

Karsh, Yousuf. *Karsh Portraits.* New York Graphic Society. Boston: Little, Brown and Company, 1976.

DAVID HUME KENNERLY

Kennerly, David Hume. *Photo Op—a Pulitizer prize-winning photographer covers events that shaped our times.* Published in cooperation with the University of Texas Center for American History. Austin: University of Texas Press, 1995.

Kennerly, David Hume. *Shooter.* New York: Newsweek Books, 1980.

ANDRE KERTESZ

Andre Kertesz. With an introduction by Daniele Sallenave. Translated from the French. New York: Pantheon Books, 1986.

Ducrot, Nicolas, ed. *Andre Kertesz—Sixty Years of Photography 1912—1972.* New York: Grossman Publishers, 1972.

Harder, Susan, with Hiroji Kubota, ed. *Andre Kertesz—Diary of Light 1912–1985.* With a foreword by Cornell Capa and an essay by Hal Hinson. New York: Aperture Foundation, Inc. in association with the International Center of Photography, 1987.

Phillips, Sandra, David Travis, and Weston J. Naef. *Andre Kertesz of Paris and New York.* New York: Thames and Hudson, 1985.

ROBERT GLENN KETCHUM

Ketchum, Robert Glenn. *Northwest Passage.* With a log by the author. With a preface by William Simon. With a commentary by Barry Lopez. New York: Aperture, 1996.

DOROTHEA LANGE

Lange, Dorothea. *Dorothea Lange—Photographs of a Lifetime.* With notes by the author. With an essay by Robert Coles. With an afterword by Therese Heyman. New York: Aperture, 1982.

Meltzer, Milton. *Dorothea Lange—A Photographer's Life.* New York: Farrar, Straus and Giroux, 1978.

BRIAN LANKER

Lanker, Brian. *I Dream a World: Portraits of Black Women Who Changed America.* New York: Stewart Tabori & Chang, 1989.

STEVE LEHMAN

Lehman, Steve. *The Tibetans—A Struggle to Survive.* A Red Wheelbarrow book. New York: Umbrage Editions; distributed by Twin Palms Publishers, Santa Fe, N.M., 1998.

ANNIE LEIBOVITZ

Annie Leibovitz—Photographs 1970–1990. New York: HarperCollins Publishers, 1991.

Leibovitz, Annie, and Susan Sontag. *Women.* New York: Random House, 1999.

JOHN LOENGARD

Loengard, John. *Pictures Under Discussion.* A Bob Adelman Book. New York: AMPHOTO, an imprint of Watson-Guptill Publications, 1987.

DON MCCULLIN

McCullin, Don. *Sleeping with Ghosts.* With notes by the author. With an introduction by Mark Haworth-Booth. New York: Aperture, 1996.

McCullin, Don. *Unreasonable Behavior—An Autobiography.* London: Vintage, 1992.

MARY ELLEN MARK

Fulton, Marianne. *Mary Ellen Mark—25 Years.* Published in association with the International Museum of Photography at George Eastman House with the support of the Professional Photography Division, Eastman Kodak Company. A Bulfinch Press Book. Boston: Little, Brown and Co., 1991.

Mark, Mary Ellen. *Portraits.* Milano: F. Motta, 1995.

Mark, Mary Ellen. *Streetwise—Photographs by Mary Ellen Mark.* With an introduction by John Irving. Text and photographs edited by Nancy Baker. New York: Aperture, 1992.

SUSAN MEISELAS

Meiselas, Susan. *Kurdistan—In the Shadow of History.* With chapter commentaries by Martin van Bruinessen. New York: Random House, 1997.

Meiselas, Susan. *Nicaragua.* Edited by Claire Rosenberg. New York: Pantheon Brooks, 1981.

CHARLES MOORE

Moore, Charles and Michael S. Durham. *Powerful Days: The Civil Rights Photography of Charles Moore.* With an introduction by Andrew Young. Text by Michael S. Durham. New York: Stewart Tabori & Chang, 1991.

MARTIN MUNKACSI

Martin Munkacsi. An Aperture Monograph. With a biographical profile by Susan Morgan. New York: Aperture, 1992.

EADWEARD MUYBRIDGE

Haas, Robert Bartlett. *Muybridge— Man in Motion.* Berkeley and Los Angeles: University of California Press, 1976.

Muybridge's Complete Human and Animal Locomotion. 3 vols. All 781 Plates from the 1887 *Animal Locomotion* by Eadweard Muybridge. Introduction to the Dover Edition by Anita Ventura Mozley. New York: Dover Publications, Inc., 1979.

CARL MYDANS

Mydans, Carl. *Carl Mydans, Photojournalist.* With an interview by Philip B. Kunhardt, Jr. New York: Harry H. Abrams, Inc., 1985.

Mydans, Carl. *More than Meets the Eye.* New York: Harper, 1959.

JAMES NACHTWEY

Nachtwey, James. *Deeds of War.* New York: Thames and Hudson, 1989.

Nachtwey, James. *Inferno.* London: Phaidon Press, Inc., 2000.

NADAR (GASPARD FELIX TOURNACHON)

Gosling, Nigel. *Nadar.* A Borzoi book. New York: Alfred A. Knopf, Inc., 1976.

ARNOLD NEWMAN

Newman, Arnold. *Artists—portraits from four decades.* With a foreword by Henry Goldzahler and an introduction by Arnold Newman. Boston: New York Graphic Society, 1980.

One Mind's Eye—The Portraits and Other Photographs of Arnold Newman. With a foreword by Beaumont Newhall and an introduction by Robert Sobieszek. Boston: David R. Godine, 1974.

TIMOTHY O'SULLIVAN

Newhall, Beaumont, and Nancy Newhall. *T.H. O'Sullivan Photographer.* With an appreciation by Ansel Adams. Rochester, N.Y.: George Eastman House, in collaboration with the Amon Carter Museum of Western Art, 1966.

BILL OWENS

Owens, Bill. *Documentary Photography.* Danbury, N.H.: Addison House, 1978.

Owens, Bill. *Surburbia.* San Francisco: Straight Arrow Books, 1973.

GORDON PARKS

Parks, Gordon. *Gordon Parks: A Poet and His Camera.* With a preface by Stephen Spendor and an introduction by Philip B. Kunhardt, Jr. New York: The Viking Press, 1968.

Parks. Gordon. *Half Past Autumn—A Retrospective.* With an essay by Phillip Brookman. Related exhibition held at the Corcoran Gallery of Art, Washington, D.C., Sept. 10, 1977–Jan. 11, 1998 and at other museums at later dates. Boston: Bulfinch Press, Little, Brown and Company, 1997.

Parks, Gordon. *In Love.* Philadelphia and New York: J. B. Lippincott Company, 1971.

Parks, Gordon. *Moments Without Proper Names.* New York: The Viking Press, 1975.

Parks, Gordon. *Voices in the Mirror— An Autobiography.* Anchor Books. New York: Doubleday, 1990.

IRVING PENN

Penn, Irving. *Moments Preserved— eight essays in photographs and words.* With an introduction by Alexander Liberman. With collaboration in the writing of the captions and text by Rosemary Blackmon. New York: Simon and Schuster, 1960.

Penn, Irving. *Worlds in a Small Room.* A Studio Book. New York: The Viking Press, 1974.

GILLES PEREZ

Perez, Gilles. *Telex Iran.* New York: Aperture, 1983.

SYLVIA PLACHY

Plachy, Sylvia. *Red Light—Inside the Sex Industry.* With text by James Ridgeway. New York: Powerhouse Books, 1996.

Plachy, Sylvia, *Signs and Relics.* With an essay by Wim Wenders. New York: Powerhouse Books, 1999.

Plachy, Sylvia. *Unguided Tour.* With an afterword by Guy Trebay. Music by Tom Waits. New York: Aperture Foundation, Inc., 1990.

ELIOT PORTER

Intimate Landscapes—Photographs by Eliot Porter. With an afterword by Weston J. Naef. The Metropolitan Museum of Art. New York: E.P. Dutton, 1979.

ELI REED

Reed, Eli. *Black in America.* With a foreword by Gordon Parks. New York: W.W. Norton & Co., 1997.

MATTHIEU RICARD

Ricard, Matthieu. *Journey to Enlightenment: The Life and World of Khyentse Rinpoche, Spiritual Teacher from Tibet.* With a remembrance by His Holiness The Dalai Lama. With excerpts from the autobiography and writings of Khyentse Rinpoche and other teachers. New York: Aperture, 1996.

EUGENE RICHARDS

Richards, Eugene. *Americans We.* With text by the author. New York: Aperture, 1994.

Richards, Eugene. *Cocaine True, Cocaine Blue—Life and Death in the Drug Zone.* New York: Aperture, 1994

Richards, Eugene. *Dorchester Days.* Introduction by Dorothea Lynch. London: Phaidon Press, Inc., 2000.

JIM RICHARDSON

Richardson, Jim. *High School: U.S.A.* New York. St. Martin's Press, 1979.

JACOB A. RIIS

Alland, Alexander, Sr. *Jacob A. Riis— Photographer & Citizen.* With a preface by Ansel Adams. Millerton, N.Y.: Aperture, 1974.

Riis, Jacob. *How the Other Half Lives—Studies Among the Tenements of New York.* New York: Dover Publications, Inc., 1971.

HERB RITTS

Ritts, Herb. *Herb Ritts—Work.* Boston: A Bullfinch Press Book. Little, Brown in association with the Museum of Fine Arts, Boston, 1996.

Ritts, Herb. *Notorious.* A Bulfinch Press Book. Boston: Little, Brown and Company, undated.

GEORGE RODGER

Rodger, George. *Humanity and Inhumanity—The Photographic Journey of George Rodger.* Text by Bruce Bernard. Picture research by Peter Marlow in association with Magnum Photos. With a foreword by Henri Cartier-Bresson. London: Phaidon Press, Inc., 1994.

ERIC SALOMON

Eric Salomon. The Aperture History of Photography Series. Millerton, N.Y.: Aperture, 1978.

Erich Salomon—Portrait of an Age. Selected by Han de Vries and Peter Hunter-Salomon. Biography and notes by Peter Hunter-Salomon. Photographic layout by Han de Vries. New York: The Macmillan Company, 1967.

FLIP SCHULKE

Schulke, Flip. *He had a Dream—Martin Luther King, Jr. and the Civil Rights Movement.* New York: W. W. Norton & Company, Inc., 1995.

Schulke, Flip, and Penelope Ortner McPhee. *King Remembered.* New York: W. W. Norton & Company, Inc., 1986.

Schulke, Flip, and Matt Schudel. *Muhammad Ali: The Birth of a Legend, Miami, 1961–1964.* New York: St Martin's Press, 2000.

SEBASTIAO SELGADO

Salgado, Sebastiao. *An Uncertain Grace.* With essays by Eduardo Galeano and Fred Ritchin. New York: Aperture, 1970.

Salgado, Sebastiao. *Migrations— Humanity In Transition.* New York: Aperture, 2000.

Salgado, Sebastiao. *Terra—Struggle of the Landless.* London: Phaidon Press, Inc., 1997.

Salgado, Sebastiao. *Workers: An Archaeology of the Industrial Age.* New York: Aperture, 1993.

BEN SHAHN

Pratt, David, ed. *The Photographic Eye of Ben Shahn.* Cambridge, Mass.: Harvard University Press, 1975.

W. EUGENE SMITH

Johnson, William S. "W. Eugene Smith: Middle Years." *The Archive.* 20 (July 1984): 4–18, 19–77.

Let Truth Be The Prejudice. With an illustrated biography by Ben Maddow and an afterword by John G. Morris. Accompanies the major retrospective exhibition, *W. Eugene Smith: Let Truth Be the Prejudice,* organized by the Alfred Stieglitz Center of the Philadelphia Museum of Art, beginning October 19, 1985 and ending April 23, 1989 in 10 American cities. New York: Aperture, 1998.

Smith, W. Eugene, and Aileen M. Smith. *Minamata.* New York: An Alskog-Sensorium Book, Holt, Rinehart and Winston, 1975.

W. Eugene Smith: His Photographs and Notes. With an afterword by Lincoln Kirstein. New York: Aperture, 1993.

Johnson, William S., ed. *W. Eugene Smith—Master of the Photographic Essay.* With commentary by William S. Johnson. Foreword by James L. Enyeart. Millerton, N.Y.: Aperture, Inc., 1981.

Willumson, Glenn G. *W. Eugene Smith and the Photographic Essay.* Cambridge, England and New York: Cambridge University Press, 1992.

W. Eugene Smith—Photographs 1934–1975. New York: Harry N. Abrams, 1998.

ALBERT SANDS SOUTHWORTH AND JOSIAH JOHNSON HAWES

Sobieszek, Robert A., and Odette M. Appel. *The Daguerreotypes of Southworth & Hawes.* New York: Dover Publications, 1980.

EDWARD STEICHEN

Steichen, Edward. *A Life in Photography.* Garden City, N.Y.: Doubleday & Company, 1981.

ALFRED STIEGLITZ

Greenough, Sarah, and Juan Hamilton. *Alfred Stieglitz—Photographs & Writings.* Callaway Editions. Washington: National Gallery of Art, 1983.

Kiefer, Geraldine Wojno. *Alfred Stieglitz—Scientist, Photographer, and Avatar of Modernism, 1880– 1913.* New York & London: Garland Publishing, Inc., 1991.

Naef, Weston. *Fifty Pioneers of Modern Photography—The Collection of Alfred Stieglitz.* The Metropolitan Museum of Art. New York: Viking Press, 1978.

Norman, Dorothy. *Alfred Stieglitz— An American Seer.* Millerton, N.Y.: Aperture, 1978.

WILLIAM HENRY FOX TALBOT

Arnold, H.J.P. *William Henry Fox Talbot—Pioneer of photography and man of science.* London: Hutchinson Benham, 1977.

Buckland, Gail. *Fox Talbot and the Invention of Photography.* Boston: David R. Godine, 1980.

Lassam, Robert. *Fox Talbot—Photographer.* With a foreword by Sir Cecil Beaton. The Old Brewery, Tisbury, Wiltshire, England: Compton Press in association with Dovecote Press, 1979.

Schaaf, Larry J. *H. Fox Talbot's The Pencil of Nature.* Anniversary Facsimile. New York: Hans P. Kraus, Jr. Inc., 1989.

JOHN THOMSON

White, Stephen. *John Thomson—Life and Photographs.* London: Thames and Hudson, 1984.

GEORGE A. TICE

Tice, George A. *George A. Tice Photographs 1953—1973.* New Brunswick, N.J.: Rutgers University Press, 1975.

LARRY TOWELL

Towell, Larry. *El Salvador.* With an introduction by Mark Danner. New York: Center for Documentary Studies in association with W. W. Norton & Co., 1997.

LINDA TROELLER

Troeller, Linda. *Healing Waters.* With a preface by Wolfgang Becker and an introduction by Yves Treguer. New York: Aperture, 1998.

DAVID C. TURNLEY

Turnley, David C. *The Russian Heart—Days of Crisis and Hope.* With an introduction by Bill Keller. New York: Aperture, 1992.

Turnley, David C. *Why Are They Weeping?—South Africans Under Apartheid.* New York: Stewart, Tabori & Chang, 1988.

DAVID C. TURNLEY AND PETER TURNLEY

Turnley, David C. and Peter. *In Times of War and Peace.* Related exhibition held in New York, N.Y. at the International Center of Photography, June 7–Sept 8, 1996 and in Verona, Italy Sept. 27–Dec. 5, 1996. New York: Abbeville Press, 1997.

CARLETON E. WATKINS

Palmquist, Peter E. *Carleton E. Watkins—Photographer of the American West.* With a foreword by Martha A. Sandweiss. Albuquerque: University of New Mexico Press, 1983.

WEEGEE (ARTHUR FELLIG)

Stettner. Louis, ed. *Weegee.* With an introduction by Louis Stettner. New York: Alford A. Knopf, 1977.

Weegee. *Naked City.* New York: Da Capo Press, 1975.

Weegee. The Aperture History of Photography Series. Millerton, N.Y.: Aperture, 1978.

Weegee's World. With essays by Miles Barth, Alain Bergala, and Ellen Handy. A Bulfinch Press book. Boston: Little, Brown and Co. in association with the International Center of Photography, New York, 1997.

EDWARD WESTON

Weston, Edward. *Fifty Years—The definitive volume of his photographic work.* Illustrated biography by Ben Maddow. Millerton, N.Y.: Aperture, 1973.

13. PICTURE-TAKING APPROACH/TECHNIQUE INCLUDING TEXTBOOKS

Callahan, Sean, and Gerald Astor. *Photographing Sports: John Zimmerman, Mark Kauffman and Neil Leifer.* Dobbs Ferry, N.Y.: Morgan & Morgan, 1975.

Feininger, Andreas. *The Color Photo Book.* Englewood Cliffs: Prentice-Hall, Inc., 1969.

Hedgecoe, John. *The Art of Color Photography.* Rev. and updated. New York: Simon and Schuster, 1989.

Horton, Brian. *The Picture—An Associated Press Guide to Good News Photography.* New York: The Associated Press, 1989.

Kobré, Kenneth. *Photojournalism—The Professionals' Approach.* 4th ed. Boston: Focal Press, 2000.

Lewis, Greg. *Photojournalism—Content & Technique.* 2d ed. Madison, Wisc. and Dubuque, Iowa: Brown & Benchmark, 1995.

London, Barbara and John Upton. *Photography.* 6th ed. New York: Addison Wesley Longman, 1997.

Photo Essay—Paul Fusco & Will McBride: How to Communication with Pictures. Los Angeles: An Alskog Book published with Petersen Publishing Company, 1974.

Spina, Tony. *On Assignment—Projects in Photojournalism.* New York: AMPHOTO, American Photographic Book Publishing, an imprint of Watson-Guptill Publications, 1982.

Stroebel, Leslie. *Stroebel's View Camera Basics.* Boston: Focal Press, 1995.

Stroebel, Leslie. *View Camera Technique.* 6th ed. Boston: Focal Press, 1993.

Weinberg, Adam D. *On the Line: The New Color Photojournalism.* With a foreword by Gloria Emerson. Minneapolis: Walker Art Center, 1986.

14. WRITING TECHNIQUES AND GRAMMAR

Barzun, Jacques. *Simple & Direct: A Rhetoric for Writers.* Rev. ed. Chicago: University of Chicago Press, 1994.

Goldstein, Norm, ed. *The Associated Press Stylebook and Libel Manual.* 34th ed. New York: The Associated Press. 1999.

Strunk, William Jr. *The Elements of Style.* 4th ed. With revisions, an introduction, and a chapter on writing by E.B. White. Boston: Allyn and Bacon, 1999.

Williams, Joseph M. *Style—Ten Lessons in Clarity & Grace.* 6th ed. New York: Longman, 1999.